The C.A.F.E. logo represents integration of the church and community. All faith-based congregations can work together to reach the community and families with basic Christianity to show *pure religion in the community. The psychology of color shows that black and white have many meanings; however, the colors can also symbolize the starkness of decison-making when one is confronted with hard *choices.

(Continued in Appendix 4)

*Free from all that would dim the transparency in belief and conduct before God and the Father is this, to go see and relieve the orphans without a father's protection and the women lacking a husband in their distress, and to keep himself untainted with guilt. James 1:27 EDNT

*My cherished band of believers, count it a jewel (precious stone) when you fall into adversity and testing that provides you a choice of direction. James 1:2 EDNT

New Testament

Narratives About the Life of Jesus
Letters to Theophilus
Letters to Assembled Believers
Relational Letters
Letters to Scattered Believers

A candid rendering of the New Testament, in chronological order by books within five (5) thematic sections, with key words and phrases in the 1611 KJV diligently compared with Koine Greek, Latin syntax and common usage to produce a devotional understanding of scripture. *Although the books are presented in groups according to theme and addressees, they are chronological by book within these groups.*

Important Note to the Reader

Although the *scripture portion begins on page 23, read the front and back material first. The Prologue, Introduction, and Appendices, will provide helpful information regarding the KJV and will explain why the author believed it was necessary to develop a devotional text for the New Testament. With deep love and commitment to the Greek of the New Testament and dedication to the original intent of scripture, this text attempts to capture the fervent religious and spiritual feeling of the passage in a devotional language designed to assist the private devotions, personal prayers and spiritual growth of believers. Since the EDNT was a 42-year project, as new knowledge was discovered, revisions and changes in the existing EVERGREEN manuscript were made. This edition shows those changes.

*See *QUICK REFERENCE* at the end (p 433) for Traditional & Alphabetical New Testament Order with page numbers. Appendix Three also includes Chronological Order.

*Whenever quoting from the Evergreen Devotional New Testament, use (EDNT).

The Evergreen
Devotional
New Testament
(EDNT)

C.A.F.E. Edition
Community and Family Education©

A Candid Rendering by

Hollis L. Green, ThD, PhD

An imprint of
GlobalEdAdvancePress

Available for this title:
Hardcover ISBN 978-1-935434-28-3
Softcover   ISBN 978-1-935434-26-9
eBook   ISBN 978-1-935434-74-0

Order from www.gea-books.com/bookstore
or anywhere good books are sold

C.A.F.E. has two tracks:
1. Bible study track (using EDNT) for basic New Testament content
2. Textbook track for practical ministry and community service:

Obtain curriculum and textbooks from gea-books.com

THE EVERGREEN Devotional New Testament (EDNT): C.A.F.E. Edition
Copyright © (2009, 2010, 2011, 2012, 2013, 2014) 2015, 2017, 2018, 2019
by Hollis L. Green

Library of Congress Control Number: 2011946084
Green, Hollis L., 1933 --
The Evergreen Devotional New Testament: Complete Edition
ISBN 978-1-935434-26-9

Subject Codes and Description: 1: REL 006410 Religion: Bible Study
– Language Study; 2: REL 006400: Religion: Bible Study - Exegeses and Hermeneutics; 3: REL 006700 Religion: Bible Study- Bible Study Guide

All rights reserved, including the right to reproduce this book or any part thereof in any form, except for inclusion of brief quotations in a review, a teaching syllabus, ministry notes, without the written permission of the author and GlobalEdAdvance Press.

Cover Design: Barton Green

The Press does not have ownership of the contents of a book; this is the author's work and the author owns the copyright. All theory, concepts, constructs, and perspectives are those of the author and not necessarily the Press. They are presented for open and free discussion of the issues involved. All comments and feedback should be directed to the Email: [comments4author@aol.com] and the comments will be forwarded to the author for response.

Published by
Post-Gutenberg Books™
An Imprint of GlobalEdAdvancePress
www.gea-books.com

C.A.F.E. CURRICULUM AND TEXT
"cutting straight the word of truth"
Text: The EVERGREEN Devotional New Testament

C.A.F.E. Enrollment and Classes -- Sunday school and youth training have suffered significant decline in recent decades, it is time for a new approach to community and family education. **C.A.F.E.** is a 4-year program sponsored by a faith-based group to teach practical ministry, community service and basic New Testament content in an informal setting. It can be used to replace the youth and adult aspects of education by faith-based groups to better reach families and the community. Students will enroll one year/or one term at a time and renew the enrollment based on interest and participation. Certificates of completion will be issued each year for those completing three Terms with a Qualification Diploma after four years.

C.A.F.E is designed for families in the community and to develop leadership for the local church, strengthen families, and equip believers for faith-based lifestyle service in the community. **C.A.F.E.** Bible Study Track: (1) Enrollment/sign-up day/ 16 Weeks/ (2)One class break for prayer and reflection/ 16 Weeks/(3) One class break for prayer and reflection/16 Weeks/ (4) Final class prayer and reflection. 1/16/1/16/1/16/1=52 Weeks. Students will enroll for one year that includes three Terms of 16 weeks. The class will be a "colloquy"—a formal discussion rather than a taught class; student participation is the objective. Students will read the assigned chapter(s) in the EVERGREEN Devotional New Testament (EDNT) before coming to class in order to be an informed participant in discussion. *See QUICK REFERENCE on page 433 for Traditional & Alphabetical New Testament Order with page numbers.*

FIRST YEAR -- Narratives about the Life of Jesus --EDNT

Learning Leader should group short chapters and divide long chapters to make 48 lessons, with 4 Sessions for prayer and reflection.

    Term One: Mark (16)

    Term Two: Matthew (28)

Lesson 1	Matthew 1 - 2:15
Lesson 2	Matthew. 2:16 - 7:12
Lesson 3	Matthew 7:13 - 12:45
Lesson 4	Matthew 12:46 - 15:20
Lesson 5	Matthew 15:21 - 18:20
Lesson 6	Matthew 18:21 - 19:30
Lesson 7	Matthew 20:1 - 22:14
Lesson 8	Matthew 22:15 - 23:36
Lesson 9	Matthew 23:37 - 25:46
Lesson 10	Matthew 26:1 - 27:44
Lesson 11	Matthew 27:45 - 28:20
Lessons 12-16	John - chapters 1-5

Term Three: John the remaining 16 chapters (6-21)

SECOND YEAR -- Letters to Theophilus --EDNT

Learning Leader should group short chapters and divide long chapters to make 48 lessons, with 4 Sessions for prayer and reflection.

Term One: Luke 1-16
Term Two: Luke 17-24 and Acts 1-8
Term Three: Acts 9-28 [29] [leader to double up on 5 chapters]

THIRD YEAR -- Letters to Assembled Believers -- EDNT

Learning Leader should group short chapters and divide long chapters to make 48 lessons, with 4 Sessions for prayer and reflection.

Term One: [I Thessalonians (5) II Thessalonians (3), Galatians (6), [2 extra classes for general discussion and review]
Term Two: I Corinthians (16) II Corinthians (12) [group chapters to complete in 16 wks]
Term Three: Romans (16)

FOURTH YEAR -- Continue Letters to Assembled Believers -- EDNT

Learning Leader should group short chapters and divide long chapters to make 48 lessons, with 4 Sessions for prayer and reflection.

Term One: Colossians (4), Ephesians (6), Philippians (4)

-- Relational Letters -- EDNT

Term Two: Philemon (1), First Timothy (6), Titus (3), Second Timothy (4), Second John (1), Third John (1)]

-- Letters to Scattered Believers -- EDNT

Term Three: Leader will have to group chapters for discussion to complete in 16 Wks.
Class 1- James (4 chapters),
Class 2- First Peter (5 chapters),
Class 3 - Hebrews chapters 1-3
Class 4 - Hebrews chapters 4-6
Class 5 - Hebrews chapters 7-10
Class 6 - Hebrews chapters 11-13
Class 7- Second Peter (3),
Class 8- Jude (1),
Class 9- First John (5),
Class 10- Revelation 1 - 3:6
Class 11- Revelation 3:7 - 7:17
Class 12- Revelation 8 - 11:14
Class 13- Revelation 11:15 - 14:20
Class 14- Revelation 15 - 18:24
Class 15- Revelation 19 - 21:27
Class 16- Revelation 22:1-21

Dedicated
To The Patrons

Many individuals have encouraged the publishing of this work. All who purchase and use this Devotional New Testament are considered supporters. Listed below are the individuals whose financial gifts enabled the completion, publication, and distribution of this project:

Rena and Paratan Balloo (Caribbean)

Glenda and Ethelbert Charles (Caribbean)

Kay and Bill Christian (USA)

Gail and Hollis Green (USA)

Leila and Basil Jackson (USA)

Lorraine Helena Mary Jackson (USA)

Martha and Ted Kittell (USA)

Mary and Glen Liebig (USA)

Dianne and Lewin Mayers (Caribbean)

Ukpabi P. MBeri and Family (W. Africa)

Lucille and Henry Parks (USA)

April and Steve Price (USA)

Debra and Subesh Ramjattan (Caribbean)

Betty and George Stout (USA)

Blessed is he who reads, and they who listen to the words of this message for the future, and is keeping those things written: for the time is at hand.

Revelation 1:3 (EDNT)

PROLOGUE

WHY A DEVOTIONAL NEW TESTAMENT?

My early study of scripture included using the King James Bible. The literary nature of this version made me appreciate English literature and gave me an incentive to memorize scripture. However, many of the words were difficult to understand and my mother guided me to find two or three references where the word was used to assist my understanding. When I still needed assistance with the meaning, she guided me to an unabridged English dictionary to determine the root meaning. This created an interest in the study of word origins and the history of changing meanings of words over time. This interest produced a Junior Thesis paper on "The Development of the English Bible" as a part of my early education.

Next, came my research paper on the causes of the American Civil War that assisted my understanding of how words mean different things to different people. Growing up in the Bible belt of the South, I was aware of segregation on the basis of race and class, and came to realize that there was a difference between a servant working as an employee of the wealthy and a "slave" who was "owned" by someone. My study also brought understanding that the Bible had been used to justify slavery by referring to slaves as servants and was being used to defend the present segregation. When it was discovered that *doulos* (a Greek word for slave) was translated "servant" in the King James and even used to justify the practice of returning run-away slaves (Paul returning Onesimus to Philemon), my study of "words" was enhanced and my venture into Civil Rights began. This verse (Philemon 1:16) in the EDNT is typical of how the verse should read: **16. Now receive him not as a slave, but beyond a slave, as my well loved brother, even more to you, both as a man and as a believer in the Lord.** (Philemon 16 EDNT). Later many English versions including the NKJV did translate *doulos* as "slave," but the damage was done.

The study of other languages including Latin, Spanish, Hebrew, and Greek gave me insight into the cultural meaning of words and the core meaning of scriptural passages. In graduate school, two doctoral dissertations; one dealing with a particular doctrine, demonstrated that it was based only on the English translation rather than the original language; second, on the study habits of pastors, gave me insight that most did not use the original language in preparing Bible-based messages. This understanding encouraged my further study of the Greek language.

Prologue

Coming to an understanding that the Bible was presented in books and letters, each with a purpose with functional benefit based on the date or chronology of the writing, brought a new perspective of the New Testament. The realization that the New Testament was progressive and chronological (by books and letters) was important to understand the way God revealed the divine message. This produced a desire to read the New Testament chronologically based on the order in time that events occurred and to clearly see the purpose of each book and letter. Gradually, I came to realize that meanings changed as words and phrases were translated from one language and culture to another. This produced a deep desire to make the English New Testament more readable and with a clearer understanding when applied to the lives of believers.

Although many others have made this effort, I felt compelled to do it for myself and my sons. Later, I was encouraged to present my work as a comprehensive unit as the Devotional New Testament. There is an urgent need for a devotional text that is true to the original manuscripts but is more easily read and understood. Hopefully, the Devotional New Testament (EDNT) will meet part of this need.

Since Holy Scripture means exactly what the first people who heard it understood it to mean, the EDNT is the result of forty-two (42) years of dedication to the original intent of words in scripture. It is my firm belief that doctrine should only be supported by the original language of scripture and that various versions or translations were designed to improve the understanding of readers, not to establish dogma. Obtaining a sense of the original intent of words improves the understanding of the inspired text. What did the Greek words mean "then" and how are they best expressed "now" to the benefit of the reader's devotional understanding? This was the primary objective of this work.

The New Testament originally, written in common Greek, did not have chapters, verses, or punctuation. The language itself clearly placed words and phrases together and in positions of emphasis. Books and letters were later divided into chapters and verses for readers to search and find particular information. The translators also added punctuations based on the placement of the words or phrases. Most translations and renderings of the New Testament capitalized the first word of each verse even if it did not start a new sentence. This confuses the English reader and causes one to give prominence and importance to subordinate thoughts rather than value the main idea. Consequently, the Evergreen EDNT does not always capitalize the beginning word of a new verse unless there is a terminal punctuation before the verse number. The new verse should be read as a continuation of the previous thought or additional development supporting the central idea of the paragraph. Also, instead of quotation marks, the EDNT uses a Capital letter to begin a quotation. The EDNT has attempted to capitalize the pronouns that refer to the Trinity. Since the KJV had so many pronouns; hopefully, this will clarify the He, Him, His, referring to the Godhead and make it easier for the reader to attribute value to the antecedent.

WHY EVERGREEN?

An evergreen tree continues to grow, making the necessary seasonal changes without the distraction of dying foliage or barren branches. There is a place in God for each believer, and through spiritual leadership and personal discipline a way for each believer to remain evergreen. A green leaf signifies growth. Seeing a green leaf on a tree one instinctively knows the tree is alive. Actually, a green leaf denotes more than life; it is the promise of fruit. A green leaf symbolizes renewal, new life, growth, but green leaves are not enough. There must be fruit. Jesus cursed the fig tree that had green leaves, the evidence of life, but no fruit, the reason for life.

Why should individual believers or a congregation drift into seasons of fruitlessness and despair? Sure, there are seasons of preparation, renewal, and growth. This, however, does not mean that the individual believer should not remain evergreen. Paul wrote about the believer's daily renewal: **This is why we are not discouraged; although the outward nature is being worn away, the inner spirit is being refreshed with continual renewal.** (2 Corinthians 4:16 EDNT)

The devotional rendering is structured to keep believers evergreen and growing. There is a present need for daily devotional readings and individual study of the New Testament. Attending a church, with all the benefits, is not sufficient for daily growth and development of the individual believer. Much of the value for the individual is lost in the programming for institutional advancement. Existing translations and versions of the New Testament are so academic they have little devotional value for the individual reader. Thus, the Devotional New Testament is presented for the personal use of believers.

Introduction

RATIONALE FOR A DEVOTIONAL NEW TESTAMENT

A Relational Document

The New Testament is a relational document designed to guide believers in their relationship with God and their behavior toward others. The EDNT contains relational letters sent to individuals, letters to scattered believers, and letters to assembled believers. These letters with relational value are presented together. Also, the nature of early converts, scattered throughout the known world without a local assembly to mother their faith, appears to be similar to the mobility of the present pluralistic society. Away from family and friends, moving from job to job and town to town, many believers are without a congregation home to nurture their faith. There is an urgent need for a devotional text that is true to the original manuscripts but is easy to read. Hopefully, the Devotional New Testament will meet part of this need

Relational and Inductive Study

Combining aspects of relational and inductive study produced the concept of a Devotional New Testament. Holy Scripture means exactly what the first person who heard it understood it to mean, not what culture, tradition, or translators interpret the words to mean. Because most translations and versions of scripture are academic with copious notes that slow the reader and hinder the devotional value, getting a sense of the original intent provides an improved understanding of the inspired text. A simple word study comparison between common Greek, Latin syntax and the language used in the KJV can clarify the actual meaning of words and produce a devotional understanding.

Mostly Pristine Issues

Although the New Testament deals with pristine issues, the basic concepts and constructs deal with a group of Christians scattered because of persecution. Without Christian assemblies converts continued to attend Jewish synagogues. Some of the synagogues were more Christian than Jewish, such as the one in Berea, but most remained bound to the old system. These letters were designed to assist both with the scattered nature of the believers without home assembly support and struggling new congregations with little knowledge of the Christian faith.

The Books and Letters have a Chronology and a Theme

The New Testament was given in books and is best understood by books. The text also has a chronology. If one accepts the concept of logical development, then reading the books in some chronological order would make sense. The books of the New Testament were written to individuals, scattered believers, and assembled believers in particular places and times. The context of these facts assists in understanding the purpose and meaning of a given book or letter. Certainly seeing the order and nature of God's revelation at various times informs a clearer understanding of the meaning of scripture. God does stack His revelation "line upon line, and precept upon precept." Although the books are presented in groups according to theme and addressees, they are chronological by book within these groups (See the Table of Contents and Appendix 3).

Use Original Language to Develop Doctrine

The devotional text does no violence to the original language because it is based on common Greek and common word meanings. Hopefully, it is objective and that personal feelings are excluded. The work is designed to make scripture clear to the devotional reader. Doctrine should be formed only from a clear understanding of the original languages, not an English translation. This text is designed for devotional reading. Academics, theologians, and Biblical scholars should themselves use the original Greek of the New Testament to develop and defend specific doctrines.

The Pristine Experience was Relational

The New Testament is relational and when personal and interpersonal relationships are properly ordered there is less need for instruction in doctrine. One should remember that the New Testament congregations did not have a New Testament. Some parts of the Old Testament were available through the Jewish traditions, but the Gentile converts did not yet have a New Testament. A few letters were circulated from assembly to assembly, but the collection of books and letters as we know them were not available. Primarily the pristine believers were concerned about a redemptive relationship with Christ and a proper relationship with others. This is what made them Christian; not the existence of sacred writings. Devotional reading of scripture is instructive as to belief and behavior. *All scripture will provide instruction in righteousness: All sacred writings are God-breathed, and serviceable for teaching, for warning, for correction, for instruction in righteousness, in order that the man of God may be adequately equipped, for every good work.* (2 Timothy 3:16, 17 EDNT)

A Candid Rendering of a Passage

Through the years in preparation to preach or teach, a candid rendering of the New Testament passage was made to frame my thinking. To arrive at the original intent of scripture was the goal. Using key words in the 1611 KJV diligently compared with Koine Greek, Latin syntax and common usage, a straightforward rendering was made. It was assumed that God did not intend the Bible to be interpreted by academics, theologians, or even preachers. To follow a New Testament model, originally scripture was read publicly to the congregation without explanation and passed on to another congregation. There was no effort to examine and describe the grammar of a sentence or a particular word in a sentence because the congregation understood the common language. There were no "read along" texts available. The congregation listened and understood.

The Devotional New Testament is an effort to place scripture into a more understandable language. The work may not demonstrate a rigid scholarship as would a word for word translation of the text. This is because the Greek word order and many of the "explanations" for translating a passage differently than other existing texts are so academic that the explanations hinder the devotional value of reading scripture. Some may think it too sermonic, but this work seeks to be devotional, not strictly scholarly. The objective was to make the text clear and understandable to the average reader the same way a pastor attempts to present scripture. This text is a candid rendering of my understanding of the text.

Speaking at the Religious Emphasis Week at a college where my mother was Dean of Women, concern gripped me because it was one of the few times my mother had heard me speak. It had been my style to first understand the passage of scripture and then transliterate it as simply as possible using common language. Normally, my approach was "The deeper meaning here is…or the original language here means, etc." As the first service progressed mother turned to a colleague and said, "He will say things that are not in your Bible, but he is a good and honest man." As I transliterated certain words and gave my free rendering, mother turned to her friend and said, "See I told you he would say things that are not in your Bible."

Yet, the Greek Professor shared with his class, "Listen in chapel and you will understand how the study of Greek is to assist the understanding of the language and not to demonstrate your knowledge." When the Professor told me his statement to the class, I was encouraged to continue the process of giving the devotional meaning of scripture in my public ministry.

Relational and Inductive Study Combined

Colleagues have encouraged me to make these practical interpretations available in book form. They are presented here as an explanation of how the candid rendering of the New Testament was reached and presented as a devotional text. It is a combination of both relational study and inductive study together with an understanding of the original language. Relational study requires one to listen, reflect, connect and act often in a subjective manner. Inductive study involves more objectivity and scholarship. Both processes have value, but need to be combined to be effective. By bringing together the basic aspects of relational and inductive study, one develops a less emotional and more intellectual approach to devotional study. A good identity for this process is a Devotional New Testament.

Both study plans have limitations. In a relational study one reads into the scripture subjectively "personal stuff" that can skew the actual meaning of the words. Inductive study requires one to be more scholarly and "read out of" the text objectively. The difficulty here is the meaning of words. Are the words colored by personal emotions or was the meaning objectively obtained. Although relational study is built on a personal relationship with God and an understanding that the study is intended to nurture and enhance this relationship, one is often left to personal devices. Inductive study requires more academic preparation to do the work effectively. Both plans use the basic steps of observation, interpretation and application in the form of three questions: What does the verse say? What does the verse mean? How does the meaning apply to me? Although there is no private interpretation of scripture, there is value in internalizing the meaning, provided it is the true meaning. This is the value of devotional reading and study.

In relational study the emotions and personal circumstance affect the study. Inductive study places value on sound biblical scholarship and intellectual study. The meaning of words is important and can be life-changing. If one does not know the Greek language (a process that can take up to twenty years to accomplish) then the recommendation is to use an Unabridged English Dictionary (UED) to obtain the actual meaning of KJV words at the time they were selected in 1611 and placed in the translation. Using an UED can assist in digging out the meaning of words. One cannot truly apply the meaning unless the true meaning of words has been determined.

A Repository of Classical Knowledge

There must be a proper worshipful approach to the study of Holy Scripture. Honest and effective study requires a level of scholarship that is not readily available. This is why the Unabridged English Dictionary is recommended. There are only a few classical scholars left in the world. The unabridged dictionary is a repository of much of the classical knowledge of the past and can be an effective tool in examining the ideas and words of a text. Also, with reference to the King James Version it is helpful to understand the meaning of words at the time of the translation. This will lead to a meaning closer to the original intent of scripture. Such an interpretation brings about objective conclusions and meaningful application to life. Devotional study uses aspects of both the relational and inductive plans.

Hearing One Side of a Two-sided Conversation

The New Testament is both books and letters written to specific persons or because of specific situations. Understanding a letter is the most difficult. It is similar to hearing one side of a two-sided conversation. One does not clearly know the person or persons to whom the letter was written. Not only is there difficulty in the technical language of New Testament letters; there is the problem of always knowing exactly what prompted the letter or what was the question or letter that was being answered. Therefore, as one interprets scripture there is a dual problem: the technical language of the text and the meaning as understood by the original reader or hearer. Of course the reason for, nature of, and exact situation the letter addresses compounds the difficulty.

Most translations and versions are so academic they are not useful for devotional reading. One friend characterized the normal process as being "So earthly minded there is no spiritual value." The Word of God was not intended to be filtered through the minds of scholars and theologians; it was to be read directly to the people to whom it was written. The Bible actually means what the first persons who heard it understood it to mean. With translations and versions of the Bible, the meaning is often hidden in the choice of words and the actual meaning of the words in the English language at the time of the rendering. With 50 years of ministry and academic leadership, a lesson of simplicity was learned. The intent is communication not sophistication or complication.

The Lapse of Time

A difficulty in Bible study is the lapse of time and the translations from one language and culture to another. Research has demonstrated that when one translates something from one language, culture, or time period to another the meaning changes. Since there are no copies of the original documents of the Bible in the handwriting of the writer, and since most of us are not classical scholars who know the nuances of many languages, the best we can do is to understand the reason for words or language choice by the selected classical scholars authorized by King James to translate the Bible in 1611.

Roots of the English Language

One of the problems understanding English versions of scripture is the language itself. The present English language originated in the Indo-European region and what is now Modern English developed in Western German vernacular, then into Low German parlance, and finally into Old English (450-1150), then Middle English (1150-1475) and finally into Modern English. In 1611 at the time of the translation of the King James Version of the Bible, English was acquiring its modern external form, but English scholars were still using subordination of clauses as a primary aspect of language.

Subordination in old grammar designated a clause that was dependent on another clause that did not itself constitute a formal sentence. A subordinate clause—also called a **dependent clause**—begins with a **subordinate conjunction** or a **relative pronoun** and contains both a **subject** and a **verb**. This combination of words does **not** form a **complete sentence**. It will instead require a reader to add additional information to finish the thought. Such clauses were introduce by subordinate conjunctions: after, although, as, because, before, even, if, even though, in order that, once, provided that, rather than, since, so that, than, that, though, unless, until, when, whenever, where, whereas, wherever, whether, while, why; or relative pronouns: that, which, whichever, who, whoever, whom, whose, whosoever, or whomever.

This linking of a subordinate clause to a main clause complicates the understanding of the modern English language reader. The old grammar defined a sentence as "One idea fully developed." This is now the definition of a Standard English paragraph. This is another reason reading the Scripture in the verse format places long sentences with multiple subordination (using colons; semi-colons, commas, etc.). Most of the more recent versions of the Bible make paragraphs out of these long sentences. Since a paragraph is now one idea fully developed, a reader of scripture should attempt to determine the "main idea" in each expository unit and not use a subordinate clause, that supports the main idea, to develop doctrine.

During the intervening years, the English language has accepted thousands of new words and refined the meaning of others; consequently, it is difficult to actually know what a present word meant several hundred years ago. For this reason, the New Testament presented here is divided into paragraphs for reading and study. A look at how the King James Bible came to be would assist the understanding of the language and the process involved. (See Appendix One)

The Canonical Order of the New Testament

The canonical order of the manuscript in the original KJV (1611) was 49 books divided into seven divisions. The Old Testament contained: (1) The Law, (2) The Prophets, and (3) The Writings. The New Testament contained: (4) The Gospels and Acts, (5) The General Epistles, (6) The Epistles of Paul and (7) The Book of Revelation. Early Church fathers altered the order into 66 books presently used in most versions. There have been numerous translations and versions of the original text and some changes in the order of the Old Testament, but the canon of the New Testament has remained the same. There is no credible question about the number (27) of books; however, these are not in chronological order. The Bible is a book of books written over many generations to show God's dealing with the human race and in particular the body of believers. The Bible forms one continuous story, a kind of string of pearls, strung together with a blood line. It is a progressive unfolding of truth "line upon line, precept upon precept" to form the story of humanity in relation to God. This devotional version places the New Testament books chronologically in order in five groups to show the development over time. It is for this reason that the New Testament books are grouped and then placed in chronological order within the section: Narratives About the Life of Jesus, Letters to Theophilus, Letters to Assembled Believers, Relational Letters, and Letters to Scattered Believers.

Guidance for the Reader

The reader should be aware of emphasis by position, proportion and punctuation. In composition (com-position) everything has a position or place. If words and phrases are in the right place, the emphasis is clear. Also, provided the punctuation is properly placed, the reader has a better understanding of the text. In addition to the process of subordination discussed before, punctuation can assist or hinder the reader's understanding. The first or last part of a book or chapter has position and the material in the middle needs proportion or more elaboration. Punctuation is the key to understanding.

Punctuation is similar to traffic signals. Some indicate full stop while others warn drivers to slow down, be cautious, or provide instruction or guidance. The eye cannot see when it is moving; it must focus. Punctuation stops the eye and places words or phrases in the emphatic position. This is why punctuation is important. A brief review of English grammar punctuation could assist the reader.

A sentence ends with a period [.] (full stop); a question mark [?] suggests an interrogatory remark or inquiry; an exclamation point [!] suggest excitement or emphasis. The semicolon [;] separates two related but independent clauses or a complex series of items that contain commas. A colon [:] introduces a list or denotes that additional information follows. The dash [-] makes a brief interruption within a statement, a sudden change of thought, an additional comment, a dramatic qualification, or to add a parenthetical statement for clarification but still relevant to the central idea. Use the comma [,] to denote that words or phrases refer to the same person or thing, or to show a break within a sentence that adds information or develops the central idea.

The New Testament originally, written in common Greek, did not have chapters, verses, or punctuation. The language itself clearly placed words and phrases together and in positions of emphasis. Books and letters were later divided into chapters and verses for readers to search and find particular information. The translators also added punctuations based on the placement of the words or phrases. Most translations and renderings of the New Testament capitalized the first word of each verse even if it did not start a new sentence. This confuses the English reader and causes one to give prominence and importance to subordinate thoughts rather than value the main idea. Consequently, the Evergreen EDNT does not always capitalize the beginning word of a new verse unless there is a terminal punctuation before the verse number. The new verse should be read as a continuation of the previous thought or additional development supporting the central idea of the paragraph. Also, instead of quotation marks, the EDNT uses a Capital letter to begin a quotation. The EDNT has attempted to capitalize the pronouns that refer to the Trinity. Since the KJV had so many pronouns; hopefully, this will clarify the He, Him, His, referring to the Godhead and make it easier for the reader to attribute value to the antecedent.

There is no reason to be in the dark.
There can be light at the *beginning* of the tunnel.

TABLE OF CONTENTS

COMMUNITY AND FAMILY EDUCATION (C.A.F.E.)
Curriculum and Text..5

PROLOGUE
Why a Devotional New Testament?..8
Why Evergreen?...10

INTRODUCTION
Rationale for a Devotional New Testament..................................11
- A Relational Document
- Relational and Inductive Study
- Mostly Pristine Issues
- The Books and Letters Have a Chronology
- Use Original Language to Develop Doctrine
- The Pristine Experience was Relational
- A Candid Rendering of a Passage
- Relational and Inductive Study Combined
- A Repository of Classical Knowledge
- Hearing One Side of a Two-sided Conversation
- The Lapse of Time
- Roots of the English Language
- The Canonical Order of the New Testament
- Guidance for the Reader
- Chronological New Testament Order

The following Sections contain the New Testament books grouped according to the theme and addressee and presented in expository units in approximate chronological order by section and book.

A Traditional list of New Testament books at the end (p433) will guide the reader to find a particular book.

SECTION ONE
NARRATIVES ABOUT THE LIFE OF JESUS

Unique perspectives..23
The Gospel According to Mark..24
The Gospel According to Matthew...58
The Gospel According to John..82

Section Two

Letters to Theophilus

Elements of Pristine Christianity..121

- My Earlier View of Luke
- The Best Greek in the New Testament
- Emphasis by Proportion
- History of the first Thirty Years
- A Clear Historical View

The Gospel According to Luke...123

The Acts of the Apostles...175

Section Three

Letters to Assembled Believers

The First Letter to the Thessalonians...229

The Second Letter to the Thessalonians......................................234

The Letter to the Galatians..237

The First Letter to the Corinthians..244

The Second Letter to the Corinthians...265

The Letter to the Romans..279

The Letter to the Colossians...300

The Letter to the Ephesians..305

The Letter to the Philippians...312

Section Four

Relational Letters

The Letter to Philemon..318

The First Letter to Timothy..320

The Letter to Titus...326

The Second Letter to Timothy...329

The Second Letter of John..334

The Third Letter of John..335

Table of Contents

Section Five

Letters to Scattered Believers

The General Letter of James..337

The First Letter of Peter..344

The Letter to the Hebrews..351

The Second Letter of Peter...369

The General Letter of Jude...373

The First Letter of John..375

The Revelation of John...381

Appendix One

The King James Version...407

- KJV Translation Process
- Translators Choice of Words
- Another Difficulty is Chronology
- Each Book Has a Message
- No Agreement on the Chronology
- New Testament Books With Authors and Themes
- Order and Record of Chronological Reading
- Important Facts About Bible Reading and Study
- New Testament Reading Plus Listening
- Steps in Devotional Reading and Study
- A Systematic Study of the New Testament
- Structured Scripture Reading
- Reading as an Art
- Learning, Listening and Learning More
- Evening and Morning Readings
- Divided into Expository Units
- Chronology to Provide Order
- A Systematic Reading

Appendix Two

Interactive Study Using Interrogatives..423

- The Learning Process
- A Methodical Path
- Interrogatives
- Useful Assumptions in Interpretation

- Inductive Study
- Observation
- Interpretation
- Always Incomplete
- Possible Areas of Concern
- Avoidable Dangers
- Evaluation and Application
- Correlation

APPENDIX THREE

New Testament Order:..429 - 430

- Chronological Order
- Alphabetical Order
- Traditional Order

APPENDIX FOUR

C.A.F.E. Logo Data:..431

Quick Reference **New Testament Order**..433

Acceptable Words

9. And moreover, because the Preacher was wise, he still taught the people knowledge; yea, he gave good heed, and sought out, and set in order many proverbs. 10. The Preacher sought to find out acceptable words, and that which was written was upright, even words of truth. 11. The words of the wise are as goads, and as nails fastened by the masters of assemblies, which are given from one Shepherd. 12. And further, by these, my son, be admonished: of making many books there is no end; and much study is a weariness of the flesh. 13. Let us hear the conclusion of the whole matter, Fear God, and keep His commandments: for this is the whole duty of man. 14. For God shall bring every work into judgment, with every secret thing, whether it be good, or whether it be evil.

Ecclesiastes 12: 9-14 (KJV)

SECTION ONE

NARRATIVES ABOUT THE LIFE OF JESUS

The Gospel According to Mark
The Gospel According to Matthew
The Gospel According to John

The Chronological order of the Narratives are: Mark, Luke, Matthew, and John. Luke is presented as one of the two Letters to Theophilus in Section Two. Each writer had a **unique perspective** on the Life of Jesus:

Mark —John Mark presented Jesus as a Person of action in the context of an evangelistic message to those living outside of Palestine who had not witnessed the events in the life of Jesus.

Matthew — Matthew, one of the original disciples, wrote to a Jewish audience to verify that Jesus was the Messiah. As one of the original 12 Disciples, Matthew had a good foundation to share the story of Jesus, the awaited King of Israel.

John — John, one of the original disciples, presented the signs and wonders of Jesus to convince the readers that Jesus was the Christ, the Son of God and that salvation came through faith.

Those passages in Matthew that are common to Mark, Luke, or John are not presented, only the references for the reader's further study.

The Gospel According To Mark

Mark's work has been called the essential gospel. John Mark presented Jesus as a person of action in the context of an evangelistic message to those living outside of Palestine who had not witnessed the events in the life of Jesus. His gospel is a foundational document for the Christian life and early Church development. A great deal is known about John Mark. His family home was a center for early Christians (Acts 12:12). He was the nephew of Barnabas and traveled with both Paul and Barnabas. (Acts 12:25). Although he left them and did not complete his first missionary journey (Acts 15:37, 38), Paul later saw him as "useful to my ministry."(2 Timothy 4:11). He was not only useful to Paul, his work on the gospel story is considered by many to be essential to the understanding of the Man, Christ Jesus. John Mark grew up in Jerusalem surrounded by stories about the Messiah. He spoke to many eyewitnesses and may have even witnessed the arrest of Jesus. (See note at Mark 14:51). His primary source for the gospel was the preaching of Peter who called Mark "my son" (1 Peter 5:13). It is believed that Mark functioned as an interpreter for Peter and many of the details of the story came directly from the anointed eyewitness memory of Peter. Matthew reproduces in his gospel about half of the actual words of Mark. Mark's manuscript was essential to the early writers and all but twenty-four verses of Mark appears either in Matthew or Luke. Others probably wrote about the life of Jesus, but Mark's details about the life of Jesus are the earliest record to survive the ages. This supports the view that Mark's work is the essential gospel.

Make Ready the Path of the Lord
Mark 1:1-13

1:1. Beginning the good news of Jesus Christ; 2. according to sacred writings of Isaiah the prophet, Watch, I send My herald before you, to prepare the way, 3. the voice crying aloud in the desert, Make ready the path for the Lord, make His path without delay. 4. John came who immersed and proclaimed baptism for the penitent sinner. 5. And people kept going out to him from the Judaean country, and also from Jerusalem, and were all immersed by him in the river of Jordan, when they confessed their sins. 6. And John was clothed with a rough coat of camel's hair, and with a strap of skin fastened about his waist; and he did eat migratory grasshoppers and wild honey; 7. and kept on saying, There is coming after me One of great strength and power, whose sandal straps I am not worthy to bend down and let loose. 8. I submerged you in water: but He shall identify you with the Holy Spirit. 9. And it happened in those days that Jesus came from Nazareth in Galilee, and was baptized by John in the Jordan. 10. And immediately as He came up out of the water, He saw the heavens split into separate parts, and the Spirit as a Dove descended down upon Him: 11. and there came a voice from above, saying, You are My beloved Son, in whom I am delighted. 12. And immediately He was spirited into the desert, 13. and He was there forty days, tempted by Satan; and dwelt among the wild beasts; and the angels served His needs.

I Will Teach My Disciples to Catch Men
Mark 1:14-28

14. After John was arrested and put in prison, Jesus went to Galilee proclaiming the good news of the kingdom of God, 15. saying, The time is satisfied and the kingdom of God is near: turn from your sins and believe the good news. 16. As He walked by the Sea of Galilee, He saw Simon and Andrew his brother at work casting a net into the sea: for they were fishermen. 17. And Jesus said to them, Come follow Me, and I will teach you to catch men. 18. And immediately they abandoned their nets, and followed Him. 19. A little further on He saw James the son of Zebedee, and John his brother, who were in their boat repairing their nets. 20. And He called them immediately and they left their father Zebedee in the boat with the hired hands, and followed Him. 21. And they entered Capernaum; and straightway on the next Sabbath He entered the synagogue and began to teach. 22. And they were amazed at His teaching: for He taught them with authority, and not as other scholars of the laws. 23. And at the moment there was a man controlled by a demonic spirit in the synagogue; and he cried with a loud, piercing noise, 24. saying* What have we to do with you, Jesus of Nazareth? Have you come to destroy us? I know you are the Holy One of God. 25. And Jesus muzzled him, saying, Do not speak and come out of him. 26. And when the demonic spirit had convulsed him, with a loud howl he came out of him. 27. And they were all amazed and began to question each other asking, What does this mean? What new teaching is this? With authority He even gives orders to demonic spirits and they obey Him. 28. And immediately His reputation spread abroad throughout the region around Galilee.

---

*v24 "Let us alone" was omitted because the phrase is not supported by original manuscripts.

This is Why I Came
Mark 1:29-45

29. Directly after leaving the synagogue, they entered the house of Simon and Andrew, accompanied by James and John. 30. But Simon's mother-in-law was prostrate with a fever, and soon after they told Jesus. 31. He took her by the hand and raised her up; and the fever left her, and she served them. 32. At sundown that evening they kept bringing all that were sick and those influenced by a demon. 33. And the whole town gathered at the door. 34. And Jesus healed many

that were sick of various diseases, and cast out demons; but did not permit the demons to speak, because they knew Him. 35. And Jesus arose while it was still dark and departed into a private place to pray. 36. And Simon and the others searched for Him. 37. And when they found Him they said, Everyone is looking for you. 38. And He answered, Let us go into the village-towns, I must proclaim My message there also: for this is why I came. 39. And He remained in Galilee and proclaimed His message in their synagogues, and continued casting out demons. 40. And a leper approached and knelt before Him, pleading, If you are willing, you can cleanse me. 41. And Jesus, moved with compassion, stretched forth His hand and touched him, and said, I will, be cleansed. 42. And immediately the leprosy departed and he was cleansed. 43. And Jesus sternly charged him, and sent him away; 44. warning him, Say nothing to any man: but show yourself to the priest, and offer what Moses prescribed for your cleansing as proof to the authorities. 45. But he went out and told the whole story, and spread the news, so that Jesus could not openly enter into any town, but stayed in private places: yet the people from every neighborhood kept coming to Him.

We Have Not Seen Anything Like This
Mark 2: 1-12

2:1. Several days later Jesus again entered Capernaum; and it was rumored that He had gone into a particular house. 2. And many gathered that there was no room inside not even outside the door: and He spoke the word to them. 3. And they came to Him, bringing a paralyzed man carried by four men. 4. And when they could not get near Him because of the crowd, they removed the roof tiles above Him: and when they had broken through they lowered the pallet on which the paralytic was. 5. When Jesus witnessed their faith, He said unto the paralytic, Young man, your sins are forgiven. 6. There were certain scholars of the law present who questioned among themselves, 7. Why does this man speak blasphemies? Who can forgive sins but God alone? 8. And Jesus understanding in His spirit that they questioned among themselves, asked, Why question these things in your hearts? 9. Whether is it easier to say to a paralytic, Your sins be forgiven; or to say, Arise, and take up your pallet and walk? 10. But to convince you that the Son of man has power on earth to forgive sins, (He said to the paralyzed man,) 11. Get up and take your pallet and go to your own home. 12. And he got up at once and took the pallet, and walked before them; and they were all amazed and glorified God, saying, We have not seen anything like this.

New Wine Must be Put in Fresh Wine-skins
Mark 2:13-22

13. And Jesus left the town and again walked by the sea; and the multitude kept coming to Him, and He continued teaching them. 14. And as He walked further, He saw Levi the son of Alphaeus at his seat in the custom house, and said, Follow Me. And Levi promptly arose and followed Him. 15. Later when Jesus sat down to eat at Levi's house, many tax-collectors and some who habitually did wrong things sat together with Jesus and His disciples: for there were many among His followers. 16. And when the scribes of the Pharisees saw Jesus eat with tax-collectors and sinners, they asked His disciples, Why does He eat with this bad company? 17. When Jesus overheard this, He said to them, The strong have no need of a physician, but those affected by an illness: I came not to call the blameless, but those who habitually do wrong to repentance. 18. And the disciples of John and the Pharisees were keeping a fast: and they asked, Why do the disciples of John and the Pharisees fast, but your disciples do not fast? 19. And Jesus answered, Can the bridegroom's guest fast, while the bridegroom is with them? As long as they have the bridegroom with them, fasting is impractical. 20. But the time will come, when the bridegroom is taken away, then in that time they will fast. 21. No one sows a patch of new cloth on an old garment: else the new patch will tear away from the old and the split is made worse. 22. And no one pours new wine into old wine-skins: else the new wine will rupture the old wine-skins, and the wine and the skins are lost: but new wine must be put into fresh wine-skins.

The Son of Man is Sovereign Over the Sabbath
Mark 2:23-28

23. One Sabbath Jesus was going through the corn fields; and His disciples began plucking ears of corn. 24. And the Pharisees said, Look, why are they doing what is not lawful on the Sabbath day? 25. And Jesus answered, Did you never read what David and his men did when they had great need and was hungry? 26. How David went into the house of God when Abiathar was high priest, and did eat the consecrated bread, which is lawful only for the priests and gave bread to those with him? 27. And Jesus said, The Sabbath was made to serve mankind, and not mankind for the Sabbath: 28. consequently, the Son of man is sovereign over the Sabbath.

Is it Lawful to do Good on the Sabbath?
Mark 3:1-6

3:1 And Jesus went again into the synagogue; and there was a man who had a withered hand. 2. And the Pharisees kept watching closely to see if He would heal him on the Sabbath; so they could accuse Him. 3. And Jesus said to the man with the withered hand, Come forward. 4. And He asked them, Is it lawful to do good on the Sabbath, or to do harm? To save life, or to kill? But they remained silent. 5. And after an angry look around, being grieved for the hardness of their hearts, Jesus said to the man, Stretch out your hand. And he stretched it out and at once his hand was restored whole as the other. 6. And the Pharisees left the synagogue and immediately took counsel with the partisans of Herod against Jesus, how they might destroy Him.

What Great Things He Did
Mark 3:7-12

7. And Jesus with His disciples withdrew to the lakeside: and a great multitude from Galilee and Judaea followed Him, 8. and when they had heard what great things He did, a growing crowd came to Him from Jerusalem, Idumaea, from east of Jordan; and from around Tyre and Sidon. 9. And because of the crowd, He directed His disciples to have a small boat ready for Him, lest the multitude should crush Him. 10. For He had healed many; and the sick and afflicted swarmed in to touch Him. 11. And the spirits, the unclean ones, when they saw Him, fell down before Him, and cried, saying, You are the Son of God. 12. And Jesus rebuked them and warned of a penalty if they should make Him known.

He Selected Twelve as Messengers
Mark 3:13-19

13. And Jesus went up to the hill country, and invited certain to come to Him: and they joined Him. 14. And He selected twelve as messengers, that they should be with Him, and that He might send them forth to preach, 15. and to have authority to cast out demons:* 16. and to Simon He gave the name, Peter; 17. and James, the son of Zebedee, and John, the brother of James; He put on them the name Boanerges, which is, the thunder-voiced: 18. and Andrew, and Philip, and Bartholomew, and Matthew, and Thomas, and James, the son of Alphaeus, and Thaddeus, and Simon, the Canaanite, 19. and Judas Iscariot, who would betray Him: and they entered a private house.

---

*v15 The words "to heal sicknesses" are not adequately supported here by original manuscripts, but the healing of the sick is supported elsewhere.

These are My Mother and My Brothers
Mark 3:20-35

20. And again the crowd gathered, so that they could not even eat bread. 21. And when His kinsmen learned of the crowd, they went out to restrain Him: for they kept on saying, He is in an excited and

agitated state. 22. And the scholars of the law who came down from Jerusalem said, He is possessed by Beelzebub, and by the prince of demons He cast out demons. 23. And Jesus called to them and spoke in parables, Is it possible for Satan to cast out Satan? 24. And if a kingdom be divided by civil strife, that kingdom cannot stand. 25. And if a household be divided against itself, that household cannot endure. 26. And if Satan rise up against himself, and be divided, he cannot stand, but his end is near. 27. No man can break into a strong man's house and plunder his goods, unless he first binds the strong man; and then he can plunder his house. 28. Truly, I tell you, all manner of sins can be forgiven and the insulting things they say and do that insults spiritual matters: 29. But he who disrespects the Holy Spirit through words or action has no forgiveness, but is guilty of an eternal sin: 30. Because they kept saying, He has an unclean spirit. 31. Then came His mother and brothers, and, standing without, sent a message for Him to come outside. 32. With a multitude about Him, they said, Your mother and brothers are outside asking for you. 33. And He asked, Who is My mother, or My brothers? 34. And looking around at those who sat with Him, Jesus said, Look, these are My mother and My brothers! 35. For whosoever does the will of God, the same is My brother, and My sister, and mother.

Listen and Pay Attention
Mark 4:1-25

4:1. And Jesus began again to teach by the lakeside: and there gathered a great crowd, so that He entered into a boat, and sat just off shore; and the crowd gathered by the shore. 2. And He taught them many things by parables, and said in the course of His teaching, 3. Listen and pay attention; the farmer went out to spread seed: 4. and as he spread the seeds, some fell by the hard path, and the birds came and consumed them. 5. And some fell on rocky soil, where the soil was shallow; and the seed immediately sprouted, because the soil had no depth: 6. But when the sun rose, it was parched; and because it had no root, it withered away. 7. And some fell among the prickly weeds, and the thistles grew up, and choked the seeds, and they yielded no harvest. 8. And other seeds fell on good soil, and sprang up and continued to grow; and yielded a harvest, some thirty, and some sixty, and some a hundred fold. 9. And Jesus said, he who has ears to hear let him listen. 10. And when He was alone with the Twelve they asked about the parable. 11. And He answered, To you is given to know the technical meaning of the kingdom of God: but to the uninitiated outside this circle, all these things are presented in stories: 12. that seeing they may see, and not perceive; and hearing they may hear, and not understand; lest at any time they should turn again, and their sins be forgiven.* 13. And He continued, Do you not understand this parable? How then will you know other parables? 14. The seed is the word. 15. And these are the ones by the hard path, where the word was sown; but when they heard, Satan immediately came and took away the word that was placed in their hearts. 16. And these are the ones sown on stony ground; who, when they heard the word, immediately receive it with gladness; 17. but they had no real roots, and so endure for only a short time: afterward, when affliction or persecution came for the word's sake, they were easily hurt. 18. And these are they who are sown among prickly weeds; such as hear the word, 19. and the cares of this world and the deceiving pleasures of riches, and the craving for material things enters in and chokes the word, and it becomes unproductive. 20. And these are they who received the word on good ground; such as hear the word, and receives it, and becomes productive, some thirtyfold, some sixty, and some an hundredfold. 21. And Jesus continued, Is a lamp put under a bushel, or under a bed? And not placed on a lamp-stand? 22. For there is nothing hid, except it will be manifested; neither is anything concealed, except it will be revealed. 23. If anyone has ears to hear, let him listen. 24. Then He added, Take care how you listen: with what gauge you use to measure, it shall be calculated to you: and to you who listen, more shall be added to you. 25. For he who has, shall be given more: and he who holds back shall be deprived of what he has.

---

*v12 This is one of the most difficult passages in the gospels. It is a quotation from Isaiah 6:9,10. The Septuagint (Greek version of the OT presents this passage in a clearer light.) The Greek clearly shows that God did not intend that the people be so dull of hearing and limited in their understanding, but that they had willingly hardened their hearts to the truth. Consequently, God could not save them. It appeared that the people had become so hardened that even if they saw and heard the truth they would not understand. Under grace when one is initiated to God's mercy, they can begin to understand the obscurity and even the ambiguity of the Kingdom of God.

It is Harvest-time
Mark 4:26-35

26. Then Jesus said, The kingdom of God is as if a man should spread seed upon the ground; 27. and then sleeps at night and gets up in the morning, and the seeds spring up and grows, but he does not know how. 28. For the earth produces a crop by itself; first the stalk, then the ear, after that the full grown corn in the ear. 29. But when the crop is ripe, immediately he uses the cutting blade, because it is harvest-time. 30. And Jesus continued, With what can we compare the kingdom of God? Or in what parable shall we present it? 31. It is similar to a grain of mustard seed, when sown it is smallest of all the seeds in the earth: 32. but once the seed is sown, it springs up, and becomes larger than

all the garden plants, and produces great branches; so that the birds may nest and shelter in its shade. 33. And with many such stories He shared the word with them, as they were able to receive it. 34. He said nothing to them without a parable: and when He was alone with His disciples, He explained all things to them. 35. And on that evening, He said, Let us cross over to the other side.

Why are You So Afraid?
Mark 4:36-41

36. And when they had sent away the crowd, they took Jesus away in the boat. And there were also with them other little boats. 37. And there arose a violent storm, and the waves beat into the boat, so that it was nearly swamped. 38. And Jesus was in the stern of the boat, asleep on a cushion: and they awoke Him, saying, Master, do you not care that we are sinking? 39. And being aroused, He rebuked the wind, Be silent! And spoke to the waves, Be muzzled! And the wind stopped beating, and there was a great calm. 40. And He said to them, Why are you so afraid? How is it that you have no faith? 41. And they were exceedingly awestruck, and asked one another, What kind of man is this, that even the wind and the waves obey Him?

Go Home to Your Friends
Mark 5:1-20

5:1. After they arrived at the other side of the lake, in the territory of the Gadarenes, 2. and Jesus stepped out of the boat, He encountered a man from the tombs under the power of an evil spirit, 3. who had settled down among the dead; and no man could restrain him, even with chains: 4. because he had been often shackled hand and foot, and the chains were found twisted apart, and the shackles broken into pieces: neither could any man bring him under control. 5. And always, night and day, he was in the mountains, and among the tombs, shrieking, and cutting himself with stones. 6. But when he saw Jesus from a distance, he ran showing respect and bowed at His feet, 7. and with a high-pitched shriek, said, What have we in common, Jesus, Son of the most high God? I implore you by God, do not torment me. 8. For Jesus had commanded, Come out of this man, you evil spirit. 9. And Jesus asked, What is your name? And he answered, Legion is my name: for we are many. 10 And they pleaded earnestly that Jesus not send them away out of the area. 11. On the hillside a great herd of pigs were feeding. 12. And the devils pleaded, Send us among the pigs, that we may possess them. 13. Without delay Jesus gave them permission. And the unclean spirits went out, and entered into the herd: and the pigs rushed headlong down a steep place into the lake, (they were about two thousand); and were all drowned. 14. And the herdsmen fled, and told the news in the town and country-side. And the people came to see what was done. 15 And they came to Jesus, and saw him who was possessed with the devil, and had the legion, sitting, and clothed, and in his right mind: and they were afraid. 16. And those who saw it told them how it happened to him that was possessed with the devil, and also concerning the pigs. 17. And they pleaded with Jesus to leave their area. 18. So Jesus entered the boat and the man who had been possessed with the devil kept begging to go with Him; 19. however, Jesus refused, but said, Go home to your friends, and tell them the Lord had compassion and did a great thing for you. 20. And he departed, and began to publish in Decapolis the great things Jesus had done for him: and all men were amazed.

Be Free from This Trouble
Mark 5:21-34

21. While Jesus returned to the other side of the lake by boat, many people gathered along the shore. 22. Then came the Head of the synagogue, Jairus by name; and when he saw Jesus, he fell at his feet, 23. And earnestly appealed, saying, My little daughter is dying: come and lay your hands on her, that she may be healed and live. 24. And Jesus went with him; and a great number of people crowded around as they went. 25. And a certain woman, who had hemorrhaged for twelve years, 26. and had suffered many things of many physicians, and had spent all her resources and was no better, but rather grew worse, 27. when she heard about Jesus, came in the crowd behind Him, and touched His robe. 28. For she kept saying, If I may touch but His clothes, I shall be healed. 29. And immediately her flow of blood was dried up; and she knew she was healed of her disease. 30. And Jesus, immediately perceiving that healing power had passed from Him, turned around in the crowd, and said, Who touched My garments? 31. And His disciples answered, You see the multitude thronging you, and asked, Who touched Me? 32. And He kept looking for the women that had done this thing. 33. But the woman fearing and trembling, knowing what was done in her, came and fell down before Jesus, and told Him the whole story. 34. And He said unto her, Daughter, your faith has healed you; go in peace, and be free from this trouble.

Be Not Afraid, Only Believe
Mark 5:35-43

35. While Jesus was still speaking, some came from the head of the synagogue's house and told him, Your daughter is dead: why trouble the Master further? 36. As soon as Jesus heard this, He said to the head of the synagogue, Be not afraid, only believe. 37. And He

permitted no one to go with Him except Peter, James, and John, the brother of James. 38. And they came to the ruler's house and saw the commotion, and the hired mourners who wept and wailed greatly. 39. And when Jesus entered, He said, Why do you make this commotion and weep? The maiden is not dead, but sleeps. 40. And they laughed in His face. But He drove them all out except the parents of the child and those with Him, and entered the room where the child was lying. 41. And He took her by the hand, and said, Talitha cumi; which is interpreted, My child, I say to you, arise. 42. And immediately the girl got up and began walking; for she was twelve years old. And they were overcome with great astonishment. 43. And Jesus repeatedly charged them that no one should hear about this; and told the parents to give the child something to eat.

Is Not This the Stone Mason?
Mark 6:1-13

6:1. And when Jesus left that district, He came into His home country; and His disciples follow. 2. And on the Sabbath day, He began to teach in the synagogue: and many hearing Him were astonished, saying, From where does this man get these things? How did He gain such wisdom and power to do such mighty things? 3. Is not this the stone mason (carpenter*), the son of Mary, the brother of James, Joses, Judah, and Simon? And do not His sisters live among us? And they were filled with resentment. 4. But Jesus said, A prophet is honored everywhere, except in his own country, among his own kin, and in his own house. 5. And Jesus could do no mighty work among them except to strengthen the weakness of a few sick folk. 6. And Jesus was awe struck at their unbelief. And He went to the adjacent villages and taught. 7. And He called the Twelve, and sent them forth in pairs; and gave them power over unclean spirits; 8. and instructed them to take nothing for their journey, except a carrying staff only; no satchel, no bread, no available funds: 9. but be shod with sandals; and not a second coat. 10. And He told them, In whatever place you go and enter a house abide there until you depart from that place. 11. And whoever does not receive you, or hear you, when you depart, shake off the dust under your feet as a testimony against them. Verily I say to you, It shall be more tolerable for Sodom and Gomorrah in the day of judgment, than for that city. 12. And they went out, and preached repentance. 13. And they cast out many devils, and anointed many sick with oil and they were healed.

---

*v3 The word here is "tekton," an artificer or technician who uses materials efficiently and systematically in building. One who understands biblical times may easily accept that Joseph and Jesus were manually skilled in using stones for building. Anyone who has traveled in the Holy Land observed that rocks greatly outnumber trees. Jesus said He would build His church upon a "rock." A concordance search would show many verses where God is seen as a Rock. Paul acknowledged this: "And all drank from the same spiritual Rock and that Rock was Christ," (1 Corinthians 10:4 EDNT).

Herodias had a Grudge Against John
Mark 6:14-29

14. And King Herod heard of Jesus; (for His name was spread abroad:) and some believed that John, the Baptist, was raised from the dead and was enabled to do mighty works. 15. Others said that it was Elijah. And others thought, this is a prophet, the same as one of the old prophets. 16. But when Herod heard this, he said, It is the very John, whom I beheaded: he has stood up from the grave. 17. For Herod himself had sent and arrested John, and bound him in prison for Herodias' sake, his brother Philip's wife: whom he had married. 18. For John had said to Herod, It is not lawful for you to have your brother's wife. 19. Therefore, Herodias had a grudge against John, and would have killed him; but she could not: 20. Because Herod feared John, knowing that he was a just and holy man, and protected him; and when he heard him, he was perplexed yet he heard him gladly. 21. And when a convenient time for Herodias came, on Herod's birthday when he made a supper to his leaders, high captains, and commanders of thousands in Galilee; 22. and when the daughter of Herodias came in, and danced, and pleased Herod and those who sat with him, the king said to the maiden, Ask of me whatever you wish, and I will give it. 23. And he swore to her, Whatsoever you ask, I will give it to the half of my kingdom. 24. And she went and asked her mother, What shall I ask? And she said, The head of John the Baptist. 25. And she came in immediately to the king, and asked, I will that you immediately serve me in this place, the head of John the Baptist on a ceremonial platter. 26. And the king was exceeding distressed, yet for his oath's sake, and for those who sat with him, he could not refuse her. 27. And immediately the king sent a guardsman and commanded John's head to be brought: and the soldier went and beheaded John in the prison, 28. And brought his head on a ceremonial platter, and gave it to the maiden: and she gave it to her mother. 29. And when his disciples heard about his death, they came and took John's body, and placed it in a tomb.

Give Them Something to Eat
Mark 6:30-44

30. And the apostles gathered themselves together with Jesus, and reported to Him all things, both what they had done, and what they had taught. 31 And He said to them, Come apart to a quiet place and

rest a while: for many were coming and going, and they had no time even to eat. 32. And they departed secretly in a boat to a secluded place. 33. And the people saw them departing, and recognized Jesus and ran around the lake and past all the towns, and arrived ahead of them. 34. And Jesus, when He landed, saw a large crowd and was moved with compassion on them, because they were as sheep without a shepherd: and He began to teach them many things. 35. And as the day grew late, His disciples came to Him, and said, This is a desolate place, and it is getting late: 36. send them away, that they may go into the country-side, and into the villages, and buy themselves bread. 37. He answered and said, You give them something to eat. And they said, Shall we go and buy bread, and give them to eat? 38. He asked, How many loaves do you have? Go and see. And when they knew, they answered, Five and two fishes. 39. And He instructed them to make everyone sit down in rows on the green grass. 40. And they sat down in rows, by hundreds, and by fifties. 41. And when Jesus had taken the five loaves and the two fishes, He looked up to heaven, and blessed, and broke the loaves, and kept giving them to His disciples to distribute; and the two fishes divided He among them all. 42. And they did all eat, and were filled. 43. And they took up twelve baskets full of the scraps of bread and fish. 44. And they that did eat of the loaves were about five thousand men.

Be of Good Cheer; It is I
Mark 6:45-56
45. And immediately Jesus pressured the disciples to get in the boat, and to go before Him to the other side to Bethsaida, while He sent the people away. 46. And when He had sent them away, He departed into a mountain to pray. 47. And when even was come, the boat was in the middle of the lake, and He was alone on the land. 48. And He saw them straining at the oars; for the wind was against them: and between three and six in the morning, He came walking on the water, and would have passed by them. 49. But when they saw Him walking on the lake, they supposed it was a ghost, and cried out: 50. for they all saw Him, and were troubled. And immediately He spoke to them, Be of good cheer: it is I; be not afraid. 51. And He got into the boat with them; and the wind ceased: and they were amazed beyond measure. 52. For they had not understood the miracle of the loaves: for their eyes were blinded. 53. And when they had crossed the lake, they came to the land of Gennesaret, and tied up the boat. 54. And when they came ashore, immediately the people recognized Jesus, 55. and ran all over the neighborhood, and began to carry in beds those that were sick, to where they heard He was. 56. And wherever He entered, into villages or towns or country, they laid the sick in the

market-places, and begged that they might touch if it were but the hem of His robe: and as many as touched Him were made whole.

Their Worship is Empty
Mark 7:1-13

7:1. And now the Pharisees came to Jesus in a group, with some scholars of the law who came from Jerusalem. 2. They saw some of His disciples eat bread with unwashed or defiled hands. 3. The Pharisees, and all the Jews, did not eat except they wash their hands, holding the tradition of the elders. 4. And when they purchased something from the market, they would not eat it without first purifying it with water. And they have many other customs, which they maintain by tradition; such as, the washing of cups, and pots, and vessels of copper. 5. Then the Pharisees and scribes asked Jesus, Why do your disciples not walk according to the tradition of the elders, but eat bread with unwashed hands? 6. He answered, you hypocrites, Isaiah prophesied and described you, This people honors me with their lips, but their heart is far from me. 7. Their worship is empty, teaching for doctrines the precepts of men. 8. You give up what God commanded and cling to the tradition of men, as the washing of pots and cups, 9. and He said to them, Full well you reject the commandments of God, that you may keep your own tradition. 10. For Moses said, Honor your father and mother; and, Whoever speaks evil of father or mother, let him be executed: 11. but you say, If a man shall say to his father or mother, It is Corban, that is to say, a gift to the temple, of all the support they might have gained; he shall be free. 12. And you permit him to do nothing more for his father or his mother; 13. making the word of God of none effect through your tradition, which you have delivered: and many such things you do.

If Any Man has Ears, Let Him Hear
Mark 7:14-23

14. And when He had called all the people to Him, Jesus said, Hearken to Me everyone and understand:15. there is nothing from without a man that entering into him can defile him: but the things which come out of him, those are what defile the man. 16. If any man has ears, let him listen. 17. And when He entered the house from the people, His disciples asked concerning the story. 18. And Jesus said, Are you without understanding, also? Do you not perceive, that whatever thing from without entering a man cannot defile him; 19. because it enters not into his heart, but into the stomach, and goes out as waste, making all foods ceremonially clean? 20. And He said, What comes out of the man that defiles, 21. it is from within, out of the heart that proceeds evil thoughts, adulteries, fornications, 22. thefts, covetousness,

wickedness, deceit, licentiousness, jealousy, blasphemy, slander, arrogance, and folly: 23. all these evil things come from within, and defile the man.

The Children's Bread
Mark 7:24-30

24. Then Jesus departed and went into the regions of Tyre and Sidon, and entered a house, and wanted no one to know where: but He could not be hid. 25. For a certain woman, whose young daughter had an evil spirit, heard of Him, and came and fell at His feet: 26. The woman was a Greek, a Syro-Phoenician by race; and she repeatedly asked Him to cast the demon out of her daughter. 27. But Jesus said to her, Let the children first be satisfied: for it is not right to take the children's bread, and to throw it to the house-dogs. 28. And she answered, Yes, Lord: yet the house-dogs under the table eat of the children's crumbs. 29. And He said to her, For this saying go your way; the evil spirit has left your daughter. 30. And she went to her house and found the demon gone, and her daughter resting on the bed.

He has Done All Things Well
Mark 7:31-8:9

31. Again, Jesus departed the coasts of Tyre through Sidon, to the sea of Galilee, through the regions of the Decapolis. 32. And they brought to Him one that was deaf, and had an obstruction in his speech; and they implored Jesus to place His hand on him. 33. And He took the man aside from the multitude, and thrust His fingers in his ears, and touched his tongue with saliva*; 34. and looking up to heaven, He moaned and said, Ephphatha, meaning, Be opened. 35. And his ears were opened, and the obstruction to his tongue was removed, and he began to speak clearly. 36. And Jesus instructed them that they should tell no one: but the more He insisted, the more they publicized it; 37. and the people were utterly astonished, and kept saying, He has done all things well: He makes both the deaf to hear, and the dumb to speak.

---

*v33 Seems an uncouth act, but "saliva" contains a clear liquid consisting of water, mucin, protein and enzymes from the salivary glands that are believed to have a healing effect.

Moved with Compassion
Mark 8:1-9

8:1. During these days a great crowd again gathered and they had nothing to eat, Jesus called His disciples, and said, 2. I am moved with compassion for this multitude, because they have continued with Me three days, and have nothing to eat: 3. and if I send them away fasting to their own houses, they will fall by the way: for some of them came a great distance. 4. And His disciples answered, How could a man find bread for this many in this remote place? 5. And He asked, How many loaves do you have? They answered, Seven. 6. And He instructed the people to sit down on the ground: and He took the seven loaves, and gave thanks, and broke them into pieces, and gave to His disciples to distribute; and they gave the bread to the people. 7. And they had a few small fishes which Jesus blessed, and instructed that they be distributed also. 8. So they did eat, and were filled: and they gathered up seven baskets of scraps. 9. And those that had eaten were about four thousand*: and He sent them away.

---

*v9 It should be remembered that at such events, women and children were not normally counted.

Only One Loaf
Mark 8:10-21

10. And immediately Jesus entered a boat with His disciples, and came to the district of Dalmanutha. 11. And the Pharisees came out and engaged Him in dispute, tempting Him by asking for a sign from heaven. 12. And He exhaled deeply in His spirit, and said, Why does this generation seek a sign? Truly, I say, There shall no sign be given to this generation. 13. And He left them, and entered again into the boat and departed to the other shore. 14. Now the disciples had forgotten to bring bread, and had only one loaf on the boat. 15. And with anxious feelings He instructed them, saying, Take heed, beware of the yeast of the Pharisees, and of the yeast of Herod. 16. And they discussed the matter among themselves, saying, It is because we have no bread. 17. When Jesus perceived this, He said, Why the discussion about not bringing bread? Do you not perceive or understand? Do you have a closed mind? 18. You have eyes and ears do you not see and hear? Do you not remember? 19. When I broke the five loaves among five thousand, how many baskets of scraps did you gather? They answered, Twelve. 20. And when the seven among four thousand, how many baskets of scraps did you gather? And they said, Seven. 21. And He said, How is it that you do not understand?

Sent to His house - Family First
Mark 8:22-26

22. And He came to Bethsaida; and they brought a blind man to Him, and pleaded that He touch him. 23. And Jesus took the blind man by the hand, and led him outside the village; and dampened his eyes with saliva and laid on His hands, and asked him can you see anything? 24. And the man looked up, and said, I see men as trees, walking. 25.

After that Jesus laid His hands on his eyes again, and his sight came into focus, and he saw every man clearly. 26. And He sent him away to his house, saying, Do not go into the village.

Your Thoughts are not God's but Men's
Mark 8:27-33

27. Then Jesus went on with His disciples into the villages of Caesarea Philippi: and on the way He asked His disciples, Whom do men say that I am? 28. And they answered, John the Baptist: but some say, Elijah; and others, one of the prophets. 29. And He questioned, But whom do you say I am? And Peter answered, You are the Christ. 30. And He cautioned them that they should tell no one. 31. And for the first time He began to teach that the Son of man must suffer many things, and be renounced by the elders, and by the chief priests, and scribes, and be killed, and after three days stand up again. 32. And He kept telling them this openly. And Peter took hold of Him, and began to express disapproval. 33. But when Jesus had turned about and looked at His disciples, He rebuked Peter, saying, Get behind Me, Satan: your thoughts are not God's but man's.

Take Up His Own Cross
Mark 8:34-38

34. And when Jesus had called the crowd and His disciples to Himself, He said, If anyone wants to follow Me, let him deny himself, and take up his own cross, and come with Me. 35. For whoever wants to save his life will lose it; but whoever loses his life for Me and the gospel, the same will save it. 36. For what will it profit a man, if he gains the whole world, and lose his own soul? 37. Or what shall a man give in exchange for his soul? 38. Whoever therefore shall be ashamed of acknowledging me and of My words in this faithless and wicked generation; of him also shall the Son of man be ashamed to acknowledge, when He comes into the glory of His Father with the holy angels.

Listen to Him
Mark 9:1-8

9:1. And Jesus said, I say the truth to you, That there are those that stand here, who shall not taste of death, until they have seen the kingdom of God come with power. 2. And after six days Jesus takes Peter, James, and John, and leads them up into a high mountain apart by themselves: and He was transformed before them in great spirituality and beauty. 3. And His clothes glistened and became exceedingly white as snow; whiter that any bleach on earth could whiten. 4. And there appeared Elijah with Moses talking with Jesus. 5. And Peter spoke loudly to Jesus, Master, it is good for us to be here: let us make three tabernacles; one for you, and one for Moses, and one for Elijah.

6. Peter was so frightened he did not know what to say. 7. And there was a cloud that overshadowed them: and a voice came out of the cloud, saying, This is My beloved Son: listen to Him. 8. And suddenly, when they had looked round about, they saw no one, save Jesus and themselves.

Coming Down from the Mountain
Mark 9:9-13

9. And coming down from the mountain, Jesus instructed them that no one was to know what things they had seen, until the Son of man stood up again from the grave. 10. And they kept asking themselves, questioning one another what the standing up from the grave should mean. 11. And they asked Him, Why do the scribes say that Elijah must first come? 12. And He answered, Elijah does come first, and restores all things; and how it is written that the Son of man must suffer many things, and be rejected. 13. But I say, That Elijah has already come, and they have done to him whatever they pleased, as it was written about him.

I Believe, Help My Unbelief
Mark 9:14-27

14. And when Jesus came to His disciples, He saw a large crowd surrounding them, and the scribes arguing with them. 15. And immediately all the people, when they saw Jesus, were greatly amazed, and running to Him greeted Him respectfully. 16. And He asked the scribes, Why do you argue with them? 17. And one in the crowd answered, Master, I have brought to you my son, who has a spirit that makes him speechless; 18. and when it seizes hold of him, he is knocked down and foams at the mouth and grinds with his teeth, and goes rigid: and I asked your disciples to cast out this spirit, and they were powerless. 19. He answered, O you faithless generation, how long will I bear with you? How long will I endure you? Bring him to Me. 20. And they brought him to Jesus: and when He saw him, immediately the spirit caused him to shake violently and uncontrollably; and the lad fell on the ground, and rolled about, foaming at the mouth. 21. And Jesus asked his father, How long has he had this? And he said, Since childhood. 22. And often it has thrown him into the fire, and into the waters, to destroy him: but if you can do anything, have compassion on us, and help us. 23. Jesus asked, Do you question if I can? All things are possible to him who believes. 24. And immediately the father of the child cried out, and said, I believe; help my unbelief. 25. When Jesus saw that a crowd was gathering, He rebuked the evil spirit, and said, You spirit of dumbness and deafness, I charge you, come out of him, and enter no more into him. 26. And the spirit gave a loud shriek, and

convulsed him sore and came out of him: and the lad was lifeless; and many said, He is dead. 27. But Jesus took him by the hand, and lifted him up; and he stood up.

By Nothing Except Prayer
Mark 9:28-35

28. And when He had entered the house, His disciples asked privately, Why were we unable to cast out the spirit? 29. And Jesus answered, This kind can come out by nothing except prayer.* 30. And they departed and made a journey through Galilee; and Jesus did not want anyone to know of this journey. 31. Because He wanted to explain to His disciples, that the Son of man is presently delivered into the hands of men, and they will kill him and after His death on the third day He would stand up again. 32. But they did not understand that saying, and were afraid to ask. 33. And they came to Capernaum: and being in the house Jesus asked them, What was the dispute among yourselves by the way? 34. But they held their peace: for by the way they had argued among themselves, who should be the greatest. 35. And He sat down, and called the Twelve, and said, If any man desire to be first, the same must make himself to be last, and a committed servant (minister) of the gospel to all.

---

*v29 Although fasting is an important scriptural teaching, the words "and fasting" were not adequately supported here by the original texts.

Whoever Receives Little Children in My Name, Receives Me
Mark 9:36-42

36. And Jesus took a little child, and placed him among them: and when He had taken him in His arms, He said, 37. Whoever receives* (for themselves) little children in my name, receives* Me: and whoever shall receive* Me, receives* not me alone, but Him who sent Me. 38. And John said, Master, we saw one casting out devils using your name, and we forcefully told him to stop, because he does not follow us. 39. But Jesus said, Do not hinder him: for there is no man who will do a mighty works in My name, who can quickly speak evil of Me. 40. For whoever is not against us is on our side. 41. For whoever gives you a cup of water to drink in My name, because you belong to Christ, I assure you, he will not lose his wages. 42. And whoever shall cause to stumble or entice to sin** one of these little ones who believes in Me, it is better for him that a large grinder-stone be wrapped around his neck, and be thrown into the sea.

---

*v37 "receive(s)" is *dechoma*i in the middle (selfish) voice and should be understood "receives for themselves." It appears that Jesus was making a point that receiving children brings personal responsibility.

**v42 "offend" Greek *skandalizo*, the English *scandalize*, means to "stumble, entrap, trip up or entice to sin." Obviously Jesus saw the abuse of children as a serious matter.

Preserving Principle of Divine Grace
Mark 9:43-50

43. And if your hand causes you to sin, cut it off: it is better for you to enter life with a permanent injury, than have two hands and go to hell, into the perpetual fire that is unquenchable*: 44.** 45. And if your foot causes you to sin, cut it off: it is better for you to enter life crippled, than having two feet be thrown into hell. 46.** 47. And if your eye causes you to sin, pluck it out: it is better for you to enter the kingdom of God with one eye, than having two eyes be thrown into hell fire: 48. where the earth-worm never dies, and the fire never goes out. 49. For every one shall be preserved with fire. 50. Salt is good: but if the salt is tasteless, wherewith will you restore it? Have the preserving principle of divine grace in your hearts, and live in peace with one another.

---

*v43 "quenched" is *asbestos* meaning perpetual, unquenchable.

**vs 44,46,and part of 45 are not supported by the original texts; however, the words and concepts omitted here are supported in other verses of this chapter.

Lack of Spiritual Perception
Mark 10: 1-12

10:1. And Jesus arose and went into the coasts of Judaea across the Jordan: and the people crowded around Him again; and, as His custom He again taught them. 2. And the Pharisees came to tempt Him and asked, Is it right for a husband to set at liberty his wife? 3. And He answered, What instructions did Moses give you? 4. And they said, Moses permitted a written bill of divorcement that included forgiveness and liberty for her. 5. And Jesus answered, Because of your lack of spiritual perception he wrote you these guidelines. 6. But from the creation, the first principle was that God made them male and female. 7. By reason of this shall a man turn loose of his father and mother, and hold fast to his wife; 8. and the two shall become one body (flesh):* so then they are no more two, but one body (family). 9. When God has conjoined two or more together, let no man separate (a family) into parts. 10. And in the house His disciples asked again about the same matter. 11. And He said, Whoever shall set his wife at liberty and add another, commits adultery against her. 12. And if a woman shall put away her husband, and add another, she commits adultery. **

---

*v8 "one flesh" is *sarx* which suggests a human body apart from the soul. Probably this is the bonding that comes with the first child and not only the emotional bonding of a couple when vows are physically consummated.

**Commit adultery in this section is *moichao* in the Greek middle (selfish) voice and is not a stand alone word; it is either a selfish act or a morally wrong attitude about marriage. Committing adultery is actually adding another which adulterates and diminishes a relationship; in fact, the selfish act releases or sets at liberty a partner. The modern legal system has altered the concept and constructs of marriage for the same reasons Moses gave his guidelines for a written bill of divorcement.

Let the Little Children Come to Me
Mark 10:13-16

13. And they were bringing little children that Jesus should lay hands on them: and his disciples harshly admonished those who brought them. 14. But when Jesus saw this, He was much displeased, and said, Allow the little children come to Me, and do not hinder them: for to the childlike belongs the kingdom of God. 15. Truly, I say to you, Whoever shall not receive*, as a little child the kingdom of God, they shall not enter the kingdom. 16. And He took them up in His arms, blessed them laying His hands on them.

---

*(See Mark 9:37 Greek middle voice note)

One Thing You Lack
Mark 10:17-22

17. And when Jesus was beginning His journey, there came one running and kneeled before Him, and asked, Good Master, what must I do to inherit eternal life? 18. And Jesus said, Why do you call Me good? There is none good but One, that is, God. 19. You know the commandments: Do not commit adultery, Do not murder, Do not steal, Do not give false witness, Do not defraud, Value your father and mother. 20. And he answered, Master, all these have I obeyed from my youth. 21. When Jesus observed him clearly He loved Him, and said, One thing you lack: go sell you possessions and give the funds to the poor, and you shall have treasure in heaven: and come back and follow Me. 22. And he was depressed at the request, and went away with great sadness: for he had much property. [And Jesus let him go.]

With God All Things are Possible
Mark 10:23-31

23. Then Jesus looked round at the crowd and said to His disciples, It is not practical for the wealthy to enter the kingdom of God! 24. And the disciples were astonished at His words. But Jesus repeated Himself, and said, Children, how impractical it is to enter the kingdom of God! 25. It is easier for a camel to go through the eye of a needle, than for a rich man to enter into the kingdom of God.* 26. And they were exceedingly astonished, saying among themselves, Who can possibly be saved? 27. And Jesus looking straight at them said, With men this is impossible, but not with God: for with God all things are

possible. 28. Then Peter began to boast, Well, we have forsaken all, to follow you. 29. And Jesus answered, I assure you, There is no man that has left house, or brothers, or sisters, or father, or mother, or children, or lands, for My sake, and the gospel's, 30. but he will receive an hundred fold presently, houses, and brethren, and sisters, and mothers, and children, and lands, though not without perseverance; and in the world to come eternal life. 31. But many who are now first shall be last; and many who are last shall be first.

---

*v25 A gate to Jerusalem, known as the needle's eye because of its narrowness, required a camel to be unloaded, and made to kneel in order to enter. This common proverbial expression was used for effect to illustrate how one must part with material wealth and stoop to the humble life of a little child to enter the kingdom. Some manuscripts use "cable-rope" similar to the Greek for "camel." Both the word "camel" and "robe" used together with "the needle eye" was to show the complexity and difficulty of the process when using material wealth for the benefit of the poor. Also, to show that the process requires child-like thinking without prejudice or irrational feelings.

It Shall Not be So Among You
Mark 10:32-45

32. And they were on the road up to Jerusalem; and Jesus walked ahead: and they were amazed; and those who followed were also afraid. And He took again the Twelve, and began to tell them what things were about to happen to Him, 33. saying, Behold, we go up to Jerusalem; and the Son of man will presently be betrayed to the chief priests, and to the scribes; and they will condemn Him to death, and will deliver Him to the Gentiles: 34. and they will mock Him, and beat Him, and spit on Him, and kill Him: and the third day He will stand up again. 35. At that moment James and John, the sons of Zebedee, came to Jesus, saying, Master, we desire that you grant us a special request. 36. And He asked, What would you that I should do for you? 37. They replied, Grant to us that we may sit, one on your right hand, and the other on your left hand, in your glory. 38. But Jesus answered, You do not know what you ask: can you drink of My cup? And be immersed in the agony that I am to endure? 39. And they said, We can. And Jesus said, You shall indeed drink of My cup; and be immersed in the agony that I am to endure: 40. but to sit on My right hand and on My left hand is not mine to grant; but it will be given to those for whom it is reserved. 41. And when the ten heard it, they became indignant toward James and John. 42. But Jesus called them to Himself, and said, You know that those who are so-called rulers over the Gentiles exercise lordship over them; and their great ones exercise authority over them. 43. But it shall not be so among you: but whoever will be great among you, shall be your servant: 44. And whoever among you

wants to take first place must become servant of all. 45. For the Son of man Himself came not to be served, but to minister, and to give His life as a redemptive price for many.

Go Your Way, Faith has Restored Your Sight
Mark 10:46-52

46. They journeyed to Jericho: and as Jesus was leaving Jericho with His disciples and a great crowd of people, the blind son of Timaeus, one Bartimaeus, sat by the roadside begging. 47. When he heard that it was Jesus of Nazareth, he began to cry out, Jesus, Son of David, have mercy on me. 48. And many admonished him to be quiet: but he shouted out more the louder, Son of David, have mercy on me. 49. And Jesus stopped and stood still and commanded the blind man be called. And they summoned the blind man, saying, Be of good comfort, stand up, He is calling for you. 50. And he, throwing off his beggar clothes, sprung up and went to Jesus. 51. And Jesus asked, What would you have Me do for you? The blind man answered, Lord, that I might regain my sight. 52. And Jesus said, Go your way; faith has restored your sight. And immediately he recovered his sight, and followed Jesus along the road.

They Answered as Jesus had Commanded
Mark 11:1-11

11:1. And when they drew near Jerusalem, and arrived at Bethphage and Bethany, near the Mount of Olives, Jesus sent two of His disciples, 2. and said, Go to the village just ahead: and as you enter you will find a colt tied, that has never been ridden; untie him and bring him. 3. And if any man asks, Why are you doing this? Say, The Lord has need of him; and without delay he will send it here. 4. And they departed, and found the colt tied outside by the door at a fork in the road: and they untied it. 5. And certain that stood there asked, What are you doing untying the colt? 6. And they answered as Jesus had commanded: and they let them go. 7. And they brought the colt to Jesus, and saddled it with their garments; and Jesus sat upon it. 8. And many spread their garments in his path: and others cut down branches. 9. And those in front and those that followed, cried, saying, Hosanna; Blessings on Him who comes in the name of the Lord: 10. blessings on the reign of our father David: Hosanna in the heavens. 11. And Jesus entered Jerusalem, and went into the temple: and when He had thoroughly looked around, and now the hour being late, He went with the Twelve to Bethany.

Nothing but Leaves
Mark 11:12-18

12. And on the next day when they left Bethany, Jesus was hungry: 13. and seeing in the distance a fig tree with leaves, He went to find fruit: and when He came to it, He found nothing but leaves; for the season for figs had not come. 14. And Jesus spoke to the tree, No man will ever eat fruit from you again. And His disciples heard it. 15. And they came to Jerusalem: and Jesus went into the temple, and began driving out those that sold and bought in the temple, and overthrew the tables of the money-changers, and the benches of those who sold doves; 16. and He would not permit anyone to carry goods through the temple. 17. And He taught them, Is it not written, My house shall be called the house of prayer for all nations? But you have made it a cave for robbers. 18. And the scribes and high priests heard it, and began to seek means to destroy Him: for they feared Him, because all the people were astonished at His instruction.

Have Faith in God
Mark 11:19-26

19. And whenever evening came, Jesus went out of the city. 20. And in the morning, as they passed by and saw the fig tree dried up from the roots. 21. Peter calling to remembrance asked, Master, look, the fig tree that you cursed is withered away. 22. And Jesus answering said, Have faith in God. 23. For I assure you, That whoever says to this mountain, be removed, and be cast into the sea; and does not doubt in his heart, but believes what he says will happen; it shall be granted. 24. That is why I say, Whatever you desire, when you pray, believe that you receive it, and you will have it. 25. And when you stand up to pray, forgive anything you are holding against anyone: so that your Father in heaven may forgive you your moral wrongs. 26. But if you do not forgive, neither will your Father who is in heaven forgive your transgressions.

I will Ask You One Question
Mark 11:27-33

27. Again they entered Jerusalem: and as Jesus was walking in the temple court, the high priests, and the scribes, and the elders, came to Him. 28. And asked, By what authority do you do these things? And who gave you this authority to do these things? 29. And Jesus replied, I will also ask you one question, and if you answer me, I will tell you by what authority I do these things. 30. Was John's baptism from heaven, or from men? Answer me! 31. And they reasoned among themselves, If we say, from heaven; He will say, Why then did you not believe him? 32. But since we fear the people, we cannot say, from

men: for the people believe that John was indeed a prophet. 33. And they answered Jesus, We cannot tell. And Jesus replied, Neither will I tell you by what authority I do these things.

Have You Never Read?
Mark 12:1-12

12:1. And Jesus began to speak to them in parables. A certain man planted a vineyard, and built a wall around it, dug a pit for the winepress, built a watch-tower, and leased it to vinedressers, and went on a pilgrimage. 2. And at harvest-time he sent a servant to the vinedressers, to collect the rent in kind from the fruits of the vineyard. 3. And they caught him, and beat him, and sent him away empty-handed. 4. Again he sent another servant; and they threw stones at him wounding him in the head, and sent him away shamefully. 5. And again he sent another and they killed him, and many others; beating some, and killing some. 6. He had only one left to send, his only beloved son; he sent him, saying, Surely they will respect my son. 7. But the tenants said among themselves, This is his heir; let us kill him, and the vineyard will be ours. 8. And they suddenly seized him, and outright murdered and forcefully removed him from the vineyard. 9. What shall the owner of the vineyard do? He will come and destroy those vinedressers, and offer the vineyard to others. 10. Have you never read this passage of scripture; The very Stone the builders rejected has become the main corner stone: 11. this was from the Lord, and it is marvelous to us? 12. And they attempted to arrest Him, but feared the people: for they knew He had spoken the parable against them: and they left Him alone, and went away.

Present to God the Things that are God's
Mark 12:13-17

13. But they sent a number of Pharisees and Herodians, to hunt a way to ensnare Him in conversation. 14. When they arrived, they said, Teacher, we know that you are true, and fear no man: for you regard not the person of men, but truly teach the way of God: Is it lawful to pay tribute to Caesar? 15. Shall we hand over tribute or not? But He, knowing their hypocrisy, replied, Why try to ensnare Me? Fetch Me a coin that I may see it. 16 And they brought one. And He asked, Whose image and superscription is this? And they answered, Caesar's. 17. And Jesus said, Present to Caesar the things that are Caesar's, and present to God the things that are God's. And they stood amazed.

The God of the Living
Mark 12:18-27

18. Then the Sadducees came, who say there is no resurrection of the dead; and they questioned Jesus, saying, 19. Teacher, Moses

described for us, If a man's brother died, and leaves a wife, but had no child, that his brother should marry his widow and raise up children for his brother. 20. There were seven brethren: and the eldest married a wife, and died leaving no child. 21. And the second married her, and died without leaving a child, and the third and likewise, 22. the seven left no children; and the woman also died. 23. Since the seven had her for a wife, in the resurrection whose wife will she be? 24. And Jesus answering said, Is your ignorance of scripture and the power of God the reason you err? 25. For when they rise from the dead, they will neither marry, nor be given in marriage; but will be as the angels in heaven. 26. And as touching the dead that they rise: have you not read in the scroll of Moses, the place about the bush? God spoke saying, I am the God of Abraham, the God of Isaac, and the God of Jacob? 27. He is not the God of the dead, but the God of the living: you therefore do greatly err!

You are not Far from the Kingdom
Mark 12:28-37

28. And one of the scribes came, and having heard the discussion, perceived that Jesus had answered admirably, asked, Which of the commandments is in first position? 29. And Jesus answered, The chief one is, Hear, O Israel; The Lord your God is one Lord: 30. And thou shall love the Lord your God with your whole heart, and with your whole existence, and with all your moral understanding, and with all your ability and strength: 31. namely this, You shall love as yourself those near you. There is no other commandment greater than these. 32. And the scribe said, Honestly, Teacher, you have truthfully said that He is One. There is none other: 33. and to love Him with all the heart, and with the bringing together of your understanding, and with all your ability and strength, and to love a neighbor as yourself, is more than all whole burnt offerings and sacrifices. 34. And when Jesus saw that he answered wisely, He said, You are not far from the kingdom of God. After that no man had the courage to ask any questions. 35. And Jesus continued teaching in the temple, How can the scribes say that Christ is the Son of David? 36. For David himself said by the Holy Spirit, The Lord said to my Lord, Sit on my right hand, until I make your enemies your footstool. 37. David himself called Him Lord; then how can He also be David's son? And the great mass of people heard Him gladly.

She Gave All Her Living
Mark 12:38-44

38. And Jesus continued teaching, Beware of the scribes, who love to walk in long robes, and love to be saluted with respect in the

marketplaces, 39. and the front seats in the synagogues, and the place of honor at feasts: 40. who prey on the property of widows, and conceal their wrong doings by the pretense of long prayers: they are adding to their punishment. 41. And Jesus sat down in front of the collection-box, and observed the people dropping money into the chests: and many that were rich cast in much. 42. But one widow dropped in two copper coins out of her poverty, worth about a penny. 43. And Jesus called His disciples, saying, I assure you, this poor widow has given more than all they who gave to the treasury: 44. for they all put in of their abundance; but she gave all she had, even all her living.

When Will This Happen?
Mark 13:1-13

13:1. And as Jesus was leaving the temple, one of His disciples said, Master, see what large stones and what wonderful buildings are here!* 2. And Jesus answered, See these great buildings? There will not be one stone left resting on another, but they will all be loosened and torn down. 3. And as He sat down on the Mount of Olives opposite the Temple; Peter, James, John and Andrew asked Him privately, 4. Tell us, when will this happen? And what will be the sign when all these things are about to take place? 5. And Jesus began to answer, Take care that no one leads you astray: 6. for many will come using My name, saying, I am Christ; and shall mislead many. 7. And when you hear the sounds of warfare and reports of battles, be not troubled: for such things must come to pass; but the end is not yet. 8. Nation shall make war against nation, and kingdom against kingdom: and there shall be storms and quakes in various places, and a scarcity of food and great suffering: these are the birth-pains of tribulations. 9. But be on guard: for they will deliver you up to the courts; and in the houses of worship you will be beaten: and be brought before governors and kings on My account, as a witness for Me. 10. And the gospel must first be proclaimed among all nations. 11. But when they arrest you, and take you away, do not be anxious beforehand what you will say: but say whatever you are given in that hour: for it is not you who speaks, but the Holy Spirit. 12. Then brother shall betray brother to the death, and the father the son; and children will turn against their parents, and shall cause them to be put to death. 13. And you shall be hated by all men for My name's sake: but he who endures to the end, the same will be saved.

---

*v1 This chapter is difficult for most readers because it is based heavily on Jewish history and Jewish ideas. According to Josephus, the Temple built by Herod was one of the wonders of the world. Some of the stones were 40 feet long by 12 feet high and 18 feet wide. It was these stones that amazed the disciples.

Pray that Your Flight is not in Stormy Weather
Mark 13:14-20

14. But when you see the [abomination of desolation]*, existing where it has no right to be, (let him who reads understand,) then let them that be in Judaea escape to the mountains: 15. And let him that is on the housetop not go down, neither enter again to take anything from his house: 16. and let him that is in the field not turn back again to take away his clothes. 17. But alas to them who are with child and those with a nursing child in those days! 18. Pray that your flight is not in stormy weather. 19. For those days shall be a time of distress, such as never was since the beginning of God's creation, neither shall ever be. 20. Except that the Lord had limited those days, no living thing could survive: however, for the sake of his own, the chosen, he did limit those days.

---

*v14 In Hebrew, the expression literally means the profanation that appalls or in English "the acts of violation of sacred things that shocks and brings horror." The origin of this phase was in the book of Daniel when Antiocheius desecrated the Temple. Paul wrote about this evil as the "man of sin (lawlessness) 2 Thessalonians 2:3. And John in Revelation 17 associated this incarnate power of evil with what was about to happen in A. D. 70 when Titus, the Emperor of Rome, brought siege to Jerusalem.

But be on Guard
Mark 13:21-27

21. And then if anyone says, Look, here is Christ; or, look, he is there; do not believe him: 22. A false Christ and false prophets will appear, and shall make signs and wonders to seduce, if possible, even the chosen. 23. But be on guard: behold, I have forewarned you about everything. 24. But in those days, after the time of trouble, the sun shall be darkened, and the moon will give no reflected light, 25. and showers of stars will continue to fall from the sky, and the powers of heaven shall shake the earth. 26. And then the Son of man will be seen coming in the clouds with great power and glory. 27. And then He will send His angels, and gather together His chosen from the four winds, from the extremities of the earth to the edges of heaven.

I Say to All, Watch!
Mark 13:28-37

28. Now learn the lesson of the fig tree; when her branches are yet young, and puts forth leaves, you know that summer is at hand: 29. So in like manner, when you see these things happening, know that I am near, even at the door. 30. I say truly, that this age shall not pass,

until all these things are accomplished. 31. Heaven and earth shall pass away: but My words shall not pass away. 32. But no one knows the day or the hour, not even the angels who are in heaven, nor the Son, but only the Father. 33. Take heed, watch: since you do not know when it will happen. 34. For it is as a man taking a far journey, who left his house, and gave authority to his servants, and to every man his task, and commanded the door-keeper to watch. 35. Watch therefore: for you know not when the master of the house is coming, at even, or at midnight, or toward daybreak, or in the early morning: 36. Beware lest He comes unexpectedly and finds you asleep. 37. And what I say to you, I say to all, Watch!

She has Done a Worthy Deed
Mark 14:1-9

14:1 After two days was the Feast of the Passover and Unleavened Bread: and the high priests and the scribes were seeking how they might take hold of Jesus by deceit, and put Him to death. 2. But they said, Not on the feast day, lest there be an uproar of the people. 3. And being in Bethany in the house of Simon the leper, as He reclined at table, a woman came having a perfume vial of precious ointment made from a rare plant (nard); and she broke the vial, and poured it on his head. 4. Some present were indignant about this, and said, Why was this waste of precious ointment made? 5. It could have been sold for more than three hundred pieces of silver, and given to the poor. And they murmured against her. 6. And Jesus said, Let her alone; why trouble her? She has done a worthy deed for Me. 7. For you have the poor with you always, and whenever you wish you may do them good: but Me you will not always have. 8. She has done what she could: she has come before My death to anoint My body for burial. 9. This is the truth, wherever this gospel is preached throughout the whole world, what she has done will be spoken of as a memorial of her.

Is it I?
Mark 14:10-21

10. And Judas Iscariot, one of the Twelve, went to the high priests, to betray Jesus. 11. They were glad to hear his proposal, and promised to give him money. And he began watching for an opportunity to conveniently betray Him. 12 And on first day of Unleavened Bread, when they sacrificed the Passover lamb, His disciples said to Jesus, Where do you want us to go and prepare for you to eat the Passover? 13. And He sent two of His disciples, and instructed them, Go into the city, and you will meet a man carrying a jar of water: follow him. 14. And whatever house he enters, say to the master of the house, The Teacher asks, Where is the guest-chamber, that I may eat the

Passover with My disciples? 15. And he himself will show you a large upper room furnished and prepared: there make ready for us. 16. And the disciples went forth, and came into the city, and found as he said: and they prepared the Passover. 17. When it was evening he came with the Twelve. 18. And while they were eating, Jesus said, I tell you the truth, one of you eating with Me will betray Me. 19. And they began to be concerned, and each one asked, Is it I? 20. And Jesus said, It is one of the Twelve who dips with Me in the bowl. 21. The Son of Man is going the way described in scripture: but regrettably a curse will be on that man by whom He is betrayed! It would have been better for that man if he had never been conceived.

They all Said the Same
Mark 14:22-31
22. And as they were eating, Jesus took a loaf, blessed it, and broke it, and gave to them, saying, Take, eat: this is My body. 23. Then He took the cup and after giving thanks, He gave it to them: and they all drank from His cup. 24. And He said, This is My blood of the covenant, being shed for many. 25. Truly I tell you, I will not drink again of the fruit of the vine, until that day when I drink the new wine in the kingdom of God. 26. And when they sang a psalm, they departed to the Mount of Olives. 27. And Jesus said, All of you will stumble and be tempted to sin: for it is written, I will fatally strike down the Shepherd, and the sheep will be scattered. 28. Nevertheless, after I stand up again, I will go before you into Galilee. 29. But Peter said, Even though, all shall be scattered from you, yet I will not stumble. 30. And Jesus said, It will be so, that this day, even in this night, before the cock crows twice, you will deny Me three times. 31. But Peter repeated emphatically, Even if I must die with you, God forbid, I will never deny you. And they all said the same.

You have had Enough Rest
Mark 14:32-42
32. And they came to a place called Gethsemane: and Jesus said to His disciples, Sit here, while I pray. 33. And He took with Him Peter, James and John, and He began to be distressed and full of heaviness; 34. and said, My heart is exceedingly stressed unto death: stay here and watch. 35. And He went a little farther, and fell on the ground and prayed, if it were possible, He might be spared the hour of trial. 36. And He said, Abba, Father, all things are possible for you; spare Me this cup: nevertheless not My will, but your will. 37. And He returned, and found them sleeping, and said to Peter, Simon, did you fall asleep? Could you not keep watch one hour? 38. Watch and pray, in case you enter into temptation. The spirit certainly is willing, but the

human body is without strength. 39. And again He went away, and prayed, and spoke the same words. 40. And when He returned, He found them asleep again, (for they could not keep their eyes open,) neither did they know how to answer Him. 41. And He returned the third time, and said, You have had enough rest: the hour is come for you to see the Son of man being betrayed into the hands of sinners. 42. Get up, let us go; look, he that betrays Me is at hand.

Let the Scripture be Fulfilled
Mark 14:43-53

43. And while Jesus was speaking, Judas came, one of the Twelve, and with him was a great multitude with swords and wooden clubs, from the high priests, the scribes and the elders. 44. And the betrayer had arranged a sign, saying, The One I kiss, is He; take Him away securely. 45. And as soon as he arrived, he went straight to Jesus, and said, Master, Rabbi and kissed Him. 46. And they seized Jesus, and arrested Him. 47. And one of bystanders* drew a sword, and struck a servant of the high priest, slashing off his ear. 48. And Jesus responded, Have you come to arrest Me as you would against a thief with swords and clubs? 49. I was daily in the temple teaching, and you did not arrest Me: but let the scriptures be fulfilled. 50. And then all abandoned Him, and scattered. 51. And there followed Him a certain young man**, with only a linen cloth around his naked body; and they tried to seize him: 52. but he left the linen cloth, and fled naked. 53. And they carried Jesus to the High Priest: and with him were assembled all the chief priests and the elders and the scribes.

---

*v47 John 18:10 identifies this bystander as Peter.

**v51 Some believe this young man was Mark himself. Since the other gospel writers did not include this incident, perhaps Mark wanted to say, "I was an eyewitness."

Peter Followed at a Distance
Mark 14:54-65

54 And Peter followed at a distance, even to the court of the high priest: and sat with the guards and warmed himself in the light of the fire. 55. And the high priests and all the Sanhedrin enquired for testimony against Jesus to put Him to death; and found none. 56. But many gave false witness against Him, but their facts were contrary. 57. And some took the witness stand and gave false testimony, saying, 58. We heard Him say, I will destroy this temple that is made with hands, and within three days I will build another made without hands. 59. But their statements did not agree either. 60. And the high priest stood up and asked Jesus, What about this witness against you? 61. But He

remained silent and did not answer. Again the high priest asked Him, Are you the Messiah, the Son of the Blessed? 62. And Jesus said I am: and you shall see the Son of Man sitting on the right hand of power, and coming in the clouds of heaven. 63. Then the high priest tore his robes, and said, What further need have we for witnesses? 64. You heard the blasphemy: what is the verdict? And they all condemned Him to be guilty of death. 65. And some began to spit on Him, and to blindfold Him, and to hit Him with their fist, and say, Prophesy: even the servants slapped His face with open hands.

And Peter Remembered
Mark 14:66-72

66. And as Peter was beneath in the courtyard, one of the maidservants of the high priest came: 67. and when she saw Peter warming himself, she looked closely at him, and said, You also was with Jesus of Nazareth. 68. But he denied, saying, I neither know nor understand what you mean. And he went out to the covered entrance; and the cock crew. 69. And the maid saw him, and began again to speak to the bystanders, This man is one of them. 70. And a second time Peter denied it. Soon after, a bystanders said again to Peter, Surely you are one of them: you are a Galilean. 71. But he began to curse and to swear, saying, I know not this man of whom you speak. 72. And the second time the cock crew. And Peter remembered the words of Jesus, Before the cock crows twice, you will deny Me three times. And when he thought about those words, he began to sob.

What Evil has He Done?
Mark 15:1-20

15:1 And first thing the next morning the chief priests held a consultation with the elders and scribes and the whole council, and put Jesus in chains, and led Him away, and handed Him over to Pilate. 2. And Pilate asked Jesus, Are you the King of the Jews? And He answered, Yes, those are your words. 3. And the chief priests kept placing charges against Him. 4. And Pilate asked again, Do you have nothing to say in your defense? See how many things they witness against you. 5. But Jesus made no further answer; so Pilate was astonished. 6. Now his custom was to release a prisoner at the feast, whomever they desired. 7. And there was one named Barabbas, who was in prison with other rioters, who had committed murder in the insurrection. 8. And the multitude went up and began to ask him for his usual favor. 9. But Pilate asked them, Will you that I release to you the King of the Jews? 10. For he perceived that the chief priests had delivered Him out of spite. 11. But the chief priests incited the crowd, to ask rather for the release of Barabbas. 12. And Pilate asked again, What would you have me to do with Him whom you call the King of the Jews? 13. And they shrieked, Crucify Him. 14. Then Pilate asked, Why, what evil has He done? And they cried out the more exceedingly, Crucify Him. 15. Pilate, determined to satisfy the people, released Barabbas, and delivered Jesus, after He was whipped severely, to be crucified. 16. Then the soldiers took Jesus away into the courtyard, called Praetorium; and they call together the guard cohort. 17. And they clothed Jesus in purple, and weaved a crown of thorns for His head, 18. and began to salute Him, Hail, King of the Jews! 19. And they hit Him on the head with a reed-stalk and spit on Him, and bowed their knees in make-believe homage. 20. And when they had mocked Him, they took off the purple clothes, and put His own clothes on Him, and led Him out to be crucified.

Truly, This Man was the Son of God
Mark 15: 21-41

21. And the soldiers compelled a passerby to bear His cross, one Simon, a Cyrenian from Africa, the father of Alexander and Rufus. 22. And they took Him to the place Golgotha, which is, being interpreted, the place of a skull. 23. And they offered Him a drugged wine mingled with myrrh: but He refused. 24. And when they had crucified Him, they divided His robe and cast lots to decide what each man should take. 25. And it was 9:00 o'clock in the morning when they crucified Him. 26. And the inscription of His charges was written over His head, THE KING OF THE JEWS. 27. And with Him they crucify two thieves; the one on His right hand, and the other on His left. 28. [Verse not supported by original manuscripts.] 29. And they that passed by blasphemed Him, shaking their heads, and with emotion said, You would destroy the temple, and build it in three days, 30. save yourself and come down from the cross. 31. Likewise the chief priests and the scribes mocking said among themselves, He saved others; Himself He cannot save. 32. Now let Christ, the King of Israel, descend from the cross that we may see and believe. And they that were crucified with Him taunted Him. 33. And when twelve o'clock came, there was darkness over the whole land until the three o'clock hour. 34. And at the three 'clock hour Jesus shouted with a loud voice, Eloi, Eloi, lama sabachthani, being interpreted, My God, My God, why have you forsaken Me? 35. And some of them that stood by were surprised when they heard it, said, He calls Elijah. 36. A bystander ran and filled a sponge with sour wine, and put it on a reed-stalk, and gave Him to drink, saying, Let Him alone; let us see whether Elijah will come to take Him down. 37. And Jesus shouted with a loud voice, and gave up the ghost. 38. And the veil of the temple was divided from the top to the bottom. 39. And when the Centurion, who stood facing Him, saw how He cried out, and

gave up the ghost, said, Truly this man was the Son of God. 40. There were also women looking on from a distance: among them were Mary Magdalene, and Mary, the mother of the younger James and Mary the mother of Joseph, and Salome; 41. (Who also, when He was in Galilee, followed Him, and ministered to Him;) and many other women that came up with Him to Jerusalem.

A Fine Linen Winding Sheet
Mark 15:42-47

42. And now when evening was come, since it was the day of Preparation, that is, the day before the Sabbath, 43. Joseph of Arimathaea, an honorable member of the Sanhedrin, who also waited for the kingdom of God, came, and went in boldly to Pilate, desiring the body of Jesus. 44. And Pilate was surprised that Jesus was already dead: and calling to him the centurion, he asked if he were already dead. 45. And when he knew it from the centurion, he released the body to Joseph. 46. And he bought a fine linen winding sheet, and took Jesus down, and wrapped Him in the linen, and laid Him in a tomb cut out of a rock, and rolled a stone over the door of the tomb. 47. And Mary Magdalene and Mary the mother of Joseph carefully watched where Jesus was laid.

He is not Here
Mark 16:1-8

16:1. And when the Sabbath was past, Mary Magdalene, and Mary the mother of James, and Salome, bought sweet spices, that they might anoint Him. 2. And when the sun was risen on the first day of the week, they came to the tomb. 3. And they kept saying to one another, Who will roll away the stone from the door of the tomb for us? 4. And when they looked, they saw that the very large stone was rolled away. 5. And entering the tomb, they were amazed to see a young man sitting on the right side, clothed in a long white garment. 6. And he said to them, Do not be amazed: You seek Jesus of Nazareth, who was crucified: He is risen; He is not here: see the place where they laid Him. 7. But go and tell His disciples and Peter that He goes before you into Galilee: there you will see Him, as He told you. 8 And they ran from the tomb trembling and amazed: and said nothing to anyone because they were exceedingly fearful.*

---

*Many of the best scholars have expressed concern that the remainder of Chapter 16 (vs.9-20) were written by someone other than Mark. Two of the oldest Greek manuscripts omit it completely and the RSV places these verses in the margin. However, the way verse 8 ends in the Greek strongly suggests that something had to follow. It is true that the Greek in vs.9-20 is different from the rest of Mark, but whether the lone manuscript was neglected and the last words lost or

Mark or someone replaced the ending with the known facts of the post-resurrection appearances of Jesus does not alter its value. This writer accepts verses 9-20 as a part of the preserved scripture because of the strong message presented to the church: namely, Christ on the Throne in Heaven, the Church to the Task on earth, and the ultimate Triumph of the Christian message.

The Believer's Commission
Mark 16:9-20

9. After Jesus stood up from the grave early on the first day of the week, He appeared first to Mary Magdalene, from whom He had cast out seven demons. 10. And she reported to those who had been with Him, as they mourned and wept. 11. When they heard that He was alive, and had been seen by her, they did not believe. 12. After that He appeared as a stranger to two of them, as they walked in the country. 13. And they went and told the others: but no one believed them. 14. Afterward He appeared to the eleven as they were eating, and reproved them for their lack of faith and stubbornness, because they did not believe those who had seen Him after He stood up from the grave. 15. And He said, As you journey to the whole world, proclaim a good message to every inhabitant. 16. He who believes and is baptized will be saved; but he who believes not will be condemned. 17. And these miracles will follow those who believe; in My name will they cast out demons; they will speak with unnaturally acquired languages: 18. they may take up serpents; and if they drink any deadly thing, it will not hurt them; they will lay hands on the sick, and they will recover. 19. So then after the Lord had spoken to them, He was received up into heaven, and sat on the right hand of God. 20. And they went out and witnessed everywhere, the Lord working with them, and validating the message with accompanying supernatural wonders.

The Gospel According To Matthew

Matthew, formerly known as Levi, probably wrote his Gospel in Palestine for Jewish Christians. It appears Matthew wanted to demonstrate the Gospel as fulfillment of the law and the prophets and show that Jesus was the Messiah by connecting the past with the present. Matthew is in reality a document to teach early Jewish converts. For this reason, those passages in Matthew that are common to Mark, Luke, or John are not presented here, only the references for the reader's further study. Matthew is recognized as one of the three Synoptic Gospels: Mark, Matthew, and Luke. Synoptic is "to see together" means generally their material is the same but presented with a different emphasis. Mark is considered the oldest of the Gospels, presenting Jesus as a Servant, Luke presents Jesus as a Man. Matthew presents Jesus as King of the Jews and later, John presented Jesus as God. It also appears that Matthew used all but 55 of the verses in Mark. Luke used 31 of the 55 not used by Matthew. It is clear that most of the content of 661 verses in Mark were reproduced in either Matthew or Luke: over 600 verses in Matthew and more than 300 in Luke. To my count there are only 24 verses in Mark that are not reproduced in either Matthew or Luke. What does this mean? They were all working with the same known facts and using these same facts validated the facts and they were used to present Jesus from a unique perspective. For that reason, I chose not to translate the whole of Matthew, only presenting those parts that are not found in Mark or Luke or are unique to Matthew. This is why all the Gospels must be read to receive a clear understanding of Jesus Christ as Servant, Man, King, and God.

Family Record of Jesus
Matthew 1:1-16 (See Luke 3:23-38)

Generations from Abraham to Christ
Matthew 1:17

17. The genealogy of Jesus are fourteen generations from Abraham to David; fourteen from David to the captivity in Babylon, and fourteen from the captivity in Babylon to Christ.

Conception and Birth of Jesus
Matthew 1:18-25

18. The conception and birth of Jesus, the Messiah happened this way: His mother, Mary, was promised to Joseph. Before they were married, she was with child by the power of the Holy Spirit. 19. But Joseph, her promised husband, being honorable and unwilling to expose her publically, considered how to handle the matter secretly; 20. as he considered these things, a messenger of the Lord appeared to him in a dream, saying, Joseph, child of David, do not fear to take Mary as your wife, for the child within her was conceived by the Holy Spirit. 21. When she brings forth a Son, you must name Him Jesus, for

He will deliver His people from their wayward path. 22. These things are a fulfillment of the words of the Lord's prophet, saying. 23. See, an unmarried daughter will conceive and birth a Son, and His name will be Emmanuel, meaning God is with us. 24. Awaking from a deep sleep, Joseph did as the Lord's messenger directed, and took Mary as his wife: but abstained from conjugal contact until she birthed her firstborn Son: and he named the child Jesus. [See Luke 1:26-38; 2:1-7; John 1:1-2, 14]

Visit of the Wise Men
Matthew 2:1-12

1. After the birth of Jesus at Bethlehem (the House of Bread) in Judaea in the reign of King Herod, some astrologers from the east arrived in Jerusalem, 2. asking, where is the child born to be king of the Jews? We observed His star in the east, and have come to pay homage. 3. When Herod the king heard these reports, he and all Jerusalem were troubled. 4. And when he had gathered all the ruling priests and rabbis together, he demanded where the Christ was to be born. 5. And they answered, According to writings of the prophets, in Bethlehem of Judaea, 6. And Bethlehem in Judaea, you are not the least among the princes of Judaea: for out of you will come a Shepherd, who will lead my people Israel. 7. Then Herod privately called the visiting astrologers and inquired diligently what time the star appeared. 8. Herod sent them to Bethlehem with orders to search carefully for the young child; and when you find Him, report to me so I may also pay homage to Him. 9. After hearing the king's instructions, they departed; and the star in the east, went before them, until it stopped above the place where the young child was. 10. When they saw the star, they were overwhelmed with intense joy. 11. And when they reached the dwelling, they saw the young child with Mary His mother, and fell down to pay homage to Him: and when they had opened their treasures, they presented to Him gifts; gold, and frankincense, and myrrh. 12. And being warned of God in a dream that they should not return to Herod, they returned to their own country by another road.

Holy Family's Flight to Egypt
Matthew 2:13-15

13. As soon as the visitors departed, behold, an angel of the Lord appeared to Joseph in a dream, saying, Arise, and take the young child and His mother, and seek refuge in Egypt, and remain there until I bring you word: for Herod will seek to destroy the young child. 14. He arose and took the young child and His mother by night, and took refuge in Egypt: 15. And remained there until the death of Herod: that the words of the Lord by the prophet might be fulfilled Out of Egypt have I called My Son.

Herod Slays Innocent Children
Matthew 2:16-18

16. When Herod saw that he was tricked by the astrologers, he was extremely angry and sent and massacred all the male children that were in the region of Bethlehem, from two years old and under, according to the time frame he learned from the astrologers. 17. Then the words of Jeremiah, the prophet, were fulfilled, 18. In Rama there was the sound of weeping and great sorrow, it was Rachel weeping for her children, and would not be comforted, because they were dead. [See Luke 2:39-52]

Return from Egypt to Nazareth
Matthew 2:19-23

19. As soon as Herod was dead, a messenger of the Lord appeared to Joseph in a dream Take the child and his mother from Egypt and 20. journey to the land of Israel: because those seeking death for the young child have died. 21. And he arose, and took the child and his mother and journeyed to the land of Israel, 22. but because he heard Archelaus was now king in Judaea instead of his father, Herod, he was afraid to return there: and being instructed by God in a dream, he took refuge in Galilee: 23. and he came to dwell in Nazareth: to fulfill the words of the prophets, Jesus was to be called a Nazarene.

The Ministry of John the Baptist
Matthew 3:1-12 (See Mark 1:1-8; Luke 3:1-20; John 1:6-8, 15-37)

Baptism of Jesus
Matthew 3:13-17 (See Luke 3:21-22; John 1:31-34)

Temptation of Jesus
Matthew 4:1-11 (See Mark 1:12-13; Luke 4:1-13)

Public Ministry in Capernaum
Matthew 4:12-17 (See Mark 1:14-15; Luke 4:14-15)

Jesus Calls First Disciples
Matthew 4:18-22 (See Mark 1:16-20; Luke 5:1-11; John 1:35-42)

Jesus Teaches a Multitude
Matthew 4:23-25 (See Luke 6:17-19)

Part of the Sermon on the Mount
Matthew 5:1-12 (See Luke 6:17-19)

Salt and Light
Matthew 5:13-14 (See Mark 9:50; Luke 14:34-35)

Let Your Light Shine
Matthew 5:15-20 (See Mark 4:21-23; Luke 8:16-18)

Teaching about the Law
Matthew 5:17-20

17. Do not think that I came to dissolve the law or the prophets: I did not come to annul, but to fulfill. 18. Truly I say. Until heaven and earth pass, not the smallest letter or the smallest part of any letter shall pass away from the law, until all things are fulfilled. 19. Whoever shall break one of these least commandments, and teach men so, he shall be the least-esteemed in the heavens: but whoever shall keep and teach others, the same shall be esteemed great in the heavens. 20. For I say, Except your righteousness surpasses the righteousness of the Scribes and Pharisees, you certainly will not find entrance to the domain of the heavens.

Teaching about Anger
Matthew 5:21-26

21. You have heard that the ancients said, You shall not commit murder; and whoever commits murder will answer to the court of justice: 22. but I say further, Whoever is angry with his brother without a cause shall be condemned by the court of justice: and whoever shall say to his brother, raca (I spit on you), shall be answerable to the Sanhedrin: but whoever shall look down on his brother as a lost soul, shall be in danger of the Gehenna of fire. 23. Therefore if you bring your gift to the altar, and remember that your brother has a grievance against you; 24. leave your gift before the altar, and first make peace with your brother and then return and offer your gift. 25. Come to agreement without delay with your adversary, when you have opportunity; or he may hand you over to the judge, and the judge deliver you to the jailer, and you be cast into prison. 26. Truly I say, You shall not be set at liberty, until you pay the full obligation.

Sin Starts in the Heart
Matthew 5:27-32 (See Mark 10:2-12; Luke 16:18; 1 Corinthians 7:1-16)

Oaths and Perjury
Matthew 5:33-37

33. Again, you have heard that the ancients said, You shall not swear to stop doing something, but shall perform your oaths to the Lord: 34. but I say to you, Swear not at all; neither by the heavens; for it is God's throne: 35. nor by the earth; for it is His footstool: neither by Jerusalem; for it is the city of the great King. 36. Neither shall you swear by your head, because you cannot make one hair white or

black. 37. But let your words simply be yes or no: for whatever is more than these has its source in evil.

Retaliation
Matthew 5:38-42 (See Luke 6:29-30)

Love Your Enemies
Matthew 5:43-48 (See Luke 6:27-36)

Almsgiving
Matthew 6:1-4

1. Take heed that you do not do your good deeds to be seen of men: otherwise you have no reward of your Father who is in heaven. 2. Therefore when you do good things, do not make a display, as the hypocrites do in the synagogues and in the streets, that they may have praise of men. Truly I say, They have received their full reward. 3. But when you do good things, let not your left hand know what your right hand does: 4. that your good deeds may be in secret: and your Father who sees in secret will reward you openly.

Prayer
Matthew 6:5-15 (See Luke 11:2-4)

Fasting
Matthew 6:16-18

16. When you fast do not have a sad countenance as the hypocrites: for they deliberate blemish their faces to appear to men to fast. Truly I say, They have their full reward. 17. But when you fast, wash your face and comb your hair; 18. so that you do not appear to fast, but your Father who sees in secret, will reward you openly.

Treasures in Heaven
Matthew 6:19-21 (See Luke 12:33-34)

Light of the World
Matthew 6:22-23 (See Luke 11:34-36)

Put the Kingdom First
Matthew 6:24-34 (See Luke 12:22-34; 16:13)

Judging Others
Matthew 7:1-6 (See Luke 6:37-42)

Seek Assistance Through Prayer
Matthew 7:7-11 (Luke 11:9-13)

Golden Rule
Matthew 7:12 (See Luke 6:31; Ephesians 4:32)

The Narrow Passage Gate
Matthew 7:13-14 (See Luke 13:24)

Good and Bad Men
Matthew 7:15-20 (See Luke 6:43-45)

Being Religious is not Enough
Matthew 7:21-23 (See Luke 13:25-27)

Don't Build on Sand
Matthew 7:24-26 (See Luke 6:47- 49)

Jesus Cleansed a Leper
Matthew 8:1-4 (See Mark 1:40-45; Luke 5:12-16)

Healing a Centurion's Servant
Matthew 8:5-13 (See Luke 7:1-10; John 4:43-54)

Peter's Mother-in-law Healed
Matthew 8:14-17 (See Mark 1:29-34; Luke 4:38-41)

Kingdom Comes First
Matthew 8:18-22 (See Luke 9:57-62)

Jesus Calms the Storm
Matthew 8:23-34 (See Mark 4:36-41; Luke 8:22-25)

Jesus Heals a Paralytic
Matthew 9:1-8 (See Mark 2:3-12; Luke 5:18-26)

Jesus Calls Matthew
Matthew 9:9-13 (See Mark 2:13-17; Luke 5: 27-32)

Fasting
Matthew 9:14-17 (See Mark 2:18-22; Luke 5:33-39)

Daughter Healed and a Woman who Touched Him
Matthew 9:18-26 (See Mark 5:21-43; Luke 8:40-56)

Healing of Two Blind Men
Matthew 9:27-31

27. And when Jesus departed that place, two blind men followed Him, crying, and saying, Son of David, have mercy on us. 28. And when He was come into the house, the blind men came to Him: and Jesus said to them, Do you believe that I am able to do this? They said to Him, Yea, Lord. 29. Then He touched their eyes, saying, According to your faith be it to you. 30. And their eyes were opened; and Jesus immediately charged them, saying, See that no man know it. 31. But when they were departed, they spread abroad His fame in all that country.

Jesus Healed a Speechless Man
Matthew 9:32-34

32. As they went out, they brought to Jesus a man unable to speak, who was demented. 33. And when the unclean spirit was cast out, the man spoke: and the people marveled, saying, This was never seen in Israel. 34. But the Pharisees said He casts out demons by the power of the chief of the demons.

Jesus Shows Compassion
Matthew 9:35-38

35. And Jesus toured all the cities and villages, teaching in synagogues, and proclaiming the gospel of the kingdom, and healing all manner of sickness and disease among the people. 36. But when He saw the crowds, Jesus was moved with compassion, because they were distressed and scattered, as sheep without a shepherd. 37. Then Jesus said to His disciples, The harvest is truly abundant, but the workers are few; 38. urge the Owner of the harvest to send workers into His harvest.

Jesus Chooses the Twelve
Matthew 10:1-15 (See Mark 3:13-19; 6:7-13; Luke 6:12-16; 9:1-6)

Disciples to be Persecuted
Matthew 10:16-23 (See Mark 13:9-13; Luke 21:12-17)

Jesus Tells Disciples to Fear Not
Matthew 10:24-31 (See Luke 12:2-7)

Confessing Christ Before Men
Matthew 10:32-33 (See Luke 12:8, 9)

Christ Brings Conflict
Matthew 10:34-39 (See Luke 12:51-53; 14:26-27)

Rewards
Matthew 10:40-42 (See Mark 9:41)

Jesus Eulogizes John the Baptist
Matthew 11:1-19 (See Luke 7:18-35)

Jesus Denounces Indifference
Matthew 11:20-24 (See Luke 10:13-15)

Revealed to Babes
Matthew 11:25-27 (See Luke 10:21-22)

The Yoke of Submission
Matthew 11:28-30

28. Come unto Me, all you who are toiling and over-burdened, and I will give you relief. 29. Take the yoke of submission upon you, and learn from Me; for I am gentle and humble in heart: and I will refresh your souls. 30. For My yoke of submission is good, and My pack is light.

Jesus is Lord Over the Sabbath
Matthew 12:1-8 (See Mark 2:23-28; Luke 6:1-5)

Jesus Heals on the Sabbath
Matthew 12:9-14 (See Mark 3:1-6; Luke 6:6-11)

God's Servant
Matthew 12:15-21

15. Because Jesus knew about the Pharisees and withdrew Himself from there: and great crowds followed Jesus, and He healed them all; 16. And warned them that they should not make Him known: 17. so the words of Isaiah the prophet might be fulfilled, 18. Behold My servant, whom I have chosen; My beloved, in whom My soul is well pleased: I will put My Spirit upon Him, and He will show judgment to the Gentiles. 19. He shall not strive, nor cry; neither will any man hear His voice in the streets. 20. A crushed reed shall He not break, and a dimly burning wick will He not quench, until He crowns His judgment with victory. 21. And His name will bring hope to the Gentiles.

Jesus and Beelzebub
Matthew 12:22-32 (See Mark 3:20-30; Luke 11:14-23

Know by His Fruit
Matthew 12:33-35 (Luke 6:43-45)

Idle Words
Matthew 12:36-37

36. But I say, for every useless expression that men shall speak, they will give account in the Day of Judgment. 37. For by your words you shall be acquitted, and by your words you shall be condemned.

Seeking a Sign
Matthew 12:38-42 (See Mark 8:11-12; Luke 11:29-32)

Return of the Unclean Spirit
Matthew 12:43-45 (Luke 11:24-26)

True Family of Jesus
Matthew 12:46-50 (See Mark 3:31-35; Luke 8:19-21)

The Sower and the Soils
Matthew 13:1-9 (See Mark 4:1-9; Luke 8:4-8)

Why Parables?
Matthew 13:10-17 (See Mark 4:10-12; Luke 8:9-10)

Parable of the Sower Explained
Matthew 13:18-23 (See Mark 4:13-20; Luke 8:11-15)

Weeds among the Wheat
Matthew 13:24-30

24. Jesus presented another parable to them. The kingdom of heaven is similar to a man who planted good seed in his field: 25. while men slept, his enemy came and sowed weeds among the wheat, and went away. 26. But when the green stalks sprang up, and brought forth fruit, then also appeared the weeds. 27. So the servants of the householder came and asked, Sir, did we not spread good seed in your field? From where then did it get weeds? 28. He said, An enemy did this. The servants said, Would you have us go and gather up the weeds? 29. But he said, No; lest while you gather up the weeds, you root up also the wheat. 30. Let both grow together until the harvest: and in the time of harvest I will say to the reapers, Gather together first the weeds, and bind them in bundles to burn: but gather the wheat into my barn.

Mustard Seed
Matthew 13:31-32 (See Mark 4:30-32; Luke 13:18-21)

Using Parables
Matthew 13:33-35 (See Mark 4:33-34)

The Weeds
Matthew 13:36-43

36. Then Jesus sent the crowd away, and went into the house: and His disciples came and asked, Explain to us the parable of the weeds of the field. 37. He answered and said, He who plants the good seed is the Son of man; 38. the field is the world; the good seed are the children of the kingdom; but the weeds are the children of the wicked one; 39. the enemy who spread them is the devil; the harvest is the end of the world; and the reapers are the messengers. 40. As the weedy grass is gathered and burned in the fire; so will it be at the end of the world. 41. The Son of man will send His messengers, and they will gather out of His kingdom all things that cause stumbling, and those who behave lawlessly; 42. And will cast them into the furnace of fire: there shall be wailing and gnashing of teeth. 43. Then shall the

righteous shine forth as the sun in the kingdom of their Father. Who has ears to hear, let him listen.

Hidden Treasure
Matthew 13:44
44. Again, the kingdom of heaven is similar to a treasure buried in a field; and when a man found it, he buried it again, and because of his joy he goes and sells all he had, and purchased that field.

Pearl of Great Price
Matthew 13:45-46
45. Again, the kingdom of heaven is similar to a merchant seeking beautiful pearls: 46. who, when he found one pearl of great price, sold all he had, and bought it.

The Drag Net
Matthew 13:47-52
47. Again, the kingdom of heaven is similar to a net that was let down into the sea, and caught all kinds of fish: 48. when the net was full, they drew the net to shore, and sat down, and gathered the good fish into baskets, but cast the bad away. 49. So shall it be at the end of the world: the messengers shall come and sever the wicked from among the just, 50. and shall cast them into the furnace of fire: there shall be wailing and gnashing of teeth. 51. Jesus asked, Have you understood all these things? They answered, Yes, Lord. 52. Then Jesus said to them, Therefore every teacher of the law, who received instruction about the kingdom of heaven is similar to a man who is a householder, and brings out of his treasure things new and old.

Rejected at Nazareth
Matthew 13:53-58 (See Mark 6:1-6; Luke 4:16-30)

Herod Confused about Jesus
Matthew 14:1-12 (See Mark 6:14-29; Luke 9:7-9)

Feeding of 5,000
Matthew 14:13-21 (Mark 6:30-44; Luke 9:10-17; John 6:1-14)

Jesus Walks on the Water
Matthew 14:22-33 (See Mark 6:45-52; John 6:15-21)

Jesus Healed the Sick
Matthew 14:34-36 (See Mark 6:53-56)

Divine Command vs. Tradition
Matthew 15:1-20 (See Mark 7:1-23)

Faith of a Gentile Woman
Matthew 15:21-28 (See Mark 7:24-30)

Jesus Heals Many
Matthew 15:29-31

29. And Jesus departed and went along the shore of the Sea of Galilee; and went up into a mountain, and rested there. 30. And great crowds came and brought with them those who were lame, crippled, blind, injured, and many others, and placed them at Jesus' feet; and He healed them: 31. insomuch that the crowd wondered, when they saw the speechless to speak, the injured made whole, the crippled to walk, and the blind to see: and they praised the God of Israel.

Jesus Feeds 4,000
Matthew 15:32-39 (See Mark 8:1-10)

Understanding the Times
Matthew 16:1-4 (See Mark 8:11-13; Luke 12:54-56)

Pharisees Rebuked
Matthew 16:5-12 (See Mark 8:14-21)

Peter Declares Jesus as Messiah
Matthew 16:13-20 (See Mark 8:27-30; Luke 9:18-21)

The Father's Revelation
Matthew 16:17-20

17. And Jesus answered Simon Peter, you are blood-related, Simon, son of Jonah: because flesh and blood has not revealed this to you, but My Father who is in heaven. 18. And I say to you, You are Peter, but on "this rock"* I will build My church; and the gates of hell will never prevail against My church. 19. And I will give to you the keys of the kingdom of heaven: and whatever you bind on earth will be bound in heaven: and whatever you loose on earth will be loosed in heaven. 20. Then Jesus charged His disciples that they should tell no man that He was Jesus, the Christ.

---

*v18 There is a play on words here: in Greek, Peter is *petros* and a rock is *petra*. The word for "rock" was used for Abraham, the foundation for Israel, also the word is used for God, Himself. (Deuteronomy 32:4, 31; I Samuel 2:2; II Samuel 22:2; Psalm 18:31; II Samuel 22:32). It appears that Jesus said to Peter, "You are a rock, but I will build My church upon Myself."

Jesus Foretells His Death
Matthew 16:21-28 (See Mark 8:31-33; Luke 9:27)

The Transfiguration
Matthew 17:1-13 (See Mark 9:2-13; Luke 9:28-36)

Powerless Disciples
Matthew 17:14-21 (See Mark 9:14-29; Luke 9: 37-43)

Jesus Again Tells of His Death and Resurrection
Matthew 17:22-23 (Mark 9:30-32; Luke 9:43-45)

Coin in the Fish's Mouth
Matthew 17:24-27

24. At their arrival in Capernaum, the collectors of the temple-tax came to Peter and asked, Does your master not pay the temple-tax? 25. He said, Yes. And when Peter went into the house, Jesus spoke first, asking, What do you think, Simon? From whom do earthly kings take toll or tribute, from their own children or from strangers? 26. Peter answered, from strangers. Jesus said, therefore the children are exempt. 27. But lest we should cause them to stumble, go to the sea and cast a hook, and take up the first fish that comes up: and when you open its mouth, you will find a shekel: take that coin to the collectors for you and Me.

Greatest in the Kingdom
Matthew 18:1-5 (See Mark 9:33-37; Luke 9:46-48)

You Must Not Offend the Little Ones
Matthew 18:6-11 (See Mark 9:42-48; Luke 17:1-2)

The Lost Sheep
Matthew 18:12-14 (See Luke 15:3-7)

A Transgressing Brother
Matthew 18:15-20

15. Furthermore, if your brother shall transgress, go in private and speak about his weakness: if he listens, you have gained your brother. 16. But if he will not listen, then take one or two more with you, so that each word may be confirmed by two or three witnesses. 17. And if he refuses to listen to them, tell it to an assembly: but if he refuses to listen to the assembly, let him be to you as a disbeliever and a tax-collector.* 18. Truly I say, Whatever you bind on earth will remain bound in heaven: and whatever you loose on earth will remain loosed in heaven. 19. Again I say, If two of you agree on earth as touching anything that they may ask for themselves, it will be done of my Father who is in heaven. 20. For where two or three are assembled together in My name, I am in the center.

*v17 This is one of the difficult passages in Matthew. It does not sound like Jesus. Most likely it is based on something Jesus said earlier and used here much later. It suggests limited forgiveness and that those Gentiles and tax-collectors were hopeless outside forgiveness. Jesus did not think in this way, He was always forgiving and was a friend to tax-collectors and sinners. He even praised them, saying that "tax-collectors and harlots" will enter the Kingdom before the religious of that day. (Matthew 9:10-13; 11:19; Luke 18:10-14)

Forgiveness
Matthew 18:21-35

21. Then came Peter to Jesus, and asked, Lord, how often shall I forgive my brother who sins against me? Would seven times be enough? 22. Jesus answered, I say not, Until seven times: but, until seventy times seven. 23. Therefore is the kingdom of heaven similar to a certain king, who would take account of his servants. 24. And when he had begun the accounting, one was brought to him, who owed ten thousand units. 25. Since he was unable to pay, his lord ordered him to be sold, together with his wife, and children, and all his possessions and payment to be made. 26. The servant fell down, and paid homage, saying, Lord, have patience with me, and I will pay in full. 27. Then the king was moved with compassion toward that servant, forgave his debt and let him go. 28. But the same servant went out, and found one of his own servants, who owed him a small sum: and grabbed him by the throat, saying, Pay me what you owe! 29. And his fellow servant fell down at his feet and begged, saying, Have patience with me, and I will pay in full. 30. And he would not: but went and had him jailed until he should pay the debt. 31. So when his fellow servants saw what was done, they were grieved and went to their king and told all that was done. 32. Then the king called him and said, You wicked servant, I forgave you all your debt, because you asked me: 33. should you not also have compassion on your fellow servant, even as I had pity on you? 34. And the king was angry and delivered him to be punished until he paid the debt in full. 35. So likewise My heavenly Father will also do to you, if you do not from your hearts forgive everyone his brother their transgressions.

Jesus Teaches about Marriage
Matthew 19:1-12

19:1 Afterwards, when Jesus finished His discourse, He departed from Galilee, He came to the borders of Judaea beyond the Jordan; 2. and a crowd followed, and He cured them all. 3. The Pharisees also came and tested Him, asking, Is it right for a man to divorce his wife on any grounds? 4. And Jesus answered, Have you never read that the Creator made human beings male and female, 5.

continuing, For this cause shall a man leave father and mother, and shall cleave to his wife: and the two shall become one flesh.* 6. So it follows they are no more two, but one body (family). What God Himself has yoked together, man must not separate into parts. 7. They ask, Why did Moses command a man to issue in writing a notice of separation before putting away his wife? 8. Jesus answered, Moses allowed divorcement because you were not teachable: but originally there was no such consideration. 9. But I say to you, Anyone who puts away his wife on grounds other than immorality, ** and weds another, adulterates his vows: (and whoever marries her doth commit adultery)*** 10. His disciples remarked, If such a case exists] between man and wife, it is not good to marry. 11. Jesus said, Everyone cannot come to this conclusion, except those who have the gift. 12. Some are born unsuited for marriage: and some made eunuchs by men: others have renounced marriage for the sake of the Kingdom of heaven. He who is capable, let him practice abstinence. [See Mark 10:1-12; Luke 16:18; 1 Corinthians 7:1-40; Romans 7:1-3]

---

*v5 "one flesh" is sarx which suggests a human body apart from the soul. Probably this is the bonding that comes with the first child and not only the emotional bonding of a couple when vows are physically consummated.

**v9 This apparent exception relative to immorality, was not recognized in Mark, Luke or by Paul, and has been explained in various ways. It appears that Jesus is speaking of a man who puts away an innocent wife in order to marry another.

***V9 (This phrase is not adequately supported by original manuscripts)

Who Will Enter the Kingdom
Matthew 19:13-15 (See Mark 10:13-16; Luke 18:15-17)

Rich Young Ruler
Matthew 19:16-26 (See Mark 10:17-27; Luke 18:18-27)

The Last Shall be First
Matthew 19:27-30

27. Then Peter answered Jesus, Behold, we have forsaken all, and followed you; what will be the reward? 28. And Jesus said, Truly I say, That you who have followed Me, when the world is reborn and the Son of man shall sit on His throne in glory, you also shall sit upon twelve thrones, judging the twelve tribes of Israel. 29. And everyone who has forsaken houses, or brethren, or sisters, or father, or mother, or wife, or children, or lands, for My name's sake, shall receive a hundredfold, and shall inherit eternal life. 30. But many who were first will be last; and the last will be first.

Workers in the Vineyard
Matthew 20:1-16

1. For the kingdom of heaven is similar to a man who was a landowner, who went out early in the morning to hire workers for his vineyard. 2. And when he had agreed with the workers for a dollar a day, he sent them into his vineyard. 3. And he went out about 9 o'clock and saw others standing idle in the marketplace, 4. And said unto them; Go work in the vineyard, and whatever is right I will pay you. And they went to the vineyard. 5. Again he went out about noon and again at three o'clock, and made the same offer. 6. And about 5 o'clock he went out, and found others standing idle, and said, Why are you idle all the day? 7. They answered, No man has hired us. He said, Go also into the vineyard; and whatever is right, you will receive. 8. When evening came, the master of the vineyard said to his steward, Call the workers and give them their wages, beginning from the last to the first. 9. And when the workers hired at 5 o'clock came, they received every man a dollar. 10. But when those hired first came, they supposed they should have received more; and they likewise received every man a dollar. 11. And when they had received it, they murmured against the master, 12. saying, These last have worked but one hour, and you made them equal to us, who have borne the burden in the heat of the day. 13. But he answered one of them, Friend, I did you no wrong: did you not agree with me for a dollar? 14. Take your wages and go: I will give to the last, even as to you. 15. Is it not lawful for me to do what I will with my own? Is your eye evil, because I am good? 16. So the last shall be first, and the first last: [for many are called, but few chosen*].

---

*v16 This phrase is not adequately supported here by original manuscripts, but may be found at Matthew 22:14)

Jesus Again Predicts His Death/Resurrection
Matthew 20:17-19 (See Mark 10:32-34; Luke 18:31-34)

A Mother's Ambition
Matthew 20:20-28 (See Mark 10:35-45)

Sight Restored
Matthew 20:29-34 (See Mark 10:46-52; Luke 18:35-43)

The King Enters Jerusalem
Matthew 21:1-11(See Mark 11:1-11; Luke 19:28-38; John 12:12-19)

Jesus Cleansers the Temple
Matthew 21:12-17 (Mark 11:15-19; Luke 19:45-48; John 2:13-22)

The Unfruitful Fig Tree
Matthew 21:18-22 (See Mark 11:12-14; 20-24)

The Authority of Jesus
Matthew 21:23-27 (See Mark 11:27-33; Luke 20:1-8)

The Two Sons
Matthew 21:28-32

28. What do you think? A certain man had two sons; and he came to the first-born and said, Son, go work today in my vineyard. 29. He answered, I will not: but afterward he repented, and went. 30. And he came likewise to the second-born. And he answered, I go, sir: and went not. 31. Which of the two did the will of his father? They answered, The first. Jesus said, Truly I say, the tax-collectors and the harlots will go into the kingdom of God before you. 32. For John came to you in the way of righteousness, and you believed him not: but the tax-collectors and the harlots believed him: and when you saw this, repented not afterward, that you might believe:

The Vineyard and the Tenants
Matthew 21:33-46 (See Mark 12:1-12; Luke 20:9-19)

Rejection of the Jews
Matthew 21:43-46

43. Therefore I say to you, The Kingdom of God shall be taken from you, and given to a people bringing forth kingdom fruits. 44. And whosoever shall fall against this stone shall be broken: but on whomever it shall fall, it will grind to powder. 45. And when the chief priests and Pharisees heard His parables, they knew He was speaking about them. 46. But when they sought to seize Him, they feared the crowds, because they regarded Him a prophet.

Marriage of King's Son
Matthew 22:1-14

1. And Jesus answered and spoke again by parables, and said, 2. The Kingdom of heaven is similar to a certain king, who made a marriage-feast for his son, 3. And sent his servants to call those who were invited to the wedding: and they would not come. 4. Again, he sent other servants, saying, Tell those invited, I have prepared my luncheon: my oxen and my fatlings are killed, and all things are ready: come to the marriage. 5. But they gave it no heed, and went their ways, one to his own farm, another to his business: 6. and the rest seized his servants, and treated them shamefully, and killed them. 7. But when the king heard, he was angry and sent his armies, and destroyed those murderers, and burned their city. 8. Then he said to his servants, The wedding is ready, but they who were invited do not

deserve to come. 9. Go therefore into the highways, and as many as you find, invite to the marriage-feast. 10. So the servants went out into the highways, and gathered together as many as they found, both bad and good: and the wedding was furnished with guests. 11. And when the king came in to see the guests, he saw there a man who did not have on a wedding garment: 12. and he asked him, Friend, why did you come here not having a wedding garment? And he was speechless. 13. Then the king told the servants, Bind him hand and foot and cast him out into the darkness; where he can weep and regret his foolishness. 14. For many are called, but few are chosen.

Jesus and Taxes
Matthew 22:15-22 (See Mark 12:13-17; Luke 20:20-26)

Life After the Resurrection
Matthew 22:23-33 (See Mark 12:18-27; Luke 20:27-40)

The Greatest Commandment
Matthew 22:34-40 (See Mark 12:28-34; Luke 10:25-28)

David's Lord
Matthew 22:41-46 (See Mark 12:35-37; Luke 20:41-44)

Jesus Condemns Scribes and Pharisees
Matthew 23:1-12

1. Jesus then spoke to His disciples and the crowd, 2. saying, The Scribes and the Pharisees occupy the seat where Moses taught: 3. all they teach you observe and do; but do not initiate their behavior: because they say, and do not. 4. For they fasten back-breaking burdens that are grievous to carry, and lay them on men's shoulders; but they themselves will not lift a finger to move them. 5. All their behavior is done is to be seen of men: they make large their prayer reminder boxes, and enlarge the borders of their garments, 6. and love the chief places at feasts, and the front seats of honor in the synagogues, 7. and respectful greetings in the markets, and to be called Rabbi by men. 8. Do not permit others to call you Rabbi: for One is your Master, even Christ; and you are all brothers. 9. And not call any man on earth your Father: for One is your Father, who is in heaven. 10. Neither be called Teacher: for One is your Teacher, even Christ. 11. But he who is greatest among you shall be your servant. 12. And whoever shall praise himself shall be humbled; and he that shall humble himself shall be exalted.

Seven Curses Upon the Pharisees
Matthew 23:13-36

13. A curse on you, Scribes and Pharisees, for pretending to have high principles! For you shut the door in the face of men seeking

the kingdom of heaven: you neither enter yourselves, neither permit those attempting to enter. 14. *[Woe to you, Scribes and Pharisees, hypocrites! for ye devour widows' houses, and for a pretence make long prayer: therefore ye shall receive the greater damnation]**. 15. A curse on you, Scribes and Pharisees, pretenders! Because you travel sea and land to make one proselyte, and when he is made, you make him twice more the child of hell than yourselves. 16. A curse on you, you blind guides, who say, Whoever shall swear by the temple, it counts for nothing; but whoever shall swear by the gold of the temple, he is bound by his oath! 17. You are blind men: for which is greater, the gold or the temple, that makes the gold sacred? 18. And, Whoever swears by the altar, it is nothing; but whoever swears by the gift that is on the altar, he is bound by his oath. 19. You are blind men: for which is greater, the gift, or the altar that makes the gift sacred? 20. Who swears by the altar, swears by it, and by all things on it. 21. And whoso shall swear by the temple, swears by it, and by Him who dwells therein. 22. And he that shall swear by heaven, swears by the Throne of God, and by Him that sits thereon. 23. A curse on you, Scribes and Pharisees, pretenders! For you tithe of sweet-smelling plants, and have omitted the weightier matters of the law, judgment, mercy, and faithfulness: these ought you have done, and not to leave the other undone. 24. You are blind leaders, who strain a gnat from your wine and swallow a camel. 25. A curse on you, pretenders! For you clean the outside of the cup and the plate, but within they are full of greed and lust. 26. You blind Pharisee, cleanse first that which is within the cup and plate, that the outside may be clean also. 27. A curse on you, Scribes and Pharisees, pretenders! You are similar to the white-washed tombs, that appear beautiful outside, but are within full of the bones of dead men and corruption. 28. So you appear outwardly as righteous to men, but within you are full of hypocrisy and lawlessness. 29. A curse on you, Scribes and Pharisees, pretenders! You erect monument tombs to the prophets, and adorn the tombs of the righteous, 30. and say, Had we lived in the days of our fathers, we would not have joined them in murdering the prophets. 31. Wherefore you are witnesses against yourselves, that you are the children of those who murdered the prophets. 32. You complete what your fathers began. 33. You serpents, you offspring of vipers, how can you escape the damnation of hell? 34. Wherefore, I continue to send you prophets and wise men, and scholars: some of them you will kill and crucify; and some of them you will punish with the whip in your synagogues, and pursue them from city to city: 35. upon you may come all the innocent bloodshed on the earth, from the righteous blood of Abel unto the blood of Zacharias, son of Barachias, whom you murdered between the temple and the altar. 36. Truly I say, this generation shall be answerable for all these things.

*v14 This verse in the KJV is not adequately supported in original manuscripts.

Jesus Weeps Over Jerusalem
Matthew 23:37-39

37. Jerusalem, Jerusalem, you who kills the prophets, and stones those who are sent to you, often would I have gathered your children together, as a hen gathers her chickens under her wings, and you would not! 38. Behold, your temple is forsaken and desolate. 39. For I say, You will not see Me again, until you say, Blessed is He who comes in the name of the Lord.

Destruction of the Temple
Matthew 24:1-20 (See Mark 13:1-2; Luke 21:5-6)

End Time Woes
Matthew 24:3-14 (See Mark 13:3-13; Luke 21:7-19)

Abomination of Desolation
Matthew 24:15-28 (See Mark 13:14-23; Luke 21:20-24)

The King's Return
Matthew 24:29-30 (See Mark 12:24-27; Luke 21:29-33)

Discourse about Last Things
Matthew 24:31-35

31. And He shall send His messengers with a great trumpet, and they shall gather together His select from the four winds and from the extremities of heavens. 32. Now learn a parable of the fig tree; when the branch becomes tender, and putts forth leaves, you know that summer is near: 33. So likewise when you see all these signs, know that He is near, even at the doors. 34. Truly I say, this generation shall not pass until all these things are fulfilled. 35. Heaven and earth shall pass away, but My words shall not pass away.

Watchfulness
Matthew 24:36-51

36. But of the actual day and hour knows no man, not the angels of heaven, but My Father only. 37. But as the days of Noah were, so shall the coming of the Son of man be. 38. For as in the days that were before the flood they were eating and drinking, marrying and giving in marriage, until the day that Noah entered the ark, 39. and knew not until the flood came, and took them all away; so shall the coming of the Son of man be. 40. Then two men will be in the field; the one taken, and the other left. 41. Two women will be grinding at the mill; the one taken, and the other left. 42. Watch therefore: for you know not the hour your Lord will come. 43. But know this, that if the master of the

house had known exactly when the thief was coming, he would have watched, and would not have suffered his house to be plundered. 44. Therefore be ready: for in such an hour as you think not the Son of man comes. 45. Who is a faithful and wise servant, whom his master appointed over his household, to give them food in due season? 46. Blessed is that servant, whom his lord finds working when he comes. 47. Truly I say, That he shall set him over the whole estate. 48. But if that wicked servant shall say in his heart, My lord delays his coming; 49. And shall begin to beat his fellow-servants, and to eat and drink with the habitual drinkers; 50. the lord of that servant shall come in a day when he does not look for him, and in an hour when he is unaware, 51. and shall punish and appoint him a place with the hypocrites: there shall be weeping and gnashing of teeth.

Ten Virgins
Matthew 25:1-13

1. Then the kingdom of heaven is similar to ten virgins, who took their lamps, and went to meet the bridegroom. 2. And five of them were foolish, and five were wise. 3. They that were foolish took lamps with no oil: 4. but the wise took oil in their vessels with their lamps. 5. While the bridegroom dozed, they all slumbered and slept. 6. And at midnight there was a shout, Behold, the bridegroom comes; go out to meet Him. 7. Then all the virgins arose, and trimmed their lamps. 8. And the foolish asked the wise, Share your oil; for our lamps are going out. 9. But the wise answered, Not so; lest there not be enough for us and you: but go rather to those who sell and buy for yourselves. 10. And while they went to buy, the bridegroom came; and they that were ready went in with him to the marriage: and the door was shut. 11. Afterward the other virgins came, saying, Lord, Lord, open to us. 12. But he answered and said, Truly, I know you not. 13. Watch therefore, for you know neither the day nor the hour.

The Talents
Matthew 25:14-30 (See Luke 19:11-27)

Good and Bad People
Matthew 25:31-46

31. When the Son of man comes in His splendor, with all the angels, then He will take His seat on the throne of His glory: 32. and all nations shall be gathered before Him: and He will divide them one from another, as a shepherd divides his sheep from the goats: 33. and He will place the sheep on His right hand, but the goats on the left. 34. Then will the King say to them on His right hand, Come, you blood-related to My Father, inherit the kingdom prepared for you from the foundation of the world: 35. For I was hungry, and you gave Me food:

I was thirsty, and you gave Me drink: I was homeless, and you took Me in: 36. Naked and you clothed Me: I was sick, and you visited Me: I was in prison, and you came to Me. 37. Then shall the righteous answer, Lord, when did we see you hungry and feed you? Or thirsty, and gave you drink? 38. When did we see you homeless, and take you in? Or naked, and clothed you? 39. Or when did we see you sick or in prison, and came to you? 40. And the King shall answer, Truly I say, inasmuch as you did this to one of the least of these My brethren, you have done it to Me. 41. Then will He say to those on the left hand, Depart from me, you cursed ones, into eternal fire, prepared for the devil and his angels: 42. For I was hungry, and you gave me no food: I was thirsty, and you gave me no drink: 43. I was homeless, and you did not take me in: naked, and did not clothe me: sick, and in prison, and you did not visit me. 44. Then will they answer, saying, Lord, when did we see you hungry, or athirst, or homeless, or naked, or sick, or in prison, and did not minister to you? 45. Then will He answer, saying, Truly, I say, Inasmuch as you did not serve one of the least of these, you did it not to Me. 46. And these will go away into eternal punishment: but the righteous into life eternal.

Plotting the Death of Jesus
Matthew 26:1-5 (See Mark 14:1-2; Luke 22:1-2)

Jesus Anointed for Burial
Matthew 26:6-13 (See Mark 14:3-9; John 12:1-8)

Judas Bargains to Betray Jesus
Matthew 26:14-16 (See Mark 14:10-11; Luke 22:3-6)

Jesus and His Disciples Eat the Passover
Matthew 26:17-25 (See Mark 14:12-21; Luke 22:7-14, 21-23; John 13:21-30)

The Last Supper
Matthew 26:26-29 (See Mark 14:22-26; Luke 22:15-20; also see 1 Corinthians 11:23-25)

Prediction of Peter's Denial
Matthew 26:30-35 (See Mark 14:27-31; Luke 22:31-34; John 13:36-38)

Jesus Prays in Gethsemane
Matthew 26:36-46 (See Mark 14:32-42; Luke 22:39-46)

The Arrest of Jesus
Matthew 26:47-56 (See Mark 14:43-50; Luke 22:47-53; John 18:3-12)

Jesus Before Caiaphas and the Sanhedrin
Matthew 26:57-68 (See Mark 1:53-65; Luke 22:54-55, 63-71; John 18:12-14, 19-24)

Peter's Three Denials
Matthew 26:69-75 (See Mark 14:66-72; Luke 22:56-62; John 18:15, 25-27)

Jesus Before Pilate
Matthew 27:1-2 (See Mark 15:1; Luke 23:1-2; John 18:28-32)

Death of Judas
Matthew 27:3-10

3. Then Judas, who had betrayed Jesus, seeing that He was condemned, repented of what he had done, and returned the thirty pieces of silver to the chief priests and elders, 4. saying, I have sinned and betrayed innocent blood. And they said, What is that to us? It is your problem. 5. And Judas left the money as a temple offering, and departed, and went and hanged himself. 6. And the chief priests took the silver pieces, and said, It is not lawful to put the price of blood into the treasury. 7. After discussing the matter, they bought with the money the potter's field, to bury the homeless. 8. That is why, to this day, the field is called, The Field of Blood. 9. Then words spoken by Jeremiah, the prophet, were fulfilled, saying, And they took the thirty pieces of silver, the price of Him, whom the children of Israel did value; 10. and exchanged them for the potter's field, as the Lord instructed. (See Acts 1: 17-19)

Jesus Again Before Pilate
Matthew 27:11-18 (Mark 15:2-5; Luke 23:3-5; John 18:323-38)

The Dream of Pilate's Wife
Matthew 27:19

19. When Pilate sat down on the judgment seat, his wife sent to him, saying, Have nothing to do with that just man: for I have suffered many things this day in a dream because of Him.

Jesus or Barabbas
Matthew 27:20-26 (See Mark 15:6-15; Luke 23:17-25; John 18:38-40)

Jesus Mocked by Soldiers
Matthew 27:27-31 (See Mark 15:16-20; John 19:2-3)

The Crucifixion
Matthew 27: 32-44 (Mark 15:21-32; Luke 23:26-43; John 19:17-27)

The Death of Jesus
Matthew 27:45-51 (See Mark 15:33-41; Luke 23:44-49; John 19:28-30)

The Resurrection of Saints
Matthew 27:52-56

52. And the tombs were opened; and many bodies of the holy ones who slept, arose, 53. and came out of the tombs after the resurrection of Jesus, and went into the Holy City, and appeared to many. 54. When the Roman centurion and the soldiers with him, watching Jesus, saw the earthquake, and those things that were done, they feared greatly, saying, Truly this was the Son of God. 55. And many women were there watching from a distance, who followed Jesus from Galilee, ministering to Him: 56. Among the women was Mary Magdalene, and Mary the mother of James and Joses, and the mother of Zebedee's sons.

The Burial of Jesus
Matthew 27:57-66 (See Mark 15:42-47; Luke 23:50-56; John 19:38-42)

Tomb Sealed and Guarded
Matthew 27:62-66

62. Now the next day, that followed the day of the preparation, the chief priests and Pharisees came together to Pilate, 63. saying, Sir, we remember what that deceiver said, while He was alive, After three days I will rise again. 64. Command therefore that the tomb be made secure until the third day, lest His disciples come by night, and steal Him away, and say to the people, He is risen from the dead: so the last error will be worse than the first. 65. Pilate said, You have a watch: go your way, make it as secure as you can. 66. So they went, and made the tomb secure, sealing the stone, and setting a guard.

Jesus is Risen
Matthew 28:1-15 (See Mark 16:1-8; Luke 24:1-12; John 20:1-10)

The Great Challenge of Jesus
Matthew 28:16-20

16. Then the eleven disciples went to Galilee, to a mountain where Jesus had arranged to meet them. 17. And when they saw Jesus, some doubted. 18. And Jesus came and spoke, saying, All authority has been committed to Me in heaven and in earth. 19. *As you personally go, (going) therefore, and make disciples of all nations, baptizing them in the name of the Father, and of the Son, and of the Holy Spirit: 20. teaching them to observe all things whatever I have commanded

you: and behold, I am with you always, even unto the end of the world. So be it.

---

*v19 A change in the KJV that made a difference was in the words of the Great Commission in Matthew (28:19, 20) *19. Go ye therefore, and teach all nations, baptizing them in the name of the Father, and of the Son, and of the Holy Ghost: 20. Teaching them to observe all things whatsoever I have commanded you: and, lo, I am with you always, even unto the end of the world. Amen.* (KJV) Consider the primary command of the verse translated "teach." The Greek word used was *matheteuo* to instruct with the purpose of making a disciple; the word suggested not only to learn but to be attached to and a follower of a teacher. Greek words have special designations, *matheteuo* here was classified as aorist imperative active which denotes a command, or entreaty and indicates the action as being accomplished by the subject of the verb. Later versions translated the word as "make disciples" which was better.

The main problem with the translation of the Commission is that it was not given to an established or organized assembly, but given to the followers of Jesus as personal guidance. Another basic problem relates to the three participles: Go [going or as you go] ... baptizing ... teaching are each participles dependent upon the main verb teach translated "make disciples." Although such a construction is not uncommon for the participles themselves to assume the force of a weak imperative, it is indirect similar to the indirect command in modern English, i.e. "As you go, close the door!" However, the command "to make disciples" is the primary command, while the participles (weak commands) going, baptizing and teaching are ways of fulfilling the primary command. Some modern translations, translate all of the four verb forms as imperatives. "Go ... make disciples ... baptize ... teach (verse 20)," but the King James translators chose to make "go" a direct command, but not baptizing and teaching. One should either make all the participles into commands or use all the verb forms as participles or imperatives as originally written.

What difference does this make? The above translation created a self-defeating theology of coercion in an effort to compel people to "go and do" rather that establish a "do as you go" life-style. The Great Commission was not a command to "go," but a program for people in the process of going into the known world to carry the good news. It was guidance to effectively follow-up those who received the teaching, embraced the teacher, and became an active learner. Why would scholars make such a decision? All academics and theologians are influence by a personal bias.

In the England of 1604-1611, the concept of building an empire was beginning. To build an empire required Englishmen to leave their island fortress and colonize the new world. The Court of Queen Elizabeth and the golden age of English art, literature, and adventure were precursors to the effort. It was 1585 when the first effort to export the golden age was made "to go across the sea" and settle the new land "Virginia," named after the Queen. Although this group nearly starved before Sir Frances Drake rescued the survivors, the concept of "go" was firmly established in the minds of English achievers. Consequently, the translators seeking to please the new king, James, used an obscure Greek rule to translate a participle into an imperative: "Go into all the world..." This created a theology of coercion that caused an artificial motivation that negates the power of personal experience which is the true means of advancing Christianity. The Commission supports a life-style of making disciples "as you go" rather than a program of "go and do."

THE GOSPEL ACCORDING TO JOHN

John, writing from Ephesus after Christianity was established in the Gentile world, obviously felt that the Gospel had to be restated so the Gentiles would see the deity of Christ and accept His authority to bring salvation. John's work was the last of the Gospels. Some see his presentation as being different from the other gospels. Any difference is based on the purpose of the Gospel, not on a lack of knowledge. John omits some parts of the story and adds others to support his purpose. John was one of the original Disciples and had a much closer relationship with Jesus than Matthew. Luke and Mark basically received their information from others, while John gave a first-hand account. Also, having the other Gospels in circulation gave John the opportunity to complete an emphasis on the Deity of Christ. John was concerned that Christianity moving into the Gentile world had not seen the early miracles of Christ that supported His Authority to bring salvation to the world. John presents the early deeds of Christ before John the Baptist was imprisoned, while the other writers give accounts of the later periods of Christ's ministry. Although, Luke's goal was to share "all that Christ began to do and teach," John was eye-witness to the earliest activity of Jesus that convinced many that Jesus was the Christ, the Son of God with divine authority to bring salvation.

Empowered to Become Children of God
John 1:1-14

1. The Word existed in the beginning, and the Word was God. 2. The Word was with God from the beginning. 3. All creation existed by His hand, and nothing was made without Him. 4. In Him was life; and that life was the light of men. 5. And the Light continues to shine and the darkness could not restrain it. 6. God sent a man whose name was John. 7. He came as a witness of the Light, that all men may accept the Light. 8. He was not the Light, but was sent to be a witness for the Light. 9. That was the True Light that came into the world to enlighten every man. 10. He came into the world that He made, and the world did not recognize Him. 11. He came to His own Creation, and was not received. 12. But to those who welcomed Him, they were empowered to become the children of God, even to those who acknowledged His authority: 13. These were not born by the desires of earthly parents, but were born of God. 14. And the Word became a human body and lived among men, (and His glory was worthy of the Father's only Son), and this glory was full of authenticity and mercy.

Behold the Lamb of God
John 1:15-34

15. John gave testimony and cried aloud, This is He of whom I spoke, He who comes after me has status above me. 16. And we have all received of His abundance, and blessing after blessing. 17. For the law

was given by Moses, but grace and truth was realized through Jesus Christ. 18. No man had seen the only begotten Son of God, who was in the bosom of the Father, who now has made Him known. 19. And this is the witness of John, when the Jews sent priests and Levites from Jerusalem to ask, Who are you? 20. And he frankly admitted, I am not the promised Christ. 21. And they asked him Who then? Are you Elijah? And he said I am not. Are you the prophet? And he answered No. 22. We must give an answer to those who sent us, What do you say about who you are? 23. He said, I am the voice of one crying in the wilderness, Make ready for the coming of the Lord, as the prophet Isaiah said. 24. And they which were sent were of the Pharisees. 25. And they asked him, if you are not the Christ, nor Elijah, neither the prophet? 26. John answered, I baptize with water: but there stands one among you, whom you do not recognize; 27. the One coming after me is ranked ahead of me, whose sandals I am not worthy to unfasten. 28. These things were done in Bethany beyond Jordan, where John was baptizing. 29. The next day John sees Jesus coming toward him, and said, Behold the Lamb of God, who is to take away the sin of the world. 30. This is He who comes after me has status above me. 31. And I knew only that He should be made manifest to Israel, therefore, I came baptizing with water. 32. And John gave more evidence, I saw the Spirit descending from heaven as a dove, and rest on Him. 33. And I did not know Him, but the One who sent me to baptize with water, the same said, Upon whom you see the Spirit descending on Him and remaining, the same is He who baptizes with the Holy Spirit. 34. And I saw and bare record that this is the Son of God.

Come and See
John 1:35-51
35. The next day after John stood with two of his disciples; 36. And saw Jesus as He walked, and said, Behold the Lamb of God! 37. And the two disciples heard Him speak, and they followed Jesus. 38. Then Jesus turned, and saw them following, and asked What do you want? They said, Rabbi, (being interpreted, Master,) where do you dwell? 39. He said Come and see. They went and saw where He dwelt, and remained with Him the rest of the day: for it was about four in the afternoon. 40. One of the two disciples of John who followed Him was Andrew, Simon Peter's brother. 41. He first found his own brother Simon, and said, We have found the Messiah, the Christ. 42. And brought Peter to Jesus. And when Jesus saw him, He said, You are Simon the son of John: you shall be called Cephas (a small stone). 43. The next day Jesus went into Galilee, and found Philip, and said to him Follow Me. 44. Now Philip was of Bethsaida, the city of Andrew and Peter. 45. Philip found Nathanael, and said, We have

found Him of whom Moses in the law, and the prophets, did write, Jesus of Nazareth, the son of Joseph. 46. And Nathanael asked, Can any good thing come out of Nazareth? Philip said, Come and see. 47. Jesus saw Nathanael coming to Him, and said, Behold a true Israelite in whom is no guile! 48. Nathanael asked, How do you know me? Jesus answered, Before Philip called you, when you were under the fig tree, I saw you. 49. Nathanael answered, Rabbi, you are the Son of God; you are the King of Israel. 50. Jesus asked, Do you believe because, I saw you under the fig tree? You will see greater things than these. 51. And Jesus said Truly, I say unto you, Hereafter you will see heaven open, and the angels of God ascending and descending upon the Son of man.

This Beginning of Miracles
John 2:1-12

1. And on the third day there was a wedding in Cana of Galilee; and the mother of Jesus was there: 2. Jesus and His disciples were invited. 3. And when the wine was depleted, the mother of Jesus told Him they have no wine. 4. Jesus said, What can I do about it? My time has not come. 5. His mother told the servants, Whatever He says, do it. 6. And there were six stone water pots for the ceremonial cleansing of the Jews, containing about twenty gallons each. 7. Jesus said, Fill up the water pots with water. And they filled them up to the brim. 8. And Jesus said, Draw out now, and take to the governor of the feast. And they obeyed. 9. When the ruler of the feast had tasted the water that was made wine, and not knowing its source: (but the servants knew) the governor of the feast called the bridegroom, 10. And said, Every man at the beginning sets forth good wine; and when men have well drunk, then poor wine: but you have kept the best wine until now. 11. This beginning of miracles did Jesus in Cana of Galilee, and demonstrated His power; and the faith of His disciples was confirmed. 12. Then Jesus went down to Capernaum with His mother, brothers, and His disciples: and they remained there a few days.

His Disciples Remembered
John 2:13-25

13. And the Jews' Passover was at hand, and Jesus went up to Jerusalem. 14. And found in the Temple dealers in cattle, sheep and doves, and the money changers seated at their tables: 15. And when He had made a lash of small cords, He drove them all out of the Temple, and the sheep, and the cattle; and poured out the changers' money, and overthrew their tables; 16. and said to those who sold doves, Take these things outside; do not make My Father's house a market house. 17. Then His disciples remembered that it was written,

Jealousy for the honor of your house has consumed me. 18. Then the Jews asked, What sign of authority can you show us for doing these things? 19. Jesus answered, Destroy this temple, and in three days I will restore it. 20. Then said the Jews, Forty-six years was this temple in building, and will you restore it in three days? 21. But Jesus spoke of the temple of His body. 22. When He stood up again from the grave, His disciples remembered what He had said; and they believed the scripture, and the word which Jesus had said. 23. Now when He was in Jerusalem at the Passover feast, many believed in His authority, when they saw the miracles which He did. 24. But Jesus did not commit Himself to them, because He knew the nature of men, 25. and needed no additional witness of man: for He knew the nature of man.

You Must be Born Again
John 3:1-12

1. There was a leader among the Jews, named Nicodemus, a member of the Jewish Council: 2. who came to Jesus by night, and said, Rabbi, we know that you are a teacher from God: for no man could do these miracles except God be with him. 3. Jesus answered, Truly, I say to you, Except a man be born again, he cannot see the kingdom of God. 4. Nicodemus asked, How can a man be born when he is old? Can he enter the second time into his mother's womb, and be born? 5. Jesus answered, Truly, I say, Except a man be born of water and of the Spirit, he cannot enter the kingdom of God. 6. That which is born by physical birth is of nature; and to be born of the Spirit is a spiritual birth. 7. Do not be astonished that I said, You must be born again. 8. The wind blows where it wishes, and you hear the sound, but cannot determine from where it comes or where it is going: so is every one that is born of the Spirit. 9. Nicodemus answered, How can these things be? 10. Jesus answered, Are you a teacher of Israel, and do not understand these things? 11. Truly, I say, we speak what we do know, and witness to what we have seen; yet you receive not our testimony. 12. If I have told you earthly things, and you believe not, how shall you believe, if I tell you of heavenly things?

God So Loved the World
John 3: 13-21

13. The Son of Man who descended from heaven, is the only one who will return to His home in heaven. 14. Just as Moses lifted up the serpent in the wilderness, even so must the Son of Man be lifted up: 15. that whoever believes may have in Him eternal life. 16. For God so loved the world that He gave His only begotten Son, that whoever believes in Him should not perish, but have everlasting life. 17. For God sent not His Son into the world to judge the world; but that the

world through Him might be saved. 18. He that believes on Him is not judged: but he that believes not has been judged already, because he has not trusted in the authority of the only begotten Son of God. 19. And the basis for this judgment is that the Light has come into the world, and men preferred darkness to the Light, because their deeds were evil. 20. Every wrongdoer hates the Light, neither comes to the Light, lest their deeds should be exposed. 21. But he who does what is right comes to the Light, so it is obvious that his works are done through God.

Jesus Must Grow Greater
John 3:22-30

22. After these things Jesus and His disciples went to the land of Judaea; there He spent time with them and kept baptizing people. 23. Also John was baptizing near Salem where there were many streams: and people kept coming to be immersed. 24. For John had not yet been imprisoned. 25. Then there arose a discussion among some of John's disciples and the Jews about ceremonial cleansing, 26. and they came to John, and said, Rabbi, look He who was with you beyond Jordan, to whom you gave witness, the same baptizes, and everyone is going to Him. 27. John said, A man can have only what heaven gives. 28. You remember and witnessed what was said, I am not the Anointed One, but that I am sent before Him. 29. He that hath the bride is the Bridegroom: but the friend of the Bridegroom, which stands and hears Him, is overjoyed at the sound of the Bridegroom's voice: thus my joy is complete. 30. Jesus must grow greater, but I must decrease.

Certified that God is True
John 3:31-36

31. He that cometh from above is superior to all: he who comes from the earth speaks the language of earth: He who comes from heaven is above all. 32. And He states what He has seen and heard; and no one accepts His witness. 33. He who receives His testimony has certified that God is true. 34. For He whom God has sent speaks the words of God: for God gives Him the full measure of the Spirit. 35. The Father loves the Son, and has entrusted Him with all authority. 36. He who trusts in the Son has everlasting life: but those who do not trust in the Son will not see life; but lives with the displeasure of God.

Sir, Give Me This Water
John 4:1-15

1. Consequently, when the Lord learned the Pharisees had heard that He made and baptized more disciples than John, 2. (although Jesus did not normally baptize, but His disciples,) 3. He left Judaea and went again into Galilee. 4. And He had to pass through Samaria. 5.

And came to Sychar, a city of Samaria, near to the piece of ground that Jacob gave to his son Joseph. 6. Wearied from His journey, Jesus sat on the well: and it was about mid-day. 7. And a Samaritan woman came to draw water: Jesus spoke to her, Give Me to drink. 8. (For His disciples were gone to the city to buy food.) 9. Why do you ask me for a drink being a Jew and I am a Samaritan? The Jews and Samaritans do not share common vessels. 10. Jesus answered, If you knew the gift of God, and who it is that asks, Give Me to drink; you would have asked and He would have given you living water. 11. The woman said, Sir, you have nothing with which to draw, and the well is deep: from where will you get the living water? 12. Are you greater than our father Jacob, who gave us the well, and drank from it himself, and his children, and his cattle? 13. Jesus answered, Whoever drinks of this water shall thirst again: 14. but whoever drinks of the water that I give shall never thirst; but the water that I shall give him shall be in him a well of water springing up to everlasting life. 15. The woman said, Sir, give me this water, that I thirst not, neither come here to draw.

God is Spirit
John 4:16-26
16. Jesus asked her, Go, call your husband, and come back here. 17. The woman answered, I have no husband. Jesus said, You have well said, I have no husband: 18. you have spoken the truth, for you have had five husbands; and the one you have now is not your husband. 19. The woman said, Sir, I perceive that you are a prophet. 20. Our fathers worshipped in this mountain; and you say, that Jerusalem is the place where men ought to worship. 21. Jesus said, Woman, believe Me, the hour will come, when you shall neither in this mountain, nor at Jerusalem, worship the Father. 22. You worship you know not what: we know what we worship: for salvation is of the Jews. 23. But the hour has come when the true worshippers shall worship the Father in spirit and in truth: for the Father seeks such to worship Him. 24. God is Spirit: and they who worship Him must worship in spirit and in truth. 25. The woman said, I know that Messiah will come who is called Christ: and when He comes, He will tell us all things. 26. Jesus said, I that speak am He.

Is This Not the Christ?
John 4:27-42
27. When His disciples returned, they were surprised that He talked with the woman: yet no one asked the woman what she wanted or why Jesus talked with her. 28. The woman then left her water pot, and went her way to the city, and said to the men, 29. Come see a man who told me all things I ever did: is this not the Christ? 30. Then they

left the city, and made their way to see Jesus. 31. Meanwhile, the disciples kept urging their Master to eat. 32. But He said, I have food of which you have no knowledge. 33. The disciples began to discuss one with another, Has someone brought Him something to eat? 34. Jesus spoke to them, My nourishment is to do the will of God who sent Me, and to finish His work. 35. Say not, there are yet four months, and then comes the harvest? Look, I say Lift up your eyes, and look on the fields; for they are white already to harvest. 36. And he that reaps already receives wages, and gathers fruit unto life eternal: that both he that sows and he that reaps may rejoice together. 37. And herein is the saying true, One sows, and another reaps. 38. I sent you to reap where you had not labored, and you inherited their labors. 39. And many Samaritans of that city believed on Him because of the woman's testimony, He told me all that ever I did. 40. So when the Samaritans came to Him, they besought Him to tarry with them: and He abode there two days. 41. And many more believed because of His own words; 42. and said to the woman, Now we believe, not because of your testimony: but because we have heard Him ourselves, and know that this is indeed the Savior of the world.

His Whole House Believed
John 4:43-54

43. Now after two days He departed and went to Galilee. 44. Jesus testified that a prophet has no honor in His own country. 45. Then when He went to Galilee, the Galileans received Him, having seen all the things that He did at the feast in Jerusalem: for they also attended the feast. 46. So Jesus came again to Cana of Galilee, where He made the water into wine. And there was a certain nobleman, whose son was sick at Capernaum. 47. When he heard that Jesus had left Judaea for Galilee, he went and besought Him that He would come and heal his son: for he was at the point of death. 48. Then said Jesus, Except you see signs and wonders, you will not believe. 49. The nobleman said, Sir, come now before my son dies. 50. Jesus said, Go your way; your son lives. And the man believed the word that Jesus spoke to him, and he went his way. 51. And as he was going home, his servants met him, saying, the boy lives. 52. Then he asked the hour when the boy began to amend. And they said, Yesterday at one o'clock the fever left him. 53. So the father knew that it was at the same hour that Jesus said, Your son lives. And he and his whole house believed in Jesus. 54. This was the second miracle that Jesus did, when He left Judaea for Galilee.

It was Jesus
John 5:1-16

1. After there was a feast of the Jews and Jesus travelled up to Jerusalem. 2. Now there is at Jerusalem by the sheep-gate, a pool called in Hebrew, Bethesda, having five porches. 3. In these porches was a great multitude of sick and blind and lame with withered limbs waiting for the moving of the water. 4. For an angel at a certain season came to the pool, and troubled the water: whoever stepped first into the water after the troubling was made whole of his disease. 5. And a certain man was there, who had an infirmity for thirty-eight years. 6. When Jesus saw him lying there and knew that he had been a long time in that condition asked, Will you be made whole? 7. The helpless man answered, Sir, I have no man, when the water is troubled, to help me into the pool: but while I am coming, another steps down before me. 8. Jesus said, Rise, take up your bed, and walk. 9. And immediately the man was made whole, and took up his bed, and walked: and it was the Sabbath. 10. The Jews told the man who was cured, It is the Sabbath: it is not lawful for you to carry your bed. 11. He answered, He that made me whole, the same told me, Take up your bed and walk. 12. Then they asked him, Who told you, Take up your bed and walk? 13. And the healed man did not know who He was, because Jesus had withdrawn because of a multitude in the place. 14. Afterward Jesus found him in the temple, and said to him, Behold, you were made whole: sin no more, lest a worse thing come upon you. 15. The man departed, and told the Jews that it was Jesus, who made me whole. 16. Consequently, the Jews began to persecute Jesus, because He had done these things on the Sabbath.

Passed from Death into Life
John 5:17-24

17. But Jesus answered, My Father continued working until now, and I am working. 18. This made the Jews even more determined to kill Him, because He not only did not keep the Sabbath, but said God was His Father, making Himself equal with God. 19. Then Jesus answered, Truly, I say, the Son can do nothing by Himself, but He does only what He sees the Father doing: whatever the Father does, the Son does the same way. 20. For the Father loves the Son, and shows Him everything He is doing: and He will show Him greater works than these, that you may be filled with wonder. 21. For as the Father raises the dead, and gives them life; even so the Son gives life to whom He chooses. 22. For the Father judges no man, but has left all judgment to the Son: 23. So that all men may honor the Son, even as they honor the Father. Whoever honors not the Son does not honor the Father who sent Him. 24. Truly, I say, He that hears My Word, and believes

on Him who sent Me, has everlasting life, and will not face judgment; but has passed from death into life.

This should be no Surprise
John 5:25-29

25. Truly, I say, the hour is coming, and now is, when the dead will listen to the voice of the Son of God: and all who hear shall come to life. 26. For as the Father is self-existent; so has He granted to the Son to have life in Himself; 27. and has also given Him authority to execute judgment, because He is the Son of Man. 28. This should be no surprise: for the hour is coming, when all that are in their graves shall hear His voice, 29. and will come forth; those who have done good, to the resurrection of life; and those who have practiced evil will rise again to be judged.

How Shall You Believe My Words
John 5:30-47

30. I can do nothing of Myself: as I hear, I judge: and My decisions are fair; because I seek not My own will, but the will of the One who sent Me. 31. If I witness of Myself, My witness is not valid. 32. There is Another who testifies of Me: and I know that the testimony He gives is valid. 33. You sent to John, and he gave witness to the truth. 34. But I do not accept the testimony of man: but I say these things that you might be saved. 35. He was a burning fire in a shining lamp: and you were pleased to walk in his light. 36. But I have a greater witness than that of John: for the works the Father has given Me to complete, these works I am doing, abide with My words that the Father sent Me. 37. And the Father, who sent Me Himself, has given witness of Me. You have neither heard His voice, nor seen His form. 38. And His Word does not abide in you; because you do not believe the One He sent. 39. You keep searching the scriptures; because you think you will find in them eternal life: and the scripture testifies of Me. 40. And you will not come to Me, that you might have life. 41. I do not look to men for praise. 42. But I know you, that in your heart you do not love God. 43. I am come in My Father's name, and you refuse Me: if another comes with no authority but himself, you will accept him. 44. How can you believe, when you accept honor from one another, and seek not the honor that only comes from God? 45. There is no need for Me to accuse you to the Father: there is one who already accuses you, even Moses, in whom you trust. 46. For had you believed Moses, you would have believed Me: for he wrote about Me. 47. But if you believe not his writings, how shall you believe My words?

This is the Prophet
John 6:1-14

1. After these things Jesus went across the Galilee, otherwise called the Lake of Tiberias. 2. And a great multitude followed, because they saw the miracles which He did for those that were diseased. 3. And Jesus went up to a mount, and sat with His disciples. 4. And the Jewish festival of the Passover was near. 5. When Jesus saw a large crowd approaching, He said to Philip, Where shall we get food that these may eat? 6. And this He said to test him: knowing what He would do. 7. Philip answered, Forty or fifty dollars would not be enough to get food for each one to get just a little. 8. One of the disciples, Andrew, Simon Peter's brother, said, 9. There is a lad here with five barley loaves and two small fishes: but what are they among so many? 10. And Jesus said, Make the men sit down. Now there was much grass in the place and the men sat down, about five thousand. 11. And Jesus took the loaves; and when He had given thanks, He distributed to those who sat down; likewise the fishes as much as they wanted. 12. When they were filled, He said to the disciples, Gather up the pieces that remain, so nothing will be lost. 13. So they collected the pieces, and filled twelve baskets with the fragments of the five barley loaves, left over after the people were filled. 14. Then those who witnessed the miracle, said Without doubt this is the Prophet that is to come into the world.

The Works that God Demands
John 6:15-29

15. When Jesus perceived that they were about to force Him to be a King, He withdrew alone to a mountain. 16. But when evening came, His disciples went down to the sea, 17. and entered a boat to sail toward Capernaum. By this time it was dark, and Jesus had not returned. 18. And a great wind arose on the water. 19. After they had rowed about three or four miles, they saw Jesus walking on the water coming near the boat: and they were afraid. 20. But He said, It is I; do not be frightened. 21. Then they gladly took Jesus into the boat: and immediately the boat reached the shore where they were going. 22. The next day, when the people on the other side of the lake saw that there had been only one boat, and that Jesus did not enter the boat with the disciples, but that the disciples went without Him; 23. (But some other small boats from Tiberias landed near the place where they had eaten and the Lord had given thanks:) 24. when the people saw that Jesus nor His disciples were not there, they took shipping, and went to Capernaum seeking Jesus. 25. And when they had found Him on the other side of the lake, they asked, Rabbi, how did you get here? 26. Jesus answered Truly, You seek Me, not because you

saw the miracles, but because you ate the loaves and were filled. 27. Labor not for the food that perishes, but for the food that endures to eternal life, which the Son of man will give to you: for on Him has God the Father placed the seal of authority. 28. Then they asked Jesus, What are the works that God demands of us? 29. Jesus answered, This is the work of God, that you believe on the One whom God has sent.

I will Certainly Not Turn Away
John 6:30-40

30. They said to Jesus, What sign will you give us, that we may see and believe? What wonders do you perform? 31. Our fathers ate manna in the desert; it is written, God gave them bread from heaven. 32. Then Jesus said, Truly, Moses did not give you the bread from heaven; but My Father gives you the True Heavenly Bread. 33. For the Bread of God is He who comes down from heaven, and gives life to the world. 34. Then they said, Lord, day by day give us that bread. 35. And Jesus said, I am the Bread of Life: he who comes to Me will never hunger; and he who believes on Me shall never thirst. 36. But as I said, You have seen Me, and still have no faith. 37. All the Father gives Me will come; and those who come I will certainly not turn away. 38. For I came down from heaven, not to carry out My own will, but the will of Him who sent Me. 39. And this is the Father's will who sent Me, that of all given Me I should lose none, but should raise them to life on the last day. 40. And this is the will of the One who sent Me, that everyone who sees the Son, and believes, may have eternal life: and I will raise him up on the last day.

I Am the Bread of Life
John 6:41-59

41. The Jews began to find fault with Him, because He said, I am the Bread that came down from heaven. 42. And they said, Is not this Jesus, the son of Joseph, whose father and mother we know? How is it that He says, I came down from heaven? 43. Jesus therefore answered and said to them, Whisper not among yourselves. 44. No man can come to Me, without being attracted to Me by the Father who sent Me: and I will raise him up on the last day. 45. It is written in the prophets, and they will all be taught of God. Everyman that has heard, and learned of the Father, comes to Me. 46. Not that any man has seen the Father, save He who is of God, He has seen the Father. 47. Truly, I say to you, He that believes on Me has eternal life. 48. I am the Bread of Life. 49. Your fathers did eat manna in the wilderness, and are dead. 50. This is the Bread which comes down from heaven, that a man may eat thereof, and not die. 51. I am the living Bread which came down

from heaven: if any man eat of this Bread, he shall live forever: and the Bread that I will give is My flesh, which I will give for the life of the world. 52. The Jews therefore contended among themselves, saying, How can this man give us His flesh to eat? 53. Then Jesus said to them, with all earnestness, I say, Except you eat the flesh of the Son of man, and drink His blood, you have no inner life. 54. Whoso eats My flesh, and drinks My blood, has eternal life; and I will raise him up on the last day. 55. Because My flesh is True Food, and My blood is True Drink. 56. He that eats My flesh, and drinks My blood, abides in Me, and I in him. 57. As the living Father has sent Me, and I live by the Father: so he that eats Me, even he shall live by Me. 58. This is that Bread which came down from heaven: not as your fathers did eat and are dead: he that eats of this Bread will live forever. 59. These things said He in the synagogue, teaching in Capernaum.

The Words of Eternal Life
John 6:60-71

60. When His disciples heard these things some said, This is a hard* teaching, who can understand it? 61. When Jesus perceived that His disciples whispered about it, He asked, Does this offend you? 62. What would you say if you saw the Son of Man ascend to where He was before? 63. It is the Spirit who gives life; the flesh profits nothing: the words that I speak to you, they are spirit, and they are life. 64. But there are some of you that believe not. Because Jesus knew, from the beginning, who did not believe, and who would betray Him. 65. And he said, Therefore, I told you, that no one is able to come to Me, except it were given to him of My Father. 66. From that time many of His followers went back, and walked no more with Him. 67. Then Jesus said to the Twelve, Will you also go away? 68. Then Simon Peter answered, Lord, to whom shall we go? You have the words of eternal life. 69. And we believe and are sure that you are the Holy One of God, the Son of the living God. 70. Jesus answered them, Have not I chosen Twelve, and one of you is a devil? 71. Jesus spoke of Judas Iscariot the son of Simon: for he, being one of the Twelve, was planning the betrayal.

---

*v60 The Greek word for "hard" is *skleros*, which does not mean hard to understand, but "hard to accept."

Jesus Stayed in Galilee
John 7:1-9

1. After these things Jesus moved about in Galilee: for He would not walk in Judaea, because the Jews were eager to kill Him. 2. Now the Jewish Feast of Tabernacles was near. 3. His brothers said to Him, Leave here and go into Judaea, so your disciples may also see the

works that you do. 4. No man does things in secret, when he seeks to be known openly. Since you do these things, show yourself to the world. 5. Even His brothers did not believe in Him. 6. Then Jesus said, This is not the time for Me: but anytime is ready for you. 7. The world cannot hate you; but Me it hates, because I show the world that its works are evil. 8. You go up to this feast: I am not going to this feast; for My time is not fully come. 9. After saying these things, Jesus stayed in Galilee.

When Messiah Comes
John 7:10-31

10. After His brothers went to the festival, Jesus went up secretly to the feast. 11. The Jews searched for Jesus at the feast, and said, Where can He be? 12. And there was much whispering among the people concerning Jesus: for some said, He is a good man: others said, No, He deceives the people. 13. But no one spoke openly about Jesus for fear of the Jews. 14. However about the middle of the feast, Jesus went up to the Temple and was teaching. 15. And the Jews questioned, saying, How can this uneducated man know His letters? 16. Jesus answered them, My teaching is not mine, but His that sent Me. 17. Any man who does God's will, shall know of My teaching, whether it be of God, or whether I speak of Myself. 18. He that speaks of himself seeks his own glory: but he who wants to honor the one who sent him, tells the truth, and there is no deception in his heart. 19. Did not Moses give you the Law, and yet none of you keeps the Law? Why then do you seek to kill Me? 20. The people answered, You have a devil: who goes about to kill you? 21. Jesus answered and said, I have done just one deed that made you wonder. 22. Moses gave you circumcision; (not because it is of Moses, but of the fathers;) and you circumcise a male child even on the Sabbath day. 23. If a male child receives circumcision on the Sabbath day so the law of Moses would not be broken; are you angry at Me, because I have made a man's whole body well on the Sabbath day? 24. Stop judging by appearances, but judge fairly. 25. Then said some from Jerusalem, Is not this He, whom they seek to kill? 26. But, here He is speaking fluently, and they say nothing. Do the rulers know indeed that this is the Messiah? 27. But this cannot be the Christ, we know from where He comes. When Messiah comes no man knows His origin. 28. Then Jesus cried out in the temple as He taught, saying, You both know He, and you know whence I am: and I am not come of Myself, but He that sent Me is true, whom you know not. 29. But I know Him: for I am from Him, and He has sent Me. 30. Now they were anxious to seize Him: but no man touched Him, because His hour had not come. 31. And many of

the people believed on Him, and said, When Messiah comes, will He do more miracles than these that this man has done?

You Cannot Even Go in that Direction
John 7:32-39
32. The Pharisees heard that the people whispered such things concerning Jesus; and the Pharisees and the chief priests sent officers to arrest Him. 33. Then Jesus said, Only a little while will I be with you, and then I return to Him who sent Me. 34. You may seek Me but will not find Me: and where I am, you cannot even go in that direction. 35. Then the Jews spoke among themselves, To what place will He go, that we cannot find Him? Will He go to the Jews scattered among the Greeks, and teach the Greeks? 36. What does He mean saying, You will seek He, and will not find He: and where I am, you cannot even go in that direction. 37. On the greatest day of the feast, Jesus stood and cried, saying, If any man thirst, let him come to Me, and drink. 38. He that believes on Me, as the scripture has said, out of the heart of one who believes shall flow rivers of living water. 39. (But this was said of the Spirit, which those who believe on Him should receive: for the Holy Spirit was not yet given; because Jesus had not yet been exalted.)

Are You Also Deceived?
John 7:40-53
40. Many of the people who heard this saying, said, Without doubt this is the Prophet. 41. Others said, This is the Christ. But some said, Shall Messiah come out of Galilee? 42. Did the scripture not say Christ comes of the seed of David, and out of the village of Bethlehem, where David lived? 43. So there was division among the people because of Jesus. 44. And some would have arrested Him; but no man touched Him. 45. Then came the officers to the chief priests and Pharisees; and they were asked, Why have you not brought Him? 46. The officers answered, No man ever spoke as this man. 47. The Pharisees responded, Are you also deceived? 48. Have any of the leaders or any of the Pharisees believed on Him? 49. This crowd does not know the law and are wicked and despicable. 50. One of them, Nicodemus, the one who came to Jesus by night, said, 51. Does the law judge a man, without a hearing, and knows what he did? 52. They answered, Are you also of Galilee? Search the record for no prophet is to come out of Galilee. *53. And every man went to his own home.* *

Sin No More
John 8:1-11*
1. Jesus went to the Mount of Olives. 2. And early in the morning He came again to the Temple, and all the people came to Him; and Jesus sat down and continued to teach them. 3. And the Scribes and

Pharisees brought a woman caught in adultery; and when they had placed her in front, 4. they said, Master, this woman was taken in the actual act of adultery. 5. In the law, Moses instructed that such a woman be stoned: but what do you say? 6. This was an effort to trap Jesus so they could accuse Him. As if He did not hear them, Jesus stooped down, and wrote with His finger on the ground. 7. When they continued asking questions, Jesus stood up and said, He who is without sin, let him cast the first stone at her. 8. And He stooped down again and wrote on the ground. 9. And all who heard went out one by one, beginning with the eldest: and Jesus was left alone with the woman. 10. Then Jesus stood and saw only the woman, and asked, Woman, where are they? Did no one condemn you? 11. She said, No man, Lord. And Jesus said. Neither do I condemn you, go and sin no more.*

---

*John 7:53-8:11 was placed in italic because the passage is not adequately supported by ancient manuscripts, and was only a footnote in the RSV. Only one of the oldest seven manuscripts has this story; however, it is a lovely and precious story that was a warning to leaders who are too strict. The story was included here because it is typical of the forgiveness of Jesus.

The Light of the World
John 8:12-22

12. Jesus continued to speak, saying, I am the light of the world: he who follows Me will not walk in darkness, but will have the light of life. 13. The Pharisees said, You testify about yourself; your witness is not true. 14. Jesus answered, Although I testify of Myself, My record is true: for I know from where I came, and to what place I go; but you cannot tell from where I come, or to what place I go. 15. You condemn on human terms; I condemn no one. 16. And yet if I decide judicially, My decision is justice: for I am not alone, but I and He who sent Me judge together. 17. It is written in your law, that the testimony of two is true. 18. I am a witness for Myself, and the Father who sent Me testifies of Me. 19. Then they asked, Where is your Father? Jesus answered, You neither know Me, nor My Father: if you had known Me, you would also have known My Father. 20. Jesus spoke these words in the treasury, as He taught in the Temple: and no man touched Him; for His hour had not come. 21. Jesus continued speaking, I go away, and you will search for Me, and will die in your sins: the place I go, you cannot come. 22. Then the Jews asked, Will He kill Himself? Because He said, the place I go, you cannot come.

Many Believed on Him
John 8:23-30

23. And Jesus said, You are from below; I am from above: you are of this world; I am not of this world. 24. I told you that you will die in your

sins: for if you will not believe that I am who I am, you will die in your sins. 25. Then they asked, Who are you? And Jesus answered, I am as you were told. 26. I have many things to call into question about you: but the One who sent Me does not conceal; and I declare to the world those things which I have heard from Him. 27. They did not understand that He spoke to them of the Father. 28. Then said Jesus, When you have lifted up the Son of Man, then you will know who I am, and that I do nothing of Myself; but I speak the things My Father taught Me. 29. And He who sent Me is with Me: the Father has not left Me alone; for I do always those things that please Him. 30. As He spoke these words, many believed on Him.

The Truth Will Make You Free
John 8:31-43

31. Then Jesus spoke to those Jews who believed, If you continue in My word, then you are without a doubt My disciples; 32. and you will know the truth, and the truth will make you free. 33. They answered, We are descendants of Abraham, and were never in slavery to any one: what do you mean saying, You will be freed? 34. Jesus answered, Truly, I say, Whoever commits sin is the slave of sin. 35. And the slave does not always remain in his master's house: it is the son who stays forever. 36. So if the Son makes you free, you will be truly free. 37. I know that you descend from Abraham; but you seek to kill Me, because My words find no place in you. 38. I speak what I have seen with my Father: and you are practicing what you learned from your father. 39. They answered, Abraham is our father. Jesus said, If you were Abraham's children, you would do the works of Abraham. 40. But now you seek to kill Me, a man who has told you the truth, which I heard from God: Abraham would not do this. 41. You are practicing what your own father does. Then they said, We are not illegitimate children; we have one Father, even God. 42. Jesus said, If God were your Father, you would love Me: for I came into the world from God; I came not of Myself, but He sent Me. 43. Why are My words not understood by you? It is because you do not listen to My words.

Why Do You Not Believe Me?
John 8:44-47

44. You are of your father the adversary, and the desires of your father you will do. He was a destroyer of life from the beginning, and did not abide in the truth, because there is no truth in him. When he speaks a falsehood, it is his character speaking: for he is a liar, and the father of fabrication. 45. And because I tell you the truth, you do not believe Me. 46. Who of you convict me of sin? And if I speak the truth, why do you not believe Me? 47. He that is of God hears God's words: since you do not hear My words, you are not of God.

Before Abraham Was, I AM!
John 8:48-59

48. Then the Jews answered, and said, Do we not say correctly you are a Samaritan, and have a devil? 49. Jesus answered, I do not have a devil; but I honor My Father, and you dishonor Me. 50. And I seek not mine own glory: there is One who seeks and judges. 51. Truly, I say, If any one keeps My teachings, he shall not experience death. 52. Then the Jews said, Now we know you have a devil. Abraham is dead, and the prophets; and you say, If any one keeps My teachings, he shall not experience death. 53. Are you greater than our father Abraham, who is dead? And the prophets are dead: who are you making yourself to be? 54. Jesus answered, If I glorify Myself, the glory is worthless: it is My Father who gives Me glory; whom you claim is your God: 55. yet you have never known Him; but I know Him: and if I say, I know Him not, I would be a liar like yourselves, but I know Him, and keep His word. 56. Your father Abraham rejoiced at the thought of seeing My day: and he saw it, and was rejoiced. 57. The Jews protested, You are not even fifty years old, how can you have seen Abraham? 58. Jesus said, Truly, I say, Before Abraham was, I AM. 59. Then they took up stones to cast at Him: but Jesus concealed Himself, and went out of the temple unobserved, *going through the midst of them, and so passed by.**

---

*Italic phrase not adequately supported by original manuscripts.

I Am the Man
John 9:1-12

1. And passing by, Jesus saw a man who was blind from birth. 2. And His disciples asked, Teacher, who sinned, this man, or his parents, that he was born blind? 3. Jesus answered, This man or his parents did not sin: but to manifest the works of God in him. 4. We must do the works of Him who sent Me, while it is day: the night comes, when no man can work. 5. While I am in the world, I am the light of the world. 6. When He had spoken, He spat on the ground, and made paste of the saliva, and anointed the eyes of the blind man with the mud, 7. and said, Go wash in the pool of Siloam, (which means, Sent). He went and washed, and came seeing. 8. The neighbors and those who knew he was blind, said, Is not this the beggar? 9. Some said, This is the man: others said, He is like him: but he said, I am the man. 10. They asked, How were your eyes opened? 11. He answered, A man called Jesus made mud, and anointed mine eyes, and said, Go to the pool of Siloam and wash: and I went and washed, and received my sight. 12. They asked, Where is He? He said, I do not know.

He is a Prophet
John 9:13-17

13. They brought the man who had been blind to the Pharisees. 14. And it was the Sabbath day when Jesus made the mud, and opened his eyes. 15. Then again the Pharisees asked how he had received his sight. He answered, He put mud on my eyes, and I washed, and now I see. 16. Then some of the Pharisees said, This man is not of God, because He keeps not the Sabbath. Others said, How can a sinful man do such miracles? So a disagreement arose among them. 17. They asked the blind man again, What can you say about the one who opened your eyes? He answered, He is a prophet.

He Opened My Eyes
John 9:18-34

18. But the Jews did not believe that he had been blind, and received his sight, until they called his parents. 19. And they asked them, Is this your son, who you say was born blind? How now he can see? 20. His parents answered, We know that this is our son, and that he was born blind: 21. but by what means he now sees, we know not; or who has opened his eyes: he is of age; ask him: he will speak for himself. 22. They said this because they feared the Jews: for the Jews had already agreed that if any man confess that Jesus was Christ, he would be excluded from the synagogue. 23. Therefore his parents said, He is of age; ask him. 24. Then again they called the man that was blind, and said, Give God the glory: we know this man is a sinner. 25. He answered, Whether a sinner or not, I know not: one thing I do know, whereas I was blind, now I see. 26. Again they asked him, What did He do to you? How did He open your eyes? 27. He answered, I have already told you and you did not listen: why do you want to hear it again? Will you become His disciples? 28. Then they despised him, and said, You are His disciple; but we are Moses' disciples. 29. We know God spoke to Moses: as for this fellow, we do not know from where He came. 30. The man answered, This is an astonishing thing, you do not know from where He came, and yet He opened my eyes. 31. We know that God does not hear sinners: but since this man is a worshipper of God, and does His will, God hears Him. 32. Since time began no one has heard of any man who opened the eyes of one born blind. 33. If this man were not of God, He could do nothing. 34. They answered, You were altogether born in sin, and you would teach us? And they expelled him from the synagogue.

Lord, I Believe
John 9:35-41

35. Jesus heard that they expelled him from the synagogue; and finding him, Jesus asked, Do you believe on the Son of God? 36. He answered, Who is He, Master, that I might believe? 37. And Jesus said, You have seen Him, and it is He who talks with you. 38. And he said, Lord, I believe. And he knelt before Jesus. 39. And Jesus said, I came into this world to force men to decide, so that they who could not see might see; and they who see might be made blind. 40. And some of the Pharisees heard these words, and asked, Are we also blind? 41. Jesus answered, If you were blind, you would have no sin: but since you claim you can see, your guilt remains.

Sheep Will Flee from a Stranger
John 10:1-6

1. Truly, I tell you, He who does not enter the sheepfold by the door, but climbs in some other way, the same is a thief and a robber. 2. But he who enters by the door is the shepherd of the sheep. 3. To him the doorkeeper opens; and the sheep hear his voice: and he calls his own sheep by name, and leads them to pasture. 4. And when he leads his own sheep out, he goes before them and the sheep follow him: for they know his voice. 5. But they will not follow, but the sheep will flee from a stranger: for they do not know the voice of strangers. 6. Jesus spoke this parable, but they did not understand what He said.

I Am the Door
John 10:7-10

7. Jesus spoke again, Truly, I am the door of the sheep. 8. All who came before Me are thieves and robbers: but the sheep did not hear them. 9. I am the door: by Me if any man enters, he shall be saved, and shall come and go and find grazing land. 10. The thief comes not, but for to steal, kill, and destroy: I am come that they might have life, and have it abundantly.

The Good Shepherd
John 10:11-15

11. I am the Good Shepherd: who gives His life for the sheep. 12. But someone motivated by money is not a true shepherd, because he does not claim ownership of the sheep, sees the wolf coming, and leaves the sheep, and runs away: and the wolf catches and scatters the sheep. 13. The hireling abandons the sheep because he is motivated by money and does not care for the sheep. 14. I am the Good Shepherd, and know My sheep, and they know the shepherd. 15. The Father knows Me, and I know the Father: and I give My life for the sheep.

One Fold and One Shepherd
John 10:16-21

16. And other sheep I have, besides this fold: those who hear My voice I will bring; and there shall be one fold, and one shepherd. 17. My Father loves Me, because I willingly give My life, that I might receive it again. 18. No man takes My life, but I willingly lay it down. I have power to lay it down, and I have power to pick it up again. This authority I have received from My Father. 19. There was division again among the Jews for these words. 20. And many said, He has a devil, and is mad; why listen to Him? 21. Others said, These are not the words of one with a devil. Can a devil open the eyes of the blind?

You are not of My Sheepfold
John 10:22-28

22. It was winter in Jerusalem and time for the Feast of Dedication. 23. And Jesus walked in the Temple at Solomon's arcade. 24. Then the Jews encircled Jesus and asked, How long will you leave us in doubt? If you are the Christ, tell us plainly. 25. Jesus answered, I told you, and you did not believe: the works that I do in My Father's name, they bear witness of Me. 26. But you believe not, because you are not of my sheepfold. 27. My sheep hear my voice, and I know them, and they follow Me: 28. And I give them eternal life; and they will never perish, neither shall any man snatch them out of my hand.

That You May Know and Believe
John 10:29-39

29. My Father who gave Me the sheep is greater than all; and no man is able to snatch them from My Father's hand. 30. I and My Father are One. 31. Again the Jews determined to throw stones at Jesus. 32. Jesus answered, Many good works have I showed you from my Father; for which of these do you wish to stone me? 33. The Jews answered, We do not throw stones for a good work; but for blasphemy; and because you, being a man, makes yourself God. 34. Jesus answered, Is it not written in your law, I said, You are gods? 35. If he called them gods, to whom the word of God came, and the scripture cannot be broken; 36. You say of the One whom the Father has sanctified, and sent into the world, You blaspheme; because I said, I am the Son of God? 37. If I do not the works of My Father, do not believe Me. 38. But if I do, although you do not trust Me, believe the works: that you may know and believe, that the Father is in Me, and I in Him. 39. Again they tried to arrest Jesus: but He escaped, 40. and went beyond Jordan into the place where John at first baptized; and there He abode. 41. And many came and kept saying, John did no miracle: but

all things John spoke of this man were true. 42. And many believed on Jesus.

Jesus Spoke Plainly
John 11:1-16

1. A certain man was sick, named Lazarus, of Bethany, the village of Mary and her sister Martha. 2. (It was this Mary who anointed the Lord with perfume, and wiped His feet with her hair, whose brother Lazarus was sick.) 3. Therefore his sisters sent to Jesus, saying, Lord, behold, he whom you love is sick. 4. When Jesus heard that, He said, This sickness is not to death, but for the glory of God, that the Son of God might be glorified. 5. Now Jesus loved Martha, and her sister, and Lazarus. 6. When Jesus heard that Lazarus was sick, He remained two days in the same place. 7. Afterword Jesus said to His disciples, Let us go again to Judaea. 8. His disciples said, Master, the Jews recently sought to stone you; are you going there again? 9. Jesus answered, Are there not twelve hours in the day? If any man walks in the day, he does not stumble, because he walks in the light of the sun. 10. But if a man walks in the night, he stumbles, because there is no light. 11. After these things Jesus said, Our friend Lazarus sleeps; but I will go and awake him. 12. Then His disciples said, Lord, if he sleep, he will get well. 13. Yet, Jesus spoke of his death: but they thought that he was only sleeping. 14. Then Jesus spoke plainly, Lazarus is dead. 15. And I am glad for your sakes that I was not there, it will help you believe; nevertheless let us go to him. 16. Then Thomas, who was called The Twin, said to his fellow disciples, Let us also go, that we may die with Him.

I Am the Resurrection
John 11:17-31

17. Then when Jesus arrived, he found that Lazarus had already been in the grave four days. 18. Now Bethany was about two miles from Jerusalem: 19. And many Jews came to comfort Martha and Mary, concerning their brother. 20. Then Martha, as soon as she heard that Jesus was coming, went to meet Him: but Mary remained in the house. 21. Then said Martha to Jesus, Lord, if you had been here, my brother would not have died. 22. I know, even now, that whatsoever you ask, God will do it. 23. Jesus said to her, your brother will rise again. 24. Martha said to Jesus, I know he will rise again in the resurrection at the last day. 25. Jesus said, I am the resurrection, and the life: he who believeth in Me, though he were dead, yet shall he live: 26. And whosoever lives and believes in Me shall never see death. Do you believe this? 27. She answered, Yes, Lord: I believe you are the Christ, the Son of God, who should come into the world. 28. And

when she had spoken, she went her way, and called Mary her sister secretly, saying, The Master is here and calls for you. 29. As soon as she heard this, she quickly arose, and went to Jesus. 30. Now Jesus had not arrived in the village, but was in the place where Martha met Him. 31. The Jews who comforted her in the house, when they saw Mary, that she rose up hastily and went out, followed her, saying, She goes to the grave to weep.

Take Away the Stone
John 11:32-44

32. Then when Mary come where Jesus was, and saw Him, she fell down at His feet, saying, Lord, if you had been here, my brother would not have died. 33. When Jesus saw her weeping, and the Jews weeping with her, He was troubled and groaned deeply. 34. And said, Where have you placed him? They said, Lord, come and see. 35. And Jesus began to shed tears. 36. When the Jews saw His tears they said, See how much He loved him! 37. And some said, He opened the eyes of the blind, could He have caused this man, not to die? 38. Jesus deeply moved went to the grave, a cave, with a stone across the entrance. 39. Jesus said, Take away the stone. Martha, the sister said, Lord, by this time the body is decaying: Lazarus has been dead four days. 40. Jesus said, Did I not tell you, that if you believe you would see the glory of God? 41. Then they took away the stone, and Jesus looked up and said, Father, I thank you for having heard Me. 42. And I know that you always listen to Me: but because of the crowd I said it, so they could believe that you sent Me. 43. And then Jesus spoke with a loud voice, Lazarus, come out. 44. And he who was dead came out, bound hand and foot with grave wrappings: and his face was covered with a napkin. Jesus said, Untie him, and let him go.

Many Believed
John 11:45-57

45. When the Jews who came to comfort Mary, saw the things Jesus did, many believed. 46. But some went to the Pharisees, and told them the things Jesus had done. 47. Then the chief priests and the Pharisees gathered a council, and asked, What shall we do? This man is doing many miracles. 48. If we leave Him alone, all men will believe on Him: and the Romans will come and take away both our sacred place and the nation. 49. And one, named Caiaphas, being the high priest that year, said, You know nothing about this, 50. nor did you consider that it is good for us that one man die, instead of the whole nation be destroyed. 51. He spoke not of himself, but being high priest, he prophesied that Jesus should die for the nation; 52. and not for that nation only, but also that He would gather the scattered children of

God into one fold. 53. From that day they took counsel to put Him to death. 54. Jesus walked no more openly among the Jews; but traveled in the country near the wilderness toward a town called Ephraim, and remained there with His disciples. 55. And the Passover Feast of the Jews was near: and many came from the countryside to Jerusalem for ceremonial cleansing before the Passover. 56. They were seeking for Jesus and spoke among themselves in the Temple, Do you think He will come to the feast? 57. Now both the chief priests and the Pharisees had given orders, that, if anyone learned where Jesus was, His whereabouts must be reported, so He could be arrested.

The Poor You Have with You Always
John 12:1-11

1. Six days before the Passover Jesus came to Bethany, where He raised Lazarus from the dead. 2. Where they made Jesus a supper and Martha served: but Lazarus sat at the table with Him. 3. Then Mary took a pound of choice spikenard perfume of great value, and anointed the feet of Jesus, and wiped His feet with her hair: and the house was filled with the fragrance of the perfume. 4. Then asked one of His disciples, Judas Iscariot, Simon's son, who would betray Jesus, 5. Why was this valuable perfume not sold and the funds given to the poor? 6. This Judas said, not that he cared for the poor; but because he had charge of the money-bag and was a habitual thief and pilfered small items from the bag. 7. Then Jesus said, Let her alone: against the day of My burying has she observed this ritual. 8. For the poor you have with you always; but Me you have not always. 9. Many Jews knew that Jesus was there, but they did not come to see Jesus, but that they might see Lazarus, whom Jesus had raised from the dead. 10. The chief priests consulted how they might also put Lazarus to death; 11. because many of the Jews were withdrawing from them to believe on Jesus

Hosanna, Blessed is the King of Israel
John 12:12-19

12. On the next day many who were attending the feast, heard that Jesus was coming to Jerusalem, 13. and took palm branches and went to meet Jesus, and cried, Hosanna: Blessed is the King of Israel who comes in the Name of the Lord. 14. And Jesus, finding a young donkey, and sat on it; as it is written, 15. Fear not, daughter of Zion: behold, your King comes, sitting on a donkey's colt. 16. His disciples did not understand these things at first: but when Jesus was glorified, they remembered those things written of Him, and what they had done to Jesus. 17. The crowd that was with Jesus when Lazarus was called out of the grave, witnessed that he was raised from the dead. 18. This

is why the crowd met Jesus, for they heard that He had done this miracle. 19. The Pharisees said among themselves, Nothing we have done has prevailed? Look, the whole world has turned to follow Him.

We Would See Jesus
John 12:20-26

20. And there were certain Greeks among those who worshipped at the Feast: 21. who came to Philip, who was from Bethsaida in Galilee, and asked, Sir, we would see Jesus. 22. Philip told Andrew: and Andrew and Philip told Jesus. 23. And Jesus answered, The hour is come, when the Son of Man should be glorified. 24. Truly, I say, Except a grain of wheat fall into the ground and die, it abides alone: but if it dies, it brings a good harvest. 25. He who loves his life will lose it; and he who denies himself in this world shall have life in eternity. 26. If anyone is ready to serve Me, let him follow Me; and where I am, there shall My servants be: if anyone is ready to serve Me, him My Father will honor.

I Will Draw All Men to Me
John 12:27-36

27. Now My heart is troubled; what shall I ask? Father, save Me from this hour? No, for this cause did I come to this hour. 28. Father, glorify your Name. Then a voice from heaven, said, I have both glorified My Name, and will glorify it again. 29. The people who stood by heard it, and said that it thundered: others said an angel spoke. 30. Jesus explained, This voice came for your sakes, not mine. 31. Now judgment has come to this world: and the Prince of this world will be expelled. 32. And if I be lifted up from the earth, I will draw all men to Me. 33. This Jesus said, signifying the manner of His death. 34. The people answered, We have heard from the law that Christ abides forever: how can you say, The Son of Man must be lifted up? Who is this Son of Man? 35. Then Jesus said, Yet a little while is the light with you. Walk while you have the light, lest darkness come upon you: for he that walks in darkness knows not where he goes. 36. While you have light, believe in the light, that you may be the children of light. These things Jesus spoke, and departed, and did conceal Himself from them.

They did not Confess Jesus
John 12:37-43

37. Although Jesus did many miracles in their presence, they did not believe in Him: 38. So the words of Prophet Isaiah might be fulfilled, Lord, who has believed our report? And to whom has the arm of the Lord been revealed? 39. The reason they could not believe, is recorded in Isaiah, 40. He has blinded their eyes, and hardened their heart; that they should not see with their eyes, nor understand with their heart, and be converted, and I should heal them. 41. Isaiah

said these things, about Jesus when he saw His glory, and spoke of Him. 42. Nevertheless, many of the chief rulers believed on Him; but because of the Pharisees they did not confess Him, lest they should be put out of the synagogue: 43. They preferred the approval of men, more than the approval of God.

I Am Come as Light
John 12:44-50

44. Jesus exclaimed, He who believes on Me, believes not only on Me, but on Him who sent Me. 45. And who sees Me, sees Him who sent Me. 46. I am come as light to the world, that whoever continues to believe on Me, should not remain in darkness. 47. And if any man hear My words, and believes not, I do not judge him: for I came not to judge the world, but to save the world. 48. He who rejects Me, and receives not My words, has one that judges him: the word that I have spoken, the same will judge him in the last day. 49. For I have not spoken of Myself; but the Father who sent Me, and gave Me instructions, what I should say, and what I should speak. 50. And I know that His instructions are life everlasting: whatever I speak, even as the Father said to Me, so I speak.

You are not All Clean
John 13:1-11

1. Before the Festival of the Passover, Jesus knew that the hour had come that He should leave this world and return to the Father, having loved His own in the world, Jesus showed love for them to the end. 2. And supper being in process, the devil having now put into the heart of Judas Iscariot, Simon's son, to betray Jesus; 3. knowing that the Father had given all things into His hands, and that He came from God, and went to God; 4. Jesus rose from supper, and laid aside His garments; and took a towel, and girded Himself. 5. Then He poured water into a container, and began to wash the disciples' feet, and to wipe them with the towel about His waist. 6. Then Jesus approached Simon Peter and Peter asked, Lord, do you wash my feet? 7. Jesus answered, What I do you do not understand now; but you will later. 8. Peter said, You will never wash my feet. Jesus answered, Unless I wash you, you will have no part with Me. 9. Simon Peter said to Him, Lord, not my feet only, but also my hands and my head. 10. Jesus said, He who is bathed need to wash only his feet, but is complete clean: and you are clean, but not all. 11. For Jesus knew who would betray Him; therefore He said, You are not all clean.

I have Given You an Example
John 13:12-20

12. So after washing their feet, Jesus put on His robe and returned to the table, and asked, Do you understand what I have done to you? 13. You call Me Master and Lord: and you are correct; because I AM. 14. If I then, your Lord and Master, have washed your feet; you ought to willingly wash one another's feet. 15. I have given you an example that you should do as I have done to you. 16. Truly, I say, The slave is not greater than his master; neither is a messenger sent greater than the one who sent him. 17. If you know these things, blessed are you if you do them. 18. I do not speak of all of you: I know those of whom I speak: but let the scripture be fulfilled, He who eats bread with Me has kicked against Me. 19. Now I tell you before hand, so when it happens, you may believe who I am. 20. Truly, I say, He who receives whomever I send receives Me and he who receives Me welcomes the Sender.

Judas Went Out into the Night
John 13:21-30

21. After Jesus said these things, He was uneasy in spirit, and solemnly said, Truly, I say, that one of you will betray Me. 22. Then the disciples kept looking at one another, wondering about whom He was speaking. 23. Now there was one of His disciples whom Jesus loved leaning close to Him. 24. Simon Peter motioned to Jesus that he would ask of whom He spoke. 25. Then lying on Jesus' breast asked, Lord, who is it? 26. Jesus answered, To whom I give this sop,* after I have dipped it. And when He had dipped the sop, He gave it to Judas Iscariot, the son of Simon. 27. And after receiving the dipped sop, Satan entered into Judas setting him apart. Then said Jesus to him, Do quickly what you have planned. 28. No one at the table understood what Judas intended. 29. For some thought, because Judas had the money-bag that Jesus was saying, Buy those things we need for the feast; or, that Judas should give something to the poor. 30. Having received the dipped bread immediately Judas went out into the night.

---

*v26 (a piece of Paschal lamb, unleavened bread and bitter herbs)

Love One Another
John 13:31-38

31. After Judas left, Jesus said, The Son of Man has now been glorified, and God is exalted in Him. 32. And if God be exalted, God shall exalt Him without delay. 33. Little children, I am with you for a little while. You will search for Me: and as I told the Jews, Where I go, you cannot follow; so now I say to you. 34. I give you a new commandment, Love one another; the same as I have loved you. 35. By

loving one another, all men will recognize you as My disciples. 36. Simon Peter asked, Lord, where do you go? Jesus answered, Where I go, you cannot follow Me now; but you will follow Me later. 37. Peter asked, Lord, why can I not follow you now? I will lay down my life for you. 38. Jesus answered, Will you lay down your life for Me? Truly, I say, The cock will not crow, until you have denied Me three times.

Ask Anything in My Name, I Will Do It
John 14:1-14

1. Let not your life be troubled: you believe in God, believe also in Me. 2. There are many dwelling-places in My Father's House: if it were not so, would I have told you that I go to prepare a place for you. 3. And since I go to prepare a place for you, I will come again, and receive you Myself; that where I am, there you may be also. 4. You know the way to My destination. 5. Thomas said, Lord, we know not where you go; how can we know the way? 6. Jesus said, I am the way, the truth, and the life: no man comes to the Father, but by Me. 7. If you had known Me, you should have known my Father also: and from now on you know Him, and have seen Him. 8. Philip asked, Lord, show us the Father, and it will satisfy us. 9. Jesus said, Have I been with you all this time, and yet you do not know Me, Philip? Anyone who has seen Me has seen the Father; why do you say, show us the Father? 10. Do you believe that I am in the Father, and the Father in Me? I do not speak of My own accord: but the Father dwells in Me and He does the works. 11. Have faith that I am in the Father and the Father in Me: or believe Me on account of My works. 12. Truly, I say, He that believes on Me, the works that I do shall he do; and greater works than these shall he do; because I go to My Father. 13. And whatever you ask in My name, that will I do, so the Father may be exalted in the Son. 14. If you shall ask anything in My name, I will do it.

Because I Live
John 14:15-26

15. If you love Me, keep My commandments. 16. And I will ask the Father, and He will give you another Advocate, that He may abide with you forever; 17. Even the Spirit of Truth; whom the world cannot receive, because it neither recognizes Him nor understands Him: but you know Him; for He abides with you, and shall be in you. 18. I will not leave you desolate: I will come back for you. 19. Yet a little while, and the world sees Me no more; but you will see Me: because I live, you shall live also. 20. At that day you shall know that I am in union with My Father, and you in Me, and I in you. 21. Those who have My commandments, and obeys them, loves Me: and those who love Me will be loved of My Father, and I will love them, and will reveal Myself to

them. 22. Judas, not Iscariot, asked, Lord, how will you reveal yourself to us, and not to the world? 23. Jesus answered, Those who love Me will keep My word: and My Father will love them, and we will dwell with them. 24. Those who do not love Me will neglect My words: and the word you hear is not mine, but the Father's who sent Me. 25. These things have I told you still present with you. 26. But the Advocate, who is the Holy Spirit, whom the Father will send in My name, He shall teach you all things, and bring all things to your remembrance, whatever I taught you.

My Peace I Give to You
John 14:27-31

27. Peace* I leave with you, My peace I give to you: but not as the world gives. Let not your life be troubled, neither fearful. 28. You heard I was going away, and would return to you. If you loved me, you would rejoice, because I go to the Father: for My Father is greater than I. 29. And now I have told you before hand, so when it happens, you might believe. 30. I will no more speak with you: for the Prince of the world approaches, but he has neither right nor power over Me. 31. I surrender to suffering and death that the world may know that I love the Father; and the Father gave Me instruction, even so I do. Arise let us go from this place.

---

*v27 Peace was the normal oriental greeting at parting. These are parting words.

Apart from Me You Can Do Nothing
John 15:1-14

1. I am the true and genuine vine, and My Father is the vine-dresser. 2. He destroys every unfruitful branch in Me: and every branch that bears fruit, He cleans so it may bring forth more fruit. 3. Now you have been cleansed through the word which I spoke to you. 4. Abide in Me, and I in you. As the branch cannot bear fruit from itself, except it abide in the vine; no more can you bear fruit, except you abide in Me. 5. I am the vine, you are the branches: He who abides in Me, and I in him, the same brings forth much fruit: for apart from Me you can do nothing. 6. If a man does not abide in Me, he is cast out of the vineyard as the unfruitful branch and is dried up; and they gather and burn them. 7. If you abide in Me, and My words abide in you, you ask what you will, and it will come to pass for you. 8. My Father was glorified in this, that you bear much fruit; and you shall become My disciples. 9. As the Father loved Me, so have I loved you: continue in My love. 10. If you keep My commandments, you shall abide in My love; even as I have kept My Father's commandments and abide in His love. 11. These things have I spoken that My joy might be in you, and that your joy may be

fulfilled. 12. This is the content of My commandment, That you love one another, as I have loved you. 13. Greater love has no man than a man lay down his life for his friends. 14. You are My friends, if you do whatever I command you.

Friends
John 15:15-17
15. I no longer call you bond-slaves; because a servant does not know what his Lord does: but you I have called friends; for all things that I have heard of my Father I have made known to you. 16. You have not chosen me, but I have chosen you, and appointed you to go out and bring in fruit, and that your fruit should remain: and that you should obtain answers to your prayers to make them fruitful. 17. These things I command you, so that you may love one another.

You will Stand as a Witness
John 15:18-27
18. Since the world hates you, know that it has hated Me before it hated you. 19. If you were of the world, the world would naturally have affection for you: but because you are not of the world, because I selected you out of the world, therefore the world hates you. 20. Remember, the word that I said, a bond-slave is not greater than his master. If they have pursued Me with hostile intent, they will also pursue you; if they have kept My word, they will keep yours. 21. But all these things will they do to you on account of My name, because they know not Him who sent Me. 22. If I had not come and spoken to them, they would not know sin: but now they have no covering to hide their sin. 23. He that hates Me also hates My Father. 24. If I had not done miracles among them that no other man had done, they would not be guilty of sin: but now they have seen and hated both Me and My Father. 25. But this came to pass, so the word might be fulfilled that is written in the law, They willingly hated Me without a cause. 26. But when the Advocate is come, whom I will send to you from the Father, even the Spirit of Truth, who proceeds from the Father, He will be a witness about Me: 27. and also you will stand as a witness, because you have been with Me from the beginning.

When the Spirit of the Truth Comes
John 16:1-15
1. These things have I spoken to you, that you should not stumble or be caused to sin. 2. They shall banish you from the synagogues: but the time will come, when everyone who kills you will think they do God a service. 3. And they will do these things to you, because they have never known Me nor the Father. 4. But I told you these things, so when the time comes, you will remember that I told you. I said nothing about

this from the beginning, because I was with you. 5. But now I go away to Him who sent Me; and none of you asked, Where do you go? 6. But because I have said these things to you, grief has gripped your hearts. 7. Nevertheless, I tell you the truth; this is beneficial for you that I go away: for if I go not away, the Advocate will not come to you; but if I depart, I will send Him to you. 8. And when He comes, the world will be convicted about sin, and convinced about unrighteousness, judgment: 9. and sinfulness, because they do not believe on Me; 10. about righteousness, because I go to My Father, and you see Me no more; 11. about judgment, because the Prince of this world is judged. 12. I have many more things to say to you, but you are not strong enough for them now. 13. However, when the Spirit of the Truth comes, He will guide you into all truth: the Spirit will not speak from Himself; but whatever He hears, that shall He speak: and He will show you future things. 14. He shall honor Me: for He will receive out of My essence, and will reveal this to you. 15. All things that the Father has are mine: therefore, the Spirit will take of My essence and reveal it to you.

I Have Overcome the World
John 16:16-33

16. A little while, and you will not see Me: and again, a little while, and you will see Me, because I go to the Father. 17. Therefore His disciples discussed among themselves, What does He imply when saying, This little while, and you will not see Me: and again, a little while, and you will see Me: because I go to the Father? 18. They said therefore, What does He mean saying, this little while? We know not what He means. 19. Now Jesus knew they wanted to ask Him, and said, Do you inquire among yourselves what I meant, saying, this little while, and you will not see Me: and again, a little while, and you will see Me? 20. Truly, I say, that you will weep aloud and express grief, but the world will rejoice: and you shall be pained in body and soul, but your sorrow will be turned into joy. 21. As a woman when she is in travail at child birth: but as soon as she is delivered of the child, she no longer remembers the suffering, for joy that a man is born into the world. 22. You now have sorrow: but I will see you again, and your heart will rejoice, and your joy no man takes from you. 23. And in that day you will not question Me. Truly, I say, whatever you ask in My name, the Father will give it to you. 24. Until now you have asked nothing in My name: ask, and you will receive, that your joy may be full. 25. These things I tell you in parables: but the time will come, when I will no more speak in parables, but I will fluently speak of the Father. 26. At that day you will ask in My name: and I will not pray the Father for you: 27. because the Father Himself loves you, because you have loved Me, and have believed that I came from God. 28. I came forth from the Father, and

came into the world: again, I leave the world, and go to the Father. 29. His disciples asked, now you speak fluently and not in parables. 30. Now are we sure that you know all things, and need not that any man should ask you: by this we believe that you came from God. 31. Jesus answered, Do you now believe? 32. Behold, the hour comes and is now here, that you will be scattered to your own homes, and will leave Me alone: and yet I am not alone, because the Father is with Me. 33. These things I have spoken, that in Me you might have peace. In the world you will have tribulation: but be of good cheer; I have overcome the world.

Authority Over All Humanity
John 17:1-10

1. These words Jesus spoke and lifted up His eyes to heaven, and said, Father, the hour has come; glorify your Son, that the Son may glorify you: 2. As you have given Him authority over all humanity, that He should give eternal life to as many as you have given Him. 3. And this is the life eternal, that they might recognize the only True God, and whom you sent even Jesus Christ. 4. I have glorified you on the earth having finished the work that I should do. 5. Father, honor Me now in your own presence with the glory I possessed before the world was. 6. I have revealed your name to those you gave Me out of the world: they belonged to you, and you gave them to Me; and they have kept your word. 7. Now they realize that you are the source of all things given Me. 8. For I have given them the words you gave Me; and they have received them, and know surely that I came from you, and they believed that you sent Me. 9. I request for them: not for the world, but for those you gave Me; for they are yours. 10. All My possessions are yours, and yours are mine; and I am glorified by them.

I Have Guarded and None Perished
John 17:11-19

11. I am no more in the world, but these are in the world, and I am coming to you. Holy Father, keep through your own authority those you gave Me, that they may be one, as we are one. 12. While I was with them, I kept them in your name: those that you gave Me I have guarded and none perished, but the son of perdition; to fulfill the scripture. 13. And now I am coming to you; and these things I speak, that they might have My joy fulfilled in themselves. 14. I have given them your word; and the world hated them, because they are not of the world, even as I am not of the world. 15. I ask not that you take them out of the world, but keep them from the evil. 16. They are not of the world, even as I am not of the world. 17. Make them holy through your truth: your word is truth. 18. As you delegated Me into the world, even

so have I delegated them into the world. 19. And for their sakes I consecrate Myself, that they also might be made sacred through the truth.

Perfect Unity
John 17:20-26
20. Neither ask I for these alone, but for those who will believe on Me through their word; 21. that they all may be as you, Father, are in Me, and I in you, that they also may be one in us: that the world may believe that you sent Me. 22. And the glory that you gave Me, I have given them; that they may be one, even as we are one: 23. I in them and you in Me, that they may be brought to perfect unity; and that the world may know that you sent Me, and have loved them, as you loved Me. 24. Father, I will that those you gave Me, be with Me where I am; that they may behold the glory you gave Me: for you loved Me before the foundation of the world. 25. Righteous Father, the world has not known you: but I have known you, and these have known that you sent Me. 26. And I have revealed to them your name, and will declare it: that the love wherewith you have loved Me, may dwell in them and be in their hearts.

Whom Do You Seek?
John 18:1-14
1. With this petition, Jesus went with His disciples across the ravine of the Cedars, and entered a garden. 2. And Judas, who was betraying Him, also knew the place: for Jesus often assembled with His disciples in that direction. 3. Judas then, having received a cohort of men and officers from the chief priests and Pharisees, came in that direction with lanterns, torches and weapons. 4. Jesus knowing all things that were coming, went forth, and asked, Whom do you seek? 5. They answered, Jesus, the Nazarene. Jesus said, I am He. And Judas who betrayed Him, was standing with them. 6. As soon as Jesus said, I am He, they stepped backward and fell to the ground. 7. Then Jesus asked again, Whom do you seek? And they said, Jesus, the Nazarene. 8. Jesus answered, I have told you that I am He: if you seek Me, let the disciples withdraw: 9. that the saying be fulfilled, Of those you gave Me I have lost none. 10. Then Simon Peter drew his sword and with a hard blow hit the high priest's servant, and cut off his right ear. The servant's name was Malchus. 11. Then Jesus said, Peter, put away the sword in the case: the cup My Father has given Me, shall I not drink it? 12. Then the cohort, the centurion, and the officers of the Jews seized and bound Jesus. 13. And led Him away first to Annas; for he was father-in-law to Caiaphas, who was the high priest that year. 14. Now Caiaphas was he, who gave counsel to the Jews that it was beneficial that one man should die for the people.

Nothing in Secret
John 18:15-27

15. And Simon Peter followed Jesus, and so did another disciple: that was known to the high priest, went in with Jesus into the courtyard of the high priest. 16. But Peter stood outside at the door. Then the other disciple, who was known to the high priest, went out and spoke to the door-keeper, and brought in Peter. 17. Then the maid-servant that kept the door asked Peter, Are you not also one of this man's disciples? He said, I am not. 18. And the slaves and officers stood by a charcoal fire; for it was cold: and they warmed themselves: and Peter stood with them and warmed himself. 19. The high priest then asked Jesus about His disciples, and His teachings. 20. Jesus answered, I spoke openly to the world; I ever taught in the synagogue and the temple, where the Jews always assemble; and have said nothing in secret. 21. Why do you ask Me? Ask those who heard Me, what I said: these witnesses know what I said. 22. And when He had spoken, one of the officers struck Jesus with the palm of his hand, saying, Why do you answer the high priest so? 23. Jesus answered, If I have spoken evil, give evidence of the evil: but if well, why strike Me? 24. Annas had sent Jesus bound to Caiaphas the high priest. 25. And Simon Peter stood warming himself. They asked, Are you not one of His disciples? He denied it, and said, I am not. 26. One of the servants of the high priest, being a kinsman of the one whose ear Peter cut off, asked, Did not I see you in the garden with Him? 27. Peter again denied: and immediately the cock crew.

Not This Man, but Barabbas
John 18:28-40

28. In the early morning they brought Jesus from Caiaphas to the Praetorium; and the Jews for fear of being defiled from eating the Passover did not enter the judgment hall. 29. Pilate went out to them and asked, What charge do you have against this man? 30. They answered, If He were not an evil-doer, we would not have delivered Him to you. 31. Then Pilate said, You yourselves judge Him according to your law. The Jews explained, It is not lawful for us to put any man to death: 32. this was fulfilling the prophecy, signifying the manner of His death. 33. Then Pilate entered the judgment hall again, and called Jesus, and asked, Are you the King of the Jews? 34. Jesus answered, Are you speaking for yourself, or did others tell you about Me? 35. Pilate answered, Am I a Jew? Your own people and the chief priests have delivered you to me: what have you done? 36. Jesus answered, My kingdom is not founded in this world: if My kingdom were of this world, then would My servants fight, that I should not be delivered to the Jews: but now My kingdom is not for the present. 37. Pilate asked,

Are you a king then? Jesus answered, You said that I am a king. To this end was I born, and for this cause came I into the world, that I might witness to the truth. Everyone that is of the truth hears My voice. 38. Pilate asked, What is truth? And then, he went out to the Jews again, and said, I find no fault in Him at all. 39. But you have a custom, that I should release one at the Passover: you choose and I will release unto you the King of the Jews? 40. Then they all shouted again, saying, Not this man, but Barabbas. Now Barabbas was a robber.

Crucify Him, Crucify Him!
John 19:1-16

1. Then Pilate took Jesus, and whipped Him. 2. And the soldiers twisted thorns into a crown and put it on His head, and threw a purple cloak about Him, 3. And said, Hail, King of the Jews! And they slapped Him with their hands. 4. Pilate went out again, and said, Behold, I bring Him to you, that you may know that I find no fault in Him. 5. Then Jesus came out wearing the crown of thorns, and the purple cloak. And Pilate said, Behold the man! 6. When the chief priests and officers saw Jesus, they shouted again, Crucify Him, crucify Him! Pilate said, You take and crucify Him: for I find no fault in Him. 7. The Jews answered, We have a law, and by our law He ought to die, because He claimed to be the Son of God. 8. When Pilate heard this, he was the more afraid; 9. and went again into the judgment hall, and asked Jesus, What is your origin? But Jesus gave no answer. 10. Then Pilate asked, Do you refuse to speak to me? Do you not know that I have the power to crucify you, and the power to release you? 11. Jesus answered, You could have no power against Me, except it were given to you from above: therefore he that delivered Me to you has the greater sin. 12. Going forward, Pilate sought to release Jesus: but the Jews shouted, If you let this man go, you are not Caesar's friend: whoever makes himself a king speaks against Caesar. 13. When Pilate heard these words, he brought Jesus forth, and sat down on a bench in a place with gravel pavement, the Jews knew as a raised place. 14. And it was about noon on the day of preparation of the Passover: and Pilate said to the Jews, Behold your King! 15. But they cried out, Take Him away, take Him away, crucify Him. Pilate asked, Shall I crucify your King? The chief priests answered, We have no king but Caesar. 16. Then Pilot delivered Jesus to them to be crucified. And they took Jesus.

And Pilate Wrote a Notice
John 19:17-27

17. And He carrying the cross for Himself, went to the place of a skull, which the Jews called Golgotha: 18. where they crucified Him, and two others, one on either side, with Jesus between. 19. And Pilate

wrote a notice, and put it on the cross. And the writing was JESUS THE NAZARENE THE KING OF THE JEWS. 20. Many Jews read this notice: for the place where Jesus was crucified was near the city: and it was written in Hebrew, and Greek, and Latin. 21. Then the chief priests of the Jews said to Pilate, Write not, The King of the Jews; but that He said, I am King of the Jews. 22. Pilate answered, What I have written, I have written. 23. Then the soldiers, when they had crucified Jesus, took His garments, and made four parts, to every soldier a part; and also His tunic: now the tunic was without seam, woven from the top to bottom. 24. They discussed among themselves, Let us not rip it, but cast lots for whose it will be: so that the scripture would be fulfilled, They parted My raiment among them, and for My vesture they did cast lots. That was what the soldiers did. 25. There stood by the cross of Jesus His mother, and His mother's sister, Mary the wife of Cleophas, and Mary Magdalene. 26. When Jesus saw His mother, and the disciple whom He loved standing by, Jesus said to His mother, Woman, behold your son! 27. Then He said to the disciple, Behold your mother! And from that hour that disciple took her to his own home.

It is Finished
John 19:28-37

28. After this, Jesus knowing that all things were now finished, that the scripture would be fulfilled, He said, I thirst. 29. Now there was a bowl full of sour wine: and they soaked a sponge in the sour wine, and put it on a javelin, and put it to His mouth. 30. When Jesus had received the sponge, He said, It is finished: and bowed His head, and yielded up His Spirit. 31. The Jews therefore, because it was the day of preparation for a high Sabbath, and to prevent the bodies remaining on the cross on the Sabbath day, besought Pilate that their legs might be broken, and the bodies be taken away. 32. Then came the soldiers, and broke the legs of the first, and of the other who was crucified with Him. 33. But when they came to Jesus, and saw that He was already dead, they did not break His legs: 34. but one of the soldiers pierced His side with a spear, and out came blood and water. 35. And he who saw it testified, and his record is true: and he knows what he said was true, that you might believe. 36. These things were done, that the writing would be fulfilled, No bone of Him shall not be broken. 37. And again a writing said, They will look on Him whom they pierced.

A New Tomb
John 19:38-42

38. And after this Joseph of Arimathaea, for fear of the Jews was a secret disciple of Jesus, requested Pilate that he might take away the body of Jesus: and Pilate gave him permission. He went and removed the body of Jesus. 39. And Nicodemus, who at first came to Jesus by

night, also came and brought about a hundred pounds of a mixture of myrrh and aloes. 40. Then they both took the body of Jesus, and wound it in linen clothes with the spices, as the manner of the Jews was to bury. 41. In the place where Jesus was crucified there was a garden; and in the garden a new tomb, where no one had been placed. 42. There they laid Jesus because of the Jews' day of preparation; for the tomb was near.

He Saw and Believed
John 20:1-10

1. Early on day one of the week when it was yet dark, Mary Magdalene came to the tomb, and saw that the stone was taken away. 2. Then she ran, and coming to Simon Peter and to the other disciple, whom Jesus loved, she said, They have taken away the Lord out of the tomb, and we do not know where they have placed Him. 3. Peter and the other disciple set out and came to the tomb. 4. They ran both together, and the other disciple outran Peter, and came first to the tomb. 5. He stooped down, and looked and saw the linen clothes; but did not enter. 6. Then followed Simon Peter and went into the tomb, and saw the linen clothes, 7. and the napkin, that was about His head, not lying with the linen clothes, but folded together in a place by itself. 8. Then went in also the other disciple, who came first to the tomb, and he saw and believed. 9. For as yet they knew not the writing, that He must rise again from the dead. 10. Then the disciples went away again to their own home.

Why Do You Weep?
John 20:11-18

11. But Mary stood outside the tomb weeping: and as she wept, she stooped to look into the tomb, 12. and seeing two angels in white sitting, the one at the head, and the other at the feet, where the body of Jesus had lain. 13. And they said to her, Woman, why do you weep? She answered, Because they have taken away my Lord, and I know not where they have placed Him. 14. And she turned and saw Jesus standing, and knew not that it was Jesus. 15. Jesus said, Woman, why so you weep? Whom do you seek? She, supposing Him to be the gardener, said, Sir, if you have taken Him away, tell me where you placed Him, and I will take Him away. 16. Jesus said, Mary! She turned herself, and spoke in Hebrew, Rabboni; which is, My Master. 17. Jesus said, Do not cling to Me; for I have not yet ascended to My Father: but go to My brethren, and say to them, I ascend to My Father, and your Father; and to My God, and your God. 18. Mary Magdalene came and told the disciples that she had seen the Lord, and that He had spoken these things to her.

So Send I You
John 20:19-23

19. Then the same day at evening, being the day one of the week, when the doors were shut where the disciples were assembled for fear of the Jews, Jesus came and stood among them, and said, Peace to you. 20. And when He had spoken, He showed them His hands and side. When the disciples saw the Lord, they were glad. 21. Then Jesus said again, Peace to you: as my Father has sent Me, even so send I you. 22. And when He said this, He breathed on them, and said, Receive the Holy Spirit: 23. If you forgive sins, they are forgiven; and if you pronounce sins remain, they will remain.

My Lord and My God
John 20:24-31

24. Thomas, one of the Twelve, called The Twin, was not with them when Jesus came. 25. The other disciples said to him, We have seen the Lord. But Thomas said, Unless I see the nail prints in His hands, and put my finger into the wound, and put my hand into His side, I will in nowise believe. 26. And after eight days again His disciples were within, and Thomas with them: then Jesus came, the doors being shut, and stood among them, and said, Peace to you. 27. Then said Jesus to Thomas, Reach your finger here, and see My hands; and put your hand into My side: and be no doubter, but believe. 28. And Thomas answered, My Lord and my God. 29. Jesus said to Thomas, because you have seen Me, you believed: blessed are they that have not seen, and yet have believed. 30. And many other signs truly did Jesus in the presence of His disciples that are not written in this book: 31. but these are written, that you might believe that Jesus is the Christ, the Son of God; and that believing you might have life through His name.

Come to Breakfast
John 21:1-14

1. After these things Jesus showed Himself again to the disciples at the Lake of Tiberias; and this is how He appeared to them. 2. There were together Simon Peter, and Thomas called, The Twin, and Nathanael of Cana in Galilee, and the sons of Zebedee, and two other of His disciples. 3. Simon Peter told them, I am going fishing. They said, We will go with you. They went out immediately and got into a boat; and that night they caught nothing. 4. But at daybreak Jesus stood on the beach: but the disciples did not know that it was Jesus. 5. Then Jesus asked, Lads, do you have any food? They answered, No. 6. And Jesus told them to cast the net on the right side of the boat, and you will find fish. They cast and now were not able to drag it for the multitude of fishes. 7. Therefore that disciple whom Jesus loved said to Peter, It is the Lord. When Simon Peter heard that it was the Lord,

he pulled his fisherman's coat around him, and did plunge into the lake. 8. And the other disciples came in a little boat; (for they were about a hundred yards from land,) dragging the net with fishes. 9. As soon then as they were come to land, they saw burning coals with fish cooking and bread. 10. Jesus said bring some fish which you caught. 11. Simon Peter went into the boat and drew the net to land full of large fishes, a hundred and fifty-three: there were so many but the net was not broken. 12. Jesus said, Come to breakfast. And none of the disciples dared ask, Who He was, knowing that He was the Lord. 13. Jesus came and took bread and gave them bread and fish. 14. This is now the third time that Jesus showed Himself to His disciples, after He stood up from among the dead.

Follow Me
John 21:15-25

15. So when they had dined, Jesus spoke to Simon Peter, Simon, son of Jonas, Do you love Me more than these? He answered, Yes, Lord; you know that I have affection for you. Jesus said, Feed My lambs. 16. He asked again a second time, Simon, son of Jonas, are you devoted to Me? He answered, Yes, Lord; you know you are dear to me. Jesus said, Shepherd My sheep. 17. Jesus asked a third time, Simon, son of Jonas, Do you have affection for Me? Peter was hurt because Jesus asked a third time, Do you have affection for Me? And Peter said, Lord, you know all things; you know that I dearly love you. Jesus said, Feed My sheep. 18. Truly, I say, When you were young, you dressed yourself, and walked wherever you wanted: but when you become old, you will stretch forth your hands, and another shall dress you, and carry you where you do not want to go. 19. This Jesus said, signifying the manner of death Peter would glorify God. And when Jesus said this, He said, Follow Me. 20. Then Peter, turning around saw the disciple following whom Jesus loved, who also leaned on His breast at supper, and said, Lord, who will betray you? 21. Peter seeing John asked, Lord, what shall this man do? 22. Jesus answered, If I will that he tarry till I come, what is that to you? Follow Me. 23. Then the report went abroad among the brethren that this disciple would not die: yet Jesus did not say, He shall not die; but, If I will that he tarry till I come, what is that to you? 24. This is the disciple who witnessed these things, and wrote these things: and his witness is true. 25. There are many other things that Jesus did, and if they all were written, I suppose that even the world itself could not hold the books that would be written. Amen.

Section Two:

Letters to Theophilus

The Gospel According to Luke

The Acts of the Apostles

ELEMENTS OF PRISTINE CHRISTIANITY

In an early and emergent form, the fundamental elements of pristine Christianity were presented in the Gospel of Luke. This Gospel was written to provide "all that Jesus began to do and teach." It is clear from the text that Luke understood that Jesus continuously taught and often repeated central truths. From the study of eye-witness accounts, Luke was convinced that the past details had present value. From these documents, Luke gathered basic constructs from which were formulated some first principles that guided the early believers. These first things have been overlooked or neglected by present leadership in Christianity. This work is an effort to draw fresh attention to early historical facts that still speak truth to believers today. Even though Luke demonstrates great academic skill in presenting the Gospel and Acts, the "inspiration" of Luke's work has not been questioned. Luke presents Jesus as the God who became man to a Roman audience who worshipped a man who claimed to be a god. Luke overwhelmingly used "Jesus" instead of "Christ" permitting others to use that term in reference to Jesus.

My Earlier View of Luke

In my earlier books, Luke was presented as a man of medicine traveling with the physically weak Paul to keep him physically able to fulfill spiritual tasks. With a first look at the Gospel of Luke and the Book of Acts, it was easy to see Luke as a professional who wanted each person to function well. Luke appeared to be concerned that the human element did not hinder the spiritual mission. Since death was considered sleep or rest and the medical term "resurrection," literally describes one who stood up again, Luke's mission was seen as making the early believers stand up and function normally in society. Luke was much more that a nursemaid to early believers, he was the historian that recorded "all that Jesus began to do and teach" and the Acts of the Holy Spirit through the Apostles as a history of those who early followed Jesus.

The Best Greek in the New Testament

The first four verses of Luke's Gospel are considered by many to be the best Greek in the New Testament. Luke was a careful and professional writer of formal documents, contributing two major volumes to the New Testament canon. Luke was both a professional and a Gentile. The strength of his academics and as the only Gentile writer of the New Testament, Luke appears closer to the mind-set of the present non-Jewish population of the world.

Emphasis by Proportion

Provided one gives proper value to emphasis by proportion, Luke's work deserves special consideration because it comprises about one fourth of the New Testament. He claims that his work was the result of both careful review of existing documents and personal primary research. In his association and companion-ship with Paul and others, Luke had sufficient opportunity to hear eye-witness stories about the life and times of Jesus. His study and research was further enhanced by careful chronology of accounts.

History of the First Thirty Years

In addition to the Gospel, Luke's second volume known as Acts of the Apostles was a history of the first thirty years of the early church. In an effort to compare Peter and Paul, the text was proportioned equally between these two early leaders. The first half of Acts is all about Peter, the Apostle to the Jews; the last half about Paul, the Apostle to the Gentiles. Luke faithfully compares Peter and Paul in many areas of their life and ministry.

A Clear Historical View

Since Luke's first volume, the Gospel, was all that Jesus began to do and teach; the second volume was dedicated to the acts and action of the early Apostles in the pristine days of the Christian movement. Together Luke's two volumes provide a clear historical view of how the church began and developed during the life of the first generation of converts. For this reason, the lessons that can be learned from Luke are vital to a clear understanding of the principles upon which Christianity was founded and the constructs that should guide present leadership.

Early Christianity was presented as one continuous work in the Gospel and Acts. Luke's Gospel did not record all that Jesus taught, but it provides the foundational principles from which to draw lessons for the present function of believers in relationship with family, friends, and the larger community of faith. Just as the Gospel did not record all the acts of Jesus, the Acts of the Apostles does not describe all the activities of the early disciples, but recorded a few gleaned facts from three decades of early church history to assist with an understanding of how the pristine church functioned.

The Acts of the Holy Spirit through the early messengers of Jesus does not have a close; it is assumed that all believers and each local congregation are to continue writing the history of God working through individuals enabled by the Spirit. The big question: what has God done in your life or place of worship lately worthy of recording in such a book? (See Notes at the end of Acts)

THE GOSPEL ACCORDING TO LUKE

Luke was a companion of Paul and a medical professional and the only Gentile writer of the scriptures. Aware of emphasis by position and proportion, Luke's Gospel and the Acts cover about one-fourth of the New Testament about the same proportion as Paul's writings. Luke's ethnic and professional background provides an academic excellence not seen in much of the writing of his day. Luke was not an eyewitness to any of the events recorded in his Gospel, but Luke 1:1-4 demonstrated his research skills and he presented the most detailed of all the Gospels, containing about one-third more data not included in the other accounts. Since Luke was a physician, he was concerned with Jesus' ability to heal and perform other miracles. Luke intended to write a book that would convince those in the Greek culture that the claims of Jesus were valid. He addressed the gospel story to the most excellent Theophilus, a title normally left for a high Roman official in the Roman government. This he did by presenting "all that Jesus began to do and teach." Luke presents Jesus as the God who became man to a Roman audience who worshipped a man who claimed to be a god. Luke overwhelmingly used "Jesus" instead of "Christ" permitting others to use that term in reference to Jesus. Luke's Gospel was to the Gentiles, presented in a universal manner with no concern for the Hebrew traditions. He dealt with prayer, women, praise and historical facts in a manner unlike other writers of scripture.

The Care of a Historian
Luke 1:1-4

1 For a large number put their hand to arrange and relate fully and make clear that which was conceived, spoken of and accepted as truth and fixed within our number. 2. Even as they yielded up and released together with other eyewitnesses what was seen and heard from servants and what was said; 3. it was accounted suitable for me having had complete and exact comprehension from the top sources to engrave for you and others in subsequent times, most excellent Theophilus, 4. that you send forth on a mission those demonstrated words that sounded down into your ear.

The Prayer You No Longer Pray God Heard
Luke 1:5-17

5. When Herod the Great was King of Judaea, a priest named Zacharias, of the division of priests named after Abijah: and his wife Elizabeth was a descendant of Aaron. 6. They were both upright and living blameless lives keeping the commandments and rules of the Lord. 7. And they had no child, because Elizabeth was infertile, and both were well advanced in years. 8. When his division was on duty and he carried out the priest's responsibility before God, 9. according to the practice of the priesthood, it fell to him by lot to enter the Temple of the Lord and burn incense. 10. The whole congregation was praying

outside at the hour of incense. 11. Then a messenger of the Lord was standing on the right side of the altar of incense. 12. And when Zacharias saw him, he was distressed and he became apprehensive. 13. But the messenger of the Lord said, Do not be afraid, the prayer you no longer pray God heard; your wife Elizabeth shall bear a son and you shall name him John. 14. And your heart will have joy and gladness; and many shall celebrate his birth. 15. For he shall be great before the Lord, and must never drink wine or strong drink; and from birth will be filled with the Holy Spirit. 16. And he shall cause many of Israel to return to serving God. 17. And he shall go forth as a heralding pioneer in the spirit and power of Elijah, to turn the affection of the fathers to the children, and the rebellious to good judgment; and to spiritually prepare Israel for the Lord.

This is God's Doing
Luke 1:18-25

18. And Zacharias said to the messenger, how shall I know this? For both me and my wife are well advanced in years. 19. And the messenger said, I am Gabriel, who stands in the presence of God; and was sent to speak to you and to show you these good tidings. 20. Because you do not believe my words, you shall be unable to speak until this thing is accomplished in God's appointed time. 21. And the people waiting for Zacharias to come out and lead them in a blessing, were amazed that he was so long in the Temple. 22. And when he came out, he could not speak: and they assumed he had seen a vision in the Temple: for he gestured to them and remained speechless. 23. As soon as he finished his priestly duties, he left for home. 23. After those days his wife Elizabeth conceived and hid herself five months, saying, 25. This is God's doing with me when he looked on me to take away my shame among men.

Call His Name Jesus
Luke 1:26-38

26. And in the sixth month God sent the angel Gabriel to Nazareth, a town of Galilee, 27. to a maiden named Mary engaged to a man named Joseph, of the house of David. 28. And the angel came and said, Greetings, you are endowed with grace, the Lord is with you. 29. And when she saw him; she was distressed at his saying, and began to reason what the greeting could mean. 30. And the angel said, Do not be afraid, Mary: for you have received the absolute loving-kindness of God. 31. And, behold, your womb shall conceive, and bear a son, and you shall call His name Jesus. 32. He shall be well-known, and be called the Son of the Highest: and the Lord God shall give Him the throne of His forefather David: 33. And He shall reign over

the house of Jacob forever; and His reign shall have no end. 34. Then Mary asked the angel, how shall this be since I have not accepted a man? 35. And the angel answered, the power of the Holy Spirit shall come and overshadow you; therefore, the child born of you shall be called the Son of God. 36. And your cousin Elizabeth also has conceived a son in her old age: who was said to be infertile and this is her sixth month. 37. For with God nothing shall be impossible. 38. And Mary said, Behold I am the Lord's servant willing to support in a subsidiary role your word. And the angel departed.

Blessed Art Thou Among Women
Luke 1:39-45

39. In the days that followed, Mary rose up and hastened to the hill country, to a city of Judah; 40. and entered the house of Zacharias and greeted Elizabeth. 41. As soon as Elizabeth heard Mary's greeting, the unborn child jumped in her womb; and Elizabeth was filled with the Holy Spirit: 42. and she lifted up her voice with great emotion and said, Blessed are you among women, and blessed is the produce of your womb. 43. What source honors me that the mother of my Lord should visit me? 44. As soon as I heard words of your greeting, the unborn child jumped for joy in my womb. 45. Blessed is the one who believes: for there shall be a fulfillment of those things told her from the Lord.

My Soul Magnifies the Lord
Luke 1:46-56

46. And Mary said, My soul overflows with praise for the Lord, 47. And my spirit delights in God my Savior. 48. For He has graciously regarded his humble servant: just watch, henceforth all generations shall call me blessed. 49. For the Almighty has done great things for me; and holy is His name. 50. On those who fear Him His mercy is from generation to generation. 51. He has demonstrated great power with His arm; He has scattered the arrogant of heart and mind. 52. He has pulled down the mighty from their high seats, and exalted the humble. 53. He has satisfied the hungry; and sent the rich away empty. 54. He has helped his servant Israel, because He remembered His mercy; 55. as He said to our fathers, to Abraham and to his seed for ever. 56. And Mary stayed with Elizabeth about three months and returned to her own dwelling.

He Shall Be Called John
Luke 1:57-66

57. The time had come for Elizabeth to deliver; and she birthed a son. 58. And her neighbors and her relatives heard how the Lord had blessed her; and they celebrated with her. 59. A week passed and they came to circumcise the child; and they called him Zacharias, after his

father. 60. But his mother responded, not so; he shall be called John. 61. They argued with her that there were not relatives by that name. 62. And they motioned to his father, what he would have the child called. 63. And on a writing tablet he wrote, his name is John. And they were all surprised. 64. And immediately his mouth was opened and his tongue broke loose and he spoke and praised God. 65. And wonder gripped all the neighbors: and this event was talked about in all the hill country of Judaea. 66. And all who heard of this pondered in their hearts, how shall this child behave for the Lord has taken hold of him.

Blessed Be the Lord God of Israel
Luke 1:67-80

67. And Zacharias was filled with the Holy Spirit and enabled to deliver a message for God, saying, 68. blessed be the Lord God of Israel; for He has visited and ransomed His people, 69. and has awakened a deliverer for us in the house of His servant David; 70. and He spoke this promise by His holy prophets since the beginning: 71. that we should be rescued from our enemies and from the power of all who look down on us; 72. to accomplish the compassion promised to our fathers and to remember His sacred covenant; 73. the promise He pledged to our father Abraham, 74. that He would grant us deliverance out of the power of our enemies that we might serve Him without dismay, 75. in consecration and uprightness in His presence all the days of our lives. 76. And this child shall be called a prophet of the Highest: for he shall go before the Lord to prepare and clear the way for Him; 77. to give understanding of salvation to his people that they can be forgiven their sins, 78. through the tender compassion of God; the heavenly sunrise will shine on us, 79. to give light to those who live in darkness and walk under the cloud of death, to direct our feet into the path of peace. 80. And the child continued to grow and became strong in spirit, and lived in the waste lands until the day he publicly announced himself to Israel.

No Guest-Chamber for Lodging
Luke 2:1-7

1. About this time there went out an edict from Caesar Augustus for a general registration of all the inhabited land. 2. (This first enrollment was taken while Quirinius was governor of Syria.) 3. And all were going to be taxed in the town to which the place of their birth belonged. 4. And Joseph also went up from Galilee, out of the city of Nazareth, into Judaea, to Bethlehem the city of David; (because he was of the house and lineage of David:) 5. to register himself with Mary his legally espoused wife, being great with child. 6. While they were there, the time came for her child to be delivered. 7. And she brought forth her

son, the first born, and wrapped Him in linen and laid Him in a manger; because they found no guest-chamber for lodging.

Good Tidings of Great Joy
Luke 2:8-20

8. Meanwhile shepherds nearby were guarding their flock during the night watch. 9. An angel of the Lord stood suddenly by them, and the radiance of divine glory shown round about them: and they were greatly frightened. 10. But the angel commanded, Stop being afraid: for, behold, I announce good news and great joy for all people. 11. Today in the city of David a Deliverer is born; who is the Anointed Lord. 12. And this shall be the sign for you; you will find an Infant wrapped in linen lying in a manger. 13. And suddenly there appeared the armies of heaven, saying, 14. Glory to God on high and peace on earth to men of good will. 15. When the angels were gone back to heaven, the shepherds said one to another, let us go straight to Bethlehem and see this thing that has happened, which the Lord made known to us. 16. And they hurried, and discovered Mary and Joseph, and the child lying in a manger. 17. When they had seen this, they made known abroad all that was told them concerning the child. 18. And all who heard the story of the shepherds were astonished. 19. But Mary guarded these treasured words, and meditated about them in her heart. 20. And the shepherds returned to their flock, glorifying and praising God for all the wonderful things they had seen and heard, just as they had been told.

A Man Whose Name Was Simeon
Luke 2:21--35

21. And when the eight days were accomplished for the rite of circumcision of the child, His name was called Jesus, the name given by the angel before He was conceived in the womb. 22. And when the days of her cleansing was accomplished according to the Law of Moses, they took Him up to Jerusalem to present to the Lord; 23. (As it has been written in the law of the Lord, Every male opening a womb shall be called holy to the Lord;) 24. and also to make an offering as stated in the law of the Lord, a pair of turtledoves or two young pigeons. 25. And, behold, there was a righteous and devout man in Jerusalem, whose name was Simeon; constantly expecting the restoration of Israel: and the Holy Spirit was upon him. 26. And the Holy Spirit revealed to him that he should not see death before he had seen the Lord's Anointed. 27. Inspired by the Spirit he came into the temple: and when the parents brought the child Jesus, to do what was customary under the law. 28. And he received him in his arms and blessed God, and said, 29. Master, now release your bond-servant to depart in peace, according to your word: 30. for my eyes have seen your saving

power, 31. that you have prepared before the face of all peoples; 32. a light to bring light to the Gentiles, and the glory of your people Israel. 33. And Joseph and His mother were amazed at those things which were spoken of Him. 34. And Simeon gave them his blessing, and said to Mary His mother, Behold, this child is set to cause the rise and fall of many in Israel; and many will speak against and oppose Him: 35. (Yes, a broad-sword shall pierce through your own soul also,) and the inner most thoughts of many will be revealed.

Anna, a Prophetess
Luke 2:36-40
36. And there was Anna, a Prophetess, the daughter of Phanuel, of the tribe of Aser: she was advanced in age, and had lived with a husband seven years from her virginity; 37. And she had been a widow until fourscore and four years, and departed not from the temple, but served God with fasting and intercessions night and day. 38. And she came forward at that instant and gave thanks unto the Lord, and spoke of the child to all who patiently waited for the coming of the Deliverer in Jerusalem. 39. And when the parents had performed all the prescribed things according to the law of the Lord, they returned to Galilee to their own city Nazareth. 40. And the child grew, and increased in spirit, filled with wisdom: and the grace of God was upon Him.

About My Father's Business
Luke 2:41-52
41. It was the practice of His parents to go to Jerusalem every year at the feast of the Passover. 42. And when Jesus was twelve years old, they made the customary pilgrimage to the feast. 43. When the feast was over, as they returned, the child Jesus tarried behind in Jerusalem; and Joseph and His mother did not know. 44. But they supposing Him to have been in the caravan, went a day's journey; and they sought Him among their kinsfolk and acquaintance. 45. And when they found Him not, they turned back again to Jerusalem, seeking Him. 46. It was not until the third day that they found Him in the Temple Courts, sitting among the scholars, both listening to them, and asking questions. 47. And all who heard Him were greatly astonished at His understanding and answers. 48. And when they found Him, they were amazed, and His mother said to Him, Son, why have you behaved this way? Behold, your father and I have sought you sorrowing. 49. And He said to them, Why did you search for Me? Know you not that I must be about My Father's business? 50. His words seemed strange to them. 51. And He went down with them and came to Nazareth, and submitted to their authority, but His mother kept all

these sayings in her heart. 52. And Jesus increased in wisdom and stature, and in favor with God and man.

What Shall We Do?
Luke 3:1-15
1. In the fifteenth year of the reign of emperor Tiberius, Pontius Pilate being governor of Judaea, and Herod the ruler of Galilee, and his brother Philip, ruler of Ituraea and of the region of Trachonitis, and Lysanias ruler of Abilene. 2. Annas and Caiaphas were the high priests, the message of God came to John, the son of Zacharias in the wilderness. 3. And he preached repentance baptism for the forgiveness of sins in all the region about Jordan; 4. as the words of Isaiah the prophet were written in the book, saying, The voice of one crying in the wilderness, prepare the way of the Lord, make His paths straight. 5. Every valley shall be filled, and every mountain and hill shall be brought low; and the crooked shall be made straight, and the rough ways shall be made smooth; 6. and all mankind shall see the salvation of God. 7. And John said to the crowds that came to be baptized, you brood of snakes, who has prompted you to seek refuge from the coming punishment? 8. Then produce fruits consistent with your repentance, and do not begin to say, we have Abraham as our father: for I say, that God is able to raise up children to Abraham out of these stones. 9. Also the axe is laid at the root of the trees: every tree that does not produce good fruit is cut down and cast into the fire. 10. And the people asked him, what shall we do then? 11. He answered them, He that has two coats, let him share with him that has none; and he that has food, let him do likewise. 12. Then, tax-collectors came to be baptized, and asked, Master, what shall we do? 13. And he said unto them, collect only the prescribed amount. 14. And the soldiers likewise demanded of him, saying, And what shall we do? And John said unto them, Do violence to no man, neither accuse any falsely; and be content with your wages. 15. And as the people were in expectation, and all men reasoned in their hearts of John, whether he were the Christ, or not;

The Heavens Were Opened
Luke 3:16-20
16. John gave them a public answer, I indeed immerse you in water; but there is come a more powerful One, His shoe straps I am not worthy to loose: He will baptize you with the fire of the Holy Spirit: 17. His winnowing shovel is ready to thoroughly cleanse the threshing-floor and to gather the wheat into His storehouse; but the chaff He will burn up with ravenous fire. 18. Many different ways indeed he evangelized the people. 19. But Herod the governor, being criticized by John for

Herodias, his brother Philip's wife, and all the evil things which Herod had done, 20. in addition, he shut down John's ministry and put him in chains in prison.

The Son of God
Luke 3: 21-38

21. After all the people were baptized, as Jesus was being baptized and praying, the heavens opened, 22. and the Holy Spirit came down upon Him in bodily form as a dove, and a voice from heaven, You are My beloved Son; in you I am well-pleased. 23. And Jesus Himself began His ministry being about thirty years old, being the supposed son of Joseph, which was the son of Heli, 24. of Matthat, of Levi, of Melchi, of Janna, of Joseph, 25. of Mattathias, of Amos, of Naum, of Esli, of Nagge, 26. of Maath, of Mattathias, of Semei, of Joseph, of Joda, 27. of Joanna, of Rhesa, of Zorobabel, of Salathiel, of Neri, 28. of Melchi, of Addi, of Cosam, of Elmodam, of Er, 29. of Jose, of Eliezer, of Jorim, of Matthat, of Levi, 30. of Simeon, of Judah, of Joseph, of Jonan, of Eliakim, 31. of Melea, of Menan, of Mattatha, of Nathan, of David, 32. of Jesse, of Obed, of Boaz, of Salmon, of Naasson, 33. of Aminadab, of Aram, of Esrom, of Phares, of Judah, 34. of Jacob, of Isaac, of Abraham, of Thara, of Nachor, 35. of Saruch, of Ragau, of Phalec, of Heber, of Sala, 36. of Cainan, of Arphaxad, of Sem, of Noe, of Lamech, 37. of Mathusala, of Enoch, of Jared, of Maleleel, of Cainan, 38. of Enos, of Seth, of Adam, who was the Son of God.

Homage to the Lord Alone
Luke 4:1-13

1. Full of the Holy Spirit, Jesus returned from Jordan, and was led into the wilderness by the Spirit, 2. and was tempted by the Adversary for forty days. In those days He did eat nothing: and was famished. 3. And the Evil One said to Him, if you be the Son of God, command these stones to become bread. 4. And Jesus answered, The scripture says. Man cannot live by bread alone. 5. And leading Him up, showed Him all the kingdoms of the inhabited earth in a single moment. 6. And the devil said, All this power and glory will I give you, for it has been turned over to me; and I give it to whomever I please. 7. If you pay homage to me all will be yours. 8. And Jesus answered, It is written.*, Render divine homage to the Lord alone. 9. And Jesus was placed on the summit wall of the temple in Jerusalem, and Satan said, If you are the Son of God, throw yourself down: 10. For it is written, He will give His angels orders to vigilantly watch over you: 11. and they will lift you up lest you strike your foot against a stone. 12. And Jesus answered, It was said, You shall not tempt the Lord your God. 13. And

having finished all the temptation, the devil departed until an opportune occasion.

---

*v8 The rebuke "Get thee behind me, Satan" was omitted because it is not adequately supported by the original language.

He Stood Up to Read
Luke 4:14-22

14. And Jesus enabled by the power of the Spirit returned to Galilee: and reports about Him went out to the countryside. 15. And He began to teach in their synagogues and was praised by all. 16. And He came to Nazareth, where He had lived as a child: and, as His custom was, He went into the synagogue on the Sabbath day, and stood up to read Scriptures. 17. And they gave Him the scroll of the prophet Isaiah. And unrolling the scroll, He found the place where it was written, 18. The Spirit of the Lord is upon me, and has consecrated me to tell glad tidings to the destitute;* and sent Me to proclaim deliverance to the captives, and the recovering of sight to the blind, and to set at liberty the downtrodden, 19. To proclaim a year when we can find acceptance with the Lord. 20. And rolling up the scroll He gave it again to the attendant, and sat down, and the eyes of the whole synagogue were firmly fixed on Him. 21. And He began speaking, Today while you were listening this scripture is fulfilled. 22. And all who were present were surprised at the gracious words from His lips. And they said, Is this not Joseph's son?

---

*v18 The words "to heal the brokenhearted" are not adequately supported here by original texts, but the concept appears elsewhere in scripture.

He Walked Through Them Unseen
Luke 4:23-31

23. No doubt you will remind Me of the proverb: Physician, heal thyself: whatsoever you did in Capernaum do also here in your home country. 24. I declare you an accurate statement, No prophet is welcomed in his home country. 25. But I speak a true statement, In Elijah's day many widows were in Israel, when there was no rain for three years and six months, a great famine was throughout all the land; 26. but to none was Elijah sent except to a widow in Zarephath, a city of Sidon. 27. And in the time of Elisha there were many lepers in Israel, and none of them was cleansed, except Naaman, the Syrian. 28. At these words the whole synagogue became enraged, 29. and rising up, they drove Jesus out of the city and led Him to the bow of the hill whereon their city was built meaning to throw Him down. 30. But He

walked through them unseen and went His way. 31. And went down to Capernaum, a city of Galilee, and taught them on the Sabbath days.

He Taught with Authority
Luke 4:32-37

32. And they were impressed with His teaching: for His word was with authority. 33. And a man in the synagogue that had a spirit of an unclean demon screamed with a loud voice, 34. saying, Leave me alone; what do we have to do with you, Jesus of Nazareth? I know you as the Holy One of God. Have you come to destroy us? 35. And Jesus admonished him, saying, Be silent and come out of him. And when the demon had hurled him into a convulsion before the crowd, he came out of him and no permanent physical damage was done. 36. And the people were in amazement and began discussing with one another, saying, His words are with authority and with power He commanded the unclean demons and they came out. 37. And the rumor about Him went to every place in the region.

He Laid Hands on Every One
Luke 4:38-44

38. And leaving the synagogue, He went to Simon's house. And Simon's mother-in-law was sick with a high fever; and those in the house made a request on her behalf. 39. And He stood over her, and commanded the fever to leave her: and immediately she arose and waited on them. 40. At sundown, all who had sick friends with various diseases brought them to Him; and He laid hands on every one and healed them. 41. And demons came out of many, crying, You are the Christ the Son of God. And He rebuked them and did not permit them to speak: because they knew He was the Messiah. 42. And when it was day, He departed and went into a barren place: and the people continually sought Him, and came and kept on asking Him not to depart from them. 43. And He said, I must preach the Kingdom of God to other cities also: for this I am sent. 44. And He preached in the synagogues of Judaea.

Let Down the Net
Luke 5:1-11

1. Now it came to pass as the crowd pressed upon Him and heard the word of God, He was standing by the lake Gennesaret, 2. And saw two boats close to shore: but the fishermen were away washing their nets. 3. And He entered a ship belonging to Simon and asked Him to push out a little from land. And He sat down, and taught the people from the ship. 4. And when He was through speaking, He asked Simon to move out into deep water, and let down your nets and draw up a catch. 5. And Simon answered, Master, we have worked all night and caught

nothing; nevertheless at your word I will let down the net: 6. And this they did and enclosed a great catch of fish: and their nets began to break. 7. And they signaled their partners in the other boat to come and help. And they came and filled both boats to the point of sinking. 8. Seeing the catch Simon Peter fell down before Jesus, saying, Leave me Lord, for I am a sinful man. 9. For he was overwhelmed and all that were with him, at the catch of fish in one drawing of the nets: 10. and likewise were both James and John, sons of Zebedee, who were associates of Simon. And Jesus said to Simon, Fear not, henceforth you will also catch men alive. 11. And when they had landed their boats, they forsook all and followed Jesus.

You Can Make Me Clean
Luke 5:12-16
12. While Jesus was in a certain city, He came upon a man full of leprosy; who seeing Jesus fell on His face and implored Him, saying, Lord, if you will, you can make me clean. 13. And He willingly touched Him, saying, I will be cleansed. 14. And He warned him not to tell anyone: but go and show yourself to the priest and make offerings for your cleansing according as Moses commanded, to certify your cure to the people. 15. But the news of Him continued to spread: and a multitude gathered to hear Him and to be cured of their ailments. 16. And He withdrew into a desolate place and prayed.

When He Saw Their Faith
Luke 5:17-26
17. On one of the days He was teaching there were Pharisees and doctors of the law present from every town of Galilee, Judaea, and Jerusalem: and the power of the Lord was present to heal the sick. 18. And men brought on a quilt-bed a paralyzed man and sought means to bring and lay him before Jesus. 19. When they could find no way to bring him in because of the crowd, they went to the roof and let him down through the tiles in front of Jesus. 20. And when He saw their faith, He said to him, Man, your sins are forgiven. 21. And the scholars and the Pharisees began to question, asking, Who is this who speaks disrespectfully of God? Who can forgive sins, but God alone? 22. But Jesus understanding their thoughts, answered, Why argue in your hearts? 23. Which is easier to say, Your sins be forgiven or rise and walk? 24. Jesus spoke to the paralyzed man, That you may know that the Son of Man has power on earth to forgive sins, Arise and pick up your quilt-bed and walk home. 25. And comfortably he got up, picked up his quilt-bed and walked to his own home, praising God. 26. And with amazement they all worshiped and praised God and were filled with wonder, saying, We have seen wonderful things today.

The Healthy Need No Physician
Luke 5:27-32

27. After this His attention was turned to a publican, named Levi, sitting in the custom house: and Jesus said to him, Follow Me. 28. And he abandoned everything and followed Jesus. 29. And Levi made a great reception in his own house: and there was a great company of tax-collectors and other guests that sat down with them. 30. But the scribes and Pharisees expressed their discontent to His disciples, saying, Why do you eat and drink with tax-collectors and people who consistently do wrong? 31. And Jesus answered, The healthy need no physician; but those who are ill. 32. I did not come for the purpose of calling the righteous, but those who habitually do wrong to feel remorse for their sins.

Then Shall They Fast
Luke 5:33-39

33. Why do John's disciples and the Pharisees fast often and make prayers and your disciples eat and drink? 34. And He said, Can you cause the attendants of the bridegroom to fast while the bridegroom is present? 35. And the days will come when the bridegroom is taken away violently, then shall they fast. 36. Then He told this story; No one tears a piece from a new garment and puts it on an old one; otherwise the new is torn and the new piece does not match the old. 37. And no man puts new wine into old wineskins; else the new wine burst the skin and the wine and the wineskin are destroyed. 38. But new wine must be poured into new wineskins; and both will be preserved. 39. No man after drinking old wine desires the new; for He says, the old is better.

Stand Where All Can See
Luke 6:1-11

1. And it came to pass on a Sabbath that Jesus went through the cornfields; and His disciples were plucking ears of corn shucking them in their hands and eating. 2. And certain Pharisees asked, Why do you do unlawful things on the Sabbath? 3. And Jesus answered, Have you not read what David did when he was hungry, and those with him; 4. How he went into the house of God and ate the bread on the Lord's Table and gave some to his companions; bread only the priests were allowed to eat? 5. He proceeded to say, The Son of man is Lord of the Sabbath. 6. On another Sabbath He was teaching in the synagogue: and in the congregation was a man whose right hand was deformed. 7. And the scholars and Pharisees watched to see if He would heal on the Sabbath Day; so they could make accusation against Him. 8. But He was aware of their thoughts, and said to the man with the

deformed hand, Rise and stand where all can see. And he got up and stood in front. 9. Then Jesus said, I will ask you one question: is it lawful to do good or evil on the Sabbath: to rescue or destroy a life? 10. And looking around at each one, He said to the man, Stretch forth your hand. He did and his hand was restored whole as the other. 11. And they were furious and discussed among themselves what they could do to Jesus.

He Chose Twelve
Luke 6:12-19

12. In those days Jesus went to the mountain to pray, and continued all night in prayer to God. 13. And when it was morning He called His disciples to come to Him: and of them He chose twelve, whom He also named Apostles; 14. Simon, (whom He called Peter,) and Andrew his brother, James and John, Philip and Bartholomew, 15. Matthew and Thomas, James the son of Alphaeus, and Simon the Zealot, 16. and Judas the brother of James, and Judas Iscariot, who became the traitor. 17. And He came down with the disciples and stood on level ground with the company of His disciples and a multitude out of Judaea and Jerusalem, and from the coast of Tyre and Sidon, who came to hear Him, and to be healed; 18. And those tormented by unclean spirits were also healed. 19. And everyone in the crowd struggled to touch Him: for power to heal them all came forth from Him.

Release Others From Blame
Luke 6:20-39

20. Then Jesus looked at His disciples and said, Blessed are the poor: for the kingdom of God is yours. 21. Blessed are the starving: for you will be filled. Blessed are those who sorrow: for God will cause you to laugh. 22. Blessed are you when men shall hate you and ostracize you from their company, and heap insults on you, and defame your name because you are loyal to the Son of Man. 23. Express joy on that day and be exceeding glad: for your reward is great in heaven: for in the same way their fathers behaved toward the prophets. 24. But sorrows await the rich! They have already summoned their aid and comfort. 25. Anguish to you who are full! For you will receive sorrow and hunger. Sadness to you who laugh now! For you will know misery and tears. 26. Despair when all men speak well of you! For so did their fathers to the false prophets. 27. But to all who hear Me I say, Love your enemies, do good to those who hate you. 28. Praise them that attempt to harm you, and pray for them who attempt to damage you out of small-mindedness. 29. And to him who strikes you with violence on one cheek offer the other also; and to him who takes your outer garment, give him also your undergarment. 30. Give to everyone who

asks: and ask not for the return of goods taken. 31. And as you wish that men may do to you, do you to them likewise. 32. For when you love those who love you, what kind of thanks is freely given? For those who habitually do wrong also love those who love them. 33. And if you are good to those who are good to you: what kind of thanks is freely given? For sinners also do the same. 34. And if you lend to those of whom you expect to receive, what thanks have you? For sinners also lend to sinners, to receive as much again. 35. But love your enemies and lend without expecting a return; and your reward shall be great; and you shall be the children of the Highest: for He is kind to the unthankful and to the evil. 36. Be compassionate, as your Father is also merciful and forgiving. 37. Do not pass judgment, release others from blame, and you shall not be condemned. 38. Give and others will press gifts into the pockets of your garment and good measure will be yours. For the same standard you use in giving shall be used to measure gifts to you.

Identify a Tree By Its Fruit
Luke 6:39-49

39. And Jesus used a story, saying: Surely the blind cannot guide the blind or both will fall into a ditch? 40. The learner is not above his teacher: but everyone who is fully taught will reach his teacher's level. 41. And why do you see the speck in your brother's eye but cannot recognize the beam in your own eye? 42. How can you say to your brother, Let me get the speck out of your eye, when you observe not the beam in your own eye? You insincere talker, begin by removing the beam from your own eye, and then you may see clearly to remove the speck in your brother's eye. 43. For a good tree does not bear bad fruit; neither does a bad tree support good fruit. 44. For a tree is identified by its fruit. From thorns men do not gather figs, nor from a blackberry bush do they gather grapes. 45. A good man produces a good treasure from his heart; and an evil man produces plunder that is evil: for from the abundance of the heart the mouth speaks. 46. And why do you call Me, Lord, Lord, and do not the things I say? 47. Whoever comes to Me, and listens to My words and behaves them, I will show you to whom he may be compared: 48. He is compared to a man who dug deep and laid a foundation on a rock and built a house: and when the flood came, the water beat violently upon that house and could not shake it: for it was founded on a rock. 49. But he who hears and does not behave the word may be compared to a man who without a foundation built a house upon the earth; against which the stream beat violently and immediately it fell; and the damage of that house was complete.

So Great Faith
Luke 7:1-18

1. When Jesus had ended His teaching to the spectators, He entered into Capernaum. 2. And a Roman Centurion's special servant was sick and about to die. 3. When he heard of Jesus, he sent the elders of the Jews to beseech Jesus to come and heal his servant. 4. And when they came to Jesus, they earnestly petition Him, saying, The Centurion was worthy for whom He should do this: 5. for he loves our Nation, and has build us a synagogue. 6. Jesus went with them and when He was nearly to the house, the Centurion sent friends saying to, Lord do not trouble yourself: for I am not worthy that you should enter my house: 7. Neither thought I worthy to come to you myself: just say a word, and my servant shall be healed. 8. For I am also a man with authority, having under me soldiers, and I say to one, Go and he goes; and to another, Come, and he comes; and to my servant, Do this and he does it. 9. When Jesus heard these things, He was impressed and turned around and said to the people that followed, I say to you, I have not found so great faith, no, not in Israel. 10. And those that were sent returned to the house and found the servant in good health.

Weep Not
Luke 7:11-18

11. And Jesus happened to go the next day to a city called Nain; and His disciples and a multitude of people went with Him. 12. As He approached the gate of the city He met a funeral possession, the only son of his mother, and she was a widow: and many people of the city were with her. 13. And when the Lord saw her, He had great understanding of her feelings, and said to her, Weep not. 14. And He touched the coffin: and the pallbearers stood still. And He said, Young man, I say to you, Arise. 15. And the corpse sat up and began talking. And Jesus delivered him to his mother. 16. And a feeling of amazement and respect mixed with fear was on all: and they worshiped God, saying, A great prophet is risen among us; and, God has visited His people. 17. And this report of Jesus went throughout all Judaea and the region about. 18. And John's disciples informed him of all these things.

Cured Many
Luke 7:19-23

19. And John called two of his disciples sent them to Jesus, saying, Are you He who should come? or do we look for another? 20. When the men came to Jesus, they said, John Baptist sent us to you, saying, Are you He who should come? or do we look for another? 21. And at the same hour He cured many of their sickness and diseases, and of

evil spirits; and to many that were blind He gave sight. 22. Then Jesus answered, Go your way and tell John what you have seen and heard; how the blind see, the lame walk, the lepers are cleansed, the deaf hear, the dead stand up again, and to the poor the gospel is preached. 23. And blessed is he, whoever shall not find an occasion of stumbling in Me.

Who Shall Prepare the Way?
Luke 7:24-35

24. And when the messengers of John departed, Jesus began to speak to the people concerning John, What did you go to the wilderness to see? Reeds shaken in the wind? 25. But what did you go to see? A man clothed in silk robes? Behold, those dressed stylishly live in kings' courts. 26. But what did you go to see? A prophet? Yes, and much more than a prophet. 27. This is he, of whom it is written, Behold, I send My messenger before your face, who shall prepare the way before you. 28. For I say, Among those born of women there is not a greater prophet than John the Baptist: but the least in the kingdom of God is greater than he. 29. And all the people that heard Him, and the tax-collectors, acknowledged God, having accepted the baptism of John. 30. But the Pharisees and lawyers rejected the counsel of God by refusing baptism themselves. 31. And the Lord said, How shall I describe this generation? And to what are they compared? 32. They are similar to children sitting in the marketplace, and calling one to another, and saying, We have piped to you, and you have not danced; we have mourned to you, and you have not wept. 33. For John the Baptist came neither eating bread nor drinking wine; and you say, He has a demon. 34. The Son of Man is come eating and drinking; and you say, Behold a glutton and a wine-drinker, a friend of tax-collectors and sinners! 35. But wisdom is justified by all who are practical.

I Have Something to Say to You
Luke 7:36-40

36. And one of the Pharisees invited Jesus to a meal. And He went to the Pharisee's house, and sat down to eat. 37. And, a woman of the city, who habitually did wrong, when she knew that Jesus was at the Pharisee's house, brought an alabaster jar of ointment, 38. and took her place behind Him weeping, and began to wash His feet with tears, and wipe them with her hair, and kissed His feet, and anointed them with the ointment. 39. When the Pharisee saw it, he spake within himself, saying, This man, if He were a prophet, would know who this woman is that touches Him: for she is a sinner. 40. And Jesus answering said to him, Simon, I have something to say to you. And he said, Master, say on.

Your Faith Has Saved You
Luke 7:41-50
41. There was a money-lender who had two debtors: the one owed ten times more than the other. 42. And when they had nothing to pay, he freely forgave them both. Tell me which of them will love him most? 43. Simon answered and said, I suppose the one he forgave most. And He said to him, You are right. 44. And He turned to the woman, and said to Simon, See this woman? I entered your house, and you gave Me no water for My feet: but she has washed My feet with tears, and wiped them with her hair. 45. You gave Me no kiss: but this woman has not ceased to kiss My feet. 46. My head with oil you did not anoint: but this woman has anointed My feet with ointment. 47. Wherefore I say, Her sins, which are many, are forgiven; for she loved much: but to whom little is forgiven, the same loves little. 48. And Jesus said to her, Your sins are forgiven. 49. And they that ate with Him began to ask themselves, Who is this that forgives sins also? 50. And Jesus said to the woman, Your faith has saved you; go in peace.

Listen
Luke 8:1-8
1. Then Jesus traveled from city to village and preached and showed the good news of the kingdom of God: and the Twelve were with Him. 2. And women, who had been healed of evil spirits and infirmities, Mary called Magdalene, out of whom He expelled seven demons, 3. and Joanna the wife of Chuza, Herod's steward, and Susanna, and many others, who supported Him with personal resources. 4. And when many were gathered together out of every city, He spake by a parable: 5. A farmer went out to sow his seed: and as he sowed, some seeds fell beside the footpath; and it was walked on, and the birds consumed it. 6. And some fell on rocky ground; and as soon as it came up, it withered away, because it lacked moisture. 7. And some fell among prickly weeds; and the thistles sprang up with it, and choked it. 8. And other seeds fell on good ground, and sprang up, and produced fruit a hundredfold. And when He had said these things, He cried, Who has ears to hear let him listen.

Bring Forth Fruit with Endurance
Luke 8:9-15
9. And His disciples asked Him, saying, What does this story mean? 10. And He said, You are given the sacred secrets of the kingdom of God: but to others it comes in stories; and they look and look again, but never understand. 11. Now the story is this: The seed is the word of God. 12. Those by the footpath are they that hear; then the devil comes and takes away the word out of their hearts, lest they should

believe and be saved. 13. The seed on the rocky ground are those who hear, receive the word with joy; but have no root, who for a while believe, and in a time of testing they fall away. 14. And the seed that fell among prickly weeds are they, who having heard, go forth, and are choked with cares and pleasures of this life, and bring no fruit to maturity. 15. But the seeds on the good ground are they, who in an honest and good heart, having heard the word, keep it, and bring forth fruit with endurance.

Hear the Word and Behave It
Luke 8:16-21

16. No man, after lighting a lamp, covers it with a vessel, or puts it under a bed; but puts it on a lamp stand, that others may see the light. 17. For nothing is hidden, that shall not be revealed; neither any thing concealed, that shall not become clear as day. 18. Be careful how you listen: for those who have will be given more and those who have not shall lose what he seems to have. 19. Then came His mother and His brethren, and could not come to Him for the crowd. 20. And He was told, Your mother and brothers stand without, desiring to see you. 21. And He answered and said, My mother and My brothers are those who hear the word of God, and behave it.

Where is Your Faith?
Luke 8:22-26

22. On a certain day, Jesus went into a boat with His disciples and said, Let us go to the other side of the lake. And they got underway. 23. As they sailed He fell asleep: and a thunderstorm came down from the heights surrounding the lake; and the boat was in jeopardy of becoming swamped. 24. And they awoke Him, saying, Master, master, we are about to perish. He arose and rebuked the wind and the surging waves: and the water became calm. 25. And He asked, Where is your faith? And being fearful they discussed the matter, asking who this man is! He commands the winds and water, and they obey Him. 26. And they arrived in the Gadarenes, across the lake from Galilee.

Resided in the Tombs
Luke 8:27-33

27. And when Jesus came ashore, a man from the city met Jesus, who had demons for a long time, and wore no clothes, neither lived in a house, but resided in the tombs. 28. When he saw Jesus, he fell down before Him, and cried with a loud voice, What have I to do with you, Jesus, you Son of God most high? I beg you do not torment me. 29. (For Jesus was commanding the unclean spirit to come out of the man. Often it had seized him: and he was kept under guard and bound with shackles; and he would break the chains, and was

driven by the devil into the desert.) 30. And Jesus asked, What is your name? And he said, Legion: because he had many demons. 31. And they besought Him that He would not command them to go into the bottomless abyss. 32. And there were many swine grazing on the hillside: and they besought Him to permit them to possess the swine. And Jesus consented. 33. Then the demons left the man and entered into the swine: and the herd stampeded over a cliff into the lake, and were drowned.

What Great Things God Has Done
Luke 8:34-39

34. When the swine herdsmen saw what was done, they fled, and told the city and the countryside. 35. Then the people went out to see for themselves; and came to Jesus, and found the man, out of whom the demons were departed, sitting at the feet of Jesus, clothed, and in his right mind: and they were afraid. 36. They who saw it told them by how the demonized man was healed. 37. Then the whole multitude of the country of the Gadarenes round about besought Jesus to depart from them; for they were taken with great fear: and He returned to the boat. 38. Now the man out of whom the demons were departed prayed that he might be with Him: but Jesus sent him away, saying, 39. Return to your own house, and describe the many things God has done. And he went his way, and announced publicly to the whole city the many things Jesus had done for him.

Your Faith Has Made You Whole
Luke 8:40-48

40. On His return the people gladly welcomed Him: and they were all waiting for Him. 41. And there came a man named Jairus, an official of the synagogue: and he fell down at Jesus' feet, and prayed that He would come to his house: 42. for his only daughter, about twelve years old, lay dying. But as he went the crowd stifled him. 43. And a woman having a hemorrhage for twelve years, who had spent all her living and could not be healed by the physicians, 44. came behind Jesus, and touched the fringe of His garment: and immediately her issue of blood stopped. 45. And Jesus said, Who touched Me? When all denied, Peter and those with him said, Master, the crowd has crushed you, and you ask, Who touched Me? 46. And Jesus said, Someone did touch Me: for I recognized that power went out of Me. 47. And when the woman saw that she was known, came trembling, and prostrating before Him, declared to Him before all the people for what cause she had touched Him and how she was cured at once. 48. And Jesus said unto her, Daughter, be of good comfort: your faith has made you whole; go in peace.

Fear Not, Only Believe
Luke 8:49-56

49. While still speaking, one came from the official of the synagogue's house, saying, Your daughter is dead; do not disturb the Master. 50. But when Jesus heard it, He said, Fear not: only believe, and she shall be made whole. 51. And when He came into the house, He allowed no one to go in, except Peter, James, and John, and the father and mother of the child. 52. And all wept, and were grieved: but He said, Weep not; she did not die, but sleeps. 53. And they ridiculed Him, knowing that she died. 54. And He put them all out, and took her by the hand, and called, saying, Child, stand up. 55. And her spirit returned, and she got up without delay: and He instructed them to give her something to eat. 56. And her parents were astonished: but Jesus charged them not to tell any one what was done.

Power and Authority
Luke 9:1-9

1. Jesus called the Twelve disciples together, and gave them power and authority to overcome all demons and to cure diseases. 2. And He sent them to proclaim the kingdom of God, and to heal the sick. 3. And He told them, Take nothing for your journey, neither staff, nor satchel, neither bread, nor money; take only one coat each. 4. And whatever house you enter, there abide, and from that place depart. 5. And whoever will not receive you, when you go out of that city, shake off the dust from your feet as a witness against them. 6. And they departed, and went through the towns, evangelizing and healing. 7. Now Herod the governor heard of all that was done by Jesus: and he was puzzled, because some said, that John had risen from the dead; 8. and some said that Elijah had appeared; and others, that one of the ancient prophets had returned. 9. And Herod said, I beheaded John: but who is this, of whom I hear such things? And he desired to see Jesus.

Those Who Had Need of Healing
Luke 9:10-17

10. When the apostles returned, they told Jesus all they had done. And He took them, and went aside privately into a desert place near Bethsaida. 11. When the people knew it, they followed Him: and He received them, and spoke to them of the kingdom of God, and healed those who had need of healing. 12. Toward the end of the day, the Twelve came and said, Send the crowd away, that they may go into the towns and country round about, and lodge, and get food: for we are in a wasteland. 13. But He said, Give them something to eat. And they said, We have only five loaves and two fishes; unless we go and

buy food for all the people. 14. For about five thousand men were present. And He said to His disciples, Make them sit down by fifties in a company. 15. And they did so, and made them all sit down. 16. Then He took the five loaves and the two fishes, and looking up to heaven, blessed them, and broke them in pieces, and gave to the disciples to set before the crowd. 17. And they did eat, and were all filled: and they gathered up twelve baskets full of broken pieces.

What is the Benefit?
Luke 9:18-27

18. And it came to pass, as Jesus was praying alone, His disciples joined Him: and He asked them, Whom say the people that I am? 19. Then answered, John the Baptist; but some say, Elijah; and others say one of the ancient prophets has stood up again. 20. He asked, But whom do you say I am? Peter answered, God's Messiah. 21. And He firmly commanded them to tell no man this thing; 22. saying, the Son of Man must undergo great suffering, and be deliberately rejected by the elders, chief priests and the scholars, and be executed, and raised the third day. 23. And Jesus said to them all, Should any one desire to follow My steps, let him disregard himself, and take up his cross everyday, and follow Me closely. 24. For whosoever attempts to preserve this life shall lose it: but whosoever suffers the loss of his life for My sake, shall be restored to eternal life. 25. What is the benefit, if a man acquires the whole world, and is defeated in his personal struggle, or forfeit his own soul? 26. For whoever dishonors Me and My words, the Son of Man shall disgrace him before His Father and the holy angels. 27. But I tell you a truth, there are some standing here, who shall never experience the sorrows of death, before they see the kingdom of God.

This is My Son, Listen to Him
Luke 9:28-36

28. About eight days after these words, Jesus took Peter, John, and James, and went to a mountain to pray. 29. As He prayed, His facial expression was changed, and His clothing became white and sparkled with light. 30. And Moses and Elijah appeared to talk with Him. 31. They appeared in heavenly splendor and spoke of His going away at Jerusalem. 32. But Peter and the others were asleep and waking up they saw His glorious appearance and the two men that stood with Him. 33. As they departed, Peter said to Jesus, Master, it is good for us to be here: let us build three places of worship: one for you, one for Moses, and one for Elijah: not understanding what he said. 34. While he spoke a cloud began to overshadow them and they were fearful. 35. And a voice came from the cloud, saying, This is My beloved Son:

listen to Him. 36. When the voice came, Jesus was found alone. And they remained silent and told no man any of those things they had seen.

God's Mighty Power
Luke 9:37-45

37. The next day when they came down from the mountain, they were met by many people. 38. A man in the crowd cried out, saying, Teacher, I beg you, come look at my son: for he is my only child. 39. At times a spirit takes him and he suddenly cries out; he has convulsions and foams at the mouth, and the spirit does not leave him until he is covered with bruises. 40. I begged your disciples to cast out this spirit; and they could not. 41. You really are a misguided and perverse generation; how long will I bear with you? Bring your son here: 42. as he was coming, the demon dashed the child violently to the ground. And Jesus firmly rebuked the unclean spirit and healed the child, and delivered him to his father. 43. And they were all struck with astonishment at the evidence of God's mighty power. But while they all wondered at the things that were done, Jesus spoke to His disciples, 44. Listen carefully: for the Son of Man will be betrayed into the hands of men. 45. The truth was hidden from them and they feared to ask Jesus about the saying.

Who is Not Against Us is for Us
Luke 9:46-56

46. Then there arose a debate among them as to who should be greatest. 47. And Jesus knowing their thoughts took a child and set the child by His side. 48. And said, Whoever receives this child in My name receives Me: and whosoever receives Me receives Him who sent Me: and the least among you shall be the greatest. 49. And John asked, Master, we saw one using your name to cast out evil spirits; and we tried to stop him because he was not one of us. 50. Do nothing to stop him: for he who is not against us is for us. 51. When the time was coming close to when Jesus was to be taken back to heaven, with resolution Jesus set His face toward Jerusalem. 52. And He sent messengers in advance: and they went into a village of the Samaritans to make arrangements for Him. 53. And they did not receive Him because His intention was to go to Jerusalem. 54. And when James and John, His disciples saw this, they asked, Lord will you be willing for us to command fire to come down from heaven and consume them, even as Elijah did? 55. But Jesus turned and rebuked them and said, 56. The Son of Man came not to destroy men's lives, but to save them. And they went to another village.

Lord, I Will Follow You
Luke 9:57-62

57. As they continued their journey, a man said, Lord, I will follow you wherever you go. 58. And Jesus said, Foxes have holes, and birds have nests; but the Son of Man has no where to lay His head. 59. And He said to another, Follow Me. But he said, Lord, permit me first to bury my father. 60. Jesus said, Let those without eternal life bury their own dead: you go and proclaim the kingdom of God. 61. And another said, Lord, I will follow you; but permit me first say good-bye to my family. 62. And Jesus said, No man, having put his hand to the plough, and keeps looking back, is ready for the kingdom of God.

Sent Them Two by Two
Luke 10:1-16

1. After these things the Lord commissioned seventy more and sent them two by two in advance to every place where He planned to go. 2. He said to them, the summer harvest is great, but the workmen are few: plead with the Lord who owns the crop to urgently send more workers to gather His harvest. 3. Go and remember I am sending you as lambs among wolves. 4. Carry no money, nor food, nor extra shoes: and exchange no greetings on the road. 5. And into whatever house you enter, first say, Peace be to this house. 6. If the character of the house is peaceful, your peace shall rest on it: if not, it shall return to you. 7. Abide at the same house, eating and drinking whatever they provide: for the worker is worthy of maintenance. Go not from house to house. 8. When you are welcomed in any place, eat what is set before you: 9. and heal the sick there, and say, The Kingdom of God has come near to you. 10. But if they do not welcome you, go to the streets and say, 11. Even the dust of your city that clings to our feet, we wipe off as a witness against you: but remember the kingdom of God came near to you. 12. And Jesus said, it will be more bearable for Sodom on the day of reckoning, than for that city. 13. Woe to Chorazin and Bethsaida; for if these powerful deeds happen in Tyre and Sidon they would have immediately repented covered with a grain-sack and ashes. 14. But it will be more bearable for Tyre and Sidon at the judgment than for you. 15. And to Capernaum, who is exalted high, shall be cast down to hell. 16. He who hears you, listens to Me; and he who disregards you, rejects Me; and those who reject Me, refuse to accept the One who sent Me.

I Have Given You Power
Luke 10:17-24

17. And the seventy returned with joy, saying, Lord, even the demons submit to us in your name. 18. And Jesus said, I watched as the

dazzling brilliance of your Adversary was suddenly quenched as he fell from heaven. 19. Observe, I have given you power to trample serpents and scorpions, and authority over all the power of the enemy: and nothing by any means shall hurt you. 20. Notwithstanding this power, do not rejoice that demons are subject to you; but rather rejoice because your names are written in heaven. 21. Then Jesus rejoiced in the Spirit and said, I thank you, Father, Lord of heaven and earth, that you have kept these things from the wise and learned, and have revealed them to the little ones: even so, Father, it was according to your will. 22. All things have been conveyed to Me by My Father: and no man knows who the Son is, but the Father; and who the Father is, but the Son, and to whom the Son may choose to reveal Him. 23. And He turned toward His disciples and said privately, Blessed are the eyes that observe the things you see: 24. For many prophets and kings have wanted to observe the things you see, and have not seen them; and to hear the things you hear, and have not heard them.

Do the Same for Others
Luke 10:25-37

25. A certain lawyer stood up and tested Jesus, saying, Teacher, what shall I do to inherit eternal life? 26. He answered, What is written in the text? How do you read it? 27. He answered, You shall love the Lord your God continually with your whole heart, and with your whole soul, and with your whole strength, and with your whole mind; and your neighbor as your own self. 28. Jesus said, That is correct: do this and you shall live. 29. And he, willing to justify himself, said to Jesus, And who is my neighbor? 30. And Jesus said, a man on his way to Jericho from Jerusalem fell among bandits, who took his cloths and beat him and left him half dead. 31. By chance a priest passed that way: and when he saw him passed by on the other side, 32, and by chance a Levite, came to the scene, looked and passed by on the other side. 33. But a Samaritan on his journey came and saw him and had compassion on him, 34. and went to him, dressed his wounds, using oil and wine and put him on his own donkey and took him to an inn and cared for him. 35. And when he departed the next day, he gave the innkeeper some money and said, Take care of him and if it cost more when I return I will pay. 36. Which of these three do you think was neighbor to the man who fell among bandits? 37. And he answered, The one who showed compassion. Then Jesus said, Go and do the same for others.

Mary Has Chosen the Good Part
Luke 10:38-42
38. On their way, Jesus entered a certain village: and a woman named Martha invited Him into her house. 39. And her sister was called, Mary, who also sat at Jesus' feet and heard His word. 40. But Martha was burdened with serving and came to Jesus and asked, Lord, do you not care that my sister has left all the serving to me alone? Tell her to help me. 41. And Jesus answered, Martha, Martha, you are anxious and burdened about many things: 42. but one thing is needful: and Mary has chosen the good part, and it will not be taken from her.

Because of Persistence He Will Rise
Luke 11:1-13
1. As Jesus ceased praying in a certain place, one of His disciples asked, Lord, teach us to pray, as John taught his disciples. 2. And Jesus said, When you pray say, Our Father, may your name be honored. Your reign begin, your will be done in Heaven and on earth. 3. Continue giving us daily the food we need. 4. And forgive our sins; for we too forgive all who are indebted to us. And keep us clear of temptation, and rescue us from evil. 5. And He said, Suppose one of you should go to a friend at midnight and say, Friend lend me three loaves; 6. for a visitor has come to my house from a distance, and I have no food to offer him. 7. And from within you hear, Trouble me not the door is shut and my children are in bed; I cannot give you anything. 8. Although he will not rise and give because of friendship, yet because of persistence he will rise and give as many loaves as he needs. 9. And Jesus said, Ask, and it will be given you; seek, and you will find; knock, and it will be opened to you. 10. For every asker receives, and every seeker finds; and to him who knocks the door will be opened. 11. If a son asks bread of his father, will he give him a stone? Or if he asks for a fish, will he give him a serpent? 12. Or if he asks for an egg, will he offer him a scorpion? 13. If you then, being human, provide good gifts for your children: how much more will your heavenly Father give the Holy Spirit to those who ask Him?

A Kingdom Divided
Luke 11:14-23
14. On an occasion Jesus cast out a dumb spirit, and when the demon was gone the man could speak, and the crowd marveled. 15. But some said, He caste out demons through Beelzebub the chief of evil spirits. 16. And others, testing Him, wanted a sign from heaven. 17. But Jesus, knowing their thoughts, said, A kingdom divided is brought to destruction; and a house divided falls. 18. If Satan also be divided, how shall his kingdom stand? Because you say that I cast out demons

through Beelzebub. 19. And if by Beelzebub I cast out demons, by whom do your sons cast them out? Let them be your judges. 20. But if by the hand of God I cast out demons, no doubt the kingdom of God is come to you. 21. When a strong man is armed and guards his homestead, his goods are safe: 22. But when a stronger one overpowers him, he takes all the weapons in which he trusted, and divides up the plunder. 23. He who is not with me is against me: and those who do not gather the sheep, scatters them.

Blessed are Those Who Hear the Word
Luke 11:24-32

24. When an unclean spirit is caste out, he searches for rest through dry places, finding none he says, I will return to the house I left. 25. And when he returns and finds the house clean and orderly. 26. He goes in and takes seven more wicked spirits and they enter and dwell there: and the last state of that man is worse than the first. 27. While He spoke, a woman in the crowd, with a loud voice said, Blessed is the Mother who birthed you and nursed you. 28. But Jesus said, Rather blessed are those who hear the word of God and behave it. 29. And as the people crowded together around Him, He said, This is an evil generation: they seek a sign: and no sign will be given, but the sign of Jonah the prophet. 30. For as Jonah was a sign to the people of Nineveh, so also the Son of Man shall be to this generation. 31. The Queen of the South shall stand in judgment and condemn the men of this generation: for she traveled a great distance to hear the wisdom of Solomon; and a greater than Solomon is here. 32. The men of Nineveh shall stand up in judgment and condemn this generation: for they repented at the preaching of Jonah: and a greater than Jonah is here.

So All May See the Light
Luke 11:33-44

33. No man who lights a lamp puts it in a closet, nor under a box, but on a lamp stand so all may see the light. 34. The lamp of the body is the eye: therefore when your eye is focused your whole body has light; but when your eye is morally bad, your body is full of darkness. 35. Take care that the reflected light in you does not come from moral darkness. 36. If you have light for the body with the absence of darkness, the whole shall be light, as when a candle shines brightly in the dark. 37. As He spoke, a Pharisee invited Him to dinner: and He went and sat down to eat. 38. And the Pharisee saw that He had not washed before dinner and was amazed. 39. And the Lord said, You Pharisees make clean the outside; but your inside is full of greed and malice. 40. Did not He who made the outside also make the inside?

41. But give alms to the poor and all things outside are clean to you. 42. A curse on you, Pharisees! For you tithe even your plants, but give no thought to justice and the love of God: this you should do and not leave the other undone. 43. A curse on you, Pharisees! For you love the best seats in the synagogues, and respectful greetings in the markets. 44. A curse on you scholars and Pharisees, insincere talkers! For you are as unmarked graves, and those who walk over them are not aware of their unconscious defilement.

You Took Away the Key
Luke 11:45-54

45. Then one of the lawyers said, Teacher, your words outrages even us. 46. And Jesus said, A curse on you lawyers also! For you load men down with intolerable burdens, but do not touch these burdens with one finger. 47. A curse on you! For you build tombs for the prophets, that your fathers killed 48. You bear true witness that you consent to the deeds of your fathers: they killed them, but you built their tombs. 49. Therefore in His wisdom God said, I will send them prophets and apostles, and some of them will be persecuted and killed. 50. The blood of all the prophets, killed from the foundation of the world, may be required of this generation; 51. From the blood of Abel to the blood of Zechariah, who perished between the altar and the sanctuary: in truth I say, it shall be required of this generation. 52. A curse on you lawyers! For you took away the key to the right interpretation of scripture, but entered not yourselves, and hindered those who were at the door. 53. As Jesus said these things, the scholars and the Pharisees became hostile and violently tried to provoke him to speak on other issues. 54. Seeking to seize something He would say that they might accuse Him.

Be Forewarned
Luke 12:1-5

1. Meanwhile as thousands gathered together and began to trample one another, Jesus spoke first to His disciples, Beware how the Pharisees reduce the importance of things by talking insincerely. 2. For there is nothing covered that will not be exposed; neither veiled, that will not be known. 3. Therefore whatever you speak in secret will be repeated openly; and that which you whisper behind closed doors will be proclaimed from the house tops. 4. As My friends, I tell you, Be not afraid of those who kill the body, and then can do no more. 5. But be forewarned whom you should fear: Fear Him, who after death has power to cast you into hell; Yes, I say, Fear Him.

You are Valuable
Luke 12:6-12

6. Are not five sparrows sold for a penny, and not one is forgotten by God? 7. Even the hairs of your head are all numbered. Fear not then: you are more valuable than many sparrows. 8. Also I say, whoever shall confess Me before men, him will the Son of Man confess before the angels of God: 9. but he who rejects Me before men shall be denied before the angels of God. 10. And whosoever speaks a word against the Son of Man, it shall be forgiven: but he who swears disrespectfully in word or action that insults the Holy Spirit it shall not be forgiven. 11. And when they bring you to trial in the synagogues, and before civil authorities, take no thought of what you will answer, or what you shall say: 12. for the Holy Spirit will teach you at the moment the words to say.

Be On Guard Against Greed
Luke 12:13-21

13. And one in the crowd said to Jesus, Teacher, speak to my brother, to give me my share of our inheritance. 14. And He said, Man, who made Me a judge or a divider of property? 15. He continued, Be on guard against greed: for a man's life is not based on wealth or possessions. 16. And He told a story about a rich farmer whose land produced plentifully: 17. and he debated with himself, saying, What shall I do, there is no room to store my harvest? 18. And he decided to demolish his barns and build larger ones; and there to store all his harvest. 19. And he said to his soul, Soul you have great wealth stored for many years: take it easy, eat, drink, and enjoy life. 20. But God said, You fool, this night you will die: then whose shall those things be, which you have stored? 21. So it is with those who store up wealth for themselves, and have not treasure with God.

Stop Worrying About Your Life
Luke 12:22-34

22. And Jesus said to His disciples, Therefore, I say to you, stop worrying about your life, what you will eat; neither about clothes for the body. 23. Life is more than food, and the body is more than clothing. 24. Consider the ravens: for they neither sow nor reap; they neither have storehouse nor barn; and God feeds them: how much more are you better than the ravens? 25. And which of you with taking thought can add a few moments to your life? 26. If you then be not able to do that thing which is least, why take thought for the rest? 27. Consider the lilies how they grow: they toil not, they spin not; and yet I say to you, that Solomon in all his glory was not robed as one of these. 28. If then God so dresses the grass, which is here today and gone

tomorrow, how much more will He dress you. Have a little more faith. 29. And seek not what you shall eat, or drink, neither be disturbed with cares. 30. For all these things do the nations of the world seek after: and your Father knows that you need these things, 31. but rather seek the kingdom of God and all these things shall be added to you. 32. Fear not, little flock; for it is your Father's good pleasure to give you the kingdom. 33. Keep your assets liquid and give alms; provide yourselves a purse that does not grow old, a treasure in the heavens that fails not, where no thief has access, neither moths can spoil. 34. For where your treasure is, there your heart will be also.

Be Ready When the Master Knocks
Luke 12:35-40

35. Make yourself ready, dressed, belt fastened and your lamps burning; 36. And behave as men who are waiting for their master to return from a marriage feast so they may immediately open the door when the master knocks. 37. Blessed are those servants whom the Lord will find watching for him, I assure you that he will tighten his belt and make his servants to set at table and he will serve them.* 38. And if he comes before or after midnight and finds them on watch, they are most fortunate of servants. 39. And know this, if the Goodman of the house had known the time the burglar was coming, he would have watched and not permitted his house to be ransacked. 40. Be you also ready for when you least expect, the Son of Man will appear.

---

*v37 The master serving the servants is a revolutionary idea.

Fortunate is the Servant
Luke 12:41-48

41. And Peter asked the Lord, are you addressing this parable to us or to everyone? 42. And the Lord answered, Who is that trusted manager with good sense whom his master put in control of his household to supply their food at the proper times? 43. Fortunate is the servant on his master's return that finds him faithful in the discharge of these duties. 44. A true saying, the master will put him in charge of the whole estate. 45. But if that servant says in his heart, my master is delayed in coming, and takes to bullying the other servants, and eats and drinks and becomes drunk; 46. that servant's master will return on a day when he expects nothing and will flog him severely and will cause him to share the lot of the untrustworthy. 47. And that servant that knows his master's plan, but does not get ready or act properly, will be flogged many times. 48. But he who knew not and did commit things worthy of flogging, will receive but few lashes. Everyone to whom

much is given, much is required; and of him to whom men commit much they will demand the more.

But Rather Division
Luke 12: 49-59

49. I came to set the world on fire; and I wish it were already started. 50. But I have an engagement and I am impatient until it is accomplished! 51. You suppose that I came to bring peace, I tell you, not so, but rather division: 52. henceforth, a family of five will be divided in one house, three against two, and two against three. 53. A father will decide one way about Me and the son another; the mother will be set against the daughter, and the daughter against the mother; and the mother-in-law will oppose the daughter-in-law, and the daughter-in-law will be at variance with the mother-in-law. 54. And He said also to the crowd, when you see a cloud rise in the west, at once you say, rain is coming. 55. And when the south wind blows, you say, it is going to be hot. 56. You talkers* can speak about the sky and the earth, but how is it you cannot interpret these time? 57. Does not your own experience teach you what is right? 58. When you are going with your opponent before a magistrate, in advance you make an effort to settle with him (out of court) lest you be dragged before the court and the judge puts you in jail. 59. You will find no dismissal and it will cost you every last fraction of a cent you possess.

---

*v56 The word is "hypocrites" and at first hypocrite meant answering or dialogue, then began to be connected with questions and answers in a play. From that the connection was made to acting a part. A hypocrite is always play-acting, often talking without knowledge or experience.

Ask Forgiveness or Perish
Luke 13:1-9

1. At this moment some came to tell Jesus about the Galileans, whose blood Pilate had mixed with the animal sacrifices. 2. And Jesus answered, Do you suppose these Galileans were sinners above all other Galileans, because they suffered this fate? 3. No, it was not so: but, if you do not ask forgiveness you will all perish the same way. 4. Or the eighteen men killed when the tower fell in Siloam, do you think they were sinners above all others in Jerusalem? 5. No, it was not so: but, if you do not ask forgiveness you will all perish. 6. And Jesus shared another story about a man who planted a fig tree in his vineyard; and he came in search of fruit and found none. 7. Then he said to his gardener, for three years I come seeking fruit of this fig tree and find none: cut it down; why should it just take up space? 8. And the gardener

answered, Lord, let it alone for a year and I will dig around it and fertilize it; 9. Then if there is no fruit, I will dig it up.

Is It Not Morally Right?
Luke 13:10-17
10. As Jesus was teaching in one of the synagogues on the Sabbath, 11. There was a woman suffering from rheumatism for eighteen years, who could not stand up straight. 12. When Jesus saw her, He called her to Him and said, Woman you are loosed from your illness. 13. And He laid hands on her: and she immediately stood up straight, and began glorifying God. 14. Because Jesus had healed on the Sabbath day, the head of the synagogue was angry and said to the crowd, There are six days for men to work; during these days come and be healed, but not on the Sabbath day. 15. The Lord answered, You idle talker, does not each one of you on the Sabbath loose his animals from the feeding stall and lead them to water? 16. And is it not morally right that this daughter of Abraham, whom Satan has bound for eighteen year, be released from her bonds on the Sabbath day? 17. Even as He spoke, His antagonists were full of embarrassment and all the people rejoiced for the wonderful things that were done.

Enter the Narrow Gate
Luke 13:18-24
18. Then Jesus said, What does the kingdom of God resemble? And to what shall I compare it? 19. It is similar to a mustard seed, that a man planted in his garden: and it grew into a tree; and the birds roosted on its branches. 20. Again He said, How will I examine the kingdom of God for similarities? 21. It is akin to yeast that a woman placed in three pounds of flour until it caused the whole batch to rise. 22. And Jesus went though towns and villages, teaching as He journeyed toward Jerusalem. 23. Then one asked, Lord, are there few that be saved? And He answered, 24. Struggle to enter the narrow door, for many will seek to find a way in and shall not find it.

Last Now, First Then
Luke 13:25-30
25. Once the head of the house has locked the door, and you stand outside and knock, saying, Lord, Lord, open to us; and he shall answer, I do not know you: 26. Then you will plead, we have eaten and drunk together and you have taught in our streets. 27. But he shall say, I do not know you; depart from me, all you workers of what ought not to be. 28. There shall be weeping and the grinding of teeth in pain and frustration, when you see Abraham, Isaac, Jacob, and all the prophets in the kingdom of God and you yourselves excluded. 29. And the people shall come from the east, west, north, and from the south,

and sit down in the kingdom of God. 30. Notice, some who are the last now will then be first. Take notice, some now last shall be first and some now first will be last.

Continue Your Journey
Luke 13:31-35

31. The same day certain Pharisees came saying, Get out and continue your journey: Herod intends to kill you. 32. And Jesus said, Go and tell that cunning fox, today, I cast out demons, and tomorrow I do cures, and the third day I will complete My task. 33. Nevertheless, I must travel the next three days: for a prophet should not meet His death except in Jerusalem. 34. Jerusalem, Jerusalem you still murder the prophets and stone the messengers sent to you; how often I desired to gathered your children together, as a hen does her clutch under her wings, and you would not! 35. Behold, your house is left unprotected: and truthfully I say, you shall not see Me until the day comes when you shall say, Blessed is He who comes in the name of the Lord.

You Shall Be Rewarded
Luke 14:1-14

1. When Jesus went to the house of the chief Pharisees to eat on the Sabbath, they were watching Him. 2. And before Him was a man afflicted with a swelling tumor. 3. And Jesus asked the lawyers and Pharisees, Is it lawful to heal on the Sabbath? 4. There was no reply. And He took hold of the man and cured him and sent him on his way; 5. to their unasked questions, Jesus said, Which of you having a son or an ox fall into a ditch, and would not hesitate to rescue him on the Sabbath? 6. And they were unable to reply to the question. 7. And He shared a story with the guests, when they were choosing the best seats; saying. 8. When you are invited to a wedding, sit not down in the best seat; lest a more honorable person be invited by the host; 9. and the host say to you, Give this man this seat; and you with embarrassment must take a humble seat. 10. But when you are invited, go and sit in a humble place; perhaps the host may say to you, Friend, take this better seat: then you will have respect in the presence of the other guests. 11. Because whoever elevates himself shall be lowered; and he who is unassuming shall be advanced in rank. 12. Then Jesus said to the host, When you have a special meal, do not invite your friends, nor your brethren, neither your kinfolk, nor your rich neighbors: lest they return the invitation, and repay your hospitality. 13. But rather invite, the poor, the crippled, and the blind: 14. and you will be blessed; for they cannot repay your hospitality and you shall be rewarded at the resurrection of the just.

There is Still Room
Luke 14:15-24

15. On hearing this, one of the guest at the table said, Blessed is he who shall eat bread in the kingdom of God. 16. Then Jesus said, A certain man planned a great dinner; and invited many: 17. and at the time of the dinner sent his servants to say to those invited, Come the dinner is ready. 18. And without exception they all declined. The first excuse was, I have bought a piece of ground and must go see it: 19. and another said, I purchased five teams of oxen and I am on my way to test them: I pray have me excused. 20. Another said, I was just married and cannot come. 21. So the servant returned and shared these things. Then the master of the house being angry said to the servant, Go out quickly to the streets and alleys of the town, and bring in the poor, the crippled, and the blind. 22. And the servant said, Lord it is done as you commanded, and there is still room for more. 23. And the master said, Go to the country lanes and the hedge-rows, and persuade them to come that My house may be filled. 24. For I say to you, not one of those invited shall taste of My dinner.

Listen to This
Luke 14:25-35

25. As great crowds followed Jesus, He turned and said, 26. Anyone who follows Me cannot be My disciple unless he loves Me more than his father and mother, wife and children, brothers and sisters, yes and his own life also. 27. And whoever does not bear his own cross and follow Me, cannot be My disciple. 28. For which of you, intending to build a lofty structure do not first estimate the cost to see if there are sufficient funds to complete the project? 29. Lest after you have made the foundation are unable to finish it, all those watching begin to ridicule him. 30. Saying, This man began to build and was unable to finish. 31. Or what king, marching to battle against another king, does not first consult whether his ten thousand men can overcome a larger force? 32. And if he decides he cannot win, before he approaches the enemy, he sends a delegation seeking conditions of peace. 33. Likewise, whoever of you that does not forsake all that he has, cannot be My disciple. 34. Salt is good, but if the salt has lost its strength; how shall you restore its taste? 35. It is neither good for the ground or the manure heap, it is simply thrown out. Let him who has ears listen to this.

Rejoice with Me
Luke 15:1-10

1. All the tax-collectors and those who habitually do wrong stood at the edge of the crowd to hear Jesus. 2. And the Pharisees and scholars

complained, saying, This man receives sinners and eats with them. 3. And Jesus told this story, saying, 4. What man of you with a hundred sheep, if he lost one, does not leave the ninety and nine in an uncultivated pasturage, and go after the lost one until he finds it? 5. And when it is found, he rejoices and places it on his shoulders. 6. And when he returns, he calls together his friends and neighbors, saying, Rejoice with me: for I have found my sheep which I lost. 7. Likewise there shall be joy in heaven over one sinner who repents, more than over ninety and nine just persons, who need no change of heart. 8. Either what woman having ten coins of silver, and loses one, does not light a lamp and clean the house, searching diligently until she finds it? 9. And when it is found she calls her friends and her neighbors together, saying, Rejoice with me: for I found the coin I lost. 10. Likewise, there is joy in the presence of the angels of God over one sinner whose heart is changed.

Squandered Inheritance
Luke 15:11-24

11. And Jesus said, a man who had two sons: 12. and the younger asked, Father, give me the share of the property that is mine. And he apportioned his means between the two. 13. And after a few days, the younger son converted all to cash and took his journey to a far country, and there he squandered his inheritance in wasteful living. 14. And when he had spent all, a famine struck that land; and he began to suffer hunger. 15. And he hired himself out to a citizen of that country; who sent him to the farm to feed pigs. 16. And he was eager to fill his belly with the bean-pods that the pigs were eating: and no one gave him anything. 17. And when he realized who he was, he said, How many hired servants in my father's house have bread enough and to spare, and I am starving to death! 18. I will get up and go to my father's house; and say to him, Father, I have sinned against heaven and before you, 19. And I am no more worthy to be called your son: make me one of your hired servants. 20. And he got up and went to his father, but when he was a long way off, his father saw him, and his heart was filled with compassion and he ran and hugged and kissed him. 21. And the son said, Father, I have sinned against God and in your sight, and am no more worthy to be called your son. 22. But his father interrupted and said to his servants, Put the best robe on him and put a ring on his hand, and sandals on his feet: 23. and kill the calf we are fattening: and let us eat and be merry. 24. For this my son I thought was dead is alive; he was lost, but is found. And they begin to celebrate.

All That I Have is Already Yours
Luke 15:25-32

25. Meanwhile the elder son was in the fields: and as he came near the house, he heard the music and dancing. 26. And he called one of the servants and inquired about the celebration. 27. And he said, Your brother has returned and your father killed the fatted calf, because he returned alive and well. 28. He became furious and would not go into the celebration: but his father came out and pleaded with him. 29. Then he answered his father, look at the many years I have served you and never disobeyed any of your instructions: and yet you never killed even a young goat for me that I might celebrate with my friends; 30. but when this one turned up, who wasted his inheritance with unworthy women, you killed the fatted calf. 31. And the father said, Son you have always been with me and all that I have is already yours. 32. It was proper that we celebrate and be glad, for your brother we thought was dead is alive; he was lost and is now found.

The False God of Wealth
Luke 16:1-13

1. And Jesus said to His disciples, The property manager of a certain rich man was accused of mismanagement. 2. And he was asked, What is this I am hearing about you? Give an account of your stewardship for you can no longer manage my property. 3. And the steward said to himself, What am I to do now that I have lost my position: I cannot dig ditches; and I am ashamed to beg. 4. I have a plan, when I am discharged, the debtors will welcome me into their homes. 5. So he called each of his master's debtors and asked the first, How much do you owe my master? 6. And he said, A hundred gallons of olive oil. And the steward said, quickly mark your bill down to fifty. 7. Then he asked another: How much do you owe? And he said, A hundred sacks of wheat. And he said, Take your bill and write eighty. 8. And the master complemented his level-headedness: for the businessmen of the world are wiser in dealing with others than those with spiritual insight. 9. And I say to you, Make friends for yourselves by the wise use of money, so when the money is gone your friends will receive you. 10. He who is faithful in small things is trustworthy in big things. 11. If you have not been faithful in the wealth of this world, who will trust you with true riches? 12. And if you have not been faithful with another man's wealth, who shall give you personal possessions? 13. No steward can serve two masters: he will hate one and love the other or attach himself to one and detest the other. You cannot serve both God and the false god of wealth.

God Knows Your Heart
Luke 16:14-18

14. And the covetous Pharisees heard all these things and ridiculed Him openly. 15. And Jesus said to them, You justify yourselves before men; but God knows your heart: for that which is highly regarded among men is disgusting in God's eyes. 16. The law and the prophets were in force until John came: since then the kingdom of God is proclaimed, and each one is urged to enter. 17. It is easier for heaven and earth to disappear, than for one mark in a word of the law that aids pronunciation to vanish. 18. An example under the law: He who puts away his wife and legally takes another, adulterates the marriage vows by adding another: and whoever takes the one that was put away legally adds another to adulterate their vows.

Lest They Come to This Place
Luke 16:19-31

19. There was a certain rich man who usually dressed in purple and fine linen, and feasted daily in luxury: 20. and a beggar named Lazarus, was laid at the rich man's gate, whose skin was full of boils. 21. Desiring to be fed with the crumbs from the rich man's table: only the dogs licked his sores to aid healing. 22. But the beggar died and was taken by angels to Abraham's bosom: the rich man died also, and was buried; 23. and from the habitation of the dead he saw Abraham at a distance and Lazarus in his arms. 24. And he cried, Father Abraham, have mercy on me and send Lazarus that he may dip his finger in water and cool my tongue; for I am in anguish here. 25. But Abraham said, Son, remember in your lifetime you received the good things, and likewise Lazarus the misfortunes of life: but now he is comforted and you are in anguish. 26. And beside this, between us there is a great fixed chasm: so that none who wish may pass either way. 27. Then the rich man said, I pray you, father, send Lazarus to my father's house: 28. for I have five brothers: that he may witness to them lest they come to this place of torment. 29. Abraham said, They have Moses and the prophets, let them hear them. 30. And he said, No father Abraham: but if one went from the dead they would repent. 31. And Abraham said, If they hear not Moses and the prophets, neither would they be persuaded though one stood up from the grave.

Unprofitable Servants
Luke 17:1-10

1. Then Jesus said to His disciples, Crimes against moral standards will come: but serious misfortune to him through whom these crimes come! 2. It would be better for him if dead weights were placed around his neck and he was thrown into the sea, than to hurt a single little one.

3. Give attention to yourselves: if your brother commits a moral or social injustice, reprimand him; and if he apologizes, forgive him. 4. And if he commits this injustice seven times in a day, and apologizes every time, you shall forgive him. 5. And His followers said, Lord, increase the substance of our faith. 6. And the Lord said, If you have faith the size of a grain of mustard seed, you may say to this mulberry tree, Pull yourself up by the roots and plant yourself in the sea; and it should obey you. 7. But which one of you having a servant plowing or herding the sheep, will say, When you come from the field, go and sit down at the table and eat? 8. Instead you say, Make ready my meal and gird yourself and serve me until I have finished, and then you may eat and drink. 9. When the servant is commanded, do you thank him? I think not. 10. So likewise when you have done all those things commanded of you, say, We are unprofitable servants: we have done that which was our duty.

Where Are the Nine?
Luke 17:11-19

11. In the course of going to Jerusalem Jesus passed through Samaria and Galilee. 12. At the entrance of a certain village, ten lepers met Him and stood at a distance: 13. And called to Him, Jesus, Master, have mercy on us. 14. And when He saw them, He said, Go show yourselves to the priests. And as they went, they were cured. 15. One of them, when he saw he was healed, turned back, and glorifying God with a loud voice, 16. and fell prostrate at his feet, giving Jesus thanks: and he was a Samaritan. 17. And Jesus asked, Were there not ten cleansed? But where are the nine?* 18. We find only this foreigner who returned to give glory to God. 19. And Jesus said, Arise, go your way, your faith has made you whole.

---

*v17 The nine were obeying Jesus and on their way to show themselves to the priests. Since the Samaritan was not allowed in the Temple, he returned to show his appreciation directly to Jesus. It appears that God works through the system, when the system works.

One Taken, the Other Left
Luke 17:20-37

20. When Jesus was questioned by the Pharisees as to when the kingdom of God should come, He answered, The kingdom of God is not observed by visible signs. 21. No one will say, here it is, there it is; because, the kingdom of God is within you. 22. Turning to His disciples, He said, The time will come when you shall desire to have a single day in the presence of the Son of Man, and you shall not have it. 23. Some will say, See here or see there: do not follow after them. 24. But as a lightning-flash shines from one end of the sky to the other; so

shall the Son of Man come in His day. 25. But first it is His destiny to undergo much suffering and rejection by this generation. 26. As it was since the days of Noah, so shall life be when the Son of Man comes. 27. People went on eating, drinking, taking and giving wives, until the day Noah entered in the ark, and the flood came and destroyed them all. 28. As it was in the days of Lot; they went on eating, drinking, buying and selling, planning and building; 29. but the same day that Lot left Sodom it rained fire and brimstone and destroyed them all. 30. It shall be the same in the day when the Son of Man is revealed. 31. In that day, if a man is on the housetop and his possessions in the house, he must not go down to save his stuff: and he that is in the field, let him not return to the house. 32. Remember Lot's wife. 33. Whoever seeks to save his life shall lose it; and whoever shall lose his life will safeguard it. 34. On that night, there will be two in one bed; the one taken, and the other left. 35. Two shall be grinding together; the one taken, and the other left. 36. Two in the field; the one taken, and the other left. 37. And they asked, Where, Lord? And he replied, Where the dead body is the vultures will gather.

Pray and Not be Faint-hearted
Luke 18:1-17

1. And Jesus told them a story to make it clear that men ought always to pray and not be faint-hearted; 2. saying, There was a city judge who feared not God, neither regarded man: 3. and a widow in the same city came to him, saying, Protect me from the man trying to destroy me. 4. And he would not for a while: but said although I fear not God, nor regard man; 5. yet because this widow aggravates me, I will avenge her, lest she weary me with her continual coming. 6. And the Lord, said, Hear what the unjust judge said. 7. And shall God not vindicate His own people, who cry day and night to Him, though He delays action? 8. I tell you that the Lord will avenge them speedily. When the Son of man comes will He find faith on the earth? 9. And Jesus told this story about some who trusted in themselves that they were righteous and detested others: 10. two men went to the temple to pray: a Pharisee and a tax-collector. 11. The Pharisee stood forward and began a self-centered prayer, God, I thank you, that I am not as other men, who steal, cheat, and violate marriage vows, or even as this tax-collector. 12. I fast two days a week and give tithes of all I possess. 13. And the tax-collector standing far back, would not lift his head or eyes toward heaven, but in despair smote his chest, saying, God be merciful to one who habitually does wrong. 14. I tell you, this man went home justified rather than the other: for every one who praises himself shall be cast down; and he who is modest and unassuming shall be praised. 15. And the people brought infants to Him that He would touch them: but

His disciples scolded them. 16. But Jesus called the children to Him, and said, Permit the children to come to Me, and do not hinder them: for of such is the kingdom of God. 17. Truly, I say, Whoever shall not welcome the kingdom of God as a little child shall in no wise enter therein.

One Thing You Lack
Luke 18:18-30

18. A man of the ruling class asked Jesus, saying, Good Teacher, what shall I do to inherit eternal life? 19. And Jesus answered, Why do you call Me good? No one is good, save God. 20. You know the commandments, Do not be unfaithful in marriage, Do not murder, Do not take what is not yours, Do not say anything false about others, Honor your father and your mother. 21. And he said, All these I have kept from my youth. 22. When Jesus heard this, He said, Yet one thing you lack: sell all your possessions, and distribute it among the poor, and you will have treasure in heaven: then return and follow Me. 23. And when he heard this, he was distressed: for he was a wealthy man. 24. When Jesus saw he was grief-stricken, He said, With great difficulty shall the wealthy enter the kingdom of God! 25. For it may be easier for a camel to squeeze through a surgical needle's eye, than for a wealthy man to enter the kIngdom of God. 26. And those who heard this asked, Who then can be saved? 27. And Jesus said, The things that are impossible with men are possible with God. 28. And Peter said, We have left all and followed you. 29. And Jesus said, Truly, I say, Those who left home, parents, brothers, spouse, or children, for the sake of the kingdom of God, 30. Will receive in this present time much more and in the world to come everlasting life.

Uttering His Testimony of God's Mercy
Luke 18:31-43

31. Then Jesus took the Twelve aside and said, Listen, we are now going up to Jerusalem, and everything written by the prophets concerning the Son of Man will be carried out. 32. For He will be delivered to the nations and ridiculed, insulted, and spit on: 33. and they will beat and put Him to death: and on the third day He will stand up again from the grave. 34. And they understood nothing of what He said because the meaning was concealed. 35. And as He came near to Jericho, a blind beggar sat by the road. 36. Hearing the crowd pass, he asked what was happening. 37. And they told him Jesus of Nazareth was passing by. 38. And he cried, Jesus, the Son of David, have mercy on me. 39. He was rebuked and told to be quiet: but he cried louder and louder, Son of David show mercy to me. 40. And Jesus stopped and commanded that the beggar be brought to Him; and when he was

near, Jesus asked, 41. What would you have Me do for you? And he said, Lord that I may see again. 42. And Jesus said, Receive your sight: your faith has cured you. 43. And instantly he could see and began following Jesus and giving God praise: and when the crowd became aware that he could see, they honored and magnified God.

And Welcomed Jesus Joyfully
Luke 19:1-10

1. As Jesus entered to pass through Jericho. 2. He saw the wealthy head of the tax-collectors, named Zaccheus. 3. Who was trying to see Jesus but could not for the crowd, because he was short in stature. 4. So he ran ahead and climbed into a mulberry tree to see Jesus as He passed. 5. When Jesus reached the tree He looked up and saw Zaccheus, calling his name said, climb down quickly, for I am going to your house today. 6. Hurriedly, he climbed down and welcomed Jesus joyfully. 7. When the crowd saw this, they murmured, He is going to be the guest of a man who habitually does wrong. 8. Stopping, Zaccheus said, Lord, the half of my goods I will give to the poor and if I have taken anything wrongly, I will restore four times the amount. 9. And Jesus said, This day has salvation come to this house, for he is a descendant of Abraham. 10. The Son of Man is here to search for and save the lost.

Do Business Until I Return
Luke 19:11-27

11. While these words were still on their mind, Jesus told a story because He was near to Jerusalem, and because they thought the kingdom of God would immediately appear. 12. Jesus said, A nobleman journeyed to a far place to obtain his kingdom and return. 13. He called ten servants and gave each about three month's wages, and said, Do business until I return. 14. But his subjects continued to detest him and sent delegates, saying, We will not accept this man to reign over us. 15. When he came back as king, he commanded those servants to whom he gave funds, to account for the profit each had gained trading. 16. The first came, saying, Lord the profit has been ten times. 17. And he said, Well done, my good servant: because you have been faithful in this small thing, you will have authority over ten cities. 18. The second one came, saying, My profit has been five times. 19. And he said likewise to him, you will have authority over five cities. 20. And another came, saying, Lord, here is the money you gave me, I have kept it safe in a napkin: 21. for I was afraid, because you are a stern man: you pick up what you never put down, and harvest what you did not sow. 22. And he said, Out of your own mouth you have judged yourself, you worthless servant, you knew I was a stern man, picking

up what I never put down and harvesting what I did not sow; 23. Why then did you not deposit my money into the bank that at my return I may receive back my money with interest? 24. And he said to those standing by, Take from him the money and give it to the servant who had the ten fold increase. 25. (And they said, Lord, he already has much money.) 26. For I say to you, that each one who has shall be given; and from him that has not, even what he has shall be taken away. 27. But bring my enemies, who would not accept my sovereignty; and slay them before me.

Wonderful Works They Witnessed
Luke 19:28-38

28. And when Jesus finished this story, He continued His journey up to Jerusalem. 29. When He almost reached Bethphage and Bethany, near the Mount of Olives, He sent two of His disciples, 30. saying, Go into the village and at the gate you will find a tethered colt, that no one has ridden, untie him and bring him to Me. 31. And if any man ask, Why do you untie that colt? Say, Because the Lord has need of him. 32. And they went and found even as Jesus had said. 33. And as they were releasing the colt, the owners asked, Why do you untie the colt? 34. And they said, The Lord has need of him. 35. And they brought the colt to Jesus: and put their garments on its back, and lifted Jesus onto the colt. 36. As He was going along, the people spread their clothes in the way. 37. And when they neared the slopes of the Mount of Olives, the whole crowd of followers began to rejoice and praise God with a loud voice for all the wonderful works they witnessed; 38. saying, Blessed be the King who comes in the name of the Lord: there is peace in heaven and glory in the highest.

Listening to Every Word
Luke 19:39-48

39. Some Pharisees in the crowd said to Jesus, Teacher, reprimand your disciples. 40. And He answered, I tell you, if these should hold their peace, the stones would cry out rejoicing. 41. And when He came near and beheld the city, He wept over it. 42. Saying, If you had known, at least on this your day, the things that belong to your peace! But now they are concealed from your eyes. 43. For the days will come that your enemies shall build siege-works about you, and surround you and hem you in on all sides, 44. And will level you to the ground, you and your children within the walls, and shall not leave one stone upon another; because you knew not the time of your visitation. 45. And He went into the temple and began casting out those who sold and bought; 46. saying, It is written My house is the house of prayer: but you have made it a den for bandits. 47. And He daily taught in the

temple. But the chief priests and the scholars, and the head of the people sought to destroy Him. 48. But they could not find a way to physically attack Him: because the people surrounded Him and were listening to every word He said.

Neither Will I Tell You
Luke 20:1-8

1. On one of the days that Jesus taught the people and preached in the Temple Courts, the ruling priests and the scholars confronted Him with the elders. 2. And asked, Tell us, by whose authority you do these things? Who gives you this authority? 3. And Jesus answered, I have one question for you. Give Me an answer: 4. The baptism of John, was it from heaven, or of men? 5. Discussing with one another, they reasoned, If we say, from heaven; He will say, Why then did you not believe him? 6. But if we say of men; the people will stone us; for they are persuaded that John was a prophet. 7. And they answered, that they did not know the origin of John's baptism. 8. And Jesus said, Neither will I tell you by what authority I do these things.

The Meaning of the Written Word
Luke 20:9-18

9. Then Jesus told a story about a certain man who planted a vineyard and leased it to vine-growers, and took a long journey to a far country. 10. And at harvest season he sent a servant to the vine-growers asking for a share of the fruit: but the vine-growers beat the servant and sent him away empty. 11. He sent another servant: and they beat him also, and spoke to him shamefully, and sent him away empty. 12. And he sent a third servant and they wounded him also, and threw him outside the vineyard. 13. Then the owner of the vineyard asked, What shall I do? I will send my beloved son: perhaps they will respect his appearance. 14. But when vine-growers saw him, they justified previous behavior, saying, This is the heir, let us kill him and the property will be ours. 15. So they threw him out of the vineyard and killed him. What therefore shall the owner of the vineyard do to those men? 16. He shall come and destroy these vine-growers, and permit others to work the vineyard. And when they heard it, they said, God forbid. 17. And Jesus looked them in the eye, and asked, What is the meaning of the written word? The stone that the builders cast away has become the main cornerstone? 18. Whoever falls on that stone shall be shattered; but on whomever it shall fall, it will grind him to dust.

Why Do You Tempt me?
Luke 20:19-26

19. And the high priests and the scholars immediately attempted to get their hands on Him; but they feared the people: for they realized the

story Jesus told was about them. 20. And they watched for an opportunity and sent spies, who presented themselves as honest men, that they might record His words and then deliver Him to the power and authority of the governor. 21. And these spies said, Teacher, we know that you teach what is right, and you never look at any man's position, but truly teach the way of God; 22. Is it lawful for us to give tribute to Caesar, or not? 23. Jesus perceived their cunning words, and asked, Why do you tempt Me? 24. Show Me a coin. Whose image does it have and what words are engraved on it? They answered, Caesar's. 25. And Jesus said, Render to the Emperor the things that are the Emperor's, and to God the things that are God's. 26. And they could not get a handle on His words to publicly use against Him: and they were amazed at His answer, and did not speak a word.

God of the Living
Luke 20:27-39

27. Then came some of the Sadducees, who deny the resurrection; and they asked Jesus. 28. Saying, Teacher, Moses wrote, If a man's married brother die without children, that his brother should take his wife and raise up a family for his brother. 29. There were seven brothers: and the first took a wife and died without children. 30. And the second took her to wife and died childless. 31. And the third took her and in like manner the seven took her to wife and left no children. At last the woman died. 33. At the resurrection whose wife of these brothers will she be? For seven had her to wife. 34. And Jesus answered, The children of this world marry and are given in marriage: 35. But they who are counted worthy of reaching the other world by standing up from the grave, neither marry, nor are given in marriage: 36. Neither can they die any more: in this respect they are as the angels; and are the children of God, being the children of the resurrection. 37. Now that the dead stand up again, even Moses showed at the bush, when he called the Lord, the God of Abraham, Isaac, and Jacob. 38. For He is God of the living and not the dead: and from His perspective all men are alive. 39. Then some of the scholars said, Teacher, you have spoken well.

Be on Guard
Luke 20:40-47

40. After that they dared not ask Him any questions. 41. And Jesus said, How say the people that Messiah is David's son? 42. And David himself wrote in the Book of Psalms, The Lord said to my Lord, Sit on my right hand, 43. until I put your enemies under your feet. 44. Since David called Him Lord, how is He then His son? 45. Then in the hearing of all the people Jesus said to His disciples, 46. Be on

guard against the scholars of the law, who desire to walk in long robes and love greetings in the marketplace, and want the best seats in the synagogues, and the places of honor at feasts; 47. who sell widow's houses, and still make long prayers for show: these shall receive greater condemnation and eternal punishment.

Do Not Panic
Luke 21:1-19

1. And Jesus observed the rich men placing their gifts into the treasury. 2. Also He saw a poor widow putting in two small coins. 3. And said, Truly this poor widow has given more that everyone: 4. for the wealthy gave out of their abundance: but she out of her scarcity has put in her whole living. 5. When some spoke of the temple being embellished with beautiful stones and dedicated gifts, He said, 6. The day will come when all these things shall be thrown down and you will see not one stone left on another. 7. And they asked, Teacher, when will this happen? And what sign will be given when these things are near? 8. And Jesus said, Be careful that you are not deceived: for many will come in My name, saying, I am Christ; then the time is near: do not follow them. 9. But when you hear of wars and disturbances, do not panic: for these things must happen first; but the end is not near. 10. Jesus continued, Nation shall rise against nation and kingdom will war against kingdom: 11. enormous earthquakes, widespread famine and deadly disease in various places; dreadful things will be imagined and horrifying signs in the heavens. 12. But before these things, men will arrest you, bring you before kings and rulers of the synagogues and deliver you to prisons, because you bear My name. 13. This will bring you an opportunity to witness. 14. Resolve in your hearts not to ponder what your defense will be: 15. I will give you wisdom to withstand your enemies and they cannot contradict nor refuse to accept your words. 16. But you will be betrayed by parents, brothers, kinfolk, and friends; and some of you will be put to death. 17. And you will be despised by all men because you bear My name. 18. But not a hair of your head shall perish. 19. And your enduring patience shall gain souls.

Panic for Anticipated Horror
Luke 21:20-27

20. When you see Jerusalem surrounded with armies, know that her destruction is near. 21. Then those in Judaea must flee to the hills; those who live in the city must leave; and those outside must not attempt to enter the city. 22. For those are the vengeful days of God, that all things written may be fulfilled. 23. But in those days, there will be anguish for those with children, and despair for those with infants, for there shall be great suffering in the land, and deep-seated anger

against the people. 24. And the citizens shall fall at the point of the sword, and be led away captive into pagan lands: and Jerusalem shall be insulted by hostile pagans, until their dominion shall end. 25. And there shall be mysterious indications in the sun, moon, and stars: and on earth the nations shall feel hopelessness and bewilderment by the roaring of the sea; 26. men's hearts will panic for the anticipated horror coming on the earth: and the heavens shall be powerfully shaken. 27. And then shall they see the Son of Man coming with full power and magnificence.

Keep Watch on Yourselves
Luke 21:28-38
28. When these events begin to happen, stand straight and look up, your deliverance is near. 29. And Jesus told this story; Always notice the trees; 30. When the leaves begin to grow, you know that summer is near. 31. Likewise when you see these things happening, know that the kingdom of God is near. 32. Truly, I say, this generation shall not pass away, until all this happens. 33. Heaven and earth shall come to an end: but My words by no means shall pass away. 34. Keep watch on yourselves, for fear that your hearts become weighted down with intoxication and nausea and the self-indulgence of life, so that day catches you suddenly and unprepared. 35. For as the sudden springing of a trap that time shall come on the whole world. 36. Guard against evil and pray always, that you may be reported worthy to avoid all these things that will happen, and have the moral strength to stand before the Son of Man. 37. During the day He taught in the temple; and at night He rested in the Mount of Olives. 38. And it was customary for the people to come early in the morning to the temple to hear Him.

Jesus Took His Place
Luke 22:1-14
1. And the feast using unleavened bread, called the Passover, was near. 2. And the high priests and scholars were seeking ways to kill Jesus; for they feared the people. 3. Then Satan found a way into Judas Iscariot, one of the Twelve. 4. And he went and discussed a scheme with the high priests and temple police, how he might betray Jesus. 5. Delighted, they agreed to give him money. 6. And he openly pledged to betray Jesus and searched for an opportunity apart from the crowd. 7. Then came the feast day, when the Passover lamb must be killed. 8. And Jesus sent Peter and John, saying, Go and prepare the Passover meal that we may eat. 9. And they said, Where shall we prepare? 10. And Jesus said, As you enter the city, you will meet a man, carrying a pitcher of water; follow him into the house he enters.

11. And say to the head of the house, The Master asks, Where is your guest room where Me and My disciples may eat the Passover meal? 12. And he will show you a large upper room with carpets and dining couches with cushions: there make ready. 13. They found everything as Jesus had said: and they made ready the Passover meal. 14. And at the time of evening meal, Jesus took His place, and the twelve apostles sat down with Him.

This Do for My Memorial
Luke 22:15-27

15. And Jesus said, With earnest longing I have desired to eat this Passover meal with you before I suffer: 16. I will not eat this meal again until it is completely fulfilled in the kingdom of God. 17. And He received a cup and gave thanks, saying, Take this and share it among yourselves: 18. for I will not drink of the fruit of the vine until the kingdom of God shall come. 19. And taking a loaf, He gave thanks, and broke it apart, and gave to them, saying, this is My body given for you: this do for My memorial. 20. Likewise, also the cup after eating, saying, This cup is the new covenant in My blood, shed for you. 21. Be warned, the hand of him who betrays Me is with Me at the table. 22. And truly the Son of Man goes freely, as was determined: but anguish and despair to the man by whom He is betrayed! 23. And they debated among themselves, who it was that should do this deed. 24. And there was also a conflict among them as to who would be counted the greatest. 25. And Jesus said, The kings of the nations exercise authority over the people and they are called benefactors. 26. But with you it will not be so: he who is greatest among you, let him become as the younger; and the elder, as he who serves. 27. For who is greater, he who eats, or he who serves? Is not he who eats? But I am among you as He who serves.

I Have Prayed for You
Luke 22:28-38

28. You are the men who continued with Me during My trials. 29. And I distribute to you authority, as the Father appointed to Me a kingdom. 30. That you may eat and drink at My table in My kingdom, and sit in authority judging the twelve tribes of Israel. 31. And the Lord said, Simon, Simon, watch out, Satan has desired to have you that he may sift you as wheat: 32. But I have prayed for you, that your faith fail not: and when you return to Me, strengthen your brethren. 33. And Peter said, Lord, I am ready to go with you, both to prison and to death. 34. And Jesus said, I tell you, Peter, before the cock crows this day, you will three times deny that you know Me. 35. And Jesus said, When I sent you without purse, satchel or sandals, lacked you anything? And

they answered, Nothing. 36. Then Jesus said, But now, he who has a purse, let him take it, and likewise his money: and he who has no sword, let him sell his cloak and buy a sword. 37. Believe Me, all that was written about Me must be fulfilled, And He was counted among the transgressors; for the things concerning Me will be accomplished. 38. And they said, Lord we have two swords. And Jesus said, It is enough.

Why Do You Sleep?
Luke 22:39-53

39. Leaving the city, as His habit was, Jesus went to the Mount of Olives; and His disciples followed. 40. When He arrived at His usual place, He said to them, Continue to pray that you enter not into temptation. 41. Then He went about a stone's throw from them, and knelt down and prayed, 42. Saying, Father, if it pleases you spare Me this cup: nevertheless not My will, but your will be done. 43. An angel appeared from heaven and strengthened Him. 44. And being anguished He prayed more earnestly: and His sweat became thickened and appeared as drops of blood falling to the ground. 45. And when He ceased praying, He found His disciples overwhelmed with anguish, but sleeping, 46. And Jesus asked, Why do you sleep? Rise and pray, so you may not be subject to temptation. 47. While He was speaking, a crowd gathered including Judas, one of the Twelve, who was in front and he walked close and kissed Jesus. 48. Jesus said, Judas, Do you betray the Son of Man with a kiss? 49. When His supporters saw what was happening, they asked, Lord, shall we fight with the sword? 50. And one of them sliced off the right ear of the servant of the high priest. 51. Stop, I permit no more of this, and He touched the servant's ear and healed it. 52. Then Jesus spoke to the high priests, the temple guards, and the elders, Do you come after Me as against a thief with swords and clubs? 53. Daily I was with you in the temple and you stretched forth no hands against Me: but you chose the hour of darkness as your time to act.

And Peter Remembered
Luke 22: 54-62

54. Then they seized Him and marched Him off to the high priest's house. And Peter followed afar off. 55. And when they had lit a fire in the middle of the courtyard, they all set down together, Peter sat down with them. 56. But a servant girl saw him from the light of the fire, and looking at him, said, This man was with Him. 57. And Peter denied her statement, saying, Woman, I do not know Him. 58. Later another saw him, and said, You are one of them, too. And Peter said, Man, I am not. 59. After about an hour another boldly affirmed, saying, Truly this

man was with Him: for he is a Galilean. 60. And Peter said, Man, I do not know what you are saying. And immediately, there was a loud cry of a rooster. 61. And the Lord turned and looked straight at Peter. And Peter remembered the word of the Lord, Before the rooster crows, you will deny Me three times. 62. And Peter left the group, and burst into tears of sorrow.

Are You the Christ?
Luke 22:63-71

63. And the men who held Jesus flogged and made fun of Him. 64. And after blindfolding Him, they hit His face with a hard blow, and asked, Now, prophet, can you tell us who hit you? 65. And they spoke many other disrespectful things against Him. 66. At dawn, the council of elders and the high priests and scholars came together, and brought Jesus into the court chamber, saying, 67. Tell us. Are you the Christ? And Jesus said, You will not believe, if I tell you: 68. and you will not answer My question, nor will you let Me go. 69. From this time forward, the Son of Man shall sit on the right hand of God in power. 70. Then they asked, Are you then the Son of God? And Jesus said, You say that I am. 71. And they said, Do we need further witness? We have heard this ourselves from His own mouth.

I Find No Fault in This Man
Luke 23:1-12

1. The whole council arose and led Jesus to Pilate. 2. And began to accuse Him, saying, We found this man teaching sedition and telling the people it was wrong to pay tribute to Caesar, saying that He Himself is Christ, a King. 3. Pilate asked, Are you King of the Jews? And He answered, You said it. 4. Then Pilate said to the high priests and to the people, I find no fault in this man. 5. And they became more spiteful, saying, He stirs up the people, teaching throughout all Jewry, beginning in Galilee to this place. 6. When Pilate heard the word Galilee, he asked if the man were a Galilean. 7. As soon as he understood that he belonged under Herod's jurisdiction, he sent Him to Herod, who was himself in Jerusalem at the time. 8. Herod seemed delighted to see Jesus, he had desired to see Him for a long time because of the many things he heard of Him; and he hoped to see Him perform some miracle. 9. Herod asked Jesus many questions; but He answered nothing. 10. And the high priest and scholars stood making relentless accusations against Jesus. 11. And Herod and his guards made light of Him and mocked Him, and dressed Him in an elegant robe and sent Him again to Pilate. 12. That same day Pilate and Herod made a friendship: before this there was hostility between them.

Herod Found Nothing Worthy of Death
Luke 23:13-25

13. Pilate called the high priests, and the leaders of the people together, 14. and said, You brought this man to me, as one who perverts the people: and I examined Him before you and found no fault touching those accusations: 15. No, nor yet Herod: for I sent you to him; and he found nothing worthy of death was done by Him. 16. I will flog Him and release Him. 17. (It was required for Pilate to release one at the feast.) 18. And they cried as a single voice, Away with this man, and release Barabbas: 19. (Who was in prison for treason and murder.) 20. Pilate willing to release Jesus spoke again to the crowd. 21. But they shouted, Crucify Him, crucify Him. 22. And Pilate said the third time, Why, what evil has He done? I have found no cause for death: I will punish Him and let Him go. 23. But they continued to shout him down, requiring that He be crucified. And the shouts of the people and the high priests prevailed. 24. And Pilate pronounced the official sentence that they required. 25. And he released to them the one guilty of treason and murder; but delivered Jesus to their will.

An African From Cyrene
Luke 23:26-34

26. As they led Jesus away to be crucified, they required one coming out of the country, Simon, an African from Cyrene, to carry the cross behind Jesus. 27. And a great company followed with women, who grieved and wept. 28. Jesus turned and said, Daughters of Jerusalem, weep not for Me, but for yourselves, and your children. 29. For the days are coming when they shall say, Blessed are infertile women and the wombs that never bore children, and the breast that never nursed an infant. 30. They shall call to the mountains, Hide us. 31. For if they do these things to a green tree [*the innocent*] what shall be done to the guilty? 32. And there were two wrongdoers taken away to be crucified also. 33. Arriving at the place called Calvary, there they crucified Jesus and the wrongdoers, one on the right hand, and the other on the left. 34. Then Jesus said, Father, forgive them for they do not understand what they are doing. And they divided His clothing and gambled for the pieces by casting pebbles or sticks.

Lord, Remember Me
Luke 23:35-43

35. The people stood gazing. As the leaders derided Him, saying, He saved others; let Him save Himself, if He be Christ, the chosen of God. 36. And the soldiers mocked Him and offered Him sour wine, 37. saying, If you are the king of the Jews, save yourself. 38. And to slander Him they wrote above the cross in Greek, Latin, and Hebrew,

THIS IS THE KING OF THE JEWS. 39. One of the crucified wrongdoers began to behave in an irresponsible way, saying, If you are Christ, save yourself and us. 40. But the other scolded him, saying, Do you not fear God, seeing you are under a guilty verdict? 41. And we indeed receive just punishment for our deeds: but this man has done nothing wrong. 42. And he said to Jesus, Lord, remember me when you come into your kingdom. 43. And Jesus answered, Truly I say, Today you will be with Me in paradise.

Joseph Took Jesus Down From the Cross
Luke 23:44-56

44. About mid-day, darkness came over all the earth until three in the afternoon. 45. The sun was darkened and the veil of the temple split in the middle. 46. Then Jesus cried with a loud voice, Father, into your hands I commit My spirit: and He breathed out His last breath. 47. When the Roman Centurion saw what happened, he glorified God, saying, Certainly, this was a righteous man. 48. And the crowd that came together to witness the spectacle, seeing the phenomenon they were disturbed and beat their breasts and returned to the city. 49. And all His friends and colleagues with the women who followed Him from Galilee, stood at a distance, watching all that happened. 50. Present was a man named Joseph, a member of the council, who was a good and upright person: 51. (Joseph had not consented to the deeds and action of the council;) he was from Arimathaea, a city of the Jews: who also patiently waited for the kingdom of God. 52. He went to Pilate and requested the body of Jesus. 53. And Joseph took Jesus down from the cross, wrapped His body in linen, and placed it in a new tomb carved in stone. 54. That was the day of preparation for the Sabbath was near. 55. The women who came from Galilee followed and saw the tomb, and how His body was placed. 56. And they returned and prepared spices and ointments: and then rested on the Sabbath day according to the commandment.

He Said This Would Happen
Luke 24:1-12

1. At first light on the first day of the week, the women and some others came to the tomb, bringing prepared spices. 2. And found the stone from the tomb rolled away. 3. They entered the tomb but did not find the body of the Lord Jesus. 4. As they were mystified about the body, there stood by them two men in bright clothing: 5. they were afraid and lowered their eyes to the ground, then the men said, Why seek you the living among the dead? 6. He is not here, but is risen: remember, He said this would happen when He was still in Galilee. 7. Saying, The Son of Man must be handed over to wicked men and be crucified, and

the third day stand up again. 8. And they remembered His words. 9. And returned from the tomb and told these things to the eleven and to all the others. 10. It was Mary Magdalene, Joanna, and Mary, the mother of James, and other women that were with them, who told these things to the apostles. 11. And the Apostles did not believer their words for they seemed to be nonsense. 12. Then Peter got up and ran to the tomb: and stooping down, saw that the linen clothes placed separately and he departed wondering what had happened.

But They Did Not See Jesus
Luke 24:13-24

13. That same day, two of His disciples went to the village Emmaus, about seven miles from Jerusalem. 14. Their conversation was about all the things that had happened. 15. While they were discussing the whole matter, Jesus Himself overtook them and walked beside them. 16. For some reason their eyes did not recognize Him. 17. And Jesus asked, What are you talking about as you walk that makes you so sad? 18. Cleopas answered, Are you a stranger in Jerusalem, and do not know the things that happened in the past few days? 19. He asked, What things? They answered, Concerning Jesus of Nazareth, who was a mighty prophet in word and deed before God and all the people: 20. and how the high priests and our leaders delivered Him to be sentenced to death and be crucified. 21. We had confidence that He was the one who would redeem Israel: and three days have passed since this happened. 22. And certain women of our group, went early to the tomb, and disturbed us with their news; 23. they did not find the body of Jesus and also said they saw a vision of angels, who told them He was alive. 24. And some who were with us went to the tomb and found it just as the women had said: but they did not see Jesus.

Jesus Explained the Sacred Writing
Luke 24:25-35

25. Then Jesus said, You are foolish and slow of heart to trust what the prophets said: 26. Was not the Messiah to suffer such things, and then enter His glory? 27. Then starting with Moses and through all the prophets, Jesus explained the scared writings concerning Himself. 28. As they reached the village of Emmaus, He pretended to go further. 29. But they pressured Him, saying, Stay with us: it is late and evening is near. And He went in to wait expectantly for something to happen. 30. And as He sat down to enjoy a meal, He took the bread and blessed it, and broke it, and gave to them. 31. And their eyes were opened, and they recognized Him; and He disappeared suddenly from their sight. 32. And they said to each other, Did not our heart burn

within us, while He talked with us on the road, and as He explained the scriptures? 33. And immediately they returned to Jerusalem, and found the eleven and some friends gathered together, 34. saying, The Lord has certainly risen, and appeared to Simon. 35. And the two began to relate what happened on the road to Emmaus, and how He was recognized when He broke bread with them.

You Must Wait Expectantly
Luke 24:36-49

36. As they were telling what happened, Jesus stood among them.* 37. And they were alarmed and overwhelmed with sudden fear, and thought they had seen Christ's spirit. 38. And Jesus asked, Why are you troubled? And why do doubts arise in your hearts? 39. Look at My hands and My feet, it is I Myself: touch Me, and know; for a spirit does not have flesh and bones, as you now see. 40. After He had spoken, He showed them His hands and feet. 41. And while they still could not believe for sheer excitement and astonishment, He asked, Have you anything to eat? 42. And they gave Him a piece of broiled fish and a honeycomb. 43. He took it and did eat before them. 44. And said, Present with you I said, that all things must be fulfilled that was written in the Law of Moses and the prophets, and the psalms, concerning Me. 45. Then He opened their understanding, that they might grasp the meaning of the scriptures. 46. And said, Scripture clearly says that Messiah should suffer, and stand up from the grave the third day: 47. and that repentance and forgiveness of sins should be proclaimed in His name among all nations, starting at Jerusalem. 48. And you are witnesses of these things. 49. And, behold, I send the promise of My Father: but you must wait expectantly in Jerusalem, until you be clothed with ability and heavenly strength.

---

*v36 The words "Peace be unto you" are omitted by the best texts.

Spiritual Delight
Luke 24:50-53

50. And Jesus took them out as far as Bethany, and lifted up His hands, and blessed them. 51. And as He blessed them, He ascended from them.* 52. And they recognized His divine nature and engaged in prayer and devotion, returning to Jerusalem with spiritual delight: 53. and continued praising and blessing God in the temple. Amen.

---

*v51 The best texts omit "and carried up into heaven."

The Acts Of The Apostles

The book of Acts is considered primarily a historical document, but it is much more. Acts provided an account of events that took place in the lives of early followers of the Resurrected Lord, including the beginnings of what was later called the church. The power of the Spirit was displayed in the daily lives of Christians, the persecution of early believers was documented, leadership, conversions, ministry and spiritual development were recorded. The Acts became an inspiration to followers of Christ as believers witnessed the acts of the Holy Spirit through dedicated and committed followers of Jesus, the Christ. The Resurrection of Jesus initiated Christianity fifty-days before Pentecost, the historic date for establishing the church. Later these followers of Jesus assembled in groups for protection and worship and the emphasis soon became an effort to build a "place" rather than developing people with a Christian lifestyle. *

More on this subject in Tear Down These Walls --Beyond Freeze Frame Thinking and Name Brand Religion. ISBN 978-1-935434-18-4 GlobalEdAdvancePRESS (2013).

The second volume of Luke's writing, the Book of Acts, documented the universal growth of pristine Christianity and became a defense of Christianity to Roman authorities by demonstrating the law-abiding character of Christian followers. The strong research skills of Luke produced a comparison of Peter and Paul. The first half was all about the Apostle to the Jews, Peter; the second half was about Paul, the Apostle to the Gentiles. Since Luke's record was closed in AD 64 there was no record of the martyrdom of either Peter or Paul (in Rome about three years later) at the hands of the Roman Emperor Nero.

The Acts of the Holy Spirit through the early messengers of Jesus does not have a close; it is assumed that all believers and each local congregation are to continue writing the history of God working through individuals enabled by the Spirit. The big question: what has God done in your life or place of worship lately worthy of recording in such a book? {See the Notes at the end of Acts)

Many Foolproof Manifestations
Acts 1:1-5

1. Beloved, Theophilus, the subject of my previous discourse was all that Jesus both began to do and teach, 2. until the day of His ascension, after that He gave instructions through the Holy Spirit to His chosen apostles: 3. To whom He presented Himself alive after His death by many foolproof manifestations, appearing over a space of forty days, and speaking of the things concerning the kingdom of God: 4. being assembled together with them, instructed them not to depart from Jerusalem, but wait expectantly for the fulfillment of the Father's promise, the assurance you heard from Me. 5. Truly John immersed in water, but you shall be immersed with the Holy Spirit in a few days.

Be My Witnesses Unto the Death
Acts 1:6-11
6. On one occasion the apostles asked Him, Lord will you now restore the kingdom to Israel? 7. He answered, It is not for you to know the period of time or the specific season, that is only in the Father's authority. 8. But you shall receive miraculous ability and strength, after the Holy Spirit is come upon you: and you shall be My witnesses unto the death both in Jerusalem, and in all Judaea, and in Samaria, and continually into the farthest part of the earth. 9. As soon as He spoke these things, He was lifted up; and a cloud closed under Him to block their sight. 10. As they looked determinedly toward heaven He disappeared, suddenly two men in white garments stood by them; 11. Who said, Men of Galilee, why do you stand looking into the sky? The same Jesus, you saw lifted up, shall return in the same way as you saw Him go back to heaven.

One of Our Number
Acts 1:12-17
12. Then they returned to Jerusalem from the Olive Orchard, which is a Sabbath day's journey. 13. As they entered the city they went up to an upstairs room, where they were staying together with Peter, James, and John, Andrew, Philip, and Thomas; Bartholomew and Matthew, James, the son of Alphaeus and Simon the Zealot, and Judas the brother of James. 14. All these agreed together constantly in prayer with the women, and Mary, the mother of Jesus and His brothers. 15. In those days Peter stood up in a gathering of brethren to speak (the gathering was about 120 persons all together,) and Peter said, 16. Brothers, the sacred writings had to be fulfilled which the Holy Spirit by the mouth of David spoke concerning Judas, who guided those who arrested Jesus. 17. For he was one of our number and part of this ministry.

By Transgression Turned Aside
Acts 1:18-26
18. Judas, had purchased a field for himself with his unrighteous reward; then fell headfirst, and his internal organs were violently disgorged. 19. Everyone in Jerusalem heard about his death and the place became known as Aceldama, meaning field of blood in Aramaic. 20. It was written in the Book of Psalms, Let his dwelling place be deserted with no habitation, and his office and responsibility given to another. 21. It is appropriate for one of the men who accompanied us all the time of our unhindered association with the Lord Jesus, 22. From His baptism by John, to the day He was taken away from us, must be proclaimed publicly to be a witness with us of His standing up

again from the grave. 23. And they named two men, Joseph, called Barsabas, surnamed Justus, and Matthias. 24. And they prayed, Lord, you know the hearts of all men, urgently show us which of these two you have chosen, 25. That He may take part of this ministry and mission deputation, from which Judas by transgression turned aside, that he might go to his own place. 26. And they drew lots; and the choice was Matthias; and he was counted with the eleven apostles.

Full of New Wine
Acts 2:1-13

1. When the Jewish Harvest Festival was completed, they were all together in agreement in one place. 2. Suddenly there came a sound carried by a violent wind from the heavens, and the roar completely filled up the house where they were gathered. 3. There appeared divided flames of fire that rested on each of them. 4. And they were all endowed with power* of the Holy Spirit and began to speak as the Spirit gave them ability to articulate an unnaturally acquired language. 5. And there were present in Jerusalem, pious Jews from every part of the known world. 6. When the noise was heard, an amazed throng gathered and every man heard them speak in his own language. 7. In their astonishment they speculated, saying one to another, Behold, are not all these who speak Galileans? 8. How does everyone hear in their native language? 9. Parthians, and Medes, and Elamites, and those living in Mesopotamia, and in Judaea, and Cappadocia, in Pontus, and Asia, 10. Phrygia, and Pamphylia, in Egypt, and in the parts of Libya about Cyrene, and visitors from Rome, Jews and new converts to our faith, 11. Cretes and Arabians, we hear them speaking in our native language the wonderful works of God. 12. And they were all amazed, and bewildered, saying one to another, What does this mean? 13. Others mocking said, These men are full of new wine.

---

*v4 See Luke 24:49, Acts 1:8, 4:31; 11:15-17; Ephesians 5:18

Listen Carefully to My Words
Acts 2:14-24

14. Then Peter, speaking for the eleven, addressed the crowd with a loud voice, and said, You men of Judaea, and all living in Jerusalem, let me explain this to you, and listen carefully to my words. 15. It is wrong to assume these men are drunk, since it is only nine in the morning. 16. But this is what was prophesied by Joel; 17. When the last days come, I will pour out a portion of my Spirit on mankind: your sons and daughters shall speak forth divine truths, and your young men shall see visions of prophetic significance, and your old men shall experience vivid images of hoped for things even sleeping: 18. and

on your believing servants will I pour out of my Spirit, and they shall speak forth under inspiration: 19. And I will show awesome sights in the heavens, and indications of tribulations on earth: blood, fire and clouds of smoke: 20. The sun shall become dark, and the moon turned as red as blood, before that great and memorable day of the Lord comes: 21. in those days, whoever calls on the name of the Lord shall be saved. 22. Men of Israel listen to my words; Jesus of Nazareth, a man endorsed by God through miracles, wonders, and signs, that you personally witnessed: 23. being delivered by determinate counsel and foreknowledge of God, you took Him, and by wicked hands brutally killed by crucifixion: 24. whom God stood up from the grave, having loosed the agony of death: because it was not possible for death to hold Him.

The Promise of the Holy Spirit
Acts 2:25-36

25. David spoke concerning Jesus. I saw the Lord always before my eyes, on my right hand, that I should not be alarmed: 26. therefore my heart rejoiced, and my tongue was joyful: also my body shall rest in hope: 27. because you will not leave my spirit in the place of departed souls, neither will you permit your Holy One to see decay. 28. You have shown me the path of life: you shall make me full of joy in your presence. 29. Men and brethren, let me speak freely about the patriarch David, who is both dead and buried, and his tomb is still with us. 30. Being a prophet and knowing what God had sworn with an oath to Him; 31. saw this before, and spoke of the resurrection of Christ and that His body would not decay. 32. This Jesus has God stood up from the grave, and we are all witnesses. 33. Therefore being exalted at the right hand of God, and having received of the Father the promise of the Holy Spirit, has dispersed this that you see and hear. 34. David never ascended into the heavens: but he said himself, The Lord said to my Lord, Sit on my right hand. 35. Until I put your enemies under your feet. 36. Therefore let all Israel know assuredly, that God has made that same Jesus, whom you crucified, both Lord and Christ.

The Lord Added to the Church
Acts 2:37-46

37. Now when they heard this, they were stabbed in the heart, and said to Peter and to the rest of the apostles, Men and brethren, what shall we do? 38. Then Peter said, Everyone must repent for the forgiveness of sins and be baptized in the name of Jesus Christ, and also you shall receive the gift of the Holy Spirit. 39. Because the promise is to you, and your children, and to all those in distant places, even as many as the Lord our God shall call. 40. And with many other

words did he testify and exhort, saying, Rescue yourselves from this troublesome generation. 41. Those who willingly received his word, were baptized: and the same day about three thousand souls were added to the believers. 42. And they continued consistently in the apostles' teachings and fellowship, and in breaking of bread, and in prayers. 43. Everyone was filled with a sense of reverence: and many signs and wonders were done by the apostles. 44. All who believed kept together, and all their possessions were shared; 45. Goods and property were sold and distributed as every man had need. 46. And they agreed to meet daily in the temple and to break bread from house to house, and they took meals cheerfully and with personal commitment. 47. Praising God and having favor with all the people. And the Lord added to the church daily those being saved.

Walking and Praising God
Acts 3:1-11

1. Peter and John went together to the temple for the three o'clock prayers. 2. At the same time a man crippled from birth was being carried to the temple gate called Beautiful who daily begged for gifts of those entering the temple; 3. seeing Peter and John about to enter the temple asked for gifts. 4. Both Peter and John with a steady stare, said, Look at us. 5. And he turned toward them expecting to receive a gift. 6. And Peter said, I have no silver or gold, but I will give you what I do have: In the name of Jesus Christ of Nazareth stand up and walk. 7. Taking his right hand, Peter lifted him up: and instantly his feet and ankle bones became strong. 8. And he jumped to his feet and walked around and went with them into the temple, leaping and praising God as he walked. 9. All the people saw him walking and praising God: 10. And realized that it was the beggar from the Beautiful gate of the temple: they were filled with speculation at what had happened to him. 11. And as the man firmly hugged Peter and John, all the people crowded into Solomon's porch, with continued amazement.

Repent and Turn Back to God
Acts 3:12-26

12. When Peter saw the opportunity he spoke to the people. Men of Israel, does this surprise you? Why are you looking intently at us, as if we by our own power or godliness made this man walk? 13. The God of Abraham, Isaac, and Jacob, the God of our forefathers, has glorified His Servant Jesus; whom you betrayed, and denied Him before Pilate's Court, when he had decided to release Him. 14. You denied the Holy and Righteous One, and asked for the release of a murderer; 15. and killed the Author of life, whom God stood up again from the dead; and we are witnesses of this fact. 16. This man you

all know who put his faith in Jesus and that Name has awakened faith and strengthen this man in your presence. 17. I know it was in ignorance that you brethren acted as your rulers did. 18. This is how the Christ fulfilled those things which God showed by the mouth of all His prophets. 19. Repent and turn back to God, that your sins may be completely cancelled, so that God may grant you a time of renewal in the presence of the Lord. 20. And sent Jesus the Messiah, who was preached before to you; 21. Heaven must retain this Christ until the restoration of all things, which from ancient times God spoke by His holy prophets. 22. For Moses said, A Prophet shall the Lord your God raise up unto you of your brethren, just as He appointed me; you must listen to everything He says. 23. And everyone who refuses to listen to that Prophet shall be utterly destroyed from among the people. 24. Likewise all the Prophets since Samuel have spoken and told of these days. 25. You are the descendents of the prophets and of the covenant which God made with our forefathers, saying to Abraham, in your descendents will all the nations be blessed. 26. It was to you first that God sent His resurrected Servant to bless those who will turn away from wickedness.

Many Who Heard the Word Believed
Acts 4:1-12

1. Before they finished speaking to the people, the Chief Priests with the Captain of the temple and the Sadducees came to them, 2. Being highly annoyed that they were teaching the people and proclaiming Jesus as an example of standing up again from the grave. 3. And they arrested them and put them in custody overnight. 4. However, many who heard the word believed and the number of men alone was about five thousand. 5. The next day, the leading men of the council, gathered together at Jerusalem, 6. including Annas, the high priest, and Caiaphas, John, Alexander, and many kindred of the high priest. 7. They brought Peter and John before them and asked, By what kind of power or name have you people done this? 8. Then Peter furnished courage by the Holy Spirit said, You leaders and men of authority, 9. if we this day be examined for the good deed done to a helpless man, by what means this man was cured; 10. then you and all Israel should know, that by the name of Jesus Christ of Nazareth, whom you crucified, whom God raised from among the dead, even by the authority of Jesus does this man stand here cured. 11. He is the stone rejected by the builders, who has become the chief stone of the building. 12. No one else can bring salvation: for there is no other name under heaven given among men, whereby we may be saved.

They Had Been Companions of Jesus
Acts 4:13-22

13. When they saw the fearlessness and fluency of speech of Peter and John, and understood that they were uncultured and uneducated men, they were astonished; and recognized that they had been companions of Jesus. 14. And seeing the man which was cured standing with them, they could say nothing against it. 15. After they ordered them outside the council, they consulted together, 16. saying, What shall we do with these men? For a notable sign has happened through them that is manifest to all inhabiting Jerusalem and we cannot deny it. 17. But to keep it from spreading further among the people, let us intimidate them to speak to no one in this name. 18. And they called them and commanded them not to speak or teach in the name of Jesus. 19. But Peter and John answered and said, Decide for your selves whether it be right to obey God or you. 20. For we cannot refrain from speaking about the things we have seen and heard. 21. So when they had further threatened them, they let them go, finding no way to punish them because of the people: since everyone was giving thanks to God for what was done. 22. For the man on whom this sign of cure was evident was more than forty years old.

They Spoke the Word with Fluency
Acts 4:23-37

23. After their release, they went to their companions and reported all that the chief priests and elders had said. 24. When they heard the story, with one accord they raised their voice to God and said, Lord, you made heaven, earth, the sea, and everything in them; 25. Who through the Holy Spirit spoke by your servant David, Why do nations rage and people devise vain things? 26. The rulers of the earth gathered together against the Lord, and against His Christ. 27. It is true that both Herod and Pontius Pilate with the Gentiles and the people of Israel gathered together against your Anointed Holy Child Jesus, 28. to do whatsoever your hand and counsel allowed to be done. 29. And, now Lord, observe their aggressive intimidation: and grant your servants fluency to speak your word, 30. by stretching forth your hand to heal; and that signs and wonders may be done through the name of your Holy Servant Jesus, 31. and when they prayed, the place where they were assembled together was shaken and they were all furnished* *(filled up)* with the Holy Spirit and began speaking the word of God with fluency. 32. And the multitude of believers was of one heart and one soul: and no one claimed the things they possessed were their own, but was common property. 33. And the apostles with great power witnessed to the resurrection of the Lord Jesus: and

God's favor was upon them all. 34. Not one among them lacked, for many owners of lands or houses sold them and brought the money, 35. and placed it at the apostles' feet; and it was distributed to every man based on need. 36. And Joseph, the one surnamed Barnabas by the apostles, (which is translated Son of Encouragement) a Levite from Cyprus, 37. who owned land sold it and brought the money and placed it at the apostles' feet.

---

*v31 Ephesians 5:18. Stop excessively drinking wine, which influences riotous living; more willingly be influenced by the Spirit; *(This is the command related to the Holy Spirit and involves an again and again experience.)*

Believers Were Added to the Lord
Acts 5:1-16

1. A man named Ananias in partnership with his wife Sapphira, sold a piece of property, 2. and kept back part of the selling price with full knowledge and consent of his wife, and brought only part of it to the apostles. 3. But Peter said, Ananias, why has Satan influenced your heart to lie to the Holy Spirit, and caused you to keep back part of the price of the land? 4. Was the land not your own to keep? And after it was sold, was it not the price under your control? Why have you conceived this thing in your heart? You have not lied to men, but unto God. 5. And hearing these words, Ananias fell down and died: and fear came on all who heard about it. 6. And the young men rose up, covered the body and carried him out and buried him. 7. After about three hours, his wife, not knowing what had happened, came in. 8. And Peter asked her, Did you sell the land for so much? And she said, Yes, for so much. 9. Then Peter said to her, how is it that you agreed together to provoke the Spirit of the Lord? Behold, the feet of those who buried your husband are at the door to carry you out. 10. Then she fell down immediately and the young men came in and found her dead and carried her out and buried her by her husband. 11. And terror came upon the congregation and on all who heard about these events. 12. And many signs and wonders were wrought among the people by the hands of the apostles; (and the common meeting place was Solomon's Porch. 13. And all the others feared to come near: yet the people praised them. 14. And believers were added to the Lord, multitudes both men and women.) 15. Insomuch that they brought their sick into the streets and laid them on pallets so that as Peter passed he might cast a shadow over some of them. 16. And crowds came from around Jerusalem and brought sick folks and some who were troubled by unclean spirits: and they all were cured.

Speak All the Words of This Life
Acts 5:17-32

17. Then the high priests and the party of the Sadducees rose up filled with jealousy, 18. and arrested the apostles and put them in the common prison. 19. But that night the angel of the Lord opened the prison doors, and led them out, and said, 20. Go to the temple, stand and speak all the words of this life, 21. hearing this, they entered the temple early in the morning and taught. But the high priest came and called the council together, and all the senate of the children of Israel, and sent to the prison for them. 22. But the officers who went to the prison did not find them and they returned, 23. saying, We found the prison safely locked and the keepers standing guard: but when we opened we found no one inside. 24. Now when the captain of the temple and the chief priests heard this, they were at a loss and wondered where this would grow. 25. Then someone came and reported that the men they put in prison were standing in the temple and teaching the people. 26. Then the officers brought them without violence: for they feared the people would have them stoned. 27. And bringing them forth, they set them before the council: and the high priest asked, 28. saying, Did we not charge you not to teach in this name? And now you have filled Jerusalem with your teaching, and intend to bring this man's death on us. 29. Then Peter with the other apostles answered, We must obey God rather than men. 30. The God of our forefathers raised from the grave this Jesus, whom you put to death by hanging Him on a tree. 31. God has exalted this Jesus to His right hand as Author of life and as Savior, to give repentance to Israel, and the forgiveness of sins. 32. And we are witnesses to the truth of these events: and so is the Holy Spirit, whom God has given to those who obey Him.

Ceased Not to Teach and Preach Jesus Christ
Acts 5:33-42

33. And hearing this, they became frustrated and took counsel to kill the apostles. 34. But a member of the council stood up, a Pharisee, and teacher of the law, named Gamaliel, a man with reputation among all the people, and commanded that the men be removed for a while; 35. and said, You men of Israel, take heed to yourselves what you intend to do touching these men. 36. Recently, Theudas rose up boasting himself to be somebody; about four hundred men joined him and he was slain and all who followed him were scattered and came to nothing. 37. After this man rose up Judas of Galilee at the time of the census, and many followed him: he also perished; and all that followed him were dispersed. 38. And now I say, have nothing to do with these men; for if this counsel or this work is of men, it will come to

nothing: 39. but if it be of God, you cannot overthrow it; lest perhaps you find yourselves fighting against God. 40. And the council followed his advice; and when they had called the apostles and beaten them, commanded that they should not speak in the name of Jesus, and let them go. 41. And the apostles left the council rejoicing that they were counted worthy to suffer shame for His name. 42. And every day in the temple and in every house, they ceased not to teach and preach Jesus Christ.

We Will Continue in Prayer and Teaching
Acts 6:1-15

1. At this time the numbers of disciples were multiplying, complaints were made by the Greek-speaking believers against the Hebrews, because their widows were overlooked in the daily care. 2. Then the Twelve called the company of disciples together and said, It is not logical that we should leave behind the word of God to make the daily distribution. 3. Wherefore, brethren, search among the Greeks for seven men of honest report, completely influenced by the Holy Spirit and wisdom, to whom we may assign this task. 4. Nevertheless, we will continue in prayer and teaching the word. 5. The company was pleased with this plan: and they chose Stephen, a man full of faith and the Spirit, and Philip, Prochorus, Nicanor, Timon, Parmenas, and Nicolas, a convert from Antioch: 6. whom they presented to the apostles: and they prayed and laid hands on them. 7. And the word of God increased; and the number of disciples in Jerusalem grew rapidly; and a large number of priests were submissive to the faith. 8. And Stephen, full of grace and power, did miracles and amazing good things among the people.

Wisdom and Spiritual Power
Acts 6:9-15

9. And some members of the Synagogue of Freed Slaves, and visitors from Cilicia and Roman Asia, attempted to argue with Stephen. 10. But could not withstand the wisdom and spiritual power of Stephen. 11. Then they secretly substituted witnesses who would falsely say, We have heard him speak offensive words against Moses and God. 12. And they stirred up hostility among the people, the elders, and the scribes, and they seized him and brought him to the Sanhedrin, 13. And brought false witnesses, who said, This man continually utters abuse against the Temple and the Law: 14. We have heard him say that this Jesus of Nazareth will destroy the Temple and change the customs that Moses delivered to us. 15. And all the Sanhedrin looked directly at Stephen and his face appeared as the face of an angel.

Are These Things True?
Acts 7:1-8
1. Then the high priest asked, Are these things true? 2. And Stephen answered, Men, brethren and fathers, listen to me: The glorious God appeared to father Abraham while he lived in Mesophotamia, before he dwelt in Haran, 3. and God said, Leave this land and your kindred, and go to the land I will show you. 4. Then he left the Chaldea and came to Haran, where you now live. 5. God gave him no ownership of the land: yet he promised that he would give it to him for a possession, and to his posterity, although he had no child. 6. And God told him, his descendants would live in a foreign land and that they would be enslaved and ill treated for four hundred years. 7. And God said, The nation that enslaves them I will judge, and after that they will be free and serve Me in this place. 8. And with Abraham God made the sacred agreement of circumcision: so Abraham became the father of Isaac and circumcised him the eighth day; and Isaac fathered Jacob and Jacob fathered the twelve who founded the Twelve Tribes.

But God was with Him
Acts 7:9-16
9. And our respected ancestors out of jealousy sold Joseph as a slave into Egypt, but God was with him, 10. and rescued him out of his distress, and enabled him to win favor and show wisdom before Pharaoh; who appointed him Governor of Egypt and put him in charge of the royal household. 11. Then came a famine over the whole of Egypt and Canaan, which caused great suffering; and our ancestors could find no food. 12. But when Jacob heard that there was grain in Egypt, he sent our forefathers on their first visit to Egypt. 13. It was on the second visit that Joseph made himself known to his brothers; and Joseph's true family was made known to Pharaoh. 14. Then Joseph sent an invitation to his father Jacob and all his family numbering seventy-five persons. 15. So Jacob went to Egypt where he and our forefathers died, 16. and their bodies were carried back to Shechem and placed in the tomb that Abraham bought for a price in Shechem from the sons of Hamon.

Till a Monarch of a Different Character Arose
Acts 7:17-29
17. But as the promised time approached, which God had affirmed to Abraham, the people grew in Egypt and multiplied, 18. until a monarch of a different character arose who knew nothing of Joseph. 19. Who dealt deceitfully with our kindred and oppressed our fathers, so that they exposed their infants to the elements so they would not live. 20. In this time Moses was born, he was a beautiful child nurtured for three

months in his father's house: 21. and when he was exposed to die, Pharaoh's daughter rescued him and nourished him as her own son. 22. And Moses was well-educated in the science of the Egyptians, and was a strong man in word and action. 23. And when he was about forty years old, he decided to visit his brethren, the children of Israel. 24. And seeing one of them wronged, he defended him and avenged the victim by striking down the Egyptian: 25. thinking his brethren would understand how God by his hand would deliver them: but they did not understand. 26. And the next day he discovered two fighting and tried to stop the quarrel, saying, Men you are brothers, why do you seek to harm one another? 27. But the aggressor pushed Moses aside, saying, Who made you our ruler and judge? 28. Do you wish to kill me as you did the Egyptian yesterday? 29. At this remark Moses fled and became a sojourner in the land of Midian, where he begat two sons.

Then the Lord Said
Acts 7:30-43

30. Forty years later in a flaming bush an angel of the Lord appeared to him suddenly in the desert of Mount Sinai. 31. Moses was surprised and as he drew near to take a look, the voice of the Lord said, 32. I am the God of your fathers, the God of Abraham, Isaac, and Jacob. Trembling with fear, Moses did not look at the bush. 33. Then the Lord said, Take off your sandals: for the place where you stand is holy ground. 34. The oppression of My people in Egypt is always before My eyes, and I have heard their cries of pain and misery and have come to rescue them. Come now, I will send you back to Egypt. 35. This Moses whom they rejected, saying, Who appointed you referee and ruler? This same Moses did God send to be a ruler and a deliverer speaking through the angel in the bush. 36. Moses brought them out after he worked wonders and signs in Egypt, at the Red Sea and in the Wilderness for forty years. 37. It was this Moses who told Israel that God would lift up a Prophet from among your brethren, just as He appointed me. 38. It was He who appeared at the assembly in the desert with the angel who spoke to Him in Mount Sinai, and with our forefathers: who received the living words to hand on to us: 39. our fathers refused to listen and spurned his authority, and turned their thoughts back to Egypt. 40. Who said to Aaron, Make gods to lead us: as for this Moses, who brought us out of Egypt, we do not know what became of him. 41. And they made a bull-calf and offered sacrifice to the idol, and rejoiced in their own handiwork. 42. Then God turned from them and gave them up to serve the Stars: as it is written by the prophets, Oh, Israel, did you offer to Me slain beasts and sacrifices for forty years in the desert? 43. No, you set up a tent to Moloch and the star-symbol

of Rephan as your god, images which you made to worship: so I will exile you beyond Babylon.

God Dwells Not in Man-made Buildings
Acts 7:44-50
44. In the wilderness our fathers had the Tabernacle of Testimony according to the instructions He gave Moses to design it. 45. The next generation inherited it and brought it with Joshua when they made the conquest of the nations, whom God drove out before our fathers unto the days of David; 46. he found favor with God and longed to build a resting-place for the God of Israel. 47. But it was Solomon who built a House for God. 48. Yet the Most High dwells not in man-made buildings; as the Prophets foretold, 49. heaven is My throne and the earth My footstool: what kind of house will you build Me? Said the Lord: or what place of rest shall I have? 50. Did not My hand make all things?

Lord, Fix Not This Sin Against Them
Acts 7:51-59
51. You stubborn people, heathen still in heart and ears, you always strive against the Holy Spirit: as your fathers did, so do you. 52. Name one prophet whom your fathers did not persecute. And they killed those who announced the coming of the Just One; whom you have now betrayed and murdered: 53. you received the law through the sensitivity of angels and have not kept it. 54. When they heard these things, they were infuriated, and they ground their teeth together in anger. 55. But Stephen, being full of the Holy Spirit, looked up to the heavens and saw the glory of God and Jesus standing on the right hand of God, 56. And said, I see heaven open and the Son of Man standing at God's right hand. 57. Hearing this, they yelled with a loud voice and stopped their ears, and rushed at him in full agreement, 58. And dragged him out of the city and stoned him: and the witnesses threw off their outer garments at the feet of a young man, Saul. 59. And they stoned Stephen while he prayed to Jesus saying, Lord Jesus, receive my spirit. 60. On his knees, he prayed with a loud voice, Lord, fix not this sin against them. After this prayer, Stephen calmly and peacefully fell asleep.

And There Was Great Rejoicing
Acts 8:1-13
1. And Saul with pleasure gave formal consent to Stephen's death. And great persecution broke out against the believers in Jerusalem; and all except the apostles were scattered throughout Judaea and Samaria. 2. And God-fearing men recovered Stephen and with deep expressions of grief together took his body to the burial place. 3. And Saul created a wild uproar and chaos in the church by forcefully

entering house after house and dragging off men and women to jail. 4. As a result those who were scattered in different directions went from place to place declaring the gospel. 5. Then Deacon Philip went to the city of Samaria and kept declaring the Christ. 6. And the people listened attentively to what Philip said and the miracles he performed. 7. And many who were possessed with unclean spirits were delivered with loud cries, and many of the disabled and paralyzed were cured. 8. And there was great rejoicing throughout the city. 9. But there was a man named Simon who claimed to have great powers and practiced witchcraft to the amazement of the Samaritans: 10. All the people gave heed to him saying, This man has the Great Power of God. 11. They all paid attention to him because for a long time he had amazed them with magic arts. 12. But when they believed what Philip preached about the kingdom of God and the name of Jesus Christ, they were baptized, both men and women. 13. Even Simon himself believed and was baptized and was constantly with Philip and was amazed by the great signs and miracles performed.

No Part or Share in This Ministry
Acts 8:14-25

14. Now when the apostles at Jerusalem heard that Samaria had received the word of God, they sent Peter and John to them: 15. who, when they arrived prayed for them to receive the Holy Spirit: 16. (for as yet none of them had embraced the Spirit: only they were baptized in the name of the Lord Jesus.) 17. Then Peter and John laid hands on them and they received the Holy Spirit. 18. When Simon saw that the Spirit was bestowed by the laying on of the apostles' hands, he offered them money. 19. Saying, Give me this authority, so that when I lay hands on someone, he receives the Holy Spirit. 20. But Peter said, Your money disappear with you, because you thought the gift of God could be purchased with money. 21. You have no part or share in this ministry: for your heart is not right with God. 22. Repent of your wrong doings and pray, if perhaps the thought of your heart may be forgiven. 23. For I recognize that you are enraged with bitterness and are a slave to wickedness. 24. Then Simon replied, Pray to the Lord for me that none of these things that you have spoken will come upon me. 25. After they had given personal testimony and declared the word of the Lord, they returned to Jerusalem preaching the gospel in many Samaritan villages as they went.

What Hinders Me From Being Baptized?
Acts 8:26-40

26. A messenger of the Lord spoke to Philip, saying, Arise and go along the desert road from Jerusalem to Gaza. 27. So he went on

his journey and saw a man of Ethiopia, an Eunuch of the Court of Candace Queen of the Ethiopians, who had charge of her treasure and had come to Jerusalem to worship, 28. and was returning and was sitting in his chariot reading the Prophet Isaiah. 29. The Spirit spoke to Philip, Go near and join yourself to this chariot. 30. And Philip ran and heard him read the Prophet Isaiah, and said, Can you understand what you are reading? 31. And he said, How can I, except someone guide me? And he invited Philip to come up and sit with him. 32. The portion of scripture which he was reading was, As a sheep led to the slaughter and as a lamb before the shearer is silent, so He opened not His mouth: 33. In His humiliation He was denied justice: and who shall declare their wickedness? For His life is taken from the earth. 34. And the eunuch said to Philip, Tell me about whom the prophet is speaking, of Himself or of another? 35. Then Philip began at the same scripture and told him the good news about Jesus. 36. As they traveled on, they came to some water: and the eunuch said, What hinders me from being baptized? 37. * 38. And he commanded the chariot to stop: and they both went down into the water, Philip and the eunuch: and he baptized him. 39. And as they came up out of the water, the Spirit of the Lord snatched Philip away, so that was the last time the eunuch saw him. 40. Philip was found at Azotus. He passed through all the cities and preached the good news until he came to Caesarea.

---

*The best text omits verse 37. *And Philip answered, If you believe with all your heart, you may. And he answered, I believe that Jesus Christ is the Son of God.*

A Light From Heaven
Acts 9:1-9

1. And Saul still breathing hard with aggressive and murderous desire against the disciples of the Lord approached the high priest. 2. And asked him for letters addressed to the synagogues in Damascus, so that if he found any men or women of the Way that he might bring them bound to Jerusalem. 3. As he journeyed near Damascus: suddenly a light from heaven flashed around him: 4. And he fell to the ground and heard a voice saying, Saul, Saul, why do you persecute me? 5. And he asked, Who are you, Lord? And the Lord said, I am Jesus whom you are persecuting: 6. But rise up and enter the city and you shall be told what you ought to do. 7. And the men who traveled with him stood speechless, hearing a voice, but seeing no man. 8. And Saul got up from the ground and when his eyes were opened he saw no man: but was led by the hand and brought to Damascus. 9. And for three days he was unable to see and neither ate or drank.

Arise and Go to Straight Street
Acts 9:10-22

10. And the Lord spoke in a vision to a certain disciple in Damascus, the name was Ananias, And he said, Yes, Lord I am here. 11. And the Lord said, Arise and go to Straight Street, and inquire in the house of Judas for one called Saul of Tarsus: for he is now praying. 12. He saw a man named Ananias coming and putting his hand on him that he might see again. 13. Then Ananias answered, Lord, I have heard from many about this man, especially the great suffering he has brought on your people in Jerusalem: 14. and has come here with authority from the chief priests to arrest all that call on your name. 15. But the Lord said, Go on your mission: for he is My chosen instrument to bear My name before the nations and their kings and the children of Israel: 16. for I will show him the great things he must suffer for My name's sake. 17. And Ananias went his way, and entered into the house; and putting his hands on him said, Brother Saul, the Lord, even Jesus, who appeared to you in the way as you came, has sent me, that you might see again, and be furnished with the Holy Spirit. 18. Immediately there fell from his eyes something similar to scales: and he received sight and rising up was baptized.* 19. And he took food and was strengthened and remained with the disciples in Damascus a few days. 20. Immediately proclaiming in the synagogues that Jesus was the Son of God. 21. All the hearers were astonished and said; Is not this the man who in Jerusalem destroyed those who called on this name, and came here for the same purpose, that he might take in chains believers to the chief priests? 22. But Saul became more forceful and confounded the Jews living in Damascus, proving that Jesus was the Messiah.

---

*v18 This is not a treatise on "baptism" only a simple explanation as to why Saul was baptized. Proselytes to Judaism were required to be baptized. Likewise, when Jews, who accepted God, the Father, accepted Jesus as the Son of God, they were baptized in the name (authority) of the Father, the Son and after Pentecost, the Holy Spirit. Water baptism was in obedience to Christ's Commission, a personal identification with the Trinity and an initiation into the Christian way of life. This is what happened with Saul.

A True Disciple
Acts 9:23-30

23. After several days had passed, the Jews consulted together to kill Saul: 24. but their plot was made known. And they watched the gates day and night to kill him. 25. But the disciples took Saul by night and let him down through the wall in a wicker-basket. 26. On Saul's arrival in Jerusalem, he tried to join the disciples: but they were all afraid of him, and could not believe he was a true disciple. 27. But Barnabas brought him to the apostles and declared how he had seen the Lord in

the way, and that he spoke to him, and how he had preached fluently at Damascus in the name of Jesus. 28. And Saul remained with the disciples and associated with them freely. 29. And he spoke fluently in the name of the Lord, and disagreed and questioned the Greek-speaking Jews: but they kept trying to kill him. 30. When the brethren knew this, they sent him by sea to Tarsus.

Get Up and Make Your Bed
Acts 9:31-43

31. Then the assembled believers throughout all Judaea, Galilee, and Samaria had peace, and were built up and multiplied by the encouragement of the Holy Spirit and walked in the fear of the Lord. 32. As Peter traveled from town to town, he came to the saints living at Lydda. 33. And there he found a man named Aeneas, who had been bedridden for eight years and was helpless. 34. And Peter said to Aeneas, Jesus Christ makes you whole: Get up and make your bed. And he arose immediately. 35. And all who lived at Lydda and in the Plain of Sharon saw him and were converted to the Lord. 36. Among the disciples at Joppa was a women named Tabitha (which is *gazelle* and is translated, Dorcas); this women was graceful, full of good works and swift to assist people in need. 37. She took sick and died: and they washed and laid her in an upper chamber. 38. Since Lydda was near Joppa and the disciples had heard that Peter was there, they sent two men, asking him to come without delay. 39. Peter went with them and they brought him to the upper room: and all the widows stood weeping showing the clothing that Dorcas had made. 40. But Peter sent everyone out of the room and went to his knees and prayed: and turning to the body said, Tabitha, get up! And she opened her eyes: and saw Peter and sat up. 41. And he gave her his hand and lifted her up, and called the believers and the widows and presented her alive. 42. The news spread over Joppa and many were converted to the Lord. 43. And Peter remained in Joppa several days and stayed with a tanner named Simon.

Observed and Remembered By God
Acts 10:1-8

1. Cornelius was in Caesarea. He was a Captain in the Roman Army, 2. a devout and God-fearing man with all his house and gave alms to the Jews and prayed to God always. 3. About three o'clock in the afternoon, he saw a vision of an angel of God coming to him saying, Cornelius. 4. And he gazed fearfully and said, What is it, Lord? The angel said, Your prayers and almsgiving are observed and remembered by God. 5. Send men now to Joppa and ask for Simon, called Peter: 6. he is lodging with Simon, a tanner whose house stands by

the sea: 7. when the angel who spoke to Cornelius departed, he called two servants and a God-fearing soldier who served on his staff; 8. after explaining what happened, he sent them to Joppa.

What God Has Cleansed
Acts 10:9-23

9. The next day as the men journeyed and came near the city, about noon, Peter went to the housetop to pray: 10. and he became hungry and desired to eat, and while they prepared a meal, he fell into a trance, 11. and saw heaven open and something like a sheet of sail-cloth being let down to earth by ropes at the four corners: 12. it contained all manner of four-footed beasts and creeping and flying things. 13. And a voice said, Rise, Peter; kill and eat. 14. But Peter said, Not so, Lord; for I have never eaten anything that is common or unclean. 15. And the voice spoke again, What God had cleansed, you must not call defiled. 16. This happened three times and suddenly it all disappeared into heaven. 17. While Peter was still perplexed over what he saw, the men sent from Cornelius asked the way to Simon's house and were standing at the gate, 18. and called out to enquire if Simon, called Peter, was lodged there. 19. While Peter was pondering on the vision, the Spirit said, Behold, men seek you. 20. Get up and go down, and go with them without doubting: for I have sent them. 21. Then Peter went down to the men; and said, I am the man you seek: what brought you here? 22. They answered, Cornelius, the Roman Captain, a just man, and God-fearing, with a good report among the Jewish nation, was divinely directed by an angel to send for you at this house, and to hear your message. 23. Then he asked them to stay the night and on the morrow Peter and certain men from Joppa traveled with them.

Present Before God to Hear
Acts 10:24-33

24. And on the next day they reached Caesarea. And Cornelius was expecting them and had called together his relatives and close friends. 25. As Peter entered, Cornelius met him and fell down at his feet to pay respect. 26. But Peter lifted him to his feet, saying, Stand up, I myself am also a man. 27. Talking with him as they entered the house, Peter found a large gathering of people. 28. And Peter said, You know a Jew is forbidden to associate with Gentiles or visit their houses, but God has showed me that I should not call any man unholy. 29. Therefore, I came to you without objection when I was invited: now I ask for what reason have you sent for me? 30. And Cornelius said, Four days ago I was in my house keeping the three o'clock prayer, and a man stood before me in shining clothing, 31. and said, Cornelius, God has heard

your prayer and remembered your almsgiving. 32. Send to Joppa and call Simon, whose surname is Peter; he is lodged in the house of one Simon a tanner by the sea side: 33. immediately, I sent for you, and it is good that you came. Now we are all here present before God to hear all the things that God commanded you to say.

God is No Respecter of Persons
Acts 10:34-43

34. Then Peter begin to speak, Truly, I perceive that God is no respecter of persons: 35. but in every nation those who reverence God and does what is right is acceptable to Him. 36. God sent His word to the descendants of Israel announcing the good news of peace through Jesus Christ: (He is Lord of all:) 37. you know how the word spread throughout Judaea, beginning in Galilee after the baptism that John proclaimed; 38. how God anointed Jesus of Nazareth with the Holy Spirit and with power: who went about doing good and healing all that were demoralized by the devil; for God was with Him. 39. And we are witnesses of all things which He did both in Judaea and in Jerusalem; whom they killed by hanging on a wooden cross: 40. this Jesus God stood up again from the grave the third day and showed Himself openly; 41. not to all the people, but to witnesses chosen before of God, even to us, who did eat and drink with Him after He rose from the dead. 42. And He charged us to announce and solemnly testify that it is He who was appointed by God to judge the living and the dead. 43. It is to Him that all the prophets testify that through His name whoever believes in Him shall receive forgiveness of sins.

Can Anyone Refuse Water Baptism
Acts 10:44-48

44. Before Peter had finished speaking, those who heard the word willingly embraced the Holy Spirit in fullness. 45. And the Jewish believers who came with Peter were astonished that the gift of the Holy Spirit had actually been poured out on the Gentiles. 46. For they heard them speak with unnaturally acquired languages and magnify God. Then Peter asked, 47. Can anyone forbid water baptism for these who have received the Holy Spirit as we did? 48. And he directed that they be baptized in the name of Jesus Christ. Then they asked him to stay a few days.

A Change of Heart That Leads to Life
Acts 11:1-18

1. The apostles and brethren in all Judaea heard that the Gentiles had also received the word of God. 2. And when Peter returned to Jerusalem, the stricter Jews took issue with him, 3. saying, You visited and ate with men who were not Jews. 4. But Peter explained the facts

from the beginning, saying, 5. I was praying in the city of Joppa and fell into a trance and saw heaven open and something like a sheet of sail-cloth being let down to earth by ropes at the four corners: 6. it contained all manner of four-footed beasts and creeping and flying things. 7. And a voice said, Rise, Peter; kill and eat. 8. But I said, Not so, Lord; for I have never eaten anything that is unholy. 9. And the voice spoke again, What God had cleansed, you must not call defiled. 10. This happened three times and suddenly it all disappeared into heaven. 11. Immediately there were three men already come where I was, sent from Caesarea to me. 12. And the Spirit told me to go with them, nothing doubting. Moreover these six brethren accompanied me, and we entered into the man's house: 13. And he told us how he had seen an Angel in his house, which stood and said, Send men to Joppa, and call for Simon, whose surname is Peter; 14. who shall tell you words, whereby you and your house will be saved. 15. And as I began to speak, the Holy Spirit fell on them, just as He did on us originally. 16. Then I remembered the word of the Lord, how He said, John indeed baptized with water; but you shall be baptized with the Holy Spirit. 17. Now since God granted to them the same gift He gave us, when we believed on the Lord Jesus Christ; who was I, that I could resist God? 18. On hearing this, they were silenced and praised God, saying, God has also granted the Gentiles a change of heart that leads to life.

Transact Their Affairs as Christians
Acts 11:19-30

19. They that were distributed in foreign lands because of the persecution of Stephen went as far as Phoenicia, speaking of Christ only to the Jews. 20. But some were natives of Cyprus and Cyrene, on their arrival at Antioch, they began to speak to the Greeks also, announcing the Lord Jesus. 21. And the power of the Lord was with them and a great number believed and turned to the Lord. 22. And when the news was reported to the assembly in Jerusalem: they sent Barnabas to Antioch. 23. When he arrived and saw the grace of God he was glad and continuously encouraged them to remain with the Lord with readiness of heart. 24. For he was a good man and full of the Holy Spirit and faith: and many people were added to the Lord. 25. Then Barnabas went to Tarsus in search of Saul: 26. and when he found Saul brought him to Antioch. And for one whole year they assembled with the congregation and taught many people. And the disciples first began to transact their affairs as Christians in Antioch.* 27. At this time prophets from Jerusalem came to Antioch. 28. And one of them came forward named Agabus and predicted by the Spirit that a famine was to visit the whole world: and it did happen in the time of Claudius. 29. Then every disciple according to his ability determined to send

relief to the brethren in Judaea: 30. this they did and sent it to the elders by Barnabas and Saul.

---

*v26 At first being Christian was a life-style recognized by others, then it became a mark of identification as a follower of Christ.

Earnest and Persistent Prayer
Acts 12:1-10

1. It was about this time that Herod the king exerted his authority to persecute some members of the Christian congregation. 2. He beheaded James the brother of John. 3. When he saw it pleased the Jews, he arrested Peter also. (This was during days of the Passover.) 4. After seizing Peter, he put him in jail under the guard of sixteen soldiers; intending to present him to the people after the Passover. 5. Peter was kept in jail: but earnest and persistent prayer was made for him by the assembly to God. 6. On the night before his trial, Peter was sleeping between two soldiers, bound with two chains: and the guards were on duty outside the door of the jail. 7. Suddenly the Angel of the Lord stood by him and a light shined in the cell and the Angel struck Peter on the side to wake him, saying, Get up quickly. And the chains fell from his hands. 8. And the Angel said, Dress yourself and put on your sandals. And he did. And the Angel said, Put your coat on and follow me. 9. And he went out and followed him; without knowing what was happening was real, but he thought he was dreaming. 10. After they had passed the first and second guard, they came to the Iron Gate leading to the city and it opened to them automatically, and when they had gone about one block: the Angel departed.

But the Word of God Grew and Multiplied
Acts 12:11-25

11. As Peter recovered his senses, he said, Now, I know for certain that the Lord has sent his Angel and rescued me from the power of Herod and from all the Jewish people hoped to see. 12. When he understood what had happened, he came to the house of Mary, the mother of John Mark: where many were gathered and praying. 13. When he knocked at the door in the gate, a maidservant called Rhoda came to listen. 14. When she recognized Peter's voice, she was overjoyed and did not open the gate, but ran and reported that Peter was standing at the gate. 15. And they said, You are mad, but she strongly affirmed that it was true. Then they said, It is his messenger. 16. But Peter continued knocking: and when they opened the gate and saw him they were astonished. 17. But he motioned with his hands for silence, and explained how the Lord brought him out of jail. And he said, Go tell these things to James and to the brethren. And he left

and went to another place. 18. In the morning there was consternation among the soldiers as to what could have happened to Peter. 19. When Herod searched for Peter and could not find him, he examined the guards and ordered them to be executed. And he went down from Judaea to Caesarea and remained there. 20. And Herod was angry with the people of Tyre and Sidon: but they went in agreement to him having made friends with Blastus, the king's household steward, they asked for peace because their country was dependent on the king for its food supply. 21. And on a fixed day, Herod arrayed in royal apparel, sat on his throne, and made an address to them. 22. And the people shouted, It is the voice of a god and not a man. 23. Instantly the Angel of the Lord struck him down because he had seized the honor due to God: and he died with his life eaten away by intestinal worms. 24. But the word of God grew and multiplied. 25. And Barnabas and Saul after they fulfilled their ministry returned from Jerusalem and took with them John Mark.

Being Sent Forth By the Holy Spirit
Acts 13:1-12

1. In the congregation at Antioch there were some prophets and teachers; namely Barnabas and Simeon called Black, and Lucius of Cyrene, and Manaen, the foster-brother of Herod the tetrarch, and Saul. 2. As they ministered to the Lord and fasted, the Holy Spirit said, Dedicate Barnabas and Saul now for the special work to which I have called them. 3. After fasting and prayer and the laying on of hands, they sent them on their way. 4. Being sent forth by the Holy Spirit, they traveled down to Seleucia and from there sailed to Cyprus. 5. When they reached Salamis, they proclaimed the word of God in the Jewish synagogues: and added John as an assistant. 6. Traveling the entire island as far as Paphos, they met a Jewish magician who posed as a prophet, whose name was Barjesus: 7. Who was a soothsayer to Sergius Paulus, the proconsul, a man of understanding; who called for Barnabas and Saul and desired to hear the word of God. 8. But Elymas, for that is the Arabic meaning of Barjesus, argued to defend his position and turn away the proconsul from the faith. 9. Then Saul, hereafter called Paul, filled with the Holy Spirit, looked him squarely in the face, 10. and said, You impostor and expert deceiver, son of the devil, and enemy of all righteousness, will you never stop trying to spoil the straight path of the Lord? 11. Now the hand of the Lord is upon you and you shall be blinded and unable to see the sun for a season. Instantly a dimness, then utter darkness fell on him; and he went about feeling for someone to lead him by the hand. 12. When the proconsul saw what had happened, he believed, being amazed at the teaching of the Lord.

A Word of Exhortation
Acts 13:13-22

13. Paul and his company sailed from Paphos and came to Perga in Pamphylia: but John deserted them and returned to Jerusalem. 14. The rest traveled from Perga the difficult journey to Pisidian Antioch* and on the Sabbath went into the synagogue and sat down. 15. After the reading of the law and the prophets, the rulers sent a message to them, saying, You men and brethren, if any among you have a word of exhortation for the people, you may speak. 16. Then Paul stood up and gesturing with his hand said, Men of Israel, and you who reverence God, listen to me. 17. The God of this people Israel chose our fathers and made them a great nation while they were outsiders in Egypt, and stretched out his arm and delivered them. 18. And for about forty years endured their conduct in the wilderness. 19. And after destroying seven nations in the land of Canaan, he divided the land for an inheritance. 20. Then he gave them Judges for about four hundred and fifty years, until Samuel, the Prophet. 21. Afterward they desired a king: and God gave them Saul the son of Cis, a man of the tribe of Benjamin, for the space of forty years. 22. After removing him, he raised up David to be their king; to whom He gave witness, and said, I have found David, the son of Jesse, a man after My own heart, who shall fulfill all My will.

---

*v14 Most likely it was Paul's health that caused the group to travel the rugged mountain road to reach the high country of Antioch in Pisidia.

The Word of This Salvation
Acts 13:23-29

23. It was through the descendants of this man that God's promise produced for Israel a Savior, Jesus: 24. when before His coming John preached the baptism of repentance to all of Israel. 25. As John was completing his course, he said, Whom do you think I am? I am not the Christ. He is coming after me whose sandals I am not worthy to untie. 26. Men and brethren, children of the family of Abraham, and all who reverence God, to you was the Word of this salvation sent. 27. For the people and their leaders in Jerusalem, refusing to recognize Him and not understanding the words of the prophets read every Sabbath, they fulfilled the words by condemning Him. 28. Though they found no cause for death, yet they demanded Pilate to crucify Him. 29. After fulfilling all that was written of Him, they took Him down from the tree and laid Him in a tomb.

All Who Believe Are Justified
Acts 13:30-41

30. But God stood Him up from among the dead: 31. and for many days He was seen by those who came up with Him from Galilee to Jerusalem, who are now His witnesses to the people. 32. We now declare the glad news to you, how the promise made to the fathers, 33. God has fulfilled the same to us their children, in that He has raised Jesus up again; as it is written in second psalm, You are my Son, this day have I begotten you. 34. And since God raised Jesus up from the dead, never to turn to decay, this He said, I will give you the holy and sure blessings of David. 35. Also He said in another psalm, You will not give your Holy One over to corruption. 36. For David, after serving God's will for his generation, died and was buried with his fathers and saw decay: 37. but Jesus, whom God raised again, saw no corruption. 38. Be it known therefore fellow Jews that through This Man is proclaimed to you the forgiveness of sins: 39. and by Him all who believe are justified from all things from which you could not be justified by the Law of Moses. 40. Take care that these words of the prophets do not apply to you; 41. Look you despisers and be unsure and vanish: for I work a work in your time, a work that you shall in no wise believe, though one relate it fully to you.

A Light to the Gentiles
Acts 13:42-52

42. And when they were gone out, the people asked that the same words be repeated to them the next Sabbath. 43. After the congregation dispersed, many of the Jews and devout converts to Judaism accompanied Paul and Barnabas: who in conversation urged them to continue in the grace of God. 44. And the next Sabbath almost the whole city came together to hear the word of God. 45. When the Jews saw the crowds, they were filled with jealousy and spoke against what Paul had said using abusive language. 46. Then Paul and Barnabas boldly and fluently said, It was necessary that the word of God should first be spoken to you: but since you violently rejected it and judged yourselves unworthy of everlasting life, now we are turning to the Gentiles. 47. For the Lord has commanded us, saying, I have placed you for a light to the Gentiles that you should be a means of salvation to the uttermost parts of the earth. 48. And when the Gentiles heard this, they rejoiced and praised God for the word of the Lord: and as many as were inclined to eternal life, believed. 49. And the word of the Lord was spread over the countryside. 50. But the Jews stirred up the wealthy women and the leading men of the city, and urged persecution against Paul and Barnabas, and drove them out of the area. 51. But they shook off the dust of their feet as a protest against them and

went to Iconium. 52. And the followers were filled with joy and with the Holy Spirit.

Bring You Good News
Acts 14:1-18

1. Also in Iconium, both Paul and Barnabas spoke in the Jewish synagogue and a large number of Jews and Greeks believed. 2. But the disobedient Jews stirred up the Gentiles and excited and embittered their minds against the brethren. 3. In spite of this they spent a long time there speaking fearlessly in the Lord, who gave witness to the words of His grace and granted signs and miracles to be done by their hands. 4. But the townsfolk were divided, some supporting the Jews and some the apostles. 5. And plans were made by both the Gentiles and the Jews with the sanction of authorities to treat them shamefully and stone them, 6. when they became aware of the plot they took refuge at Lystra and Derbe, cities in Lycaonia, and the surrounding countryside: 7. where they continued to preach the gospel. 8. In Lystra there was a cripple man who had no use of his feet and had never walked since birth: 9. this man heard Paul speak: and steadfastly observed him, and Paul recognized that he had faith to be cured, 10. and said in a loud voice, Stand up on your feet. And the man jumped up and began walking about. 11. When the crowd saw what had happened, they called out in the Lycaonian language, The gods have come down in human form. 12. And they called Barnabas, Jupiter and Paul, Mercury, because he was the main speaker. 13. Then the priest of the temple of Zeus at the gateway of the city, brought oxen and head-wreaths of flowers to the gates, and would have joined the people in offering sacrifice. 14. When Barnabas and Paul heard about this, they tore their clothes and rushed out into the crowd shouting, 15. Men, why are you doing this? We are mortal men the same as you and bring you good news that you should turn from these superstitions to the living God who made heaven and earth and the sea and everything that is in them: 16. In past generations God permitted all nations to walk in their own ways. 17. Nevertheless He has not left Himself without evidence of His kindness by giving us rain from heaven and fruitful seasons filling our hearts with food and happiness. 18. Even this appeal was inadequate to restrain the people who wanted to honor them and make a sacrifice.

Opened the Door of Faith
Acts 14:19-27

19. A group of Jews from Antioch and Iconium came and incited the crowd and after they had stoned Paul, dragged him out of the city thinking he was dead. 20. However, as the disciples stood around

him, Paul stood up and went into the city: and the next day he and Barnabas departed to Derbe. 21. And when they had proclaimed the good news to that city and taught many, they returned to Lystra, Iconium, and Antioch, 22. Strengthening the souls of the disciples and urging them to continue in the faith and warning them that through many tribulations we enter the kingdom of God. 23. And when they had appointed elders in every congregation and, after prayer and fasting they entrusted them to the Lord in whom they had believed. 24. After traveling through Pisidia they reached Pamphylia. 25. And after they proclaimed the word in Perga, they went to Attalia: 26. and from there they sailed back to Antioch to where they had been commissioned by the grace of God for the work they had been accomplished. 27. And when they arrived, they gathered the congregation together and gave a report of all God had done and how He had opened the door of faith to the Gentiles. 28. And they stayed at Antioch with the disciples for a long time.

God Made No Distinctions
Acts 15:1-12

1. But a group of men from Judaea came to Antioch and taught the brethren, saying, Unless you are circumcised as Moses prescribed you cannot be saved. 2. When Paul and Barnabas vigorously opposed them and questioned their teaching, it was determined that Paul and Barnabas and some of the group, should go to Jerusalem and discuss the question with the apostles and elders. 3. The assembly sent them on their way and they passed through Phoenicia and Samaria, reporting the conversion of the Gentiles: this brought great rejoicing to the brotherhood. 4. Arriving at Jerusalem, they were received by the congregation and the apostles and elders, and reported all that God had done. 5. But certain of the converted Pharisees, said, that it was necessary to circumcise converts and to require them to keep the Law of Moses. 6. The apostles and elders came together to consider the question. 7. After a heated discussion, Peter stood up and said, Brethren, you well know that in the past God made a choice that through my words the Gentiles should hear the gospel and learn to believe. 8. And God who knows the hearts of men, gave evidence of this by bestowing on them the Holy Spirit just as He did on us; 9. And God made no distinctions between us and them by cleansing their hearts by faith. 10. Why do you now attempt to provoke God and put a yoke on believers which neither our fathers nor we were able to bear? 11. But we believe that through the grace of the Lord Jesus Christ, we were saved just as they are. 12. They all kept silence and began to listen to Barnabas and Paul reporting what signs and miracles that God had performed through them among the Gentiles.

Brethren, Listen to Me
Acts 15:13-21

13. And when they completed their report, James responded, saying, Brethren, listen to me: 14. Simon has explained the way God at first visited the Gentiles to gather from them a people for His name. 15. This is in full agreement with the words written by the prophets; 16. There will come a time when I will return and rebuild the tent of David that has fallen down; and from the ruins I will set it up afresh: 17. so that the rest of mankind might seek after the Lord, and all the Gentiles, among whom My name is called, said the Lord, whose work this is. 18. God has known from the beginning what He does now. 19. It is my judgment, therefore, that we do not further trouble those among the Gentiles who have turned to God: 20. but that we send a written message that they abstain from food sacrificed to idols, from sexual immorality, from things strangled, and from tasting blood. 21. For Moses has had in every city those who proclaim his Law for generations, because it is read aloud in the synagogues every Sabbath.

Be Strong!
Acts 15:22-29

22. Then it seemed good to the apostles and elders, and the whole assembly, to send selected men from the congregation to Antioch with Paul and Barnabas; namely, Judas, called Barsabas, and Silas, who were leaders among the brethren: 23. and the assembly sent a written message; The apostles and elders and brethren send greetings to the Gentile brethren in Antioch, Syria, and Cilicia: 24. since we have heard that some who came from us have disturbed you by teaching things not authorized by us: 25. it seemed good, being assembled with one accord, to send chosen men to you with our beloved Barnabas and Paul; 26. men who have risked their lives for the name of the Lord Jesus Christ. 27. We have sent Judas and Silas, who shall confirm this message by their words. 28. For it seemed good to the Holy Spirit and to us, not to impose any extra burden on you, apart from the necessary ones: 29. that you abstain from food sacrificed to idols, from tasting blood, from things strangled, and from sexual immorality: if you guard against these things, you will be doing right. Be strong!

Establishing and Strengthening the Assembled Believers
Acts 15:30-41

30. So when they were sent they arrived at Antioch: where they called together the whole assembly and delivered the message: 31. and when the message was read, they rejoiced for the comfort and support. 32. And Judas and Silas, both being inspired speakers, encouraged the brethren with many words and strengthened their faith. 33.

And after remaining a while, they were released in peace to return to the apostles. 34. But some delayed departure. 35. Paul and Barnabas, with some others stayed in Antioch teaching and preaching the word of the Lord. 36. After a while Paul said to Barnabas, Let us go again and visit the brethren in every city where we have ministered the word of the Lord, and see how they do. 37. But Barnabas insisted on taking along John Mark. 38. But Paul thought it not good to take John since he had abandoned them at Pamphylia and continued not in the work. 39. So a sharp disagreement arose between them and they went their separate ways: Barnabas took Mark and sailed to Cyprus; 40. and Paul chose Silas and started his journey being recommended by the brethren unto the grace of God. 41. And he journeyed through Syria and Cilica, establishing and strengthening the assembled believers.

Established in the Faith
Acts 16:1-8

1. Then Paul came to Derbe and Lystra and found a disciple named, Timothy, whose mother was a Jewess who believed in Christ, but his father was a Greek: 2. who had a good report from the brethren that were at Lystra and Iconium. 3. Desiring to take Timothy on his journey, Paul caused him to be circumcised because the Jews in the area knew his father was a Greek. 4. As they traveled through the cities, they delivered the instructions sent by the apostles and elders that were at Jerusalem. 5. So the assembled believers were established in the faith and increased in number daily. 6. After going throughout Phrygia and Galatia, they were forbidden by the Holy Spirit to preach the word in Roman Asia, 7. When they reached the borders of Mysia and attempted to enter Bithynia, the Spirit of Jesus did not permit them to enter. 8. And they passed by the outskirts of Mysia and came to the coast of Troas.

The Place of Prayer
Acts 16:9-18

9. And Paul had a night vision; a man of Macedonia stood pleading with him, saying, Come over into Macedonia and help us. 10. As soon as he saw the vision, immediately we* made a serious effort to go into Macedonia, convinced that God had called us to evangelize there. 11. Therefore, setting sail from Troas, we sailed before the wind straight to Samothrace and the next day to Neapolis; 12. from there we made our way to Philippi, a Roman outpost and the main town in that part of Macedonia; and spent several days there. 13. And on the Sabbath we went outside the gate along the river to a place of prayer and sat down and talked with the women gathered there. 14. And a woman named Lydia, a seller of purple cloth from the town of Thyatira, who

worshipped God, listened to us: and the Lord opened her heart and she gave heed to the words of Paul. 15. After she and her household were baptized, she appealed to us, saying, If you have judged me to be faithful to the Lord, come into my house and abide there. And she pressured us. 16. And one day as we were on our way to the place of prayer, we met a slave girl possessed with the spirit of a prophetic demon, who brought her master much gain by soothsaying: 17. This slave girl followed us crying, These men are the servants of the most high God, who show us the way of salvation. 18. And this she did for many days. But Paul distressed, turned and said to the spirit, I command you in the name of Jesus Christ to come out of her. That very moment the spirit left her.

---

*v10 Note the introduction of the pronoun "we" marking the presence of Luke himself.

What is Necessary for Me to Be Saved?
Acts 16:19-34

19. And when her masters saw that their hope of future profits were gone, they seized Paul and Silas, and dragged them before the authorities in the public square, 20. bringing them to the Roman officials, saying, These men, being Jews, do disturb the peace of our city, 21. and advocate customs which are not lawful for us to receive or practice, being Romans. 22. And the crowd was aroused against them: and the Roman officials stripped them of their clothes and ordered them to be beaten. 23. After a brutal flogging they were cast into prison, and gave the jailor orders to guard them securely: 24. receiving such a strict order, the jailor put them in the inner dungeon and secured their feet with stocks. 25. At midnight Paul and Silas prayed and sang praises to God: and the prisoners heard them. 26. Suddenly there was a violent earthquake that shook the foundations of the prison: and at once all the doors were opened and everyone's bands were loosed. 27. And the jailor was startled out of sleep and seeing the prison doors open, drew his sword to kill himself thinking the prisoners had all fled. 28. But Paul shouted out, Do yourself no harm: for we are all here. 29. Calling for a light, the jailor rushed in and fell trembling at the feet of Paul and Silas, 30. and leading them outside said, Sirs, what is necessary for me to be saved? 31. And they said, Believe on the Lord Jesus Christ and you and your house shall be saved. 32. And they explained to him the word of the Lord and to all that were in his house. 33. And he took them the same hour of the night and washed their stripes; and he and his household were baptized without delay. 34. And he brought them to his house and set food before them and rejoiced, believing in God with his whole house.

They Saw and Encouraged the Brethren
Acts 16:35-40

35. In the morning, the Roman officials sent the constables with the message, Release those men. 36. And the jailor reported the message to Paul, saying, The Roman officials have sent an order for your release: so leave now and go in peace. 37. But Paul said, They publicly flogged us without trial being Roman citizens and dragged us to prison: and now they want to push us out in secrecy? No truly, let them come personally and take us out. 38. And the constables told these words to the officials: and they were frightened hearing that they were Roman citizens. 39. And they came to the prison and apologized and asked urgently for them to leave the city. 40. So they left the prison and went to the house of Lydia: and when they saw and encouraged the brethren, they continued their journey.

And Some Believed
Acts 17:1-9

17:1 And traveling through Amphipolis and Apollonia, they came to Thessalonica, where the Jews had a synagogue: 2. and Paul following his custom, went to the synagogue and for three Sabbaths reasoned with them out of the scriptures, 3. openly affirming, that it was necessary for Christ to suffer death and stand up again from the grave; and that this Jesus, whom I declare to you, is the Christ. 4. And some believed and spent time in the company of Paul and Silas; many God-fearing Greeks and influential women also believed. 5. But the unbelieving Jews moved with open resentment and recruited a mob of wicked and vicious men from the marketplace, and threw the city into confusion, and besieged the house of Jason intending to bring Paul and Silas out to the people. 6. When Paul and Silas were not there, the mob took Jason and some brethren to the officials of the city, accusing them, Those who upset the whole world have come here also; 7. and Jason received them: and all these do contrary to the decrees of Caesar, saying that there is another king, One Jesus. 8. Hearing the accusations troubled the mob and the officials of the city. 9. And when Jason and the others posted bail, they were released.

Searched Daily the Scriptures to Verify
Acts 17:10-15

10. Immediately the brethren sent Paul and Silas by night into Berea: when they arrived they went to the Jewish synagogue. 11. And they were more gracious than the Jews in Thessalonica, because they were eager to receive the word and search daily the scriptures to verify what was said. 12. Consequently many believed; also many influential Greek women and men also believed. 13. But when the

Jews of Thessalonica learned that Paul preached the word of God at Berea, they came and stirred up the people. 14. Immediately the brethren sent Paul down to the sea coast: but Silas and Timothy remained there. 15. And Paul's escort took him as far as Athens: and receiving a message for Silas and Timothy to quickly come to Paul, they began their return.

What Will This Fast-talking Scrap-picker Say?
Acts 17: 16-21
16. While Paul waited for them at Athens, his spirit was stirred when he saw the whole city filled with idols. 17. So he reasoned in the synagogue with the Jews and daily in the market with the God-fearing people who met with him. 18. Then some Epicurean and Stoic philosophers stumbled upon him. And some said, What will this fast-talking scrap-picker say? Others said, He seems to be presenting some strange gods: because he speaks about Jesus and the resurrection. 19. Taking hold of him, they led him to the Areopagus *(Mars' Hill)*, saying, Can we learn more about this new teaching you speak about? 20. For you introduce strange terms and we want to know what they mean. 21. (For all Athenians and visitors to the city spent their leisure time either telling or listening to some new ideas.)

God Overlooked This Past Lack of Knowledge
Acts 17: 22-31
22. And standing in the center of the Areopagus, Paul said, Men of Athens, I perceive that in all things you are fearful of deities. 23. For as I passed through your city and saw the objects of your worship, I found an altar inscribed, TO AN UNKNOWN GOD. The God you unknowingly worship, I announce to you. 24. The God who ordered the universe and all the things in it, the One being Lord of heaven and earth does not dwell in hand made shrines; 25. neither is He served by human hands, as though He needed something from man, seeing He gives to all life, breath, and all things; 26. and has made of one blood all nations of men who dwell on the earth, determined the history of nations and their territory; 27. so they should search for God and hopefully find Him although He is not far from all of us. 28. For in Him we live and move, and have our being; as certain also of your own poets have said, For we are also His offspring. 29. Since we are the offspring of God, we ought not to think that the Deity has any similarity to anything made of gold, silver, or stone that is sculptured by the art and imagination of man. 30. Then God overlooked this past lack of knowledge, but now commands all men everywhere to repent: 31. because he has set aside a day in which he will judge the world with justice by the Man He

has chosen and has provided assurance to mankind by standing Him up from among the dead.

Among Those Who Believed
Acts 17:32-34

32. On hearing of the resurrection of the dead some mocked: but others wanted to hear more on this matter. 33. Paul departed the Council. 34. However, certain men followed him and believed: among those who believed was Dionysius, one of the judges of the Court of Areopagus, and a woman named Damarius, and several others.

My Conscience is Clear
Acts 18:1-8

1. After leaving Athens, Paul's next stop was Corinth; 2. there he found a Jew named Aquila, born in Pontus, he and his wife, Priscilla had recently come from Italy; (because Claudius had ordered all Jews to leave Rome:) and visited them. 3. And because he was of the same trade, he lodged and worked with them: for by their occupation they were tent makers. 4. And he explained the word in the synagogue every Sabbath and tried to persuade both Jews and Greeks. 5. And when Silas and Timothy came from Macedonia, Paul was busy teaching the word and witnessing to the Jews that Jesus was the Christ. 6. And when they organized a resistance and used foul language, he shook the dust from his clothes and said, Your blood be on your own heads: my conscience is clear; from this time forward I will go to the Gentiles. 7. And he left and entered the house of a God-fearing man, named Justus, who lived next to the synagogue. 8. And Crispus, a leading man in the synagogue believed on the Lord with all his house; and many Corinthians came to believe and were baptized.

Speak and Refuse to be Silenced
Acts 18:9-17

9. And the Lord said to Paul in a night vision, Put aside your fears, but speak and refuse to be silenced: 10. for I am with you and no man shall lift a finger to harm you: for I have many believers in this city. 11. And he lived there a year and six months, teaching the word of the Lord among the people. 12. Now when Gallio was proconsul of Achaia, the Jews made a concerted attack on Paul, and dragged him before the court, 13. saying, This man is persuading people to worship God in an unlawful manner. 14. Just as Paul was about to speak, Gallio said to the Jews, If this were a matter of wrongful acts or wickedness that involved Jews, I should have reason to bear with you: 15. but if they are questions about words and names and your own law, you can handle it yourselves; for I will not judge such matters. 16. And he drove them from the court. 17. Then the Greeks took Sosthenes,

a leader of the synagogue, and kept beating him in view of the court. And Gallio took no notice of what was happening.

Explained the Way of God More Completely
Acts 18:18-28

18. And Paul stayed there a good while and then said his farewell to the brethren and sailed to Syria, and Priscilla and Aquila went with him; but because of a private vow, Paul's head was shaved at Cenchrea. 19. And they came to Ephesus where Paul left his companions: but he himself entered the synagogue and had discussions with the Jews. 20. And when they asked him to stay longer, he declined; 21. but said his farewell, saying, I will come back again if it is the will of God. And he sailed from Ephesus. 22. When he landed at Caesarea he went up to Jerusalem and greeted the assembled believers, then went down to Antioch. 23. And after some time, he departed for the country of Galatia and Phrygia traveling systematically strengthening all the disciples. 24. And a Jew named Apollos, born at Alexandria, a learned man and mighty in the scriptures, came to Ephesus. 25. This man was instructed in the way of the Lord and with burning zeal, spoke and taught diligently the things of the Lord, though he knew only the baptism of John. 26. And he began to speak boldly in the synagogue: when Aquila and Priscilla listened to him speak, they took him to their house and explained the way of God more completely. 27. And when he expressed a desire to go into Achaia, the brethren wrote, encouraging the disciples to receive him: on his arrival he was most helpful to those who had believed through grace: 28. and he powerfully and publicly confronted the Jews, showing by the scriptures that Jesus was the Christ.

Those Who Expressed Sorrow for Sins
Acts 19:1-7

1. During the stay of Apollos at Corinth, Paul traveled through the upper districts to reach Ephesus: and found some disciples of John, 2. he asked them, Did you receive the Holy Spirit having believed? And they answered, We did not even hear of the existence of a Holy Spirit. 3. And he said, How then were you baptized? They answered, With John's baptism. 4. Paul said, John's baptism was for those who expressed sorrow for sins, always telling the people that they must believe on One coming after him, namely, on Jesus. 5. When they heard this, they were baptized in the name of the Lord Jesus. 6. And when Paul laid hands on them, the Holy Spirit came on them; and they spoke inspired words with unnaturally acquired languages. 7. The number was about twelve.

The Word of God Increased in Effectiveness
Acts 19:8-20

8. And Paul went into the synagogue and spoke boldly for three months, lecturing concerning the things of the kingdom of God. 9. But when some grew obstinate in unbelief and slandered the Way before the crowd, Paul departed and separated his converts, lecturing daily in the school of Tyrannus. 10. This happened for a space of two years; so that all who lived in Roman Asia, both Jews and Greeks heard the word of the Lord Jesus. 11. And God worked special works of power by the hands of Paul: 12. so that people carried to the sick pieces of cloth that had touched his body, and they were cured of diseases and evil spirits were driven out. 13. Then some of the itinerant Jews who pretended to have power to caste out evil spirits began to call out the name of the Lord Jesus, saying, We command you by Jesus whom Paul preaches. 14. And the seven sons of Sceva, a Jewish Chief Priest, were trying to do this. 15. And an evil spirit spoke and said, Jesus I know and Paul I know; but who are you? 16. Then the man with an evil spirit leaped on them and violently overpowered them so that they fled out of the house stripped of their clothes and wounded. 17. And this became known to all the Jews and Greeks living at Ephesus; and they were all frightened and the power of the name of the Lord Jesus was increased among the people. 18. And many who became believers, publicly confessed and openly admitted their practices. 19. Those practicing magical arts brought their books and burned them publicly: and the value of these books was several thousand dollars. 20. So the power of the word of God increased in effectiveness.

There Are No Handmade Gods
Acts 19:21-31

21. With this accomplished, Paul determined in his spirit, to visit Macedonia and Achaia, and then go to Jerusalem, saying, Following Jerusalem it is fitting that I see Rome. 22. So he sent two ministers to Macedonia, Timothy and Erastus; but he remained in Roman Asia for a season. 23. About this time there was great commotion concerning the Way. 24. There was a silversmith named Demetrius, who made silver images of Diana*, and made great profits for the craftsmen; 25. whom he called together with others who did similar work, and said, Sirs, you understand that by this craft we have our livelihood. 26. Furthermore, you see and hear, that not only in Ephesus, but in almost all of Roman Asia, this Paul has persuaded and turned away many people, saying that there are no handmade gods: 27. and not only is there danger that our trade will be discredited, but the Temple of the goddess Artemis* will be neglected and her splendor be destroyed, and her worship in Asia and the whole world will be diminished. 28. As

they listened they became enraged and cried out, Great is Artemis* of the Ephesians. 29. And confusion spread through the whole city: and they seized two of Paul's Macedonian companions, Gaius and Aristarchus, and together rushed them into the amphitheatre. 30. And when Paul wanted to enter and address the people, the disciples prevented him. 31. And some of the public officials, who were Paul's friends, sent warnings for Paul not to risk entering the amphitheatre.

---

*v24 The Temple of Artemis, one of the seven wonders of the ancient world, was in Ephesus. The Greeks used the name Artemis while the Romans used Diana.

Most Did Not Understand
Acts 19:32-41

32. Some were shouting one thing and some another: for the assembly was confused and most did not understand why they had gathered. 33. And the Jews moved alongside Alexander pushing him forward. And Alexander motioning with his hand to get silence, would have made his defense to the people. 34. But when they realized he was a Jew, for two hours they shouted in unison, Great is Artemis of the Ephesians. 35. And when the Town Clerk succeeded in calming the people, he said, You men of Ephesus, what man is there that does not know that the Ephesians worship the great goddess Artemis and the symbol of her that fell from heaven? 36. Seeing that these things cannot be contradicted, you should keep calm and not behave recklessly. 37. The men you have brought here are not robbers of temples, nor have they used abusive speech against our goddess. 38. However, if Demetrius and the craftsmen has a case against any man, the courts with appointed judges are open: let them bring charges against one another. 39. But if you have concerns about other matters, it should be determined in a legal assembly. 40. For we are in danger of being charged for the uproar, there being no cause to explain this gathering. 41. With these words, he dismissed the assembly.

On The First Day of the Week
Acts 20:1-12

1. When the confusion was passed, Paul sent for the disciples and encouraged them and took leave for Macedonia. 2. And he journeyed through the districts speaking encouraging words to the disciples and came into Greece, 3. and stayed there three months, and just as he was about to set sail for Syria he learned of a plot against him by the Jews, and determined to return by way of Macedonia. 4. And his travel companions as far as Asia were Sopater, son of Pyrrhus of Berea, Aristarchus and Secundus from Thessalonica, Gais of Derbe and Timothy, Tychicus and Trophimus of Roman Asia. 5. These went

ahead and waited for us* at Troas. 6. After five days we sailed from Philippi for Troas and stayed there seven days. 7. And on the first day of the week when the disciples gathered to break bread, and planning to depart on the morrow, Paul had serious discussion with them until midnight. 8. There were many lamps in the upper chamber where they were gathered. 9. And a young man named Eutycus sat in a window and fell into a deep sleep: and as Paul prolonged his speech, the young man was overcome with sleep and fell from the upper loft and was picked up dead. 10. And Paul went down and took him in his arms and said, Stop the commotion, his life is still in him. 11. Then Paul went upstairs again and broke bread and ate, and talked with them until daybreak and finally departed. 12. And when they brought the young man in alive there was great rejoicing.

---

*v5 "us" indicates that Luke had again joined Paul.

Kept Back Nothing That was Good
Acts 20:13-21

13. Meanwhile, we had gone aboard to sail to Assos intending to pick up Paul there as he had arranged to make the journey on foot. 14. He met us at Assos and joined the ship and we sailed to Mitylene. 15. Then one day later came to the coast of Chios; and on the second day we arrived at Samos; and the third day we came to Miletus. 16. Paul had decided to sail past Ephesus to avoid spending more time in Asia, he wanted to hurry on and if possible reach Jerusalem and celebrate the Day of Pentecost. 17. But from Miletus he sent a message to the elders of Ephesus. 18. And when they joined him, he said, You know, from the first day I came to Asia, the kind of life I lived among you, 19. And how humbly I served the Lord and the many tears and trials I encountered by the plots of the Jews: 20. and you know I delivered the message to you and kept back nothing that was good for you, having taught you publicly and from house to house. 21. Witnessing to the Jews and to the Greeks about the necessity of repentance before God and faith toward our Lord Jesus Christ.

Declaring the Whole Counsel of God
Acts 20:22-27

22. And now, you see that I go to Jerusalem compelled by the Spirit, not knowing what will happen there: 23. except that the Holy Spirit bears witness in every city, that bonds and afflictions await me. 24. But none of these things move me, neither count I my life of value to myself, so that I might finish my course with joy, and the ministry that I received from the Lord Jesus, to witness the gospel of the grace of God. 25. And now, I tell you to whom I have gone preaching the

kingdom of God, that you shall see my face no more. 26. Wherefore, I solemnly affirm to you today that I am innocent of the blood of all men. 27. For I have not fallen short in declaring the whole counsel of God to you.

An Example of Working Hard
Acts 20:28-38

28. Be watchful for yourselves and the whole flock, over which the Holy Spirit has placed you in charge, and commanded that you shepherd the God's assembly which he purchased with his own blood. 29. For I know that after my departing, a pack of heinous wolves shall enter among you, and will do great damage to the flock. 30. Also men shall arise from among you speaking false things, to draw away disciples after them. 31. Therefore, be on guard and remember that for the space of three years I never stopped warning you night and day with tears. 32. And now, brethren, I commend you to God, and to the word of His grace, which is able to make you strong, and give you an inheritance among the consecrated ones. 33. I have never asked for silver or gold or clothing from anyone. 34. You have seen yourself that these hands have supplied not only my own needs, but for the people with me. 35. In all things, I gave you an example of working hard and that one must provide for the poor. Remember the words of the Lord Jesus, when He said, It is more blessed to give than to receive. 36. When he had finished speaking, he knelt and prayed with them all. 37. And they all erupted in tears and fell on Paul's neck and kissed him, 38. grieving most over what he said that they would not see his face again. And they followed him to the ship.

The Lord's Will Be Done
Acts 21:1-14

1. Having torn ourselves away from them we set sail and ran before the wind to Cos, and the next day to Rhodes and from there to Patara: 2. finding a ship bound for Phoenicia, we went aboard and sailed. 3. And coming in sight of Cyprus, we left it behind and sailed to Syria and landed at Tyre: for there the ship was to unload her cargo. 4. And finding disciples, we tarried seven days: who said to Paul through the Spirit that he should not go to Jerusalem. 5. When we accomplished our visit we continued our journey; and all the disciples with their wives and children escorted us out of the city: and the whole group knelt on the shore and prayed. 6. We then said farewell and boarded the ship and they returned home. 7. And when we completed the course from Tyre we arrived at Ptolemais and saluted the brethren and stayed there one day. 8. And the next day Paul's company departed and came to Caesarea: and entered the house of Philip the evangelist, who was

one of the seven; and lodged with him. 9. Philip had four unmarried daughters who prophesied. 10. Since we stayed there many days, a prophet named Agabus came down from Judaea. 11. And when he came to us, he took Paul's belt and bound his own hands and feet and said, This is what the Holy Spirit says, So shall the Jews at Jerusalem bind the man who owns this belt and shall deliver him into the hands of the Gentiles. 12. On hearing these words, both we and the brethren at Caesarea began to entreat Paul not to go up to Jerusalem. 13. Then Paul answered, What do you mean weeping and breaking my heart? I am ready not only to be bound, but also to die for the name of the Lord Jesus. 14. And when he could not be persuaded, we ceased, saying, The Lord's will be done.

The Things God Had Done
Acts 21:15-25

15. A few days later we packed our baggage and set out for Jerusalem. 16. Some of the disciples of Caesarea went with us to introduce an early disciple, Mnason of Cyprus, with whom we were to lodge. 17. When we arrived in Jerusalem, the brethren gave us a warm welcome. 18. And the next day Paul went with us to James; and all the elders were present. 19. After greeting them, he described in detail the things God had done among the Gentiles through his ministry. 20. When they heard his account they began praising God, and said, You see, Brother, that thousands of Jews believe and are all zealous of the law: 21. and they have been given information that you teach the Jews among the Gentiles to depart from Moses, instructing them not to circumcise their children or observe Jewish customs. 22. What will you say? A crowd will gather when they hear you have come. 23. We suggest you take this course: we have four men who are personally under a vow; 24. join them and make a vow* yourself and bear their expense for the shaving of their heads: then all will see that there is no truth in the reports they heard about you; that you walk orderly and keep the law. 25. As to the Gentiles who believe, we have sent a message that they abstain from food sacrificed to idols, from tasting blood, from things strangled, and from sexual immorality.

---

*v24 (See Acts 18:18) This was a Nazarite vow.

Paul Joined the Men
Acts 21:26-32

26. And the next day Paul joined the men after placing himself under a vow and they entered the temple to declare the days of purification until the sacrifice for each one was offered. 27. Just before the seven days ended, the Jews from Asia saw him in the temple and stirred up

all the people and took hold of Paul, 28. shouting, Men of Israel come and help: this is the man who teaches against the people, and the law, and this place; he also brought Greeks into the temple and desecrated this holy place. 29. (They had seen Paul in the city with Trophimus an Ephesian, whom they thought had entered the temple.) 30. And the whole city was in an uproar and a crowd gathered quickly and pulled Paul out of the temple: and closed the temple doors. 31. While they were noisily demanding his death, news came to the commander of the Roman Cohort that all Jerusalem was in an uproar. 32. Without delay he ordered his officers and soldiers into the crowd: and when they saw the garrison commander and the soldiers, they stopped beating Paul.

I Ask Your Permission to Speak
Acts 21:33-40

33. Then the commander arrested Paul and ordered him to be bound with two chains; and demanded to know who he was and what he had done. 34. Some shouted one thing and some another: and when he could not get the facts because of the commotion, he ordered Paul to be taken to the soldiers' quarters. 35. And when he reached the steps, the soldiers carried him because of the violence of the crowd. 36. And the crowd followed, shouting, Kill him. 37. As Paul was being taken into the barracks, he said to the commander, May I speak with you? Who said, Can you speak Greek? 38. Are you not the Egyptian who raised an insurrection and led four thousand Bandits into the desert? 39. But Paul said, I am a Jew of Tarsus, a city in Cilicia, a citizen of an important city: and I ask your permission to speak to the people. 40. And when he had authorized him to speak, Paul stood on the steps and with a gesture called for the attention of the people. And when a great hush came over the crowd, Paul spoke to them in the Hebrew language.

Who Are You Lord?
Acts 22:1-21

1. Brothers and fathers, listen to my defense I now put before you. 2. (When they heard him speaking in the Hebrew language they were more attentive: and Paul said,) 3. Without question I am a Jew, born in Tarsus, a city in Cilicia, but nurtured in this city under the care and guidance of Gamaliel and educated according to the strict system of our ancestral law, as zealous for God as any of you here today. 4. I am the man who persecuted this Way to the death, continually binding both men and women and throwing them into prison. 5. And to that the High Priest and the whole council may bear me witness. In fact, they gave me letters of introduction to the Jews at Damascus, to

bring those who were bound to Jerusalem for punishment. 6. And as I journeyed, near to Damascus suddenly about noon a bright light from heaven flashed around me. 7. And as I fell to the ground, I heard a voice saying, Saul, Saul, why do you persecute me? 8. And I asked, Who are you Lord? Then the voice said, I am Jesus the Nazarene, whom you are persecuting. 9. My companions saw the light; but they did not hear the voice that spoke to me. 10. And I asked, What must I do, Lord? And the Lord answered, Get up and go into Damascus; and there you will be told about all that you are destined to do. 11. When I could not see because of the bright light, my companions had to lead me by the hand until I reached Damascus. 12. And Ananias, a strict observer of the law, who had a good reputation among all the Jews living there, 13. called on me and standing by me, said, Saul brother, Look up. Instantly I saw and looked up at him. 14. And he said, You have been marked out by the God of our fathers, to learn His will and see the Righteous One and hear His voice. 15. For you shall be His witness to all men of what you have seen and heard. 16. Why delay, be baptized and be cleansed of your sins by calling on the name of the Lord. 17. One day when I had returned to Jerusalem and was at prayer in the temple, I saw a vision: 18. and saw Him saying, leave Jerusalem at once for they will not accept the truth you tell about Me. 19. Lord, I said, they know that I used to imprison and flog those who believe in you: 20. and when the blood of your martyr Stephen was shed, I was standing there in agreement with his slayers and kept the clothes of those stoning him. 21. And He said, Depart for I will send you far away unto the Gentiles.

Take Heed What You Do
Acts 22:22-30

22. They listened to Paul until he said Gentiles, then they called out their disapproval, saying, Kill him for he is not fit to live. 23. As they shouted and cast off their clothes and threw dust into the air, 24. the commander ordered Paul to be brought into the barracks, and be examined by flogging; so he might fully know why the people shouted against him. 25. As they tied him up with pieces of leather, Paul said to the officer standing by, Is it lawful for you to flog a man who is a Roman with no legal sentence? 26. When the officer heard this, he went to the commander and told him, Take heed what you do: for this man is a Roman. 27. Then the commander asked Paul, Tell me, are you a Roman? Paul replied, Yes! 28. And the commander said, With a great sum did I obtain this freedom. And Paul said, But, I was free born. 29. Then those who were about to flog him, immediately left, and the commander was alarmed because he had bound a Roman. 30. On the next day, desiring to know the reason he was accused by

the Jews, the commander released Paul from his chains and ordered the chief priests and all their council to assemble, and he brought Paul down with him to confront them.

A Good Conscience Before God
Acts 23:1-10

1. And Paul looking steadily at the Sanhedrin, said, Men and brethren, I have lived with a good conscience before God until this day. 2. And the high priest Ananias ordered those who stood to smite Paul on the mouth, 3. Then Paul said, God is about to strike you, you white-washed sepulcher: how dare you sit to judge me in accordance with the law and order me to be struck unlawfully? 4. Those who stood by said, Do you mean to insult God's high priest? 5. Then Paul said, Brethren, I did not know he was the high priest: it is written, You shall not defame the ruler of the people. 6. When Paul realized that there were two factions among them, Sadducees and Pharisees, he shouted to the Sanhedrin, Men and brethren, I am a Pharisee, the son of a Pharisee: of the hope and resurrection of the dead I am on trial. 7. At these words, there arose an argument between the Pharisees and the Sadducees: and the crowd was divided. 8. For the Sadducees claim there is no resurrection and that there is neither angel nor spirit, but the Pharisees believe in both. 9. There was a great uproar; and the scribes who were Pharisees rose up in opposition, saying, We find this man not guilty: suppose a spirit or an angel did speak to him, 10. And when a great disagreement arose, the commander, fearing that Paul could be pulled into pieces, ordered the soldiers to go down and by force bring Paul into the barracks.

Take Courage, Paul
Acts 23:11-21

11. That night the Lord stood by him, and said, Take courage, Paul: as you have witnessed truthfully about me in Jerusalem, so must you testify also at Rome. 12. At daybreak, some of the Jews banded together and bound themselves under a curse, saying they would neither eat nor drink until they killed Paul. 13. And there were more than forty in this swearing together. 14. And they went to the chief priests and elders and said, We have taken a solemn oath to eat nothing until we assassinate Paul. 15. We want you, with consent of the council, to indicate to the commander that he bring Paul down to you tomorrow as though you intended to examine him further: and we, before he comes near are prepared to assassinate him. 16. But Paul's nephew hearing of the plot went to the barracks to inform Paul. 17. Then Paul called one of the officers, and said, Take this young man to the commander: for he has something important to tell him. 18. So the officer

took him to the commander and said, Paul the prisoner called me and asked me to bring this young man to you, he has something important to tell you. 19. Then the commander took him by the hand and going aside asked him privately, What do you want to tell me? 20. And he said, The Jews have agreed to ask you to bring Paul down tomorrow to the council, as though they would examine his case. 21. You must not listen to them, more than forty men are lying in ambush for Paul, and have bound themselves with an oath that they shall neither eat nor drink until they have assassinated him: and now they are ready, awaiting your consent.

I Will Hear the Case When Accusers Arrive
Acts 23:22-35

22. And the commander dismissed the young man and cautioned him to tell no one what he had reported. 23. And he called two officers, saying, Make ready two hundred soldiers to go to Caesarea, and seventy horsemen and two hundred spearmen, by nine o'clock tonight; 24. And provide horses for Paul to ride and bring him safely to Felix the governor. 25. And he sent a letter to the governor: 26. Greetings to his Excellency Felix, the Governor, from Claudius Lysias. 27. This man I send to you was apprehended by the Jews and would have been killed, but I rescued him with my troops because I understood he was a Roman. 28. Desiring to know with certainty the offense of which they accused him, I brought him before the Sanhedrin; 29. And I discovered the charges had to do with their own law and that there was nothing against him that might be reason for prison or death. 30. And when I was informed that there was a plot against the man, I sent him immediately to you, and directed his accusers also to present their charges against him to you. Farewell. 31. Then the soldiers following their orders took charge of Paul and brought him by night as far as Antipatris. 32. The next day the soldiers returned to their barracks and the troopers escorted him the rest of the way. 33. Arriving in Caesarea they delivered the letter to the governor and presented Paul before him. 34. When Felix had read the letter, he asked to what province Paul belonged. And when he answered, Cilicia; 35. Felix said, I will hear the case when accusers arrive. And he ordered Paul to be kept by Herod's praetorian guard.

Examine Him Yourself
Acts 24:1-9

1. And after five days Ananias, the high priest, arrived with a group of elders, and an official spokesman named Tertullus, to present their case against Paul. 2. When Paul was summoned, Tertullus proceeded to accuse him, speaking to Felix, Seeing by you we have great peace

and tranquility, and that because of your wisdom improvements have been made for this nation, 3. and all of us everywhere are aware of our debt to you, most noble Felix. 4. While I do not wish to weary you, I beseech you to grant us a brief hearing. 5. For we have found this fellow both annoying and troublesome, and one who stirs up sedition among the Jews all over the empire, and a ringleader of the Nazarene party: 6. who also attempted to profane the temple: but we caught him and would have tried him by our own law. 7. But Commander Lysias, by force took him, 8. ordering his accusers to come to you. Examine him yourself and you will learn all the things whereof we accuse him. 9. And the Jews supported the truth of the accusations.

Keep a Clear Conscience Before God and Man
Acts 24:10-21

10. When the governor motioned Paul to speak, he cheerfully answered, Knowing your many years of administering justice in this province, I cheerfully make my own defense: 11. for you can easily verify the facts, that it is not more than twelve days since I went up to Jerusalem to worship. 12. They did not find me in the temple quarreling with any man, or creating a disturbance among the people, neither in the synagogue nor in the city: 13. neither can they sustain the charges which they make against me. 14. But I certainly admit to you, that after the Way they call heresy, so I serve the God of my fathers, and I believe in the scriptural authority of the Law and the Prophets. 15. And I have a hope resting in God, that they also accept, that there will be a resurrection of the dead, both the just and the unjust. 16. For this reason I always endeavor to keep a clear conscience before God and man. 17. Now after a long absence, I came to bring gifts to my nation. 18. While I was engaged in this, certain Jews found me in the temple completing a period of purification, but I was not disorderly or with any crowd. 19. There were some Jews from Roman Asia who should have appeared before you and accuse me. 20. Since they are not here, let these men accuse me and say if they found me guilty of a crime, when I was before the Sanhedrin. 21. Unless it was the one remark I shouted out, concerning the raising of the dead that I am judged this day by you.

When I Have a Suitable Time
Acts 24:22-28

22. At this, Felix having accurate knowledge of the Way, adjourned the hearing, and said, When Lysias, the commander comes, I will decide this case. 23. And he ordered the Centurion to keep Paul under guard, but to permit his friends to attend to his needs. 24. A few days later, Felix brought his wife Drusilla, a Jewess, and sent for Paul and

listened to what he had to say concerning the faith in Christ. 25. And as he spoke of righteousness, self-control, and the coming judgment, Felix was terrified and answered, You may go for the present; when I have a suitable time, I will call you. 26. He also hoped that Paul would pay some fine, so he sent for him often to converse with him. 27. But after two years, Felix was succeeded by Porcius Festus, and Felix willing to gain favor with the Jews, left Paul in custody.

I Do Not Seek to Escape Death
Acts 25:1-12

1. When Festus arrived in the province, after three days he went from Caesarea to Jerusalem. 2. Then the high priest and Jewish leaders informed him against Paul, and kept beseeching him, 3. asking support against Paul, and that he be sent to Jerusalem, all the while plotting to kill him on the road. 4. But Festus decided that Paul should be kept at Caesarea, planning to go there shortly. 5. He said, Let those among you in power, accompany me and there accuse this man if there be a crime committed. 6. After staying among them for about ten days, he went to Caesarea; and the next day took his place in the judge's seat. 7. And when Paul was brought in, the Jews stood around him making grievous charges against him, which were not supported by the facts. 8. Defending himself, Paul maintained, I have committed no offense against the Jewish law, or the Temple, neither against Caesar. 9. But Festus, desiring to gain favor with the Jews, asked Paul, Are you willing to go to Jerusalem and be judged of these things before me? 10. I take my stand before Caesar's authority, where I have a right to be judged, for I have committed no offense against the Jews, as you are well aware. 11. For if I am a criminal and have committed an offense worthy of death, I do not seek to escape death: but since there is no truth in these accusations, no man can deliver me to them as a favor. I make my appeal to Caesar. 12. When Festus had conferred with his council, he answered, Since you have appealed to Caesar; to Caesar you shall go.

I Wish to Hear This Man Myself
Acts 25:13-22

13. When several days had passed, King Agrippa and Bernice came to Caesarea to pay respects to Festus. 14. And when they had been there many days, Festus informed the king of Paul's case, saying, There is a man here who was left in prison by Felix: 15. when I was in Jerusalem, the chief priests and the Jewish elders made charges against this man, asking for a sentence hostile to him. 16. To whom I answered, that it was not the practice of Romans to give up any man on the basis of allegations until he came face to face with his accusers

and was given opportunity to defend himself concerning the charges. 17. So after they assembled here, without delay on the next day, I sat in the Judge's seat and ordered the man brought before me. 18. Against whom when the accusers stood up around him brought no charges of wrong-doing as I expected: 19. but had questions against him about their own religion, concerning the One Jesus, who had died, but Paul affirmed to be alive. 20. When I was at a loss how to inquire into such questions, I asked him if he would go to Jerusalem and be judged there. 21. But when Paul appealed to receive a hearing of Augustus, I ordered him kept until I might send him to Caesar. 22. Then Agrippa said to Festus, I wish to hear this man myself. Festus said, Tomorrow you shall hear him.

A Specific Charge to Put in Writing
Acts 25:23-28

23. And on the morrow, when Agrippa and Bernice entered the place of hearing with great pomp and ceremony, with military officers and the chief men of the city, Festus ordered Paul brought forth. 24. And Festus said, King Agrippa, and all present with us, you see this man, about whom a multitude of Jews have interceded with me, both at Jerusalem and here, loudly clamoring for his execution. 25. But it was clear to me that he had committed nothing worthy of death and since he himself had appealed to Augustus, I have determined to send him to Rome. 26. But I have nothing definite to write about him to the Emperor. For this reason, I have brought him before you all, and especially before, you King Agrippa, that after you have questioned him, I might have a specific charge to put in writing. 27. For it is not proper to send a prisoner to Rome and not signify the charges against him.

The Hope of the Promise
Acts 26:1-8

1. Agrippa said to Paul, You have permission to speak for yourself. Then Paul stretched out his hand and began his defense: 2. King Agrippa, I count myself blessed to make my defense before you this day against all the charges brought against me by the Jews: 3. mainly because you know all the customs and disputes of the Jews: I ask that you listen to me patiently. 4. My boyhood conduct was from the beginning among my own nation and in Jerusalem and is known to all the Jews: 5. they have known me from the first, if they tell the truth, that according to the strictest form of our religion I lived as a Pharisee. 6. And now I stand here to be judged based on the hope of the promise made by God to our fathers: 7. and because of this promise our twelve tribes served God with anticipation night and day. It is for this hope, King Agrippa, I am accused of the Jews. 8. Why should it be judged incredible that God has power to raise the dead?

It is True
Acts 26:9-23

9. It is true that I once thought it my duty to take extreme and hostile measures against the name of Jesus of Nazareth. 10. These things were done in Jerusalem: I locked up many of the saints in prison by the authority of the chief priests; and when they were condemned to death, I voted against them. 11. And in every synagogue I often tortured them and forced them to blaspheme; and being furiously enraged against them I went even to distant cities to persecute them. 12. On one such occasion I was traveling to Damascus armed with authority and a commission from the chief priests, 13. about noon I saw a light from heaven brighter than the sun flashing around me and my companions. 14. We all fell to the ground and I heard a voice speak to me in the Hebrew language, Saul, Saul, why do you persecute me? It is hard for you to learn submission. 15. And I asked, Who are you, Lord? And He said, I am Jesus whom you persecute. 16. But rise and stand on your feet: because I have appeared to you for the purpose of making you a minister and a witness both of what you have seen and those things that I will show you; 17. rescuing you from the hands of the Jews and from the Gentiles, to whom I now send you, 18. that their eyes may be opened so they may turn from darkness to light and from the control of Satan to God and receive pardon for their sins and be given a place among those consecrated by faith in Me. 19. After that experience, King Agrippa, I did not disobey the heavenly vision: 20. but first I told the inhabitants of Damascus and Jerusalem, and then the rest of Judaea and finally to the Gentiles, that they should repent and turn to God, and live a life consistent with that change of heart. 21. For this cause the Jews trapped me in the temple and attempted to kill me. 22. Having obtained an alliance with God, I continue to this day witnessing to everyone, saying nothing other than what the prophets and Moses said would take place: 23. how that Christ must suffer and be the first to rise from the dead and show light to the Jews and to the Gentiles.

Paul Did Nothing Worthy of Death or Chains
Acts 26:24-35

24. As Paul was speaking in his defense, Festus said in a loud voice, Paul, you are hysterical. Much book learning has made you irrational. 25. But Paul said, I am not fanatical, most noble Festus: but I speak nothing but straight truth with seriousness. 26. And King Agrippa is aware of these matters and I can speak freely before him: for I am convinced that all this is common knowledge to him; for these things were not done in some secret corner. 27. King Agrippa, Do you believe the prophets? I know that you believe. 28. Then Agrippa said to Paul,

Almost you persuade me to become a Christian. 29. And Paul said, I pray to God that not only you, but also all who hear me this day, were both almost and altogether as I am, except these chains. 30. Then the King rose to his feet and so did the governor and Bernice, and all those who sat with them: 31. and when they stepped aside, they talked among themselves, saying, Paul did nothing worthy of death or chains. 32. Then Agrippa said to Festus, This man might have been released if he had not appealed to Caesar.

Voyage Filled with Hardship and Loss
Acts 27:1-10
1. When it was finally determined that Paul would sail to Italy, they delivered him and some other prisoners to Julius, an officer of the Augustian Cohort. 2. We went aboard a ship about to sail from Adramyttium intending to pass by the coast of Asia: Aristarchus, a Macedonian from Thessalonica was with us. 3. The next day we docked at Sidon and Julius treated Paul kindly giving him permission to go and see friends to receive any needed care. 4. And putting to sea from there we sailed and because of contrary winds the ship kept to the sheltered side of Cyprus. 5. And when we had crossed the sea of Cilicia and Pamphylia, we landed at Myra in Lycia. 6. There the Roman officer found a ship of Alexandria bound for Italy; and he transferred us to that ship. 7. After several days of slow progress, we arrived with difficulty at Cridus, and since the wind was still against us, we sailed along the sheltered side of Crete toward Salmone: 8. and with difficulty came to a place called The Fair Havens near the town of Lasea. 9. Since the voyage had taken a long time and the journey was already dangerous because the autumn Fast of the Atonement had already past, Paul cautioned them. 10. After careful observation, I see this voyage filled with hardship and loss, not only to the cargo and the ship, but the loss of our lives.

Thinking They Had Found a Way Forward
Acts 27:11-19
11. However, the officer listened to the helmsman and the owner of the ship more than the warning of Paul. 12. And since the haven was not suitable to winter a ship, most of the crew wanted to continue the journey hoping to reach Phoenix and winter there which is a harbor of Crete and favorable to the southwest and northwest winds. 13. So when a southerly breeze began to blow, thinking they had found a way forward, they raised the anchor and sailed close to the coast of Crete. 14. Not long after sailing there arose a violent wind like a typhoon or Northeaster. 15. And when the ship was caught by this wind and could not face it, the crew let the wind drive the ship. 16. And running under

the shelter of an island called Clauda, with much difficulty the lifeboat was secured: 17. and after hoisting it on board, they used ropes to brace the ship; and fearing they would run onto the sandbank, lowered the top sail and boarded up the ship, and then drifted. 18. The ship continued to be tossed by the wind and the waves and the next day the crew began to throw the cargo overboard. 19. And the third day with our own hands we tossed overboard the gear and rigging of the ship.

Fear Not, Paul, You Must Stand Before Caesar
Acts 27:20-32

20. For many days we had no glimpse of the sun or stars and the storm continued to rage, all hope that we would be saved was lost. 21. And when they had been long without food, Paul came forward and said, With all respect, you should have listened to me and not have sailed from Crete, 22. yet as things are, I urge you to take courage for there will not be a single life lost among you, only the ship will be lost. 23. Because last night there stood by me an angel of God to whom I belong and whom I serve, 24. Saying, Fear not, Paul, you must stand before Caesar: and behold, God has given you all those who sail with you. 25. With all respect I ask you to be of good courage: for I believe God and it shall be exactly as it was told to me. 26. However, we must run aground on an island. 27. During the fourteenth night of the storm, as we were driven back and forth in the Adriatic Sea, a crew member felt we drew near land; 28. and taking a sounding found it 120 feet deep, and a little later, sounded again, and it was ninety feet. 29. Then fearing we could be cast upon a rocky shore, they dropped four anchors from the stern and anxiously waited for daylight. 30. And as the crew was trying to abandon the ship and had let down the lifeboat into the sea, under pretense of carrying anchors to steady the front of the ship, 31. Paul said to the Roman officer and soldiers, unless these men remain on the ship, they cannot be saved. 32. Then the soldiers cut the ropes that held the lifeboat and let it drop.

Then Paul Took Bread and Gave Thanks
Acts 27:33-38

33. And just before daybreak, Paul implored them all to take food, saying, Since this is the fourteenth day that you have not eaten. 34. For your health, I ask you to take some food: for there shall not a hair fall from the head of anyone of you. 35. Then Paul took bread and gave thanks to God in the presence of them all and began to eat. 36. Then all felt encouraged and took some food. 37. In all there were 276 on board the ship. 38. After the hearty meal they further lightened the ship by throwing the cargo of wheat into the sea.

When It was Day
Acts 27:39-44

39. When it was day, they could not recognize the land: but they discovered an inlet with a sandy shore, into which they were determined, if possible, to run the ship aground. 40. And cutting away the anchors, they committed the ship to the sea and unlashed the ropes that tied the rudders, and raised the mainsail to the wind and steered toward the shore. 41. But being caught in a cross current, they grounded the ship and the front of the ship stuck in the sand and could not be moved, and the stern was broken by the violence of the waves. 42. The soldiers plan was to kill the prisoners lest some should swim and escape. 43. But the Roman officer, desiring to save Paul, prevented this plan and ordered those who could swim to go first into the sea and make for land: 44. and the rest were ferried across on planks and some on other pieces of the wreckage. In these ways, they all escaped safely to land.

All Safely Ashore
Acts 28:1-10

1. When they were all safely ashore, they recognized the island as Malta. 2. And the foreign-speaking natives were remarkably friendly for they started a fire and welcomed us out of the cold and the rain. 3. When Paul gathered a bundle of sticks and put them on the fire, a venomous snake came out of the heat and attached itself to his hand. 4. And when the natives saw the poisonous creature hanging on his hand, they said one to another, This man must be a murderer although saved from the sea, justice would not permit him to live. 5. And Paul shook the viper off into the fire and suffered no harm. 6. The natives expected to see inflammation or sudden death: but when they had watched him for a long time and observed no misfortune come to him, they changed their mind and said he was a god. 7. Near this place there were lands belonging to the chief man of the island, named Publius: who gladly received us and made us his guests for three days. 8. And it so happened that the father of Publius was taken with fevers and dysentery: Paul visited him and after prayer laid hands on him and he was restored to health. 9. Because of this, others who were sick on the island came to him and were made well: 10. who also gave us many gifts; and when we departed they supplied the provisions needed for the journey.

Compelled to Appeal to Caesar
Acts 28:11-22

11. After three months we sailed on a ship of Alexandria that had wintered on the island, and named for its figurehead and guardian The

Twin Brothers. 12. We docked at Syracuse and stayed there three days. 13. And from there we circled around and came to Rhegium: a day later the south wind blew and we arrived at Puteoli the next day: 14. where we found brethren who invited us to stay for seven days: then we went toward Rome. 15. When news went out that we were coming, the brethren came as far as the Market of Appius and the Three Taverns to welcome us. When Paul saw them he thanked God and was greatly encouraged. 16. And when we finally reached Rome, the Centurion delivered the prisoners: but Paul was permitted to dwell by himself guarded by a single soldier. 17. Three days after arriving, Paul called the Jewish leaders together: and when they were assembled, he said, Men and brethren, although I committed no crime against the people or customs of our fathers, yet I was delivered as a prisoner from Jerusalem into the hands of the Romans. 18. They examined me and were ready to release me because they found nothing worthy of death in me. 19. But when the Jews opposed my release, I was compelled to appeal to Caesar; not that I had cause to accuse my nation. 20. For this reason I have called to see you and speak with you: because of the hope of Israel I am bound with this chain. 21. And they said, We have received no letters from Judaea and no brother has come here to report or speak about you. 22. But we think it fitting that we hear your views concerning these destructive heresies that are spoken against every where.

Some Believed and Others Refused
Acts 28:23-31

23. And when they had arranged with him a day, many came to his lodging; and when he had given further details and witnessed about the kingdom of God, attempting all day to persuade them about Jesus by appealing both to the Law of Moses and the Prophets. 24. And some believed and others refused to accept what he said. 25. Unable to agree among themselves, they departed, but not before Paul made a final statement, The Holy Spirit spoke the truth through Isaiah the prophet to our fathers, 26. saying, Go and tell the people, you shall hear and not understand; see and not recognize the truth: 27. for the heart of this people has become hardened, and their ears are muted, and they have closed their eyes; for fear they might see and hear and understand with their heart, and be turned about so I could reconcile them to Me. 28. Understand, that this message of God's salvation is now sent to the Gentiles and they will listen. 29. After this, the Jews departed. 30. For two whole years Paul remained there earning his own living* and welcoming all who came to hear him. 31. He continued to proclaim the kingdom of God and taught about the Lord Jesus Christ with fearless fluency without hindrance from anyone.

*v30 Paul lived at his own expense and was not idle. It was from this place that he wrote letters to Philemon, the Colossians, the Ephesians, and the Philippians. Paul was not alone. Scripture supports that Luke, Aristarchus, Timothy, Tychicus, Epaphroditus and Mark visited him there. (2 Timothy 4:11; Philippians 1:1; Colossians 1:1; Philemon 1, Ephesians 6:21, Philippians 4:18 and Colossians 4:10)

The Abrupt End of Acts

Why the abrupt end of the Acts of the Apostles? The Acts of the Holy Spirit through the early messengers of Jesus does not have a close; it is assumed that all believers and each local congregation are to continue writing the history of God working through individuals enabled by the Spirit. The big question is: what has God done in your life or place of worship lately worthy of recording in such a book? Below are possible explanations for this abrupt ending:

1. Luke intended to write a sequel. Luke deliberately wrote books and may have planned to do another volume of pristine church history.
2. The Holy Spirit desired that each person in each generation should keep written journals or a record of God's dealing with them, their family, friends and congregation. If this were done, their journal would read similar to a chapter in the Acts. Would it not be wonderful if each believer had a record of God's intervention in their personal lives, answered prayers, spiritual enablement for special tasks, and the general working of the Holy Spirit in their local assembly? During times of trouble or despair, the reading of such a record would be a source of spiritual encouragement. Memories are often short and fading, a written record would be an authentic record of spiritual blessings. When these were reviewed it would refresh the memories of God's interventions in your spiritual journey.
3. There was actually another chapter to Luke's account, but it was lost or left out of the canon of scripture for some reason. Any serious student of Biblical languages: (Hebrew and Greek) can easily see that different manuscripts, translations, and versions of sacred writings have differences that could be attributed to human error or intentional omission. Just as individuals today twist and misinterpret scripture to justify their personal beliefs, it could be that some additions and omissions from scripture were intentional.
4. A view in certain quarters of England is the idea that the Anglo-Saxon peoples are the lost ten tribes of Israel who were carried into captivity by Assyria in 722 B.C., and never heard of since. There is a historical record of a long-lost chapter (29) of the Acts of the Apostles, containing the account of Paul's journey to Spain and Britain. Naturally, the authenticity of the document is in question. The text made its first appearance in London in 1871. According to the editor, it was translated in the late 18th century by the French naturalist Sonnini de Manoncourt from a Greek manuscript discovered in the archives at Constantinople and presented to him by the Sultan Abdoul Achmet. It was discovered in an English translation of Sonnini's Voyage en Grèce et en Turquie in

the library of Sir John Newport, MP (1756-1843) after Newport's death. However, no evidence of such a manuscript has been found, and from internal evidence, cultural anthropology considers it most likely to be a hoax, and is classified among the writings of disputed authenticity of which some were included in the Vulgate and Septuagint, but not in the Hebrew or Protestant canon. However, it is an example of what could have happened following the abrupt close of Acts Chapter 28. It is presented here simply as an illustration not as an authentic or authorized part of Acts.

A Possible Lost Chapter of Acts (29)
29:1-26

1. And Paul, full of the blessings of Christ, and abounding in the spirit, departed out of Rome, determining to go into Spain, for he had a long time proposed to journey there, and was minded also to go from thence to Britain. 2. For he had heard in Phoenicia that certain of the children of Israel, about the time of the Assyrian captivity, had escaped by sea to "the Isles afar off" as spoken by the Prophet, and called by the Romans, Britain. 3. And the Lord commanded the gospel to be preached far hence to the Gentiles, and to the lost sheep of the House of Israel. 4. And no man hindered Paul; for he testified boldly of Jesus before the tribunes and among the people; and he took with him certain of the brethren which abode with him at Rome, and they took shipping at Ostrium and having the winds fair, were brought safely into a haven of Spain. 5. And much people were gathered together from the towns and villages, and the hill country; for they had heard of the conversion to the Apostle, and the many miracles which he had wrought. 6. And Paul preached mightily in Spain, and great multitudes believed and were converted, for they perceived he was an apostle sent from God. 7. And they departed out of Spain, and Paul and his company finding a ship in Armorica sailing unto Britain, they were therein, and passing along the south Coast, they reached a port called Raphinus. 8. Now when it was voiced abroad that the Apostle had landed on their coast, great multitudes of the inhabitants met him, and they treated Paul courteously and he entered in at the east gate of their city, and lodged in the house of an Hebrew and one of his own nation. 9. And on the morrow he came and stood upon Mount Lud and the people thronged at the gate, and assembled in the Broadway, and he preached Christ unto them, and they believed the Word and the testimony of Jesus. 10. And at even the Holy Ghost fell upon Paul, and he prophesied, saying, Behold in the last days the God of Peace shall dwell in the cities, and the inhabitants thereof shall be numbered: and in the seventh numbering of the people, their eyes shall be opened, and the glory of their inheritance shine forth before them. The nations shall come up to worship on the mount that testified of the patience and long suffering of a servant of the Lord. 11. And in the latter days new tidings of the Gospel shall issue forth out of Jerusalem, and the hearts of the people shall rejoice, and behold, fountains shall be opened, and there shall be no more plague. 12. In those days there shall be wars and rumors of war; and a king shall rise up, and his sword, shall be for the healing of the nations, and his peacemaking shall abide, and the glory of his kingdom a wonder among princes. 13. And it

came to pass that certain of the Druids came unto Paul privately, and showed by their rites and ceremonies they were descended from the Jews which escaped from bondage in the land of Egypt, and the apostle believed these things, and he gave them the kiss of . And Paul abode in his lodgings three months confirming in the faith and preaching Christ continually. 15. And after these things Paul and his brethren departed from Raphinus and sailed unto Atium in Gaul. 16. And Paul preached in the Roman garrison and among the people, exhorting all men to repent and confess their sins. 17. And there came to him certain of the Belgae to enquire of him of the new doctrine, and of the man Jesus; And Paul opened his heart unto them and told them all things that had befallen him, howbeit, that Christ Jesus came into the world to save sinners; and they departed pondering among themselves upon the things which they had heard.18. And after much preaching and toil, Paul and his fellow laborers passed into Helvetia, and came to Mount Pontius Pilate, where he who condemned the Lord Jesus dashed himself down headlong, and so miserably perished. 19. Immediately a torrent gushed out of the mountain and washed his body, broken in pieces, into a lake. 20. And Paul stretched forth his hands upon the water, and prayed unto the Lord, saying O Lord God, give a sign unto all nations that here Pontius Pilate which condemned your only begotten son, plunged down headlong into the pit. 21. And while Paul was yet speaking, behold, there came a great earthquake, and the face of the waters was changed, and the form of the lake like unto the Son of Man hanging in an agony upon the Cross. 22. And a voice came out of heaven saying, Even Pilate hath escaped the wrath to come for he washed his hands before the multitude at the blood-shedding of the Lord Jesus. 23. When, therefore, Paul and those that were with him saw the earthquake, and heard the voice of the angel, they glorified God, they were mightily strengthened in the spirit. 24. And they journeyed and came to Mount Julius where stood two pillars, one on the right hand and one on the left hand, erected by Caesar Augustus. 25. And Paul, filled with the Holy Ghost, stood up between the two pillars, saying, Men and brethren these stones which ye see this day shall testify of my journey hence; and verily I say, they shall remain until the outpouring of the spirit upon all nations, neither shall the way be hindered throughout all generations. 26. And they went forth and came unto Illtricum, intending to go by Macedonia into Asia, and grace was found in all the assemblies, and they prospered and had peace. Amen!

Note: The big question is not the authenticity of this document (Acts 29), but what has God done in your life or place of worship lately worthy of recording?

Section Three:

Letters to Assembled Believers

The First Letter to the Thessalonians
The Second Letter to the Thessalonians
The Letter to the Galatians
The First Letter to the Corinthians
The Second Letter to the Corinthians
The Letter to the Romans
The Letter to the Colossians
The Letter to the Ephesians
The Letter to the Philippians

Few discern the importance of the nine letters addressed to assembled believers. Although all scripture is "profitable" to the believer, these letters are of special value. They are not only to believers they are about believers. These letters are foundational documents of Christianity and preserve the inspired oral teaching of the pristine church. There is a marked appropriateness of these letters for the present day. These letters preserve the warm and passionate personal touch of early Christian leaders. Such letters are unique among historic documents related to religion and contain not only practical truths for believers but also concealed nuggets of spiritual treasure awaiting the serious reader.

THE FIRST LETTER TO THE THESSALONIANS

Paul wrote to the Thessalonians from Corinth around AD 50-51. The congregation was established the year before during a short stay of the missionary team. The Jews of Thessalonica rejected Paul's ministry of three Sabbaths in the synagogue, but the team moved to the city and the people heard the good news gladly. A New Testament congregation was born: a gathering of believers who belonged to the Lord. While on his way to Corinth, Timothy was sent to check on the condition of the new believers. Timothy reported that the converts were doing well, but there were some misconceptions regarding the Second Coming of Christ. It is this writer's judgment that Paul's writing to the Thessalonians was one message in two parts. The content of both parts were parallel and based on the Timothy Report. Paul encouraged the believers to be steadfast in persecution specifically describing events preceding the Parousia. He illustrated the stability of the believer's life and encouraged converts to reject worldliness and live by moral principles. Paul both answered their misunderstandings and reviewed both the conduct of the team and the content of the preaching during their short stay in Thessalonica. It appears that Paul believed the imminent return of Christ was essential to the spiritual function of the assembled believers and their daily lifestyle.

Togetherness in Christ
1 Thessalonians 1:1-5

1. Paul, and Silas, and Timothy, to the believers assembled at Thessalonica, in union with God the Father and the Master Jesus Christ: favor to you and peace of heart, from God our Father, and the Lord Jesus Christ. 2. We always give thanks to God for you all, without ceasing making mention of you in our intercessory prayers; 3. remembering your faith that produced works, and love that prompted labor, and hope in the Lord Jesus Christ that brought about endurance before God and our Father; 4. knowing beloved that you have been chosen of God. 5. For our good news came not only in human speech, but also in words with innate power, and in the Holy Spirit, and crammed full of conviction, as you know what kind of leaders we were among you for your sake.

You Became Imitators
1 Thessalonians 1:6-10

6. And you became imitators of us, and of the Master, having accepted the word on a narrow path, but with joy of the Holy Spirit: 7. so you became a model for all the believers in Macedonia and Achaia. 8. For from you echoed out the word of the Master not only in Macedonia and Achaia, but also in every place your trust God-ward is overflowed abroad, so that we do not need to speak a word; 9. for others are

telling of their own accord, what welcome you gave us, and how your turned from idols to serve the living and sincere God; 10. and to confidently wait the return of God's Son from heaven, whom He raised from a corpse, even Jesus our rescuer from the coming wrath.

Fluency of Speech
1 Thessalonians 2:1-12

1. For you know, brethren, that the good effect of our entering in unto you, continues: 2. but even after cruel and unfair treatment at Philippi, with Godly fluency in speech we brought you good news with much anxiety and conflict. 3. Yet our appeal to you was not based on false or degraded thinking nor on cunning craftiness: 4. but passing God's scrutiny, He judged us fit to be entrusted with the good news: when we speak, it is not to please men, but God who examines our hearts. 5. You know that we never used the language of flattery, and God knows we never attempted to enrich ourselves: 6. for we never sought praise from you or others, when we might have been burdensome to you as apostles of Christ. 7. But we were tender among you, even as a nursing mother warmly takes pleasure in her children: 8. so affectionately longing for you, we were willing to share with you, not only the gospel of God, but also well-pleased to share our lives, because you were valued by us. 9. You remember our long and hard labor night and day, because we would not burden you for expenses, but freely preached the gospel of God unto you. 10. You are witnesses and so is God, how upright, honest and blameless was our conduct among you that believe: 11. as you know how we encouraged, comforted, and charged every one of you, as a father treats his children, 12. that you would lead a life worthy of God, who has called you unto the glory of His kingdom.

The Word of God is Truth
1 Thessalonians 2:13-16

13. This is why we give thanks to God without let up, because the word of God you heard from us, you willingly welcomed not as the words of men, but as the true word of God who sets in operation an effectual work in you that believe. 14. For you became imitators of the believers in God's assemblies in Judaea who gathered in Christ Jesus, for you also have suffered similar things of your own tribesmen, just as they have from the Jews: 15. the men who killed the Lord Jesus and their own prophets also persecuted us. They displeased God and showed themselves the enemies of mankind; 16. hindering us from speaking to the nations that they might be saved, they keep filling up the measure of their sins, and now God's final vengeance has fallen on them.

Satan put Obstacles in our Way
1 Thessalonians 2:17-20

17. We beloved being orphaned from you for a short while in person, not in spirit, but desiring abundantly to see your face with great longing. 18. I, Paul, planned a journey to you more than once, but Satan put obstacles in our way. 19. For you alone are our hope, our joy, and crown of rejoicing in the presence of our Lord Jesus Christ at His coming. 20. All our pride and delight is in you.

Good Remembrance
1 Thessalonians 3:1-10

1. When we could no longer bear up under the strain of separation, it seemed good to be left in Athens alone; 2. I sent Timothy, our brother, fellow-laborer in the gospel of Christ and minister of God, to establish you and comfort you concerning your faith: 3. there must be no wavering because of these trials: you know that this is our appointed lot. 4. When we visited you, we told you that we must suffer tribulations; now you see it has come to pass. 5. When I could no longer endure, I sent to know your faith, lest by some means the tempter had tempted you, and our labor was unproductive. 6. But now that Timothy has returned from you and brought us good news of your faith and love, and that you always had good memory of us, desiring to see us as we also longed to see you. 7. Brethren your faith has brought us comfort in the midst of difficulties and trials. 8. For now life is worth living, if you stand fast in the Lord. 9. What thanks can we return to God for you and all the rejoicing we have because of you before God; 10. night and day we keep on praying that we might see your face and complete all that is lacking in your faith?

Strengthen Your Hearts
1 Thessalonians 3:11-13

11. Now may God Himself and our Father, and the Lord Jesus Christ, direct our journey to you. 12. And may the Lord increase you and cause you to abound in love one toward another, and toward all men, even as we do toward you: 13. in order that He may strengthen your hearts so you may be blameless in holiness before God, who is our Father, at the coming of our Lord Jesus with all His saints.

The Will of God
1 Thessalonians 4:1-8

1. Finally brothers, we urge you in the Lord Jesus, that, as you have received instructions from us as to how you must behave to please God, so you should follow the pattern more and more. 2. For you know the instructions we gave you through the Lord Jesus; 3. for this is the will of God, even your separation from sexual immorality and

that you resist fornication: 4. each one of you must learn to control the sensual impulses that are natural in the body and do it with honor; 5. not as the natural urge toward carnal desires as the Gentiles do in their ignorance of God: 6. none of you should be excessive, and take advantage of his brother in business dealings. Because the Lord is the avenger of such excess, as our testimony forewarned you. 7. For God did not call us on the basis of impurity but in the sphere of consecration. 8 Therefore he who rejects this instruction does not reject man, but rejects the God who gave us the Holy Spirit.

Learned the Lesson of Love
1 Thessalonians 4:9-12

9. There is no need that I write to you concerning same blood affection, because you have learned for yourselves God's lesson about the love we ought to show to one another. 10. And indeed you practice love toward all the believers in Macedonia: but we beseech you, that you increase your love more and more; 11. work at being calm and mind your own business, and work with your hands as we instructed you, 12. that you may behave honestly to those outside the fellowship, and that you may need no one to support you.

Dead in Christ Shall Rise First
1 Thessalonians 4:13-18

13. I do not want you to remain in the dark about the believers who are asleep, that you sorrow not as others who have no hope. 14. Since we believe that Jesus died and rose again, even so those who sleep in Jesus will God bring with Him. 15. This we say by the word of the Lord, that those who survive unto the coming of the Lord shall not take precedence over those who have gone to their rest. 16. For the Lord Himself will descend from heaven with marching orders, with the voice of the archangel, and with the trump of God: and the dead in Christ shall rise first: 17. then we who are alive will be snatched up suddenly together with them in the clouds, to meet the Lord in the air, and we shall be with the Lord forever. 18. Wherefore encourage one another with these words.

Keep On Doing What You Have Been Doing
1 Thessalonians 5:1-11

1. You have no need that I write you about the times and the seasons of these things. 2. For you know perfectly that the day of the Lord will come as a thief in the night. 3. For when men say, all is quiet, all is safe, that sudden destruction comes as a woman in the travail of birth; and there is no escape. 4. Brethren you are not living in the darkness, for the day to take you as a thief by surprise. 5. As believers you are not in the dark because you are the children of light, and the children

of the day. 6. We must not sleep as others do, but let us be watchful and sober. 7. Night is the time for sleeping and the drunkard's time for drinking. 8. We must remain sober as men of the daylight. We must put on the breastplate of faith and love, the helmet, which is the hope of salvation. 9. God has not destined us for vengeance; He means us to gain salvation through our Lord Jesus Christ, 10. Who died for us, that, whether we wake or sleep, we should live together with Him. 11. Go on encouraging one another and building up one another's faith, as you have been doing.

Know Those Who Labor Among You
1 Thessalonians 5:12-15

12. We request brethren that you know those who labor among you, and are over you in the Lord, and give you special directions; 13. and respect them highly in love for their work's sake. And be at peace among yourselves. 14. We urge you, brothers, warn the idle, comfort the faint-hearted, support the physically weak, be long-suffering with everyone. 15. Be certain that no one retaliates evil for evil to any one; but always pursue that which is good, but among yourselves, and to all men.

Hold Fast That Which is Good
1 Thessalonians 5:16-22

16. Rejoice evermore. 17. Pray without ceasing. 18. In everything give thanks: for this is the desire of God in Christ Jesus concerning you. 19. Quench not the Spirit. 20. Despise not prophesying. 21. Test all things; cling fast to that which is good. 22. Vigorously abstain from all appearance of evil.

Preserved Blameless
1 Thessalonians 5:23-28

23. May the God of peace sanctify you completely; and I pray God that no part be lacking in your spirit and soul and body, and you be kept blameless unto the coming of our Lord Jesus Christ. 24. Faithful is He who calls you, who will also guarantee your worthy report. 25. Brethren, pray for us. 26. Greet all the brethren with the deep emotion of Christian love (an holy kiss) 37. I order you under special vow of the Lord that this epistle be read to all. 28. May the grace of our Lord Jesus Christ remain with you! Amen.

THE SECOND LETTER TO THE THESSALONIANS

Paul wrote to the Thessalonians from Corinth around AD 50-51. The congregation was established the year before during a short stay of the missionary team. The Jews of Thessalonica rejected Paul's ministry of three Sabbaths in the synagogue, but the team moved to the city and the people heard the good news gladly. A New Testament congregation was born: a gathering of believers who belonged to the Lord. While on his way to Corinth, Timothy was sent to check on the condition of the new believers. Timothy reported that the converts were doing well, but there were some misconceptions regarding the Second Coming of Christ. It is this writer's judgment that Paul's writing to the Thessalonians was one message in two parts. The content of both parts were parallel and based on the Timothy Report. Paul encouraged the believers to be steadfast in persecution specifically describing events preceding the Parousia. He illustrated the stability of the believer's life and encouraged converts to reject worldliness and live by moral principles. Paul both answered their misunderstandings and reviewed both the conduct of the team and the content of the preaching during their short stay in Thessalonica. It appears that Paul believed the imminent return of Christ was essential to the spiritual function of the assembled believers and their daily lifestyle.

Your Faith Grows Exceedingly
2 Thessalonians 1:1-6

1. Paul, and Silas and Timothy, to the believers gathered in Thessalonica in God our Father and the Lord Jesus Christ: 2. grace and peace to you from God our Father and the Lord Jesus Christ. 3. Brothers it is our duty and right to always thank God for you, because your faith grows exceedingly, and the love of everyone abounds toward each other; 4. so that we ourselves glory in you in the assembled of God for your endurance and faith in all your persecutions and trials: 5. this is proof positive of the righteous judgment of God, that you may be counted worthy of the kingdom of God, for which you also suffer: 6. since it is a righteous thing with God to inflict suffering upon those who are now troubling you;

A Believed Testimony
2 Thessalonians 1: 7-12

7. You who are troubled may rest with us when the Lord Jesus is revealed from heaven with His mighty angels, 8. in flaming fire with great force and fury bringing deserved punishment on those who do not recognize God, and do not obey the good news of our Lord Jesus Christ: 9. the presence of the Lord and the glory of His power shall punish them with everlasting destruction. 10. Because our testimony among you was believed, in that day He shall come to be glorified in His saints and to be admired by all who believe. 11. Because of this we are praying constantly for you, praying that God may find you

worthy of His calling and complete all the pleasure of His goodness and power of faith that works: 12. that the name of our Lord Jesus Christ may be honored in you and you in Him, according to God's favor and the Lord Jesus Christ.

Do Not Be Quickly Troubled
2 Thessalonians 2:1-5

1. By the coming of our Lord Jesus Christ and by our gathering together with Him, I implore you, 2. Do not be quickly troubled or unsettled in mind, neither by some alleged message from the Spirit, nor by rumor, nor by letter attributed to me, that the day of Christ is at hand. 3. Do not be deluded by any means: for that day will not come, except there first come a departure* and the man of sin is exposed, the offspring of hell's everlasting punishment; 4. who opposed and exalted himself above all that is called God, or above everything revered; so that he attempts to take the seat in God's Temple proclaiming himself as God. 5. Do you remember that I told you these things when I was with you?

---

*v3 The word derived from Greek αποστασία (apostasia), meaning "departure" is used as a defection or revolt and is normally understood to mean a total desertion or departure from one's religion. It is translated here as "departure" because it is conceivable that this is the rapture of the believers (1 Thessalonians 4: 16, 17) not a revolt or rebellion against God. It is clear that Paul knew how to write "some shall depart from the faith" (1 Timothy 4:1). The KJV (1611) translated the word as "falling away" a seafaring term used to describe the casting off of a ship from shore, literally "to become gradually diminished in size." The Geneva Bible (1587); Coverdale Bible (1535) and Tyndale NT (1526) all translated αποστασία (apostasia) as "departing." Still some who do not believe in the rapture of believers see "apostasia" as a departure from religious convictions.

Now You Know
2 Thessalonians 2: 6-12

6. And now you know what the restraining influence is that will be revealed on God's timetable: 7. for the secrecy of wickedness is now in operation: only He who now obstructs will continue to hinder until He be removed out of the way. 8. And then the Lawless One will be revealed, whom the Lord will consume with the word of His mouth, and shall annihilate him by the radiance of His presence; 9. the Lawless One will come with the aid of Satan's influence with power and counterfeit signs and wonders; 10. and with all the delusions of unrighteousness in those who perish; because they did not receive the love of truth that they may be saved. 11. This is why God permitted a deceiving influence among them, so they give credit to falsehood; 12. that they all could be condemned who refused to believe the truth, but gave preference to disobedience.

Stand Fast and Hold the Way of Life
2 Thessalonians 2: 13-17

13. Beloved of the Lord, we are obligated to always give thanks to God for you, because God from the beginning has chosen you to be saved by the consecration of the Spirit and by faith in the Truth: 14. He called you through our gospel to obtain the glory of our Lord Jesus Christ. 15. Therefore, beloved, stand fast and hold the way of life you have been taught, whether by the spoken word or by letter. 16. So may God and our Lord Jesus Christ Himself who has showed such love to us, giving us unfailing comfort and enduring hope through His grace, 17. encourage your hearts and confirm you in all right behavior, action and speech.

The Lord is Faithful
2 Thessalonians 3:1-9

1. Finally, pray for us, that the word of the Lord may hold its onward course and be extolled and triumph, even as it did with you: 2. and that we may be preserved from wrong-headed and malicious men for all men do not have faith. 3. But the Lord is faithful, who shall strengthen you, and protect you from evil. 4. And we have assurance in the Lord concerning you, sure that you are doing and will do as we instructed you. 5. And may the Lord guide your hearts into a deeper realization of God's love and into steadfastness as you patiently wait for Christ. 6. Now we instruct you, brethren, in the name of our Lord Jesus Christ, that you shun any brother whose life is disorderly, and not after the way of life you received from us. 7. For you know how you should imitate us: for we behaved ourselves orderly among you; 8. neither did we eat without paying for it; but toiled hard night and day, that we might not be a burden to anyone: 9. not that we did not have the right of support, but to make ourselves an example for you to follow.

Be Not Weary in Well-Doing
2 Thessalonians 3: 10-18

10. When we were with you we instructed you that if any would not work, neither should they eat. 11. For we understand that some among you behave in an undisciplined manner refusing to work at all, but interfere in others affairs. 12. Now with the authority of the Lord Jesus Christ, we urge such people to attend quietly to their own affairs and earn their own living. 13. But, brethren, be not weary in well-doing. 14. And if any man obeys not the instructions of this letter, note that man, and shun him, that he may feel shame. 15. Yet do not consider him an enemy, but caution him as you would a brother. 16. And may the Lord of peace grant you peace everywhere and continually. The Lord is with you all. 17. The salutation of Paul with mine own hand, which is my signature in every letter I write. 18. The favor of our Lord Jesus Christ is with you all. Amen.

THE LETTER TO THE GALATIANS

Paul and Barnabas established the assembly in Galatia around AD 50 during the first missionary journey. Paul wrote this letter to the Galatian believers from Corinth around AD 52. The intention was to pass through Galatia to get to Philippi, but Paul was unable to travel due to illness. During his stay in the city the gospel was preached and warmly received. Later false teachers convinced some to follow the ritual laws of Judaism presuming to add to the gospel. Paul was angry and wrote this letter to refute the false teachings. Paul knew that rituals and rules would lead to spiritual bondage. This did not define Paul's understanding of the Christian message. He taught that it was a relationship with God that produced spiritual freedom.

A Servant of Christ
Galatians 1:1-10

1. Paul, sent with a message, commissioned not by man nor through man, but by Jesus Christ and God the Father, who raised Christ from a corpse; 2. I and all the brethren with me send greetings to the assembled believers of Galatia: 3. favor to you and peace from God the Father, and from our Lord Jesus Christ, 4. the very One who gave Himself for our sins, that He might rescue us from the present wicked age, according to the will of God our Father. 5. To God be ascribed all glory forever. Amen. 6. I am both astonished and irritated that you were so soon removed from him who called you into the grace of Christ to a counterfeit gospel: 7. that is not a gospel, but some shake you back and forth to produce a complete change in the good news of Christ. 8. Even if I or an angel from heaven, preach a gospel that contradicts what I preached to you, let God's curse be on him. 9. This I repeat again now, if any man preached a gospel that contradicts what I preached to you, let God's curse be on him. 10. For do I now attempt to persuade men, or God? Is it not contrary to the facts of the gospel that I seek to please men? For if I yet pleased men, I could be no servant of Christ.

They Gave God the Glory
Galatians 1: 11-24

11. But to make clear, brethren, the gospel which was preached by me is not after man. 12. I did not receive it or learn it from man, but by the direct revelation of Jesus Christ. 13. You have heard of my lifestyle in times past in the Jews' religion, how with fanatical zeal I persecuted the church of God, and tried to destroy it: 14. and advanced in the Jews' religion above many of my equals, being exceedingly zealous of the way of life of my fathers. 15. But when it pleased God to set me apart at birth, and call me by His grace, 16. to unveil and make known His Son in me, that I might proclaim Him to the non-Jewish

world; instead of consulting with any man: 17. neither went I up to Jerusalem to present myself to the apostles; but I went into the desert of Arabia and returned to Damascus. 18. After three years I went up to Jerusalem to see Peter, and stayed with him fifteen days. 19. I saw no other apostles except James the Lord's brother. 20. I am speaking the truth in writing this to you. 21. Afterwards I went into the regions of Syria and Cilicia; 22. and was unknown by face to the congregations of Judaea which were in Christ: 23. they had only heard, that he who persecuted us in the past now preaches the faith he once destroyed. 24. And they gave God the glory for me.

The Right Hand of Fellowship
Galatians 2:1-10

1. Then fourteen years later I took Barnabas and Titus as traveling companions and again went up to Jerusalem. 2. This time by revelation and communicated privately to those of reputation the gospel which I preached to the Gentiles, to make sure that my course of action was sound. 3. But Titus being a Greek was not compelled to be circumcised: 4. the question of circumcision came up because some false brethren spied out our liberty in Christ Jesus that they might bring us into bondage: 5. we refused to yield for a moment to their subjection that the gospel might continue in truth with you. 6. But of those who seemed to be in leadership, (whoever they were, it makes no difference to me. God is no respecter of persons) from those reputed leaders I received nothing to add to my gospel. 7. On the contrary, they saw that the gospel to the Gentiles had been committed to me, as the gospel to the Jews was given to Peter; 8. (for He who worked effectually in Peter to the apostleship of the Jews, the same was mighty in me toward the Gentiles:) 9. perceiving the favor God had bestowed on me, James, Cephas, and John, who were regarded as pillars of the congregation, gave to me and Barnabas the right hand of fellowship, that we should minister to the Gentiles, and they to the Jews. 10. The only suggestion from them was that we should remember the poor; which I endeavored to do with diligence.

Crucified With Christ
Galatians 2:11-21

11. But when Peter visited Antioch, I opposed him to his face, because he was wrong. 12. He was eating with the Gentiles until visitors came from James: but when they came, he withdrew and ate separately, fearing the Jews. 13. And the other Jews put on false appearance to conceal facts, and even Barnabas was carried away with their hypocrisy. 14. But when I saw that their conduct did not follow the true path of the gospel, I spoke to Peter before them all, If you, being a Jew live as the Gentiles do, and not as the Jews, why compel the Gentiles to

live as do the Jews? 15. We who are Jews by birth and not sinning Gentiles. 16. Since we know that a man is justified by simple faith in Jesus Christ and not by the works of the law, even as we believed in Jesus Christ and were justified by faith and not by works: for by the works of the law shall no flesh be justified. 17. But while we seek to be justified by Christ, we are found sinners, is Christ the minister of sin? God forbid. 18. For if I build up the very thing I pulled down, I make myself a transgressor. 19. For I became dead to the law, that I might live unto God. 20. I was crucified with Christ: nevertheless I live, yet not I, but Christ lives in me: and the life that I now live in the flesh I live by the faith of the Son of God, who loved me, and gave Himself for me. 21. I do not nullify the grace of God: for if justification came by the law, then Christ's death was useless.

The Just Shall Live by Faith
Galatians 3:1-14

1. Unwise Galatians, who has fascinated you by their charm, that you do not obey the truth, whose eyes have witnessed the crucified Christ among you? 2. This one question I ask, Did you receive the Spirit by keeping the law or by hearing and believing? 3. Are you so unwise? Having started in the Spirit are you now made complete by the flesh? 4. Have you experienced so many things with no purpose? Was your experience of no spiritual value? 5. Is it the works of the law that furnished you the fullness of the Spirit and miracle working power or hearing and believing the gospel? 6. Even Abraham's faith in God was counted to him for righteousness. 7. You know that they which have faith are the children of Abraham. 8. The scripture anticipating that God would justify the Gentiles through faith, proclaimed the good news to Abraham, saying, In you all nations will be blessed. 9. All who believe share Abraham's faith and his blessing. 10. All are cursed who rely on obedience to the law: for it is written, Cursed is every one that does not continue to do all those things written in the book of the law. 11. It is evident that no man is justified by the law in the sight of God: the just shall live by faith. 12. The law does not rest on faith, but on doing and the man who does the law shall live by the law. 13. Christ ransomed us from the curse of the law, being made a curse for us: it is written, Cursed is every one that hangs on a tree: 14. Christ died that the blessing of Abraham might come to the Gentiles through him; so we might through faith receive the promise of the Spirit.

All One in Christ
Galatians 3:15-29

15. Even in human arrangements once a covenant is confirmed, no party to an agreement can alone set it aside as no longer binding nor can one add a codicil. 16. The promise was to Abraham and his

offspring; it does not say, To your descendants, but in the singular, meaning Christ. 17. A covenant which came four hundred and thirty years before the Law, cannot be cancelled by the Law and cause the promise to be set aside. 18. For if the promised heritage depended on the Law, it is no more a promise: God made it to Abraham as a promise. 19. What then was the use of the Law? It was a temporary addition to make men conscious of wrong doings, until the seed should come to whom the promise was made; its terms were dictated by angels, acting through a spokesman. 20. Now a third party is not a mediator of one, but God is One. 21. Does the Law frustrate or infringe on the promise? God forbid: for if a law had been given that could give life, then righteousness would have been by the law. 22. But in scripture the Law makes all men guilty, that the promise by faith in Jesus Christ might be given to them who believe. 23. But before faith came, we were shut up in bondage to the law, until faith was afterwards revealed. 24. Wherefore the law was a truant officer to keep us in school and a teacher's aide to guide our learning until the True Teacher, Christ, came that we might learn justification by faith. 25. But after faith came, we no longer needed a truant officer or a teacher's aide. 26. For we are all the children of God by faith in Christ Jesus. 27. For as many as have been identified with Christ by baptism have been clothed with the attributes of Christ. 28. In Christ there is neither Jew nor Greek, bond nor free, male or female; for you are all one in Christ Jesus. 29. And if you belong to Christ, then you are Abraham's offspring and Abraham's promise is your promise.

God Sent His Son
Galatians 4:1-20

1. When the inheritor becomes an heir while still a minor, he is the same as a servant, though he owns the whole estate. 2. But is under guardians and trustees until he reaches the maturity prescribed by the father. 3. Even so, as immature children we were little more than servants to the traditions placed on us; 4. but when the fullness of time came, God sent His Son, made of a woman, made under the law, 5. to ransom those under the law, that we might receive the adoption of sons. 6. Since you are sons, God has sent the Spirit of His Son into your hearts, crying, *Abba,* Father. 7. Wherefore you are no more a servant, but a child; and if a child, then an heir of God through Christ. 8. Howbeit then, when you were ignorant of God you were in bondage to gods that were not gods at all. 9. But now after you learned to know God and God knows you, how turn you again to the weak and childish teachings, desiring again to be in a condition of servitude? 10. Observing days, months, times, and years. 11. I am fearful that my labor on your behalf was wasted. 12. Brethren walk in liberty as I

do for I was once in bondage as you are: your past behavior has not injured me. 13. You remember at first how through my physical frailty I preached the gospel to you. 14. And you resisted any temptation to loath or reject me in the flesh, but received me as a messenger of God, even as Christ Jesus. 15. Where is the sacredness about which you spoke? The record is clear, if possible you would have plucked out your own eyes and given them to me. 16. How have I now become your enemy, because I tell you the truth? 17. Some seek your favor, but without honorable goals, but they seek to isolate you and have your zeal for their own. 18. But to always be passionately influenced is a good thing, and not only when I am present with you. 19. You are my little children and I have a mother's birth pains again until Christ is formed in you, 20. I stand in uncertainty about you and wish I could be present with you and speak to you in a more pleasant tone.

Children of Promise
Galatians 4:21-31

21. Tell me, you who want to be under the law, have you listened to the law? 22. It is written that Abraham had two sons, one by a maidservant and the other by a free-woman. 23. But the son of the maidservant was born as the ordinary course of nature; but the son of the free-woman was by promise. 24. This is an allegory representing two covenants; one from Mount Sinai, which produced bondage through Agar. 25. For this Agar is Mount Sinai in Arabia and represents earthly Jerusalem where she and her children are in bondage. 26. But the heavenly Jerusalem is free, which is the mother of us all. 27. For it is written, Rejoice you barren who have no children; break forth and rejoice, you who never knew a mother's pains: for the deserted woman shall have more children than she with a husband. 28. Now we, brethren, as Isaac was, are the children of promise. 29. But as then he who was born after the flesh persecuted him that was born after the Spirit, even so it is now. 30. Nevertheless what is written in scripture? Cast out the maidservant with her son: for the son of the maidservant shall not be heir with the son of the free-woman. 31. So then, brethren, we are not children of the maidservant, but of the free.

The Hope of Justification
Galatians 5:1-12

1. Christ freed us, therefore continue to stand firm for this freedom, and stop allowing yourself to be entangled with a yoke of slavery. 2. Behold, I Paul speak to you, that if you allow or accept your personal circumcision, Christ will not be an advantage to you in anything. 3. For I testify again to every man who is tolerant of his own circumcision, that he is a debtor to the whole law. 4. Christ has become idle and of

no effect in you, whoever is trying to be justified by the law is rejecting justification by faith. 5. We by faith wait expectantly and patiently through the Spirit with the hope of justification by faith. 6. In Jesus Christ, the tradition of circumcision or the absence of it means nothing; but only faith that effectively works by love. 7. You were running the race well; who cut in to obstruct your obedience to the truth? 8. This readiness to believe without evidence does not come from the one who called you. 9. It is true that a little yeast can change the whole batch of dough. 10. I am persuaded in the Lord to have confidence in you, that you will not be led astray: but whoever is shaking your faith will pay the penalty at judgment. 11. And brethren, if I preach circumcision, why do I still suffer persecution? Then the offence which the cross causes would cease. 12. I wish they who upset your mind would make eunuchs of themselves.

By Love Serve One Another
Galatians 5:13-26

13. Brethren, God called you to freedom; but do not make your freedom an excuse for a corrupt nature, but by love serve one another. 14. For the whole law is fulfilled in one word, even love; you shall love your neighbor as yourself. 15. But if you bite and devour one another, take heed lest you are destroyed by one another. 16. This I say, continue to walk in the Spirit, and you will not at all satisfy the desires of the flesh. 17. The flesh and the Spirit are opposing each other: the flesh combats the Spirit, and the Spirit combats the flesh: this is why you cannot do all the things you would do. 18. But if you are guided by the Spirit, you no longer need to follow the law. *19. Now the behavior that belongs to the flesh is obvious, they are: (*sensual sins*) unfaithfulness in marriage, unrestrained living, unbridled acts of indecency; 20.(*religious sins*) the worship of idols, the use of drugs and magical powers; (*temperamental sins*) hostility, strife, jealousy, violent flare-ups of temper, self-seeking ambitions, adherence to contradictory teaching; 21.(*personal sins*) desires to appropriate what others have, drunkenness and carousing, and similar things: I warned you before that people who do such things will have no part in the kingdom of God. 22. But the fruit of the Spirit is love, and love brings joy, peace, longsuffering, kindness, goodness, faith, 23. tolerance and self-control: and no law exists against any of these. 24. And those who belong to Christ have nailed the flesh to the cross with its passions and appetites. 25. Since we live in the Spirit, we should be guided by the Spirit in our orderly walk. 26. Let us not have excessive pride or boastfulness about personal abilities, infuriating one another or causing others to be envious.

*vs 19-22 Paul changes the figure "works (are)--behavior of the flesh" to "fruit (is) of the Spirit;" the fruit is "plucked" from the tree of agape.

Bear One Another's Burdens
Galatians 6:1-10

1. Brethren, if a man should make an unintended error due to weakness, you who are regenerated, repair and adjust him with a teachable spirit; continue considering yourself, lest you also be tempted to make a false step. 2. Practice in sharing the heavy burdens of others, and you will fulfill the principle of Grace. 3. If a man supposes himself to be something when he is really nothing, he deceives himself. 4. Let every man test himself for innocence, and then he shall rejoice in himself and not in another. 5. For every man must carry his own personal load. 6. Let him who receives instructions in the word share in support of the teacher's living. 7. Be not deceived; no man can avoid God: for whatever a man may sow this also he will reap; 8. for he who plants proceeds in the field of the material shall have a spoiled harvest; but he who plants proceeds in the field of the spiritual life shall harvest life everlasting. 9. And let us not become weary in doing what is right: for if we do not weaken our resolve, in due season we will collect the good harvest. 10. As we have opportunity, let us practice generosity to all, especially to those who are of the congregation of faith.

New Life in Christ
Galatians 6:11-18

11. You see what big letters I have used to write with my own hand. 12. Those who desire to make a pleasing personal appearance are the same who seek to compel you to be circumcised; this they do to avoid the persecution from the Cross of Christ. 13. The circumcision party does not keep the law themselves; but want you to comply with the law, so they can boast of your conformity. 14. God forbid that I should boast of anything save the Cross of the Lord Jesus Christ, by whom the world was nailed to the Cross for me, and I was crucified to the world. 15. For in Christ Jesus it makes no difference whether one conforms to the ordinances of the law or not, but what counts is the new life in Christ. 16. And may peace and mercy be upon all who walk according to the rule of Christ, for they are the true Israel of God. 17. In the remaining time, let no man weary me with questions: for I also bear in my body the scars* of persecution that mark me as a slave of the Lord Jesus. 18. Brethren, the grace of our Lord Jesus Christ be with your spirit. So let it be!

---

*v17 Paul's new scars were a better witness to his commitment to Christ than the old scars of circumcision. It was a custom to brand or mark slaves and Paul indicated that he continually wore on his body the scars of persecution.

THE FIRST LETTER TO THE CORINTHIANS

During the two years Paul spent in Ephesus, he wrote the first letter to the Corinthians about AD 57. He received reports of factions in the assembly, sexual misconduct, deceptive observance of the Lord's supper, abuse of spiritual gifts, and misunderstandings regarding basic teachings including the resurrection. This letter gave instruction designed to eliminate divisiveness and restore balance in the congregation. The people's loyalties were divided among: Paul, Apollos, Peter, and Christ. God never intended for believers to be spiritually dependent on a man, but on the Holy Spirit and each other. This goes to the essence of the church and its function.

All Speak the Same Thing
1 Corinthians 1:1-10

1. Paul called by the will of God to be a messenger of Jesus Christ, and Sosthenes, the brother, 2. to the assembly of God gathered in Corinth, to those set apart in Christ Jesus, called to consecration with all those in every place who habitually call upon the name of our Lord Jesus – their Lord and ours: 3. Grace and peace with wholeness and prosperity from God our Father, and from the Lord Jesus Christ. 4. I thank my God always concerning you, for the grace of God which is given you by Jesus Christ; 5. that in every respect you are enriched by Him, in fluency of speech and in all understanding; 6. even as our testimony of Christ was confirmed in you: 7. so that you lack no gift; waiting and anticipating the coming of our Lord Jesus Christ: 8. Who will also make firm unto the end, that you may be without accusation in the day of our Lord Jesus Christ. 9. God is faithful, by Whom you were called into the fellowship of His Son Jesus Christ our Lord. 10. Now I encourage you, brethren, by the name of our Lord Jesus Christ, that you all speak the same thing unto reconciliation and that there be no divisions among you; but that you be joined together in harmony and intentions with the same mind and with the same conclusion.

Is Christ Divided?
1 Corinthians 1:11-17

11. It has come to my attention, my brethren, by means of the house of Chloe, that there are quarrels and strife that ignites a party spirit of contentions among you. 12. This is what I mean: every one of you says, I belong to Paul, and I belong to Apollos, and I belong to Cephas, and I belong to Christ. 13. Is Christ divided? Was Paul crucified for you? Were you baptized in the name of Paul? 14. I am thankful to God that I baptized none of you, but Crispus and Gaius; 15. lest any could say that I had immersed in mine own name. 16. And I immersed also the household of Stephanas: besides, I do not remember baptizing any other. 17. For Christ sent me not to baptize, but to preach the

gospel with eloquent wisdom, lest the Cross of Christ should be made of none effect.

Glory in the Lord
1 Corinthians 1:18-31

18. The message of the Cross is foolishness to those in the path to ruin; but to us who are saved it is the power of God. 19. It is written, I will destroy the wisdom of the learned, and bring to naught the understanding of the discerning. 20. Where is the one who questions? Where is the expert in law? Where are the debaters of this world? Has God not completely made the philosophy of the world nonsense? 21. Afterwards, in the wisdom of God, the world through human knowledge knew not God, it pleased God that by the content of the proclamation to save those who believe the message. 22. For the sign-seeking Jews and the wisdom-loving Greeks; 23. but we preach Christ crucified, to the Jews an occasion of stumbling, and to the Gentiles nonsense: 24. but to those who are called, both Jews and Greeks, Christ is the power and the wisdom of God. 25. Because the foolish thing of God is wiser than men; and the weak thing of God stronger than men. 26. Look at your calling, brethren, not many of you are wise by the standard of men, not many from the ruling class, not many are called of noble parents: 27. but God has chosen the average to bewilder the wise; and God has chosen the weak things of the world to amaze the strong; 28. and the poor of the world, and the insignificant, hath God chosen, and God gave an affirmative vote to things which are not, to bring to naught things that are: 29. that no human pride could boast in His presence. 30. But it is through Christ Jesus that you exist, Whom God made unto us wisdom, justification, sanctification, and atonement: 31. that according to scripture, if anyone boasts, let the boast be in the Lord.

The Power of God
1 Corinthians 2:1-5

1. And, brethren, when I came to you, it was not with rational eloquence or wordy cleverness, I made a solemn proclamation concerning the witness of God. 2. I deliberately decided my message among you would be nothing but Jesus Christ crucified. 3. The method was to process the message in weakness, fear, and much trembling. 4. And my speech and proclamation were not with persuasive language or subtle arguments based on man's wisdom, but in the manifestation of power by the Spirit: 5. my motive was that your faith should not rest in the wisdom of men, but the power of God.

The Mind of Christ
1 Corinthians 2: 6-16

6. We do speak wisdom among the mature; yet not the wisdom of this world, nor of the leaders of this world that will come to naught: 7. but we speak the wisdom of God, a divine secret, even hidden wisdom, which God designed before the world to bring us to glory: 8. which none of the present rulers of this world understood: for had they known this wisdom, they would not have crucified the Lord of glory. 9. Written in scripture, eye has not seen, nor ear heard, neither has entered into the heart of man, the things that God has prepared for those who love Him. 10. But God has unveiled them to us by His Spirit: for the Spirit searches all things, and affirms the deep things of God. 11. For what human being can know the thoughts of a man, save the spirit of man which is in him? Even so no man knows the things of God, but the Spirit of God. 12. We have not received the spirit of the world, but the Spirit that is of God; that we might know the things that are freely given to us by God. 13. We do not speak of these things in language taught by men, but that which the Holy Spirit teaches; explaining spiritual things in spiritual words. 14. The natural man does not accept the things of the Spirit of God: for they are nonsense to him: they just do not make sense to him: neither can he understand them, because they are only discerned spiritually. 15. But the man with spiritual insight can judge the worth of everything, yet no one can give an informed judgment of him. 16. For who knows the mind of the Lord, that he may instruct him? But we have the mind of Christ.

Laborers Together With God
1 Corinthians 3:1-15

1. Brethren, I could not speak to you as unto spiritually mature men, but as to men with carnal appetites, even as infant Christians. 2. I gave you spiritual milk and not solid teachings: for until then you were not able to digest strong teaching, nor are you able even now. 3. For you are yet self-sufficient without dependence on God: because there is among you strife, jealousy and party feelings, are you not still controlled by your own nature, and behave as the unconverted? 4. While you continue to say I am of Paul or I am of Appollos, are you not controlled by men? 5. Who is Apollos: who is Paul, but servants by whom you believed, each doing the work given them by God? 6. I did the planting, Apollos watered; but God caused the growth. 7. So neither the planter nor the one doing the watering deserves credit, but God who gave the growth. 8. Now he who did the planting and the one doing the watering are part of the same process: and every man will receive a reward according to his work. 9. For God is working and the laborers are together: you are God's farm, you are God's field

to be worked and God's building to be constructed. 10. According to the favor of God given to me, as a wise master builder, I have laid a foundation, and another will build on it. But let every worker take heed how he builds on the foundation. 11. There is no other foundation for the building but the one laid on Jesus Christ. 12. The material used to build on this foundation may be gold, silver, precious stones, wood, dry grass and straw; 13. the quality of each man's work will come to light: the daylight will show it, because the day will arise in a blaze of light: and the light shall test every man's labor and building material. 14. If a man's work abides which he has built, he will receive a reward. 15. If any man's work is consumed, he shall suffer loss, but he himself shall be saved; as one passing through fire.

Everything is Already Yours
1 Corinthians 3:16-23

16. Do you not know that your body is God's temple, and the Spirit inhabits you? 17. If any man desecrate God's temple, God will destroy him, for God's temple is holy, you are that temple. 18. Let no man successfully deceive you. Since any man who seems to be worldly wise must become foolish in order to become sensible. 19. For the world's wisdom is stupidity to God. It is written, He entraps the wise in their own craftiness. 20. Again, The Lord knows the thoughts of the wise, that they are unproductive. 21. Therefore place no confidence in men. Everything is already yours; 22. whether Paul, Apollos, Cephas, or the world, life, death, things present and things to come are all yours, 23. and you belong to Christ and Christ belongs to God.

Before the Lord Comes
1 Corinthians 4:1-5

1. Let a man see us as ministers of Christ, and trustees of the hidden truths of God. 2. Now it is demanded of any trustee that he be trustworthy. 3. But it is a small thing that I could be judged by you or any man: I affirm that I judge not myself. 4. For I am not justified by what I know about myself: it is the Lord who judges me. 5. Therefore make no premature judgments before the Lord comes, He will bring to light the hidden things and will expose the opinions of the hearts: each one will receive his due reward from God.

Follow My Footsteps
1 Corinthians 4:6-16

6. I have made Apollos and myself examples of these things for your sakes; that you may learn not to think of men above what is written, that no one should boast of one man above another. 7. Who made one superior to another? And what do you have that was not a gift? If you did receive gifts, why do you boast as if the gift was an achievement?

8. Now you are full of riches and reign as kings without us: I would to God you had entered the kingdom that we could have sovereignty with you. 9. It appears that God has placed us as sent messengers at the end of the procession, as gladiators awaiting death as a spectacle in the arena, to be stared at by men and angels. 10. Are we stupid and you are wise in Christ; are we weak and you are strong; you honored and we despised? 11. Do we not both suffer hunger and thirst and are ill-clad and battered about with no certain dwelling place; 12. we still work at manual labor: but we meet abuse with blessings: we suffer and endure persecution: 13. being insulted, we pray: we are considered to be scum of the earth and the scraping off the shoes of others. 14. I write this not to your shame, but as my beloved children, I warn you. 15. For though you have ten thousand tutors in Christ, you have only one father in Christ Jesus, I have begotten you through the gospel. 16. Wherefore, I beseech you, follow my footsteps.

The Spirit of Meekness
1 Corinthians 4:17-21
17. For this reason I sent Timothy, my beloved son and faithful in the Lord, he will bring to your remembrance all my ways which are in Christ, the same as I teach every where and in every assembly. 18. Some of you are filled with self-importance because you think I am not coming to visit. 19. But if it please the Lord, I will come to you shortly, and I will test not the fine words of those who are puffed up, but I will test their power. 20. For God's kingdom is not in words, but in powerful deeds. 21. You choose, am I to come with a rod of discipline or in the spirit of meekness?

Bread of Sincerity and Truth
1 Corinthians 5:1-13
1. It is reported that there is sexual immorality among you, and such immorality that is not even named among the nations, that one should sleep with his father's wife. 2. And you are arrogant instead of being over-whelmed, that the man who has done this might be removed from your company. 3. Although absent in body, but present in spirit, I have already judged concerning the man who has done this deed, 4. by the authority of the Lord Jesus, call a gathering and my spirit will be present with the power of our Lord Jesus Christ, 5. to deliver such a one to Satan for the destruction of the flesh, that his spirit may be saved in the day of the Lord Jesus. 6. Your pride and boasting is not good. Do you not know that a little leaven can make the whole lump sour? 7. Cleanse out all the old evil, that you may be a fresh lump of unleavened dough. For Christ is our Passover sacrificed for us: 8. therefore, let us keep the festival, not with old leaven, neither with the

influence of malice and wickedness; but with the unleavened bread of sincerity and true facts. 9. I wrote you a letter not to associate with people who live in immorality: 10. yet not altogether from people of the world, or with the covetous or thieves, or worshippers of idols; for then you would have to leave this world. 11. But now I have written to you not to associate intimately with any man so called a brother who is sexually immoral, a covetous man, an idolater, or one who speaks reproachfully or a habitual drinker or a greedy man, with such do not even eat. 12. For is it my business to judge those outside the assembly? Is it yours to judge those within the assembly? 13. But the outsiders God will judge, therefore, you put away from among yourselves that wicked person.

The World Shall Be Judged
1 Corinthians 6:1-8

1. I challenge any of you who has a complaint against another to go to law before the unjust, and not before the saints. 2. Do you not know that it is the saints who shall judge the world? And if the world will be judged by you are you unworthy to judge the smallest matters? 3. Do you not know that we shall even judge angels? How much more things that pertain to everyday life? 4. If you have matters to be judged about this life, set them before the least esteemed in the assembly. 5. I speak to arouse your sense of shame. Can you not find one man with enough sense to judge between his brethren? 6. Yet brother goes to law against brother and that before unbelievers. 7. Going to law with each other is evidence that your faith is not working. Why not rather be wronged? Why not rather be deprived? 8. But you do wrong and cheat your brethren.

Your Body is a Temple
1 Corinthians 6:9-20

9. Surely you know that the wicked shall not come into the kingdom of God. Be not deceived: neither those who live in sexual immorality, or worship idols, nor those unfaithful in marriage, nor sissy men, nor those given to sexual perversion, 10. nor thieves, nor greedy, nor drunkards, nor those given to slander, nor swindlers, shall fully possess the kingdom of God. 11. And such were some of you: but you are washed, you are cleansed, you have a right standing with God in the name of the Lord Jesus, and by the Spirit of our God. 12. All things are allowable to me, but all things are not profitable: all things are lawful, but I will not be brought under the power of anything. 13. Food is for the stomach and the stomach craves food: but God will destroy both. Now the body is not for immorality, but for the Lord; and the Lord is the answer to man's deepest cravings. 14. And God has made the Lord

Jesus to stand up again from the grave by His own power. 15. Do you not know that your bodies are the members of Christ? Shall one take the members of Christ and make them the members of a prostitute? God forbid. 16. What? Do you not know that he who keeps company with a prostitute is joined to her body? For two, God says, shall be one body.* 17. But he that keeps company with the Lord is one spirit. 18. But continually and habitually flee immorality. Every sin that a man commits is outside the body; but he that commits immoral acts sins against his own body. 19. What? Do you not know that your body is a temple of the Holy Spirit which is in you, which you have of God, and you are not your own? 20. For a great price was paid to ransom you: therefore, honor God with your body.

---

*v16 The Hebrew language makes clear that two becoming "one flesh" does not define the sex act; it points to the combining of two gene pools into the formation of a new body, a real person; that is a child or offspring. The Hebrew word (*basar*) means flesh, body, living creature, or blood relation. The Hebrew word used in Genesis 2:7 for "soul" (*nephesh*) was used for life in Leviticus 17:11 "The life (*nephesh*) of the flesh (*basar*) is in the blood." The word for life is the same one used for Adam becoming a "soul." The word for flesh (*basar*) is the same as Genesis 3:24 for one flesh. It appears that Genesis 3:24 "Therefore shall a man leave his father and his mother, and shall cleave unto his wife: and they shall be one flesh (*basar*)," clearly indicates that a sexual union may produce a new body, a real person, a blood relation. In conception the blood is furnished by the father's sperm and the mother's womb nurtures the unborn offspring. (See notes at Matthew 19:5; Mark 10:8; Ephesians 5:31)

Not Under Bondage
1 Corinthians 7:1-24

1. Now to answer the question in your letter to me: a single man should not be involved in sexual relations. 2. Nevertheless, to avoid immorality, let every man keep to his wife, and every woman keep to her husband. 3. Let the husband provide habitual consideration to the wife: and likewise the wife to the husband. 4. The wife cannot claim her body as her own, but the husband: and likewise the husband cannot claim his body as his own, but the wife. 5. Do not withhold sexual intimacy from one another, except by consent for a season that you may give yourselves to prayer; and come together again, that Satan may not keep on tempting you because of irrepressible desires. 6. I state this as allowable not as a binding rule. 7. I would that all men were as I am, but each man has his own particular gift from God. 8. A word to the unmarried and widows, it is good for them to remain as they are. 9. But if they cannot contain their passion, let them marry: for it is better to marry than to struggle with sexual passion. 10. And unto the married the Lord commands, Let not the wife leave her husband: 11. But if she leaves, let her remain unmarried, or be reconciled to her husband:

and let the husband not send away his wife. 12. But to the rest I speak, not the Lord: If a brother has an unbelieving wife and she is pleased to reside with him, let him not send her away. 13. And the woman who has an unbelieving husband who is pleased to reside with her, let her not leave him. 14. For the unbelieving husband is separated from immorality by the wife, and the unbelieving wife is separated from immorality by the husband: else their children would be defiled; but now the children are consecrated. 15. But if the unbelieving partner desires to leave, a brother or sister is not under bondage in such cases: but God intended that man and wife live together in peace. 16. For there is no knowledge that the wife will save the husband, or whether the husband will save the wife. 17. But each man should walk as God has allotted to him, as the Lord has called him. And this is my order for all the assembled believers. 18. If a man is called being circumcised, let him not conceal the fact. If any man is called uncircumcised, let him not be circumcised. 19. Neither act is anything, but the keeping of the commandments of God. 20. Let each man remain in the calling wherein he was called. 21. Were you a slave when you believed, stop worrying about it: but if you are made free, live according to your calling in Christ. 22. When a man is called in the Lord being a slave, he is the Lord's freeman: likewise when one is called, being free he becomes Christ's bond-servant. 23. You were bought out of slavery; do not become the servants of men. 24. Brethren, let each man abide with God where he is called.

Serve the Lord Without Distraction
1 Corinthians 7:25-40

25. Now concerning your unmarried daughters I have no direct commandment of the Lord: yet I give you my decision as one who is faithful because of the mercy of the Lord. 26. By reason of the present anguish, I say it is good to remain as you are. 27. Are you tied to a wife? Stop seeking to untie the knot. If you are unmarried, stop seeking a wife. 28. But if you marry you have not sinned; and if your young daughter marries, she has not sinned. Nevertheless, she will have additional burdens in these troubled times: I want to spare you this. 29. Brethren, the time is short: let those who have wives live for Christ as though they had none; 30. there is no time to weep; no time for rejoicing, no time to buy and enjoy possessions; 31. and you must limit contact with the world: for the things of this world pass away. 32. But I would have you free from cares and anxieties. The unmarried cares for the things that belong to the Lord, how to please the Lord: 33. but the married man must be concerned about material things and how he may keep his wife happy. 34. There is a difference between a wife and an unmarried daughter. The unmarried

woman cares for the things of the Lord, that she may be holy both in body and in spirit: but the married woman cares for material things, how she may keep her husband happy. 35. I am saying this for your benefit: not to put a restraint upon you, but for what is suitable for you, and that you may serve the Lord without distraction. 36. But if any man thinks he is behaving unsuitably toward his betrothed, if she has passed the bloom of youth and wants to marry, let them marry, there is no sin in this. 37. Nevertheless the man of steadfast purpose, and under no compulsion and has his own desires under control, and has determined in his heart to keep her as his betrothed does well. 38. So he who marries his betrothed does well; but he who keeps her as his betrothed does better. 39. The wife binds herself to wedlock as long as her husband lives; but if he is deceased, the widow is free to marry whomever she wishes, but only in the Lord. 40. It is my judgment that she would enjoy life better if she remained unmarried. I believe this is the will of the Spirit.

An Idol is Nothing
1 Corinthians 8:1-13

1. Now to deal with the idolatrous sacrifices, we all have some knowledge of this matter. Knowledge makes one arrogant, but true love enlightens. 2. And if any man thinks he has superior knowledge, he has not gained the knowledge he should have. 3. But if a man loves God, this man is known of God. 4. As concerning idolatrous sacrifices, we know that an idol is nothing and that there is only one God. 5. Although there are so-called gods, both in heaven and on earth, (there are many gods, and many lords,) 6. but to us there is but one God, the Father, the source of all things, and we by Him; and one Lord, Jesus Christ, creator of all things, and our way to God. 7. Howbeit all men do not have this understanding: for some by habit eat things offered to an idol; and their conscience being weak is defiled. 8. What we eat does not recommend us to God: neither do we gain by eating or are we made worse by not eating. 9. You must be careful that your freedom does not become a cause for stumbling by the weak. 10. If a weak brother sees you eating in the idol's temple, are you not encouraging the weak to eat food offered to idols; 11. shall the weak brother for whom Christ died perish, because of your so-called knowledge? 12. But when you wrong the brethren and wound their weak conscience, you sin against Christ. 13. Wherefore, if eating food sacrificed to idols causes my brother to stumble, I purpose to eat no butcher's meat while the world stands, lest I cause my dear brother to stumble.

Power in the Gospel
1 Corinthians 9:1-18

1. Am I not free? Am I not an apostle? Have I not seen Jesus Christ our Lord? Are you not my labor in the Lord? 2. If others do not accept me as an apostle, you are bound to recognize my commission. 3. This is my vindication to those who question my authority, 4. can I not claim the same privilege as other apostles to eat and drink? 5. Have I no right to take a Christian sister, or a wife about with me, as the other apostles and the Lord's brother and Peter? 6. Is it only Barnabas and I who are unable to refrain from working? 7. Does a soldier ever go to war at his own expense? Who plants a vineyard and does not eat of the fruit? Or who feeds a flock and does not taste the milk? 8. Do I speak as a man, does not the law say the same thing? 9. For it is written in Moses' law, You shall not muzzle the ox that treads out the corn. Does God take care of oxen? 10. Does He not speak assuredly these words for us? No doubt for us was this written: that he who plows should plow in hope; and he who threshes in hope should be partaker of his hope. 11. If we have sown to you spiritual seeds, is it a great thing that we should reap some material benefits? 12. If others have authority over you, do we not have greater rights? Nevertheless we have not exercised this power; but endured all things, lest we should hinder the gospel of Christ. 13. You know that those who serve in the temple take their food from the temple. And those who attend regularly at the altar share in the sacrificial offerings. 14. In the same way the Lord has commanded that they who preach the gospel should live of the gospel. 15. But I have never availed myself of these rights: nor have I written for this purpose: I had rather die, than any man should make my glorying an empty boast. 16. For though I preach the gospel, I have no ground for boasting because I am compelled to preach; I affirm, woe is me if I preach not the gospel! 17. Since I preach willingly, I have a reward: but if unwillingly, I have a stewardship of the gospel entrusted to me. 18. What then is my reward for preaching? That I am able to present the gospel without charge, and so make only a sparing use of my rights which the gospel gives me.

By All Means Save Some
1 Corinthians 9:19-27

19. For though I am free from the authority of all men, yet have I made myself servant to all, that I might win more converts, 20. and with the Jews I lived as a Jew, that I might win Jews to Christ; to those under the law, I put myself under the law, that I might win them; 21. to those

without law, as without law, (being under the law of Christ,) that I might win them that are without law. 22. To the weak I became weak, that I might win the weak: I am made all things to all men that I might by all means save some. 23. I am still doing this to advance the gospel, so that I may become a joint-partaker of the gospel with you. 24. Do you not know that they who run in a race all run, but only one receives the prize? So run that you may obtain the prize. 25. And every man who enters the race practices rigid self-control. They do this to win a wreath that will soon wither, but we seek a crown that will not fade. 26. I run but not aimlessly; so I fight, but not as a shadow boxer: 27. but I beat my body black and blue, and bring it into subjection: lest by any means, when I have preached to others, I myself should be rejected as a worthless coin.

Written for Our Admonition
1 Corinthians 10:1-13

1. Brethren, I want you to know how our fathers were protected and guided by the cloud and passed safely over the sea; 2. and all were identified with Moses and immersed in the cloud and in the sea; 3. and all ate the same spiritual manna; 4. and all drank from the same spiritual Rock and that Rock was Christ. 5. But God was dissatisfied with most of them: and many died in the wilderness. 6. Now these events are examples to us, that we should not desire evil things, as they desired. 7. Neither worship idols, as some of them did; as it is written: the people sat down to eat and drink, and rose up to worship an idol. 8. Neither let us practice immorality, as some did, and twenty-three thousand died in one day. 9. Neither let us tempt the Lord, as some tempted and continued to perish day by day from serpents. 10. Neither give over to audible expression of complaints as some did and were destroyed by the Angel of Destruction. 11. Now all these things happened to them as examples and are written for our warning, and judgment has come to the heirs of wrath. 12. Wherefore let him who thinks he stands today take heed that he does not fall tomorrow. 13. No test has come your way but such as is common to man: God is faithful, who will not permit you to be tempted beyond your endurance; but will with each test also show you a way of escape, so that you may be victorious.

We being Many are One
1 Corinthians 10:14-22

14. Wherefore, my dearly beloved, continually flee from idolatry. 15. I speak to you as wise men; make your own decision about what I say. 16. Is not the consecrated cup we bless a fellowship with the blood of Christ? Is the bread we break not a fellowship with the body of Christ?

17. For we being many are one bread and one body: for we all partake of that one bread. 18. Consider the practice of Israel: do not those who partake of the sacrifices share in the altar? 19. What am I saying? Am I saying that an idol-god actually exists or that which is sacrificed to idols is of any value? 20. But I say, that any thing the Gentiles sacrifice is sacrificed to devils, and not to God: and I would not that you should have fellowship with devils. 21. You cannot at the same time drink the cup of the Lord and the cup of devils: you cannot be partakers of the Lord's table and the table of devils. 22. Do we intend to provoke the Lord's anger? Surely, you do not think we are stronger than God.

Do All to the Glory of God
1 Corinthians 10:23-33

23. All things are lawful for me, but all things are not beneficial. All things are lawful, but all things do not build up the body spirituality. 24. Let no man seek his own benefit, but every man continually seek the welfare of others. 25. Whatever is sold in the market eat asking no questions for conscience sake: 26. for the whole earth and everything in it belongs to the Lord. 27. If an unbeliever invites you to a feast and you are inclined to accept, eat whatsoever is set before you asking no questions for conscience sake. 28. But if your friend should declare, this was offered in sacrifice to idols, do not eat for his sake who told you, and for conscience sake: for the earth is the Lord's and the fullness thereof: 29. I mean your friend's conscience not your own: so why is my liberty judged by another man's conscience? 30. If I partake of food after I have given thanks, how can I unjustly be criticized for eating that for which I gave thanks? 31. Whether you eat, or drink, or whatever you do, do all to the glory of God. 32. Give no occasion to stumbling, neither to the Jews, nor to the Gentiles, nor to the assembly of God: 33. even as I try to please everybody in all things, not seeking personal profit, but seeking the profit of others, that they may be saved.

We Have No Such Custom
1 Corinthians 11:1-16

1. Be imitators of me, even as I imitate Christ. 2. Now I praise you for remembering what I taught you. 3. But there is one matter I need you to know, that Christ is the Head of every man; and a wife is responsible to her husband; and Christ is responsible to God. 4. *Every man praying or prophesying, having a covering or veil hanging down from the head dishonors God. 5. But every woman who prays or prophesies without a covering or a veil dishonors her husband: for it is the same as if she were shaven as an adulteress. 6. For if the woman be not covered, let her also be shorn: but if it be a shame for a woman to

be shorn or shaven, let her head be veiled. 7. For a man has no need to cover his head, forasmuch as he is the image and glory of God: but the woman is the glory of the man. 8. For the first man did not come from a woman; but the woman came from the man. 9. Neither was man created for the woman; but the woman was made for the man. 10. For this cause ought the woman to have the sign of authority on her head because of the angels. 11. Neither is the man independent of a woman, in the Lord, the woman is not independent of the man. 12. For just as a woman was made out of a man, even so is the man made by the woman; but all things of God. 13. You make the judgment: is it becoming for a woman to pray to God unveiled? 14. Does not even nature teach you that it is unnatural for a man to have long hair, is it not degrading to him? 15. But if a woman has long hair, it appears to be her glory: for her hair was given as a covering. 16. But if any man wishes to dispute the matter, we have no such custom, neither in the assembled believers of God.

---

*v4 Since the custom of head coverings demonstrated what was visible in nature, it appears that Paul saw the need for a Gentile assembly in Greek territory to follow the Greek tradition rather than the Jewish one. Roman men also covered their heads when performing religious duties.

Let a Man Examine Himself
1 Corinthians 11:17-34

17. In giving this charge I mention a practice that I cannot commend, you gather for worship not for good, but for the worse. 18. In the first place, when you come together, I hear there are divisions among you and I have reason to believe it. 19. There must be dissent and factions among you, so those approved may become obvious among you. 20. You come together socially to eat, but it is not the Lord's Supper. 21. For some being hungry eat hurriedly before the poor and some are frequently drunk. 22. You do have houses to eat and drink in, don't you? Or do you look down on the poor and embarrass the assembly? What shall I say about this? Certainly, I will not praise you for this behavior. 23. For I have received an understanding from the Lord of that which I deliver to you, that the Lord Jesus the same night in which He was being betrayed took bread: 24. after He gave thanks, He broke it, saying to the disciples, this represents My body given for you: this do often to recall to memory My sacrifice. 25. In the same manner when supper was ended He took the cup, saying, this cup represents the New Testament ratified by My blood: every time you do this recall to memory My sacrifice. 26. As often as you repeat this, eat the bread and drink the cup, you proclaim the Lord's death until He returns. 27. And in conclusion, whoever shall eat this bread and drink this cup

of the Lord, in an unworthy manner, shall be guilty of violating the body and blood of the Lord. 28. Each time let a man examine himself before he eats of that bread and drinks of that cup. 29. The reason for self-examination before eating and drinking is to prevent partaking in an unworthy manner when one does not properly consider the Lord's assembly. 30. For this reason many are powerless and sick among you and many die. 31. For if we judge ourselves rightly, we should not be judged by God. 32. But when we are judged, we are disciplined of the Lord that we should not be condemned eternally with the world. 33. Wherefore, my brethren, when you come together to eat, wait in turn for a proper distribution. 34. If any man is hungry, let him eat at home; that there be no confusion when you come together to eat. Other things about the Lord's Supper will I set in order on my next visit.

Dividing to Every Man
1 Corinthians 12:1-11

1. Now concerning spiritual things, brethren, I do not want you to be without knowledge. 2. You remember when you were pagans and were controlled and blindly led astray to worship unintelligent idols. 3. I have you to understand that no man speaking by the Spirit can curse Jesus: and no man can truly say Jesus is Lord, but by the Holy Spirit. 4. Now there are a variety of grace-gifts, but the same Spirit. 5. And there are different services to the congregation, but the same Lord. 6. And there are a variety of supernatural workings, but it is the same God who works all things in all. 7. But the repeated presence of the Spirit is given to make clear the advantage to the assembly. 8. For to one the Spirit gives the communication of spiritual wisdom; to another the word of practical knowledge by the same Spirit; 9. to another faith that produces incredible deeds by the same Spirit; 10. to another the operations of powers; to another foretelling and forth telling; to another the ability to distinguish between different kinds of spirits; to another unnaturally acquired languages; to another the translation of unnaturally acquired languages; 11. But all these instantaneous and enabling gifts operate by the same Spirit, distributed individually to each one according to His purpose.

The Same Care One for Another
1 Corinthians 12:12-31

12. Just as the body is one with many members, and all are members of one body, although many they are one in Christ. 13. For by one Spirit were we all spiritually transformed into one body, whether we are Jews or Gentiles, whether bond or free; we have all had hands laid on us and been furnished one Spirit. 14. For the body is not one member, but many. 15. If the foot were to say, because I am not the

hand, I do not belong to the body: is it not still part of the body? 16. And if the ear were to say, because I am not the eye, I do not belong to the body: is it not still part of the body? 17. If the whole body were an eye, how could we hear? If the whole body were an ear, how could we smell? 18. Now God has placed all the parts in the body as it pleased Him. 19. And if all were one part there would be no body. 20. But now they are many members yet but one body. 21. And the eye cannot say to the hand, I have no need of you: nor can the head say to the feet, I have no need of you. 22. No, those organs of the body which seem to be weak are necessary: 23. and those parts that seem to be without honor, upon those we bestow more clothing; and on our private parts we also clothe with modesty. 24. The good parts need no adornment: but God has balanced the body together, having given a noble function to the parts that lack honor: 25. that there be no discord in the body: but that members should have the same care one for another. 26. That all members should suffer and rejoice together. 27. Now you are the body of Christ and individual members. 28. And God has placed certain people in the assembly, first some to be messengers, secondarily some to be inspired preachers, thirdly instructors, after that special powers, then gifts of healings, helps, administrators, unnaturally acquired languages. 29. Are all messengers? Are all preachers? Are all instructors? Are all workers of miracles? 30. Have all the gifts of healing? Do all speak languages unnaturally acquired? Do all interpret? 31. But set your hearts on the best spiritual graces: and yet I can show you a way beyond all comparison.

The Greatest of These is Love*
1 Corinthians 13:1-13
1. Even if I could speak the languages of men and angels and not have love*, I would become an echoing gong or a clanging cymbal. 2. Even if I have the gift of speaking forth God's word, and understand sacred secrets, and all knowledge; and though I have absolute faith and be able to move mountains, and have not love, I am nothing. 3. And though I distribute all I possess to provide for the poor, and though I seal my witness at a burning stake, and have not love, there is no benefit for me. 4. Love is long-suffering and sympathetic; love has no jealousy, love is not anxious to impress others, does not hold inflated ideas of self-importance, 5. has good manners, is not self-seeking, is never provoked, does not keep score of wrongs; 6. takes no pleasure in wrongdoing, but rejoices when truth is victorious; 7. there is no limit to endurance, love has endless faith and great expectations, there is no end to love's tolerance. 8. Love stands when all else disintegrates: but preaching, the use of unnaturally acquired languages and present and fragmentary knowledge will be rendered entirely idle. 9. For we

presently speak based on limited knowledge. 10. But when Christ returns, then our limited function will become inoperative. 11. When I was a child, I spoke, understood, and reasoned as a child: but becoming a man, I outgrew childish ways. 12. At the present we see only blurred reflections in polished metal; but then face to face the blurred image will be gone and we will see ourselves as God sees us. 13. Now there are three things that endure forever faith, hope, and love; but the greatest of these is love.

---

*Love in this chapter is *agape* or benevolent love, doing what the one who loves deems needed by the one loved, and reflects God's willful direction toward mankind and not necessarily what one desires. It is a one-way love.

Pursue Love and Be Zealous for Spiritual Things
1 Corinthians 14:1-25

1. Pursue love and be zealous for spiritual things, but be more willing to speak the message of God. 2. For speaking in a language not naturally acquired speaks not to men, but to God: for no man hears with the understanding, although he may be speaking sacred secrets in the Spirit. 3. But he that speaks forth the word speaks to the edification, encouragement and comfort of men. 4. He who speaks in a language not naturally acquired encourages himself; but he who speaks forth the word builds up the congregation. 5. I would that you all spoke languages not acquired naturally; but rather that you speak forth the word; for greater is he that speaks forth the word than he who speaks in languages not acquired naturally, unless he translates for the building up of the congregation. 6. Suppose I were to come to you speaking languages you do not know, what shall I benefit you, except I teach you by either revelation, knowledge, or divinely enabled preaching? 7. Even inanimate objects make sounds, such as a flute or harp, but unless each sound is distinctive, how shall one recognize the melody and attribute it to the flute or harp? 8. If the vibrations of the trumpet are not clear, who will be called to the battle? 9. Likewise if you do not speak clearly in an understandable language, how shall it be known what was spoken? You would be making meaningless sound. 10. There are many kinds of voices in the world, and none without meaning. 11. Therefore, if one does not understand the language, we will be hearing and speaking garbled nonsense. 12. Since you have set your hearts on spiritual endowments, be eager to excel in building up the assembly. 13. Wherefore let him who speaks in a language not normally acquired call upon God for an interpretation. 14. If I pray in an unknown language, my spirit prays, but my understanding is unfruitful. 15. What follows? I will pray in the Spirit and pray for the understanding also: I will sing in the Spirit, and sing with the understanding also. 16.

If you pronounce a blessing with the Spirit, how can the uninstructed say Amen if he cannot understand what you said? 17. To be sure you are giving thanks, but others are not enlightened or strengthened. 18. I thank God I speak with more languages than you all: 19. yet in the assembly I had rather speak five words with understanding, that by my voice I might teach others, than ten thousand words in a language unknown to the people. 20. Brethren do not be child-like in understanding: nevertheless, keep your child-like innocence, but have adult understanding. 21. The Lord said, it is written in the law, with strangers will I speak in other languages to the people: and yet they will not hear Me. 22. Wherefore, unnaturally acquired languages are a spiritual wonder to the unbelieving: but speaking forth plainly the word of God provides nothing to the unbeliever, but is for those who believe. 23. Suppose at a meeting of the whole congregation that everyone spoke in unknown languages, would not the unlearned present think everyone was mad? 24. But if all were inspired to speak forth a witness and an unlearned unbeliever attended the meeting he is convicted in his conscience and called to account: 25. and the secrets of his heart are made manifest; and he will prostrate himself before God and declare that God is truly among you.

Let Everything Be Well-mannered
1 Corinthians 14:26-40

26. To sum up, brethren, when you come together everyone should participate, one has a hymn, another has a teaching, an unnaturally acquired language, a scared truth, or a translation. Let everything be done to build up the congregation. 27. If any one speaks in a language unnaturally acquired, let it be by course of two or three; and let one interpret. 28. But if there be no interpretation, let the speaker not disrupt the service and speak silently to himself and to God. 29. Speakers should also be limited to two or three and the others judge what is said. 30. If while another is speaking someone seated has an inspired word, let the first speaker stop before another speaks. 31. You can all speak your testimony one after another, so that all may understand and all be encouraged. 32. The spirit of a true speaker is under that person's control. 33. For the God who inspires is not given to confusion, but of harmony as with all the saints in the congregations. 34. Wives* should not question the speaker's message or mumble among themselves during the service: according to the law, wives were to be deferential to their husbands. 35. And if they wish to understand what the speaker said, let them ask their husbands at home: for it is not good taste for a wife to speak out during the assembly. 36. What? Did

the word of God originate in your congregation? Or did it come only to you? 37. If any man claims to be inspired to preach or have some spiritual endowment, let him acknowledge that the message I write has the authority of the Lord. 38. But if any man does not know, let him remain ignorant. 39. Wherefore, brethren, cultivate inspired speaking, and do not forbid anyone to speak in a language that was unnaturally acquired. 40. Let every thing be well-mannered and done in an orderly manner.

---

*v34 Paul was concerned about order vs confusion. He does not forbid women in general to speak, but is concerned about the wives of the speakers speaking out, talking, when "the others judge" what was said.

If Christ Be Not Raised
1 Corinthians 15:1-19

1. This is to remind you, brethren, the saving message on which you stand is the authoritative good news I declared unto you and you received; 2. provided you hold fast the essence of the words delivered to you since you became believers in Christ. 3. For I transmitted to you what I first received, how the scriptures proclaimed that Christ died for our sins; 4. according to the writings He was laid to rest and stood up again the third day: 5. and that He was seen by Cephas, then by others of the Twelve: 6. After that, over five hundred brethren saw Him at the same time; most of whom survive to this day, but some have passed to their rest. 7. After that He appeared to James; then to all the apostles. 8. Finally, He appeared even to me, as an imperfectly formed fetus brought forth before the due date. 9. Compared to the other apostles, I am the weakest and not deserving of the office because of my efforts to hunt down and destroy the called ones of God. 10. But by the effective working of His undeserved favor I am what I am now: and His grace extended to me was fruitful; and by His grace I labor to the point of exhaustion through the strengthening power of God in me. 11. Regardless of who preached the resurrection, you believed. 12. Since you believed what was preached that Christ stood up again from the grave, how can some deny bodily resurrection of all believers? 13. But if there be no standing up of the dead, then is Christ not Risen: 14. and if Christ be not Risen, then your faith is wasted? 15. And we have affirmed a false witness, because we testified that God lifted up Christ: if Christ be not raised then the dead will not rise. 16. If the dead rise not then is Christ still in the grave: 17. and if Christ was not raised, your faith is wasted; you remain in your sins. 18. Then all who died believing in Christ have perished. 19. If our hope in Christ is only for the living, we are headed for disappointment.

Bad Company Spoils Good Behavior
1 Corinthians 15:20-34

20. But the truth is Christ was raised from the grave, and became the first installment of the resurrection harvest of those who sleep in Christ. 21. Since death came by man, resurrection from the dead came by man. 22. For in Adam all died, even so in Christ shall all live. 23. But each man in his turn: Christ the first harvest installment and afterward those who belong to Christ at His coming. 24. After an interval comes the end, when Christ shall turn over His royal powers to God, the Father; after He has abolished and put to an end all governments, authority and power. 25. Christ must reign until all enemies are put under His feet. 26. The last enemy to be destroyed is death. 27. For the Father has put all things under His authority. In that quotation "all things," it is self-evident that the Father is excluded from the subjection. 28. When all things are subdued, then shall the Son also become subject to the Father, that God may be utterly supreme. 29. Otherwise what will they gain who are immersed vicariously for the dead, if the dead rise not? What good then is a proxy baptism? 30. Why do we stand in a constant and continued state of danger? 31. I affirm by my delight in you which I have in Christ Jesus, I die day by day. 32. If as a man I suffered maltreatment from evil men at Ephesus, what have I gained if there is no life after death? Why not just eat and drink and die? 33. Do not permit yourself to be fooled: bad company spoils good behavior. 34. Come to your senses and stop sinning; for some of you are truly ignorant of God: I say this publicly to your individual shame.

How are the Dead Raised?
1 Corinthians 15:35-50

35. Someone may ask, how are the dead raised? And what sort of body will they wear? 36. Foolish questions, you know that a seed does not germinate without dying itself. 37. And when you sow a seed and the sprout comes up, it is different from the seed you planted, but it is a naked seed of wheat or something else. 38. But God gives the seed a body that pleases Him. 39. All forms of life are not the same: but there is one body for men and another kind for beasts, another for fish, and another for birds. 40. There are bodies in the heavens and bodies on the earth: but the splendor of the heavenly is one and the splendor of the earthy is another. 41. The sun is glorious in one way and the moon in another way, and another splendor for the stars: for one star differs from another in brightness. 42. This is how it will be when the dead are raised. It is sown a perishable body; it is raised an imperishable body: 43. It is sown in humiliation; it is raised in beauty: it is sown in weakness; it is raised in power: 44. it is sown a natural body and raised a spiritual body. There is a human body and there is a spiritual body.

45. It is written, the first man Adam was made a living creature; the last Adam was made a life-giving Spirit. 46. The spiritual did not come first, but the natural: and afterward the spiritual. 47. The first man was of the earth, the Second Man is from heaven. 48. The earth-minded are as the earthy man: and the heavenly man is patterned after the heavenly. 49. As we have borne the image of the earthy, we shall also bear the image of the heavenly. 50. Now I tell you this, brethren, the body made of flesh and blood cannot come into the kingdom of God; neither does the perishable body live forever.

Death is Swallowed Up in Victory
1 Corinthians 15:51-58
51. Behold, I show you a sacred secret; we shall not all die, but we will all be transformed, 52. in a nanosecond, the blink of an eye, as the last trumpet sounds the dead shall be raised imperishable, and we shall be made different. 53. For the dead shall put on an imperishable body, and the living shall put on immortality. 54. So when the dead shall put on an imperishable body, and the living shall put on immortality, then shall be brought to pass the saying, Death has been completely swallowed up in victory. 55. Death where is your venomous sting? Grave, where is your triumph? 56. Sin is the sting of death; and the law is the strength of sin. 57. But thanks to God, who gives us the victory through our Lord Jesus Christ. 58. Therefore, my beloved, be unwavering, holding your ground and always flourishing in the work of the Lord, forasmuch as you know that your hard work is always fruitful in the Lord.

As God Has Prospered
1 Corinthians 16:1-12
1. Now concerning the gathering of funds for the saints, follow the directions I gave to the congregations of Galatia. 2. On the first day of each week remember how God has prospered you and put aside your gifts in a safe place, so no collections will be necessary when I come. 3. When I arrive whomever you approved by letters, I will send with your freewill gifts to Jerusalem. 4. And if it is advantageous that I go, they shall go with me. 5. I plan to pass through Macedonia and I will visit you when I do. 6. And it may be that I will remain with you through the winter, that you may assist me on the next phase of my journey. 7. I will not see you now as I pass, but if the Lord permits, I trust to remain a while with you. 8. My plans are to stay in Ephesus until Pentecost. 9. For a great and powerful door is open to me here, and there are strong forces that oppose me. 10. Now if Timothy comes, see that he abides without opposition: for he carries out the work of the Lord, as I do. 11. Let no man look down on him: but send him on his way with

harmony that he may join me, because we all wait for him. 12. I have repeatedly urged Apollos to visit you and he will come but now is not a convenient time.

My Love Be With You All
1 Corinthians 16:13-24

13. Always be alert and stand fast in the faith, do not be fainthearted but show manly courage. 14. Let love control everything you do. 15. I have a sincere request of you, brethren, (you remember the house of Stephanas, how they were the first converts of Achaia and how they appointed themselves to the service of the saints,) 16. Follow their example and that of every one who cooperates with us and works to the point of exhaustion. 17. I am pleased with the coming of Stephanas, Fortunatus, and Achaicus, they have supplied what was lacking by your absence. 18. They have refreshed both yours and my spirit: therefore, acknowledge the worth of such men. 19. The assembled believers of Asia send their love. Aquila and Priscilla send greetings in the Lord, with the gathering that is in their house. 20. All the brethren greet you. Give one another a sacred greetings even a holy kiss. 21. The final greeting is from me, Paul written with my own hand. 22. If any man does not love the Lord Jesus Christ, let him be accursed, for the Lord cometh. 23. The sacred mercy of our Lord Jesus Christ be with you. 24. My love to all who are in union with Christ Jesus. Amen.

THE SECOND LETTER TO THE CORINTHIANS

Paul wrote his second letter to the Corinthians in Macedonia late in AD 57 to reinforce the authenticity of his apostleship. In this letter Paul expressed his love for the people probably because he had been somewhat harsh in the first letter. He expressed appreciation for financial support for the Jerusalem believers during a severe famine.

Cooperated by Praying Together
2 Corinthians 1:1-11

1. Paul, appointed by God to be a messenger of Jesus Christ, and Timothy the brother, to the congregation at Corinth, and all the virtuous people in Greece: 2. spiritual favor and peace from God the Father and from the Lord Jesus Christ. 3. Praise God, even the Father of our Lord Jesus Christ, the Father of compassion, and the God who stands beside you to encourage; 4. Who stands beside us to encourage during any kind of affliction that we in turn may be able to encourage others every time afflictions arise, by the consolation we received of God. 5. As the sufferings of Christ overflows to us, our consolation and encouragement flows from Christ. 6. And if we have miserable problems, it is for your reassurance and deliverance, that if you suffer the same difficulties you can be encouraged that we were made free from worry to the effect that you can be delivered. 7. Our hope is firmly grounded in you, knowing, that as you share in our sufferings you will also share in our encouragement. 8. I do not want you to be uninformed about the trouble that happened in Asia, we were pressed beyond the normal power of endurance, burdened down with injustice utterly without a way of escape; we even lost hope of life: 9. the official sentence of death remained upon us, we could not trust in ourselves, but in God who raised the dead: 10. Who rescued us from so great a peril, and continues to deliver: in Whom we put our trust for future deliverance. 11. You also cooperated by praying together for us, that the blessing of many who confidently lifted their face to the Lord for us would receive the thanks of many on our behalf.

Simplicity and Godly Sincerity
2 Corinthians 1:12-24

12. For our confidence and our witness as to right and wrong is in simplicity and godly sincerity, not with human wisdom, but by the grace of God we have so behaved in the world and above all with you. 13. For I write nothing other than what you read publicly, and recognize as my letters, and I trust you will continue to acknowledge and understand completely; 14. you have partly understood us, that we are your source of pride and joy, even also you are our source of

boasting on the day of the Lord Jesus. 15. Because of this confidence, I originally intended to visit you twice, so that you would have two opportunities for spiritual communication; 16. to visit you both on my way and again coming out of Macedonia, and to be outfitted by you for my journey to Judaea. 17. You really don't think I was irresponsible, do you? Do you think that my plans were according to human impulse that with me there was yes, yes, and no, no? 18. But as surely as God is true, my word had no equivocation or mixture of yes and no. 19. For the Son of God, Jesus Christ, who was preached among you by us, even by me, Silvanus and Timothy, was not yes and no, we never wavered between yes and no. 20. For to all the promises of God we supplied the affirmative yes, and in God is the final Amen, through us (*so be it*) to the glory of God. 21. And now He who established us with you in Christ, and has anointed us with the Spirit is God; 22. Who has also sealed us and given a down payment of the Spirit in our hearts. 23. I call this God, the One whom I just described, and He should punish me if I lie, that to spare you I came not yet to Corinth. 24. Not to exercise authority over your faith, but we are fellow workers of your joy: for your faith is steadfast.

Confirm Your Love
2 Corinthians 2:1-11

1. But I resolved in my mind that I would not come again to you with emotional and spiritual stress. 2. For if I cause you sorrow, who is to give me pleasure, but the same ones I grieved? 3. And those were the reasons I wrote this letter to you, so when I came, I would not be grieved by those I ought to celebrate; I have confidence that your joy and my joy are related. 4. For in much distress and anguish of heart I wrote to you with tears; not that you should be grieved, but that you might know how intense my love is for you. 5. But if a certain man has caused heartache; he has not anguished me, but in part he has distressed you all that I may heap up a burden of words against you. 6. Sufficient for such a person is the penalty he placed on the people. 7. So be gracious to forgive him, and encourage him to move forward, lest perhaps such a one become engulfed with much sorrow. 8. Wherefore I request that you officially confirm your love toward him. 9. For to this end I also wrote that I might have confirmation of your obedience in such things. 10. When you forgive it must be a continuing state of forgiveness: if I forgave any thing, for your sakes I forgave it in the Person of Christ; 11. lest Satan outsmart us: for we know of his schemes.

God Always Causes Us to Triumph
2 Corinthians 2:12-17

12. Furthermore, when I came to Troas to preach the gospel of Christ and a door was opened to me by the Lord, 13. I had no peace in my spirit, because I found not Titus my brother: so I gave my goodbye and pressed on into Macedonia. 14. Now thanks to God who always causes us to triumph in Christ, and makes us the sweet fragrance of His knowledge in every place. 15. For we are the sweet incense of Christ offered to God, that makes manifest those being saved and those who are perishing: 16. to the one we are the odor of death that precedes the grave; and to the other the fragrance of life that promises life eternal. And who is sufficient for such responsibility? 17. For we are not as many who pawn off a corrupt gospel for gain: but as men of sincerity, commissioned by God, we speak the authentic message in the presence of Christ.

The Epistle of Christ
2 Corinthians 3:1-11

1. Are we beginning afresh to recommend ourselves? Or do we need as others, letters of commendation to you or letters of recommendation from you? 2. You are our letter of recommendation written in our hearts, known and read of all men: 3. you are an open letter from Christ transcribed by us, written not with ink, but with the Spirit of the living God; not on tables of stone, but on pages of the human heart. 4. Such pure confidence we have through Christ toward God: 5. not that we were sufficiently qualified ourselves, but our sufficiency comes from the Sufficient One; 6. Who also made us ministers of the new covenant; not with letters of the alphabet, but of the Spirit: the letter of the law punishes with death, but the Spirit gives life to the soul. 7. But if the disposition of death written and engraved on tablets of stone were ushered in with splendor, so that the children of Israel could not gaze steadily on the face of Moses for the brightness of his countenance; which was a transient splendor; 8. will not the disposition of the Spirit be brighter? 9. For if the disposition of condemnation was presented in splendor, much more will the disposition of righteousness exceed in brightness. 10. By comparison that which was made glorious had no glory at all, because of the glory that surpassed it. 11. For if that which was to be abolished had some splendor, much more that which remains forever is glorious.

Changes into the Same Image
2 Corinthians 3:12-18

12. Seeing that we have such hope, we use great boldness of speech: 13. And not as Moses who put a veil over his face so the children

of Israel could not steadfastly look to the old order that was passing away: 14. but their minds were hardened: until this day the same veil is still present when the Old Testament is read; which veil was done away in Christ. 15. But even to this day there is a veil upon their heart when Moses is read. 16. When their hearts turn to the Lord, the veil will be taken away. 17. Now the Lord is that Spirit: and where the Spirit of the Lord is there is freedom. 18. But we all with unveiled faces look into polished metal and see ourselves in the mirror of the Lord and are transfigured in ever increasing splendor into the same image from glory to glory, even as by the Spirit of the Lord.

Your Servants for Jesus' Sake
2 Corinthians 4:1-6

1. Therefore seeing we have this commission, as received by the mercy of God, we do not get discouraged; 2. but have renounced disgraceful and underhanded ways, we do not practice trickery or adulterate the word of God; only by openly declaring the truth we recommend ourselves to the honest judgment of man in the sight of God. 3. But if our gospel is veiled, it is veiled to the lost: 4. whose unbelieving minds are blinded by the god of this world, lest the image of God and the glorious light of the gospel of Christ should shine unto them. 5. For we preach not ourselves, but Christ Jesus the Lord; and ourselves your servants for Jesus' sake. 6. The same God who caused light to shine out of darkness has caused His light to shine within our hearts, to give the light of understanding of the glory of God in the face of Jesus Christ.

This Treasure in Earthen Vessels
2 Corinthians 4:7-18

7. But we have this treasure in earthen vessels that the all-prevailing greatness of the power may be of God, and not from us. 8. We are pressed on every side, yet not hemmed in, we are bewildered, but never at a loss; 9. persecuted, but not abandoned; knocked down, but never counted out; 10. always exposed to the dying of the body but remembering the death of the Lord Jesus, that the life of Jesus might be revealed in our body. 11. For though we live we are perpetually delivered unto death for Jesus' sake, that the life of Jesus may be made operative in our mortal body. 12. So death operates in us, but life in you. 13. We have the same Spirit that engenders faith, as it is written, I believed, and therefore have spoken; we also believe, and therefore speak; 14. knowing for certain that He who raised up the Lord Jesus shall raise us up also by Jesus, and present us together with you. 15. For we suffer all things for your sakes, that the abundant favor might abound through the thanksgiving of many and have good

consequence to the glory of God. 16. This is why we are not discouraged; although the outward nature is being worn away, the inner spirit is being refreshed with continual renewal. 17. For our momentary afflictions are a weightless trifle compared to the exceeding and eternal weight of glory; 18. while we fix our gaze on things not seen rather than concentrate on visible things: for the things seen are temporary; but the things not seen are everlasting.

We are Always Full of Assurance
2 Corinthians 5:1-10

1. For we know that when our earthly tent is dismantled, we have an eternal heavenly building from God not made with hands. 2. Because of this we cry out desiring earnestly to move into a permanent home in heaven: 3. being permanently housed in heaven, we shall not be found destitute. 4. While in a temporary tent we are burdened with earthly emotion about dying, desiring that mortality would be swallowed up of life. 5. Now God has prepared us for this by giving us the down payment of the Spirit as a guarantee of eternal life. 6. Being therefore always fully assured knowing that while we are present in the body, we are absent from the Lord: 7. (For we walk by faith, not by vision): 8. I repeat, we are full of assurance and willing to be absent from the body to be present with the Lord. 9. Wherefore we devote ourselves zealously to please the Lord whether at home or absent. 10. The sum total of us must appear before the judgment seat of Christ; that the whole character of every one may be made manifest to receive a recompense for things done in the body whether good or worthless.

A New Creation
2 Corinthians 5:11-21

11. Understanding that all must stand before the judgment seat, we attempt to persuade men; but we are made clear before God; and I trust that my true self continues to be made clear in your consciences. 12. We are not requesting your approval again, but providing you a way to refute those who glory in appearance and not in heart. 13. If we appear confused, it is for God's cause: or whether we are clear-headed, it is for your cause. 14. Because the love of Christ presses on all sides; that if one died for all, that means that the sum total of all were dead: 15. since He died for all, then no one should live unto themselves, but live for Him who died for them and rose again. 16. In conclusion, we should know no one after the flesh: I affirm that we have known Christ after the flesh, yet henceforth we know Him no more as a mortal man.* 17. Therefore if any man be in Christ, he is a new creation: observe, the old things have passed away; all things have become new. 18. All things are of God, who has brought us together in Himself

by Jesus Christ, and has given to us the ministry of bringing people together; 19. how that God was in Christ bringing together the world to Himself, not counting their false steps and blunders against them; and has committed us to speak intelligent words that bring man and God together. 20. Now seeing we are representatives for Christ, as though God did make His appeal through us: we implore you in Christ's stead, come together with God. 21. For God caused Christ to become sin for us, who knew no sin; that we might come into right standing with God in Christ.

---

*v16 Paul evidently wanted the Corinthians to view the Cross through the empty tomb.

The Day of Salvation
2 Corinthians 6:1-10

1. As we work together with God, we appeal to you not to accept the grace of God and let it go to waste. 2. (God said, I have heard your prayers at a convenient time, and in the day of salvation I have brought you relief in a difficult situation: observe, now is the time for coming together; now is the day of deliverance.) 3. Habitually we give no occasion of stumbling that the ministry be discredited: 4. on the contrary, we seek to commend ourselves as God's ministers, by steadfast endurance, in troubles, in hardships, in difficulties, 5. in flogging, in bonds, in angry mobs, in hard labor, in sleepless nights, in hunger; 6. by innocence, by understanding, by long-suffering, by kindness, by the Holy Spirit, by authentic love, 7. by speaking the truth, by God's power, by weapons of righteousness, the sword of the Spirit in the right hand and the shield of faith in the left hand, 8. by loss of civil rights yet remaining a citizen of the kingdom, by haters, but still loved by God: called a wandering quack, but my message is true; 9. declared worthless without credentials by the Jews, but well known by the saints; always facing death, but truly alive; chastised, but not killed. 10. Sometimes grieved but always rejoicing; penniless, but enriching the souls of many; having nothing, and yet possessing everything.

They Shall Be My People
2 Corinthians 6:11-18

11. Men of Corinth, I have kept nothing back from you, and have opened by heart to you. 12. There is no narrowness in us, but you are constrained in your own hearts. 13. Can you not return my affection, (I speak to you as my children,) permit your hearts to be opened. 14. Stop being harnessed together in an alien yoke with unbelievers: for what sharing or participation has righteousness with lawlessness?

And what close relationship has light with darkness? 15. And what harmony has Christ with the worthless prince of darkness? Or what can a believer share in common with an unbeliever or freethinker? 16. And what common ground can the temple of God have with idols? For believers are the temple of the living God; as God said, I will dwell in them, walk in them, and I will be their God and they shall be my people. 17. Wherefore come out from among them and separate yourselves, says the Lord, and have no contact with impurity and I will receive you. 18. And will be a Father to you and you shall be My sons and daughters, says the Lord Almighty.

You are in Our Hearts
2 Corinthians 7:1-3
1. Since these are the promises, dearly beloved, let us finally cleanse ourselves absolutely from all that pollutes the body or spirit, and continue reverence to God by fully consecrating ourselves. 2. Open your hearts to us; we have wronged no man, we have corrupted no man, we have taken advantage of no man. 3. I speak not to blame you: I have told you before, that you are fully planted in our hearts and nothing in life or death can part us from you.

I Have Confidence in You
2 Corinthians 7:4-16
4. Great is my fluency of speech toward you and great is my pride in you: I am filled with encouragement in spite of my suffering, my joy is over-flowing. 5. Even after reaching Macedonia, our body had no rest, but we were troubled on every side, conflicts outside and foreboding within. 6. Nevertheless God who encourages the down-hearted, gave us comfort by the coming of Titus; 7. And not only were we encouraged by his arrival, but by the comfort he received from you, when he told us of your longing, your mourning, and your fervent mind toward me; I rejoiced the more. 8. For though I caused you pain with a letter, I do not change my feelings about the matter, though I did change my mind when I perceived the letter grieved you for a season. 9. Now I rejoice, not that I grieved you, but that you sorrowed to repentance: being made sorry after a godly manner, so that you received no lasting damage. 10. For godly sorrow has the out working of penitence to a recovery not to be revisited, but worldly sorrow brings death. 11. Notice the same thing, that godly sorrow produced an earnestness in you, I affirm, you were cleared, I affirm your righteous anger, I affirm your wrath against wrong, I affirm your passionate desire, I affirm your enthusiasm, I affirm, the vengeance with which you demonstrated yourself to be pure in the matter. 12. Consequently, I wrote to you not for the offender, not for his cause that suffered wrong, but that our care

for you in the sight of God might clearly appear to you. 13. Now this is the ground for my encouragement: I affirm that I rejoiced beyond measure because of how pleased Titus was because all of you had refreshed his spirit. 14. Although I have been boastful of you to him, I have not been disappointed; but as we spoke about you in truth, even so our pride before Titus was found to be true. 15. And his affection is more than ever drawn toward you when he remembers the reverence and respectful way you received him. 16. I rejoice that I have complete confidence in you.

The Genuine Nature of Your Love
2 Corinthians 8:1-15

1. Moreover, brethren, we call your attention to the assembled believers of Macedonia who have already received a deposit of the grace of God; 2. how their heavy affliction has proved their joy and steadfastness and out of their deepest poverty has come the richness of their generosity. 3. Spontaneously and voluntarily, I bare record and affirm, that beyond their means without request and without coercion they willingly gave of themselves; 4. urging us with much petition to receive their gifts for the poor, and take upon us the sharing of the relief work for the holy ones in Jerusalem. 5. And this they did, not as we expected, but they by God's will have altogether given their own selves to the Lord and to us. 6. This caused us to urge Titus to complete the task he had begun, that you might also have the same grace of giving. 7. Since you abound in almost everything, in faith and teaching, in knowledge of the truth and thoroughness, and in your benevolent love, see that you also abound in the grace of giving. 8. I speak not by order, because a command could not do what the eagerness, earnestness, and diligence of the Macedonians has done to test the genuine nature of your love. 9. For you already know the graciousness of our Lord Jesus Christ, that although He was rich, for your sakes He impoverished Himself, that you through His poverty might become rich. 10. My advice is expedient and advantageous for you, since you began a year ago and were first to propose action with a desire to do. 11. Now it is urgent that you perform the doing of it; as there was willingness before, so may there be an accomplishment according to your resources. 12. For where there is first a willingness a gift is measured by what one has and not according to what one does not have. 13. For I do not mean that others should be eased and you burdened: 14. but by equalizing the matter, that now your abundance may be a supply for their want, so at another time their abundance may supply your want: that there may be equality: 15. as it is written, He that gathered much had nothing left over; and he who gathered little had no lack.

Honest Arrangements
2 Corinthians 8:16 -24
16. But thanks to God, who kindled in the heart of Titus the same heartfelt care for you. 17. He not only accepted by appeal, but his devotion to you was so great he went to you of his own accord. 18. And we have sent with him a beloved brother whose praise is in the good news throughout all the congregations; 19. and not only that, but he was selected by the assembled believers to travel with us with this generous gift, which is administered by us to honor the Lord and show our willingness to help: 20. avoiding all suspicion or blame, we took precaution in the administering of this large fund: 21. providing for honest arrangements both in the sight of the Lord, and also in the eyes of men. 22. Along with them I am sending another brother, whose devotion we have often tested in many ways, but now more conscientious because of the great confidence I have in you. 23. As for Titus, he is my partner and fellow worker concerning you: as for our brethren they are messengers of the congregations, and an honor to Christ. 24. Wherefore demonstrate your benevolent love to them before the assembled believers, and justify my pride in you.

God Loves a Prompt and Willing Giver
2 Corinthians 9:1-15
1. It would be redundant for me to write you about service to the saints: 2. for I know your mental readiness and boasted of it to the Macedonians that Achaia stood ready a year ago with zeal that has stimulated many. 3. So you would be truly ready, I sent the brethren lest my boasting about you should be fruitless: 4. for if I bring men from Macedonia with me and they find you unprepared, we would feel ashamed of our present pride to say nothing of your feelings. 5. This is why I thought it necessary to send the brothers beforehand to complete the collection which you promised, because I want the giving to be forthcoming and not out of obligation. 6. Remember the saying, he who sows in a miserly manner shall reap miserly; and he who sows generously shall reap an abundant harvest. 7. Let every man give as he purposed in his heart; not reluctantly or under constraint: for God loves a prompt and willing giver. 8. Now God is continually able to overflow you with self-sufficiency always making you competent to pour out to the good of others: 9. as it is written, His generosity is scattered to the poor; His love-deeds are never forgotten. 10. Now He who supplies plenty of seed for the planting also furnishes bread for your table, and multiplies the seed sown and increases the fruit of your benevolence; 11. your being enriched unto all liberality causes us to give thanks to God. 12. The rendering of this benevolence not only supplies the needs of the saints, but causes a wealth of thanksgiving to God; 13.

by evidence of this service they glorify God for your conviction and response to the gospel of Christ and for your liberality in sharing with others; 14. and by their intercession for you their earnest desire goes out to you to surpass your grace and generosity. 15. Thanks to God for His indescribable generosity to you.

Self-approval Counts for Nothing
2 Corinthians 10:1-18

1. I Paul myself now implore you by the humble and patient steadfastness of Christ, who when I am face to face with you am downcast, but when absent I become courageous: 2. but I pray that it will not be necessary for me to speak freely when I am present, wherewith I dare to be stout-hearted and show strong courage toward those who think I rely only on human powers. 3. Human beings we may be, but we do not fight our battles in human strength: 4. the weapons we use to fight are not human, but mighty through God to demolish strongholds; 5. casting down the conceits of men against the knowledge of God, and bringing every human thought into obedience to Christ; 6. when your submission reaches completion, I am prepared to settle all scores with the disobedient. 7. Look at what is before your eyes and face the obvious. If anyone has been persuaded to trust in themselves as belonging to Christ, let him think again, that we also belong to Christ. 8. Since the Lord has given us authority to build you up and not break you down, I shall not be put to shame: 9. I should not appear to frighten you by my letters. 10. Some say my letters are burdensome and grievous; and that I am weak in body and my speech deserves to be treated with contempt. 11. Let this one think this, because such as we may be burdensome and grievous by letters, even more will we be when we are face to face. 12. For we do not have the boldness to compare ourselves with some who approve themselves: but they measuring themselves by their own yardstick, and comparing themselves within their own little circle, do not make sense. 13. We will not measure ourselves beyond the criteria distributed to us by God, a calculation that reaches even to you. 14. For we are not over-stretching our commission when we count you in our territory, because our preaching came as far as you with the gospel of Christ; 15. we are not boasting of things built by other men's labor; but having increased hope that our labor shall be enlarged through your growing faith and will increase our influence abundantly, 16. to preach the gospel to the Gentiles in the regions beyond you without crossing into another man's carefully marked territory. 17. But he that boasts let him do so within the territory marked by the Lord. 18. Only after testing does approval come from the Lord, self-approval counts for nothing.

That I May Present You Chaste and Undefiled
2 Corinthians 11:1-15

1. I wish you could endure a little thoughtlessness: but indeed you already put up with me. 2. For I am zealous over you with godly suspicion: for I have joined you together with one husband that I may present you chaste and undefiled to Christ. 3. But I fear lest by any means you be deceived through cunning craftiness as the serpent totally seduced Eve, so your minds should be led astray from a single-hearted loyalty toward Christ. 4. For if a specific person well-known to you preaches another Jesus, whom we have not proclaimed, or if you receive another spirit which you have not received, or another gospel, which you have not accepted, you would do well to be patient. 5. For I reckon myself in no way behind those you consider super-apostles. 6. Although I may be unskilled in speaking, but not in knowledge; but we clearly made you to understand the full truth. 7. Have I committed some wrong by honoring you by freely preaching the gospel and working without charge? 8. I took from other congregations more than their share in order to do service to you. 9. And when I was with you and my resources failed, I was not a burden to you, because the brethren from Macedonia supplied what was lacking to me: in all things I kept my fixed policy not to be burdensome to you, and this I will continue to do. 10. I take a solemn personal pledge: no man shall block me from my accomplishments in the regions of Achaia. 11. Does this mean that I do not love you? God knows I love you. 12. I will continue to preach as I have that I may cut off the fault-finding concerning my practice of preaching without compensation, that their boasting will stop when they also find themselves preaching without compensation. 13. For these are false apostles, deceitful workers, transforming themselves into the messengers of Christ. 14. And no wonder; for Satan himself changed his appearance into an angel of light. 15. Therefore it is no great thing if Satan's agents also masquerade as ministers of righteousness; whose end shall be judged according to their deeds.

Through a Window in a Basket
2 Corinthians 11:16-33

16. I repeat, let no man look upon me as a fool; if you do, show me the tolerance you show fools, and listen to what I say. 17. That which I speak, I speak not after the Lord, but it is confident boasting. 18. Since many boast of their human qualities, I will boast also. 19. Being sensible you gladly tolerate the foolish. 20. For you suffer, if a man makes slaves of you, if a man devoured you, if a man defrauded you, if a man takes advantage of you, if a man smite you on the face. 21. I am almost ashamed to speak that I was weak among you. However, where any man is foolishly bold, I am bold also. 22. Are they Hebrews? So

am I. Are they Israelites? So am I. Are they the seed of Abraham? So am I. 23. Do they foolishly claim to be ministers of Christ? I am more; in manual labor more abundant, in flogging above calculation, in bonds more frequent, in perils of death often. 24. Five times I received forty stripes save one of the Jews. 25. Three times I was beaten with Roman rods, once I was stoned, three times I suffered shipwreck, a night and a day I was adrift in the open sea; 26. in my journeys I have been in perils from rivers and floods, from robbers, in perils from my own countrymen, in perils by the pagans. I have faced dangers in the city, in the backwoods, in the sea, and in perils among false Christians; 27. I have suffered weariness and pain, sleepless nights, often hungry and thirsty, without food, I have known cold and the lack of clothing. 28. In addition to other external calamities, upon me was the daily care of all the congregations. 29. Is there anyone's weakness I do not share? Who stumbles that I am not set on fire with indignation? 30. If I need to boast, I will boast of my health related weaknesses. 31. God and Father of our Lord Jesus Christ, who is blessed forever, knows I speak the truth. 32. In Damascus, the local administrator under King Aretas, kept the walled city and the inhabitants with a garrison, desiring to take me into custody: 33. and through a window in a basket I was let down over the wall and my escape was successful.

My Grace is Sufficient for You
2 Corinthians 12:1-10

1. I must go on boasting although it is not profitable. I will proceed to the visions and the revelations the Lord has given to me. 2. I know a man in Christ who fourteen years ago, (I do not know whether it was a vision or an actual physical experience: God knows;) was caught up to the third heaven. 3. And I knew such a man, (whether in the body, or out of the body, I cannot tell: God knows;) 4. this man was caught up to paradise and heard sacred secrets, of which no man can speak. 5. Of such a one will I boast: yet not of myself, but I will boast in my weaknesses. 6. For though I would desire to boast, I shall not be foolish; for I will say the truth: but now I hold back, lest any man should think more of me than is justified by my words and deeds. 7. For fear that I should be lifted up because of the nature of the revelations a stake was placed in my flesh as a messenger of Satan to torment me, lest I should become exalted beyond reason. 8. Because of this thorn in my flesh, I sought the Lord three times for deliverance. 9. And God said, my grace is sufficient for you: for my strength is made perfect in weakness. Most gladly therefore will I rather boast in my weaknesses, that the power of Christ may rest upon me. 10. I take pleasure, therefore, in my weakness, ill-treatment, necessary hardships, troubles and

difficulties, when they are distresses for Christ's sake: for when I am weak, then am I strong.

God Will Humble Me Among You
2 Corinthians 12:11-21

11. You have compelled me to become a fool in boasting: for I ought to have been commended of you: for in nothing am I less than the best of your super-apostles, though I am nothing. 12. The marks of a true apostle were patiently shown when I was face to face with you, my deeds were mighty and followed by signs and wonders. 13. What makes you feel inferior to other congregations, except that I did not require your financial support? Forgive me this wrong. 14. See, I am prepared to visit you for the third time; and I will not burden you: for I seek not your resources, but you: for the children ought not to lay up for the parents, but the parents for the children. 15. And I will gladly spend both my energies and my funds for you; although the more abundantly I love you, the less you seem to love me. 16. Be it so, although I did not burden you: nevertheless, you think I was crafty and caught you in a trap. 17. Did I take your wealth by any one I sent to you? 18. I actually begged Titus to visit you and sent a beloved brother with him. Did Titus take any funds from you for himself? Did we not take the same steps in the same spirit? 19. Again, do you think that we are defending ourselves to you? We do all things, dear brothers, only to build you up. 20. I fear that when I come I shall find you not as I want you to be, and that you should find me other than you desire: lest there be strife, quarreling, jealous envying, sudden flare-up of burning anger, selfishness, intrigue, speaking against others, backbiting, whispering, inflated opinions, and disorder: 21. and lest, when I come again, God will humble me among you and I shall have tears to shed over many who continue in sensuality and have persisted in sexual immorality, and have not repented of impurity and immorality in which they have indulged.

Examine Yourselves – Live in Peace
2 Corinthians 13:1-14

1. This is the third time I will visit you. Any charge must be sustained in the mouth of two or three witnesses. 2. I warned you on my second visit and warn you again, and now in my absence I write to those who before have sinned, and to all that when I come again, I will not spare anyone: 3. since you seek evidence that Christ is speaking in me, which to you-ward was not weak, but mighty in you. 4. Although he was crucified in weakness, yet he lives by the power of God. We also are weak in Him, but strong enough to deal with you by the power of God toward you. 5. Examine yourselves and see what kind of persons

you really are whether you are in the faith; test your own selves. You know yourselves that you are degenerates except Jesus Christ be in you. 6. I trust you shall know that we are not degenerates, but genuine believers. 7. Our prayer to God is that you do no wrong; not that we may appear to meet the test, but that you should do what is right, even if we seem to be discredited. 8. For we have no power to do anything against the truth, but only for the truth. 9. I am glad to be weak when you are strong: and we also desire your true spiritual maturity. 10. Therefore, I write with this tone being absent, lest being face to face I should use the power of severity which power God has given to me for your edification and not your destruction. 11. Finally, brethren, we wish you goodbye. Be mature, be of good courage, be of one mind, live in peace; and the God of love and peace shall be with you. 12. Greet one another with Christian love even a holy kiss. 13. All the believers send greetings to you. 14. The grace of the Lord Jesus Christ, and the love of God, and the fellowship of the Holy Spirit always be with you all. Amen.

THE LETTER TO THE ROMANS

Paul wrote the letter to the Romans about AD 58 to introduce himself and express a desire to visit. Since Paul was not known to the congregation, he did not write to correct problems. The letter was a systematic presentation of relational realities well-organized around major themes: grace, faith, righteousness, and justification. The message was clear, Gentiles should be involved in the assembly. Salvation was not just for the Jews.

Obedience of Faith
Romans 1:1-7

1. Paul, a bondservant of Jesus Christ, commissioned as an apostle, marked off and set apart unto the good news of God, 2. (that He proclaimed beforehand by His prophets in the holy scriptures,) 3. the good news concerning His Son, Jesus Christ our Lord, according to human records He was of the seed of David; 4. and decreed to be the Son of God with power, according to the Spirit and disposition of holiness, by standing up from the grave: 5. through whom we received the grace of apostleship, to bring about an obedience of faith among all the Gentiles, to honor His name: 6. among whom you are also the called ones belonging to Jesus Christ: 7. to all who are called to be beloved saints in Rome: blessings and peace from God our Father, and the Lord Jesus Christ.

The Just Shall Live By Faith
Romans 1:8-17

8. First, I continue to thank my God through Jesus Christ for all of you, because your faith is proclaimed all over the world. 9. Calling God to witness, whom I serve with my spirit in the gospel of His Son, how spontaneously I always include you in my prayers; 10. making requests that my whole journey to you would be prosperous by the will of God. 11. I have a yearning to see you and impart some spiritual endowment to establish you in the faith; 12. that I may be encouraged together with you by our mutual faith. 13. I want you to know, brethren, that I often purposed to visit you that I might gather a harvest among you as with other Gentiles, but I was hindered. 14. I am under obligation to the Greeks and to the Barbarians; both to the wise and the foolish. 15. As far as I am able, I am ready to preach the gospel to you at Rome also. 16. For I am never reluctant to preach the gospel: for it is the power of God unto salvation to all who believe; to the Jew first, and also to the Greek. 17. For in the gospel God reveals His worthy activity that begins and ends with faith: the permanent and authoritative character of the written word affirms, the just shall live by faith.

Professing to be Wise, They Became Fools
Romans 1: 18-32

18. On the other hand, the deep seated anger of God against sin is revealed in the wrath from heaven against all wickedness (premeditated evil acts) toward God or all efforts to suppress the truth about social justice toward men; 19. because that which can be known of God lies plain before their minds. 20. For the invisible qualities of God from the creation are clearly seen, being understood through things God made, even His eternal power and Godhead; so that man has no justifiable excuse before God: 21. because they knew that God existed and did not glorify Him as God, neither were they thankful; but became unproductive in their thinking, and their unwise heart was darkened. 22. Professing to be wise, they became fools, 23. and changed the wonder of the incorruptible God into idols made into images of corruptible humans, and birds, and beasts, and creeping things. 24. Wherefore God gave them over to moral pollution through the desires of their own hearts, to bring shame on their own bodies between themselves: 25. who changed the truth of God into a lie, and worshipped and served the creature more than the Creator, who is blessed for ever. It is affirmed. 26. For this God gave them up to depraved passions: for even their women did exchange the natural use of their bodies into that which is against nature: 27. Likewise men, giving up natural relations with woman, burned in their lust toward other men behaving in an inappropriate manner, and incurring an inevitable and personal penalty for this behavior. 28. Since they did not wish to retain God in their knowledge, God gave them over to their own mind and own behavior; 29. being filled up with wrongdoings, immorality, wickedness, greed, depravity, covetousness, maliciousness, 30. backbiters, haters of God, despiteful, proud, boasters, inventor of evil things, disobedient to parents, 31. without clear understanding, covenant breakers, without natural affection, cruel, unmerciful: 32. who knowing the judgment of God, that certain things are worthy of death, not only do the same, but have pleasure in them that do such things.

No Partiality or Favoritism with God
Romans 2:1-16

1. Therefore you are without excuse, as a human being passing unfavorable judgment on another, you have condemned yourself; you criticize but do the same things. 2. But we are confident that the content of God's judgment is based on truth against those who commit such things. 3. Do you think that you will escape the condemnation of God that do the same things you criticize others for doing? 4. Or do you entertain wrong ideas about God's truce, His kindness and longsuffering; not knowing that the kindness of God causes you to turn

away from evil and begin a new moral life? 5. But because a hard and unrepentant heart stores up against you God's anger in heaven on the day of God's judgment; 6. when He will settle accounts with each man according to his deeds: 7. and eternal life to those who steadfastly do well and seek glory, honor, and immortality: 8. but to those who are controversial and do not obey the right, but yields to the wrong, a rage of righteous anger, 9. constraint and trouble from the Jews first, and also from the Gentiles, on every soul of man who constantly does evil; 10. but praise, honor, and peace, to every man who consistently does good, to the Jews first, and also to the Gentiles: 11. for there is no partiality or favoritism with God. 12. For as many as have sinned without law shall perish without law: and as many as sinned under the law shall be judged by the law; 13. it is not those who hear the law read that are righteous before God, but it is the doers of the law that are declared righteous. 14. For when Gentiles who have no law, do by instinct what the law requires, they demonstrate they have a moral law in themselves: 15. which shows the law is written in their hearts, their conscience as an automatic response bearing witness, and at the same time either accusing or excusing themselves; 16. and there will come a day when God by the gospel of Jesus Christ will judge the secret sins hidden in the heart.

No Lessons for Yourself
Romans 2:17-29

17. If you call yourself a Jew and rest on the law, and boast of God's favor, 18. and know His will and endorse the exceptional things, being instructed in the law; 19. are you confident that you can guide the blind and be a light to those in darkness, 20. be an instructor to the unwise, and a teacher of infants, because you have heard the framework of knowledge and the truth of the law? 21. Therefore you who teach others, have you no lessons for yourself? Are you a thief that teaches against stealing? 22. Are you an adulterer who forbids adultery? Do you abhor idols, but plunder temples? 23. Do you boast of the law and then dishonor God by breaking the law? 24. It is written, the Gentiles commit blasphemy against the name of God because of you. 25. For circumcision has value only if you obey the law: but if you break the law your circumcision counts for nothing. 26. And if the heathen follow the moral requirements of the law, shall his righteousness be counted for circumcision? 27. And shall those who are naturally uncircumcised, if they follow the law, judge you, who keep the letter of the law and yet are lawbreakers? 28. For a man is not a real Jew who is only outwardly visible; neither is circumcision only outward in the flesh: 29. a true Jew is one who is inwardly right with God; and circumcision is of

the heart, in the spirit, and not in the letter of the law; whose praise is not of men, but of God.

Let God be True
Romans 3:1-8

1. Does being a Jew bring favorable circumstance? Does circumcision produce a benefit? 2. In many ways, primarily, because it was to them that God gave the foreshadowing of His revelation. 3. Even if some did not believe, would their unbelief nullify the faith of God? 4. God forbid: I affirm, let God be true, and every man a liar; as it is written, that you might be vindicated by your words, and win the verdict when you are judged. 5. But if our unrighteousness magnifies the righteousness of God, what shall we conclude? In human terms, would God be wrong to punish us? 6. By no means: otherwise if God does not inflict punishment on us, how will God punish the world? 7. But if my uttering an untruth abounds to God's glory; why am I still judged as a sinner? 8. And rather not, as some slanderously affirm that we say, Let us do evil, that good may come? Their condemnation is deserved.

There is no Defense
Romans 3:9-20

9. What do we excel above the Gentiles? We have no advantage: we have previously charged that both Jews and Gentiles are under sin; 10. as it is written, There is not one righteous man: 11. there is none who discerns and seeks after God. 12. They have all turned aside from the right path; they have become utterly worthless; not one of them does good things, not even one. 13. Their throat is an open grave; with their tongues they practice deceit; the quick fatal poison of a cobra is in their words: 14. their mouth is full of cursing and bitterness: 15. their feet are quick to violently spill blood for money: 16. devastation and desolation are in their behavior: 17. they have never known the way of peace: 18. they are bold faced without the fear of God. 19. Now we understand that whatever the law says, it says to those under the law: that there is no defense and the whole world is answerable before God. 20. Therefore no human being may be justified by their deeds before the law: for by the law man understands he is a sinner.

For There is No Difference
Romans 3:21-31

21. But now the righteousness of God without the law is apparent, the law and the prophets bear witness; 22. even the right standing with God is by faith of Jesus Christ upon all who believe: for there is no difference: 23. for all have missed the mark, and continually fall short of the manifestation of God's perfection; 24. being justified by

free grace through the ransom paid in Christ Jesus: 25. whom God set forth to make atonement through faith in His blood, to manifest His righteousness for the remission of sins previously committed during God's forbearance; 26. to vindicate His righteousness at the present time: that He might be righteous and justify those who believe in Jesus. 27. The basis for boasting is excluded, not by law or works, but by the law of faith. 28. Therefore we conclude that a man is given right standing with God on the basis of faith without observance of the law. 29. Does God belong only to the Jews? No, He is also the God of the Gentiles. 30. Seeing there is one God, who shall justify the Jew by faith, and the Gentiles through faith. 31. Does faith overthrow the law? God forbid: I affirm, we establish the law by faith.

March in the Steps of Faith
Romans 4:1-12

1. What standing do we have based on Abraham as our father? 2. If Abraham were declared righteous by his works, he has grounds for boasting; but not before God. 3. What does the scripture say? Abraham believed God, and it was entered into the account book as righteousness. 4. Now if a man labors, his wages are not counted as a gift, but as an obligation. 5. But to the man who does not labor, but believes in the One who justifies the ungodly, his faith is counted as righteousness. 6. Just as David spoke of the blessedness of the man who was assigned right standing with God without works, 7. saying, Fortunate are they whose wrong doings are forgiven, and whose sins were absolved. 8. Fortunate is the man for whom the Lord will not remember his sin. 9. Did this innocence come to Jews only, or do Gentiles also enjoy this blessing? We say that faith was counted to Abraham for a right standing with God. 10. How was this calculated? Was it after circumcision or before? It was before the ritual. 11. And he was afterward given the mark of circumcision as a guarantee of the righteousness coming from faith before the ritual: that he might become the father of all who believe, although they do not practice the ritual; that a right standing with God might be assigned to them also: 12. and the Father of those who not only follow the ritual, but those who also march in the steps of faith of father Abraham, which he had before the ritual existed.

Strong in Faith
Romans 4:13-25

13. For the promise that Abraham should inherit the earth was not given to him and his descendants through the law, but through the righteousness of faith. 14. For if those who follow the law are heirs, faith is nullified: 15. for where there is law there is the assurance of

punishment: for where no law exists there can be no transgression. 16. Therefore, it is through faith that the promise might be by grace; to the end the power to withhold or bestow grace might be sure to all the descendents: not only to those who follow the law, but also to those who follow the faith of Abraham; who is the father of us all, 17. as it is written, I made him a father of many nations, in the sight of the God in whom he believed; the God who brought the dead to life, and speaks of the future with certainty. 18. Abraham with no hope believed in hope, that he might become the father of many nations; according to the promise, So shall your seed be. 19. He was not weak in faith even when he realized the impotence of his hundred year old body neither did he consider the deadness of Sara's womb: 20. he neither wobbled nor stumbled at the promise of God because of unbelief; but was strong in faith, and praised God in advance for the blessing; 21. and being fully persuaded that what God had promised, He was able to perform. 22. This faith was counted to him for righteousness. 23. This was not recorded only for his sake that his faith was attributed to him; 24. but for us also, faith shall be attributed to us provided we believe on Him who raised up Jesus our Lord from the grave; 25. Who was betrayed and crucified for our willful transgressions, and was raised again for our full acquittal.

Christ Died for Us
Romans 5:1-11

1. Since we stand declared righteous by faith, let us enjoy the possession of peace with God through our Lord Jesus Christ: 2. by Whom we have access by faith into the grace wherein we stand, and we rejoice in the hope of God's glory. 3. And not only, but we also glory in hardships and sufferings: because we know that troubles produce patient endurance; 4. and patient endurance approves character; and character brings hope: 5. and a faithful trust in God's promises will never put us to shame; because the love which God has for us is poured out in abundance in our hearts by the Holy Spirit which is God's gift. 6. For when we were yet powerless, at God's time, Christ died for the ungodly as a finished deed. 7. One would hardly give his life for a blameless man: yet possibly instead of a good man some would be courageous enough to die. 8. But God demonstrated His love toward us, in that, while we remained sinners, Christ died for us. 9. Much more since we are now justified by His blood, we shall be rescued from final punishment through Him. 10. For if, when we were enemies, we were changed by the death of God's Son, much more, we are being changed by His life. 11. And not only so, but we also pray and rejoice in God through our Lord Jesus Christ, by His suffering we have exchanged our old life for new life at one with God.

All Have Sinned
Romans 5:12-21

12. Wherefore, as by one man sin entered into the world, and death by sin; and so death passed upon all men, for that all have sinned: 13. sin was in the world before the law: but sin is not reckoned when there is no law. 14. Nevertheless death had a time in power from Adam to Moses, even over those who had not transgressed in the same manner as Adam, who was a type of the One that was to come. 15. But the free gift is not the same as the unintentional transgression of Adam. For if through an unintentional side-step of one many are dead, much more the free grace of God and the free gift of grace is by one man, Jesus Christ, was freely given to many. 16. The effect of God's free gift is much greater than the effect of Adam's transgression, for condemnation came because of one act by one man, but the free gift of God covers many transgressions and brings justification. 17. For if by one man's offence death was given power over man; much more power in life is received by abundant grace and the gift of righteousness by one, Jesus Christ. 18. Therefore as by the offence of one judgment and condemnation came upon all men; even so by the righteous act of One, the free gift came to all men bringing justification of life. 19. For as by one man's disobedience many were made sinners, so by the obedience of One many were made righteous. 20. Moreover the law came and the transgressions abounded. But where sin flourished, grace flourished much more: 21. and sin had the power of death even so might grace have power through righteousness unto eternal life by Jesus Christ our Lord.

Walk in Newness of Life
Romans 6:1-13

1. What shall we conclude? Shall we persist in sinning that the gift of grace may flourish? 2. May it not be: how shall we who have died to sin, continue to live therein? 3. Are you ignorant that all who were identified with the name of Jesus Christ were immersed into His death? 4. Therefore we were identified with Him by baptism into death: that as Christ was raised up from the dead by the power of the Father, likewise we should behave in newness of life. 5. For if we were grafted together through baptism into the death, we shall also stand up in His likeness: 6. For we know that our sinful self was crucified with Him, that the sinful body might be rendered powerless, that henceforth we should not be in bondage to sin. 7. For the one who is dead is released from the pattern of sin. 8. And since we died together with Christ, we believe that we will be raised with Him: 9. knowing that Christ standing up from the grave dies no more; death can rule no more over Him. 10. For His death was a once for all death to sin: but since He now lives,

He lives forever unto God. 11. In the same way, count yourselves dead to sin, but alive unto God through Jesus Christ our Lord. 12. Let not sin have sovereignty over your mortal body that you would listen to the passions of the flesh. 13. Never allow your body to be used as a sinful weapon of unrighteousness: but commit yourselves to God, as one who stood up from the grave, and your body to God as a holy weapon of righteousness.

Gift of God is Eternal Life
Romans 6:14-23

14. For sin shall not have authority over you: for you are not under the law, but under grace. 15. What? Are we to continue sinning because we are under grace and not under the law? God forbid. 16. Do you not know that if you submit yourselves to blind obedience, you become a servant whether to sin unto death or obedience unto righteousness? 17. But God be thanked, that you were once bond-servants to sin, but now your heart is obedient to the structured teaching delivered to you. 18. And when you were freed from being a servant of sin, you became a bond-slave of righteousness. 19. I speak about slaves because you readily understand: for you once offered your bodies to the slavery of immorality which leads to more and more wickedness; even so now yield your bodies as bond-slaves to righteousness which leads to purity. 20. For when you were the slaves of sin you were unable to serve righteousness. 21. What harvest did you gain from those things whereof you are now embarrassed? For the ultimate end of those things is death. 22. Being now freed from the bondage of sin, you become enslaved to God, you have your harvest unto holiness, and the ultimate end is everlasting life. 23. The take-home pay of sin is death; but the free gift of God is eternal life through Jesus Christ our Lord.

The Law Had Power Over a Man
Romans 7:1-12

1. You understand, brethren, because you know the law, how the law had power over a man as long as he was alive. 2. According to the law a married woman was bound to her husband as long as he lived; but if the husband died, she was freed from the law's obligation to her husband. 3. So while her husband lived, if she became intimately joined to another, she would be called one who adulterated the law by adding a paramour: but if her husband was dead, she was free from the law; and free to add another husband. 4. Wherefore, my brethren, the crucified body of Christ made you dead to the law; that you could be joined to another, even to Christ who stood up from the grave, that we should produce a harvest for God. 5. For when we were obeying our lower nature, the emotional hardships of sins, which came by the law,

did operate in our bodies to produce a harvest unto death. 6. But we are now released from the bondage of the law that we should serve in newness of life and not in past obedience to the letter of the law. 7. What shall we conclude? Is the law sin? God forbid. No, I would not have known sin but for the law: I would not have known longing for the forbidden, except the law said, You shall not covet. 8. But sin found an occasion in the commandment and stirred up all kinds of covetous ways. For without the law sin was dead. 9. There was a time when I was alive without the law: but when I understood the precept, the sense of sin sprang into life, and I died. 10. And the precept designed to bring life, brought me a sentence of death. 11. For sin found an occasion by the guideline to deceive me, and by the principle brought death to me. 12. Undoubtedly the law is holy, and the instruction holy, and just, and good.

Delight in the Law of God
Romans 7:13-25

13. Would that which was good bring death to me? God forbid, but sin, worked death in me by that which was good, that transgression might become visible as sin; so the instruction showed how transgression was exceedingly sinful. 14. For we know that the law comes from heaven: but I am of the earth, sold under sin. 15. For what I do I do not tolerate: for what I would do, I do not do: but what I detest, that I do. 16. If then my actions are against my will, I approve that the law is good. 17. Now it is no more I who does wrong, but sin that dwells in me. 18. For I know that there is nothing good in my earthly nature: for the desire to do right is there, but I cannot find the power to do the good things. 19. For the good things I want to do, I do not do: but I do the wrong things that I do not want to do. 20. Now if I do what I do not want to do, it is no more me doing the wrong, but sin that resides in me. 21. I discovered this principle of law, when I would do good evil is present with me. 22. At heart I consent gladly to the law of God as far as my new nature is concerned: 23. but I see another principle working in my body, warring against the law of my mind, and bringing me into bondage to the law of sin which operates in my human nature. 24. I am an unacceptable man! Who shall deliver me from the body of this death? 25. I thank God for deliverance through Jesus Christ our Lord. So with my intellect I constantly serve the law of God; but the principle of sin remains in my mortal body.

The Spirit is Life
Romans 8:1-11

1. Consequently, there is no disapproval for them who are in Christ Jesus.* 2. For the spiritual principle of life in Christ Jesus has made

me free from the law of sin and death. 3. For what the law could not do because of the weakness of human flesh, God sent His own Son in the form of sinful humanity, and because of sin, disapproved sin in the flesh: 4. in order that the righteous requirements of the law might be satisfied in us, who behave not after human nature, but after the Spirit. 5. For those who follow their human nature are earthly minded, but those who are after spiritual things follow the Spirit. 6. Death comes from being carnally minded; but to be spiritually minded is life and peace. 7. Because the human mind is hostile toward God: for it does not willingly submit to the law of God, neither can the carnal be subject to God. 8. So then the earthly minded cannot please God. 9. But you are not controlled by human nature, but by the Spirit, if so be that the Spirit of God abide in you. Unless a man has the Spirit of Christ he does not belong to Christ. 10. And if Christ be in you, the body is dead because of sin; but the Spirit is life because of right standing with God. 11. But if the Spirit of Him that raised up Jesus from the grave dwell in you, He that caused Christ to stand up from the grave shall make alive your mortal bodies by His Spirit that dwells in you.

---

*v1 The phrase *who walk not after the flesh, but after the Spirit* is not adequately supported here by original manuscripts, but the concept is found elsewhere.

Received the Spirit of Adoption
Romans 8:12-27

12. It follows that you owe nothing to human nature, to live after the flesh. 13. For if you live under the control of your human nature, you are on the path to death: but if by the Spirit you put to death the deeds of the body, you shall live. 14. For only those who are led by the Spirit of God are the children of God. 15. For we have not received the essence of bondage again we urgently cry, Father, Father: 16. the Holy Spirit joins with our human spirit confirming that we are the children of God: 17. since we are children, then heirs, and fellow-heirs with Christ; if we suffer together we may also be glorified together. 18. For I consider the sufferings we now endure not worthy to be compared with the glory about to be revealed in us. 19. All creation is yearning expecting to see the appearance of the children of God. 20. For all creation was made subject to putrefaction, not willingly, but by reason of hope that it would be redeemed, 21. because creation itself will be delivered from the bondage of corruption into the glorious freedom that belongs to the children of God. 22. Creation and human beings suffer together until the present. 23. And not only them, but also the believers of today, who are the first harvest of the Spirit, even we ourselves whimper waiting the full adoption, the redemption of the body. 24. For in hope were we saved: but hope is waiting for

something we do not yet possess, so if a man possess hope why does he yet hope? 25. But if we hope for that we see not, then do we with enduring patience wait for it. 26. In the same manner the Spirit supports our weaknesses: for we know not what we should pray for as we ought: but the Spirit Himself makes intercession for us with groans too deep for words. 27. And God who searches all hearts knows the mind-set of the Spirit, because He makes intercession for the saints according to the will of God.

All things Work Together for Good
Romans 8:28-39

28. We know for those loving God that He continually works all things together for good, to those who are the called ones according to His purpose. 29. Because those He knew beforehand, He determined before to be conformed to the image of His Son, that He might be supreme among the brotherhood. 30. Moreover those whom He long ago destined for this purpose, He also called; and whom He called He placed in a right standing and those in right standing He glorified. 31. What is the conclusion? Since God is on our side, does it really matter who is against us? 32. He handed over His own Son to death for us all. With Christ will He not freely give us all things? 33. Who can lay any charge upon God's chosen ones? It is God who gives them a right standing with Him. 34. Who is He that judges us? It was Christ who died, I further affirm, that it was Christ who rose again and is even now at the right hand of God, making intercession for us. 35. Who shall separate us from the love of Christ? Shall trouble or misfortune, or harassment, or starvation, the absence of clothing, or the threat of danger, or the sword? 36. As it is written, For your sake we are slaughtered all the day long; we are accounted as sheep for the slaughter. 37. In all these things, I vote no because we are more than conquerors through Him who loves us. 38. For I am convinced, that neither death nor life, nor messengers from heaven, nor rulers from earth, nor powers, nor things present, nor things to come, 39. not anything above or below, nor any power in the whole creation, shall be able to separate us from the love of God, which is in Christ Jesus our Lord.

The Words of Promise
Romans 9:1-13

1. I speak the truth in Christ, my conscience bears witness in the Holy Spirit that this is no falsehood, 2. that there is a great weight of sorrow upon me and continual anguish in my heart. 3. For I was wishing that I myself would be set apart from Christ for destruction for my brethren, my kinsmen according to the flesh: 4. who are Israelites; to whom belongs adoption and God's presence and covenants, the law, Temple

worship, and divine promises; 5. descendents from the patriarchs and from their lineage came Christ, whom God exalted above all and blessed forever, Amen. 6. It is not as though the word of God had no effect. For they are not all Israel who are of Israel: 7. they are not all children of Abraham because they are Abraham's descendents: but, the line of Isaac is Abraham's promise. 8. That is, all his descendents are not the children of God: but the children of promise are counted for true descendents. 9. For these are the words of promise, At a time fixed I will come and Sara shall have a son. 10. And not only this; but when Rebecca had also conceived by our father Isaac; 11. (before the children were born, neither having done good or evil, that the purpose of God according to His choice might stand, not on anything man does, but on the call of God;) 12. she was told, the elder son shall serve the younger son. 13. As it is written, I prefer Jacob in a moral or social sense. But for Esau I have strong moral hostility.

He Will Finish the Work
Romans 9:14-33

14. What do we conclude? Is there injustice in God? God forbid. 15. For He said to Moses, I will have compassion in word and deed on whom I choose, and I will manifest sympathy with the grief and misery of whomever I choose. 16. So it is not a question of human will or action, but the showing of divine mercy. 17. A holy document said of Pharaoh, It was for this purpose that I raised you up, that I might show My power in you, and that My name might be proclaimed throughout all the earth. 18. So God shows compassion on one and hardens the heart of another as He chooses. 19. Perhaps you will ask me, why does God yet find fault? For who has power to resist His purpose? 20. I vote, no man, who are you to answer back against God? Shall the molded clay say to the potter who formed it, why have you made me this way? 21. Has not the potter absolute power over the clay, of the same lump to make one vessel for noble use and another for common use? 22. What if God, willing to display His anger, and to make His power known, was patient and long-suffering with vessels of wrath prepared for destruction: 23. and did so that He might make known the full value of the vessels prepared for compassion, which He made ready beforehand, 24. even us, whom He has called, not the Jews only, but also the Gentiles? 25. As He said also in the Book of Hosea, Those who were not My people I will call My people; and she who was not beloved, I will call My beloved. 26. And in the same place where they were told, You are not My people; there they will be called the children of the living God. 27. And Isaiah proclaimed aloud concerning Israel, Although the number of the children of Israel is as the sand of the sea, a remnant shall be saved: 28. for the Lord will consummate

His work on the earth, and justly cut it short. 29. And as Isaiah said before, Unless the Armies of the Lord had spared some of our race, we would be as Sodom and Gomorrah. 30. What do we conclude? The Gentiles, without the righteousness of the law to guide them, nevertheless attained to righteousness, even a righteousness conditioned on faith. 31. But Israel, which followed after the law of righteousness, hath not attained to the law of righteousness. 32. Because they sought it not by faith, but by the works of the law. They hesitated at the stumbling block; 33. As it is written, Behold, I lay in Zion a stumbling block and a rock of transgression: and whoever believes in Him shall not be reluctant to accept the Messiah.

Believe in Your Heart
Romans 10:1-11
1. The sincere desire of my heart on behalf of Israel is that they might be saved. 2. I bear record that they possess a sincere devotion to God, but not according to true insight. 3. Not knowing the righteousness of God, but going eagerly ahead to establish a righteousness of their own, they would not submit themselves to a right standing with God. 4. Christ is the termination of the law to bring righteousness to every one who believes. 5. For Moses wrote about the righteousness that was based on the law That the man who practiced the law shall live by the law. 6. But the righteousness which results from faith, speaks this way, Say not in your heart, who shall ascend into heaven? And bring Christ down from above: 7. who shall descend into the deep? And bring up Christ again from the grave. 8. What does the word that we preach say? It is near you, even in your mouth, and in your heart; 9. if you acknowledge with your mouth the message that Jesus is Lord, and believe in your heart that God stood Him up from the grave, you shall be saved. 10. For with the heart man believes and is justified; and with the mouth he confirms his salvation. 11. The scripture declares that whoever believes on Him shall not be disappointed.

There is No Difference
Romans 10:12-21
12. There is no difference between the Jew and the Greek: for the same Lord over all is abounding to all who call on Him. 13. For everyone who calls upon the name of the Lord shall be saved. 14. How shall they call on Him in whom they have not learned to believe? And how shall they believe in Him of whom they have never heard? And how shall they hear without a messenger? 15. And how shall they proclaim, except they be sent? As it is written, Fully developed are the swift feet of those who proclaim the glad tidings of the gospel! 16. But they have not all learned to obey the gospel. For Isaiah said, Lord,

who has believed what they heard? 17. So faith comes by learning to listen to the word of Christ. 18. But I ask did they not hear? Yes, the word went into all the inhabited earth, and the message reached the bounds of habitation. 19. But I ask did Israel not understand? First Moses said, I will make you jealous of a people who are not a nation, and by a nation with limited understanding will I anger you. 20. Then Isaiah boldly said I was found of those who were not seeking; I made Myself known to those who never asked about Me. 21. But to Israel God said constantly I stretched forth My hands to a disobedient and obstinate people.

Life From the Dead
Romans 11:1-15

1. I ask: has God rejected His people? God forbid. I myself am an Israelite, a descendant of Abraham, of the tribe of Benjamin. 2. God has not repudiated the people He marked out as His own. Do you not know what the scripture says about Elijah? How he pleaded with God against Israel, saying, 3. Lord, they have killed your prophets, and pulled down your altars; and I am left utterly alone, and they seek to destroy my life. 4. But what did God answer? I have reserved seven thousand true men who have not bowed a knee to the image of Baal. 5. Presently there is a remnant selected by grace. 6. Since the selection was by grace, there is no need for works: otherwise grace is not a gift. 7. What then? Israel did not find what was sought; but the selection of grace obtained it, and most became hardened. 8. According to the record, God gave them a spiritual insensibility, and they could not see or hear spiritual things unto this day. 9. Also David said, Let their feasts become an anchor, a net, and a stumbling block to keep them at ease: 10. let their eyes be darkened with no clear vision, and their backs continually be bent under burdens. 11. I ask then, have they stumbled to rise no more? God forbid: rather their false step brought salvation to the Gentiles, and to stimulate them to rivalry. 12. Now if their decrease enriched the world, and their withdrawing enriched the Gentiles; how much more will result with their full restoration? 13. This word is for the Gentiles, as an apostle to the Gentiles, I exalt my office: 14. if by any means my office may stimulate Israel to rival the Gentiles that I might save some. 15. For if their exclusion meant the inclusion of the world in salvation, what would their restoration be but life for a corpse?

God is the Source
Romans 11:16-36

16. When the first loaf is holy: the whole batch is consecrated: and if the root of the tree is holy, so are the branches. 17. And if some branches

were broken off, and you being of a wild olive tree were grafted into the tree, and became also a partaker of the root and richness of the olive tree; 18. you must not look down on the branches that were broken off, but remember you do not support the root, the root supports you. 19. You may say, the branches were broken off that I might be grafted into the tree. 20. But it was from lack of faith that they were broken off, and you stand in their place by faith. Stop being proud, but be on guard: 21. for if God spared not the natural branches, pay attention lest He also not spare you. 22. Consider both the kindness and strict justice of God: on them who fell, strict justice; but toward you, kindness, if you continue steadfast in His goodness; otherwise you will also be pruned from the tree. 23. And should they not remain in unbelief, God is able to graft them in again. 24. For if you were cut out of a wild olive tree and grafted contrary to nature into a good olive tree: how much more shall these, who are the natural branches, be grafted into their own olive tree? 25. For I would not have you ignorant of this hidden truth, lest you deceive yourselves; that a partial hardening has befallen Israel, until the full number of Gentiles come to faith. 26. Then at the end the whole of Israel will find salvation: as it is written, There shall come out of Zion the avenger of blood, and shall take away wickedness from Jacob: 27. for this is My covenant that I shall take away their sins. 28. Regarding the gospel, they are opponents of God which is to your advantage: but from the stand point of God's selection, they remain beloved for sake of their ancestors. 29. God's free gifts and His calling are not subject to recall. 30. For in times past you did not believe in God, yet you obtained mercy through their disobedience: 31. so even now these being disobedient, yet through your compassion they may also obtain forgiveness. 32. For God has shut all together in the same net of unbelief, that He might have mercy on all. 33. There is a fathomless depth in God's wisdom and knowledge! His judgments are unsearchable, and His footsteps cannot be tracked! 34. Who can figure out the mind of the Lord? Or who could be His advisor? 35. Who has first given to God that He should pay back again? 36. For God is the source, preserver, and ruler of all things: to God is glory throughout all ages. Amen.

Be Sober-minded
Romans 12:1-8

1. I implore you, brethren, by the compassions of God that you place yourselves as a living sacrifice, consecrated and pleasing to God, which is your reasonable worship. 2. And be not fashioned according to this age: but be transformed by a new mental attitude, that you may confirm for yourselves what is good, acceptable, and the complete will of God. 3. For I say this through the grace given unto me, to every

man that is among you, not to be high-minded more than he ought to be minded; but to be sober-minded, according to the measure of faith God has given. 4. For as the human body has many parts, and all parts do not have the same function: 5. so we, being many form one body in Christ, and each one is mutually dependent on another. 6. Having gifts that differ according to the grace given to us; if your gift is inspired speech, practice according to your proportion of faith; 7. if your gift is serving others, minister well: and the teacher concentrate on teaching; 8. the one who exhorts, must give attention to consolation; he who gives food, clothing or shelter for the poor, let it be done with no partiality; he that governs must do it with diligence; the one who shows compassion must do it with cheerfulness.

Overcome Evil With Good
Romans 12:9-21

9. Let love be without pretense. Hate wrong behavior. Cleave to the good. 10. Have tender affection for the believers; go before one another as an honorable guide; 11. do not delay your enthusiasm; be on fire in the spirit; serving the Lord as a slave; 12. rejoice in hope; remain steadfast in time of trouble; be persistent in the habit of prayer; 13. contribute your share with reference to the needs of the saints; give attention to hospitality. 14. Bless all who persecute you: bless and curse not. 15. Share the happiness of those who rejoice, and share the sorrow of those who are sad. 16. Maintain harmony with one another. Set your mind on high things, but accept humble ways. Do not think too highly of yourself. 17. Never pay back injury for injury. Aim to do what is honorable in the sight of all men. 18. As much as you can, live peaceable with all men. 19. Never avenge yourselves dearly beloved, but leave room for Gods anger: for it is written, Vengeance is mine; I will repay, said the Lord. 20. There is another test, if your enemy hunger, feed him; if he thirst, give him drink: for in so doing you will make him feel a burning sense of shame. 21. Never permit evil to conquer you, but get the better of evil by doing good.

Love Your Neighbor
Romans 13:1-14

1. Let every person line up under governing authorities. For all authority comes from God: the existing authorities have been established by God. 2. Whoever therefore resists authority is opposing God's established order: they that resist will bring judgment on themselves. 3. Those with good conduct have nothing to fear because established authorities are against the wrongdoer. Do you want to have no fear of authorities? Then do what is good, and you will receive praise: 4. for the magistrate is the minister of God to you for good. But if you

do wrong, you have reason to be alarmed; for the sword of justice is not without meaning: for the magistrates are the ministers of God to execute punishment to the evil doer. 5. Therefore you must line up under authority, not only to escape God's anger, but also because it is the right thing to do. 6. For this cause also pay your taxes: for the authorities are God's ministers, devoting themselves to this work. 7. Pay what you owe: taxes to whom taxes are due; custom duties to whom payment is due; look at and pay attention to those entitled to respect; honor to those entitled to honor. 8. Leave no debt unpaid, except the debt of love to others: for he who loves his neighbor has done what the law demands. 9. The commandments are: You must not adulterate (contaminate) your marriage vows by adding another, You must not murder, You must not steal, You must not desire what others have, and if there be any other commandment, it simply means, You shall love your neighbor as yourself. 10. Love does not intentionally do wrong to a neighbor: love, therefore, satisfies the law completely. 11. The time is now that you must awake to reality: for salvation is nearer than when we first believed. 12. The night is almost over and dawn is near: let us therefore lay aside the clothing of the night, and put on the weapons of light. 13. Let us behave honestly in the day light; not in partying and intoxicated behavior, not in secret places of immorality, not in conflict and greed. 14. But clothe yourselves with the Lord Jesus Christ, and make no plans to fulfill the desires of the flesh.

God is Able to Make Him Stand
Romans 14:1-13

1. Receive the weak in faith into your fellowship, but not for the purpose of quarreling about what is right and wrong. 2. One man feels he can eat anything: another eats only vegetables. 3. Those who eat meat should not look down on the vegetarian; neither should those who eat no meat judge the others who eat: God has accepted both. 4. Who are you to judge another man's servant? He will be judged by his own master. The servant of God will stand: for God is able to make him stand. 5. One man considers one day special: another believes every day is the same. Each one should reach a conclusion on this point for himself. 6. He that looks upon a special day observes it unto the Lord. Those who eat meat and those who do not, both give God thanks. 7. No one lives or dies to himself. 8. For whether we live or die, we belong to the Lord. 9. For this purpose, Christ both died and arose to life, that He might be Lord both of the living and the dead. 10. Why do you pass judgment on your brother? Why do you look down on your brother? We shall all stand before the judgment seat of Christ. 11. It is in scripture, As surely as I live, every knee will bow before Me, and every tongue shall acknowledge God. 12. So then every one of us

shall give account of himself to God. 13. Let us stop passing judgment on one another: but rather determine that no man will do anything to cause his brother to stumble and fall.

Nothing Unclean of Itself
Romans 14:14-23

14. I am convinced by the Lord Jesus, that nothing is unclean of itself: but to him who considers any thing to be unclean, to him it is unclean. 15. If because of the food you eat your brother is distressed, you are not walking in love. Do not tear down with your food a man for whom Christ died. 16. Do not let what is good for you be bad for another: 17. for God's kingdom does not consist of food and drink; but moral decency, and mutual agreement among believers, and much happiness through the Holy Spirit. 18. For all who serve Christ in this way are approved by God and acceptable by men. 19. Let us pursue the things that make peace, and the things that edify one another. 20. Do not permit food to break down the work of God. All things of themselves are pure; but it is wrong for anyone to eat and cause another to stumble. 21. It is not good either to eat meat or to drink wine, nor any thing that causes your brother to stumble. 22. Do you have faith? Keep your convictions about food and drink between you and God. Happy is the man who has no misgivings about what he eats or drinks. 23. And if you have doubts do not eat, because whatever is not of faith is sinful.

Written for Our Learning
Romans 15:1-12

1. It is the duty of the strong to support the weak and immature, and not just please themselves, 2. let each one seek to please and build up his neighbor. 3. For even Christ pleased not Himself; but, as it is written, The ill-treatment that was against you, became abuse on Me. 4. Whatever was written before was prepared for our instruction, that we through endurance and encouragement from scripture produce hope. 5. Now the God of enduring patience and assurance grant you to be of one mind toward each other according to Christ Jesus: 6. that with one accord and one voice you may glorify God, even the Father of our Lord Jesus Christ. 7. Wherefore welcome others into your fellowship just as Christ received us to the glory of God. 8. Now I say that Jesus Christ was a messenger to Israel to confirm the promises made to the fathers: 9. and that the Gentiles might exalt God for His compassion; as it is written, For this purpose, I will sing praises of Israel to the Gentiles, and sing in honor of your name. 10. And again God said, Rejoice you Gentiles with God's people. 11. And again, Praise the Lord, all you Gentiles; and all the people eulogize Him. 12. And again

Isaiah said, A descendent of Jesse will come who will rise up and rule over the nations, in Him shall the heathen hope.

The Power of the Spirit
Romans 15:13-21

13. May God the source of hope fill you with happiness and harmony in believing, that your whole life may overflow with hope, through the power of the Holy Spirit. 14. I have personal confidence in you, my brothers, that you are full of integrity, amply furnished with understanding, and able to admonish one another. 15. Nevertheless, brethren, I have written fearlessly to you to remind you of the grace given to me by God. 16. That I should be the messenger of Jesus Christ to the Gentiles, proclaiming the gospel of God, so that the offering up of the Gentiles might be acceptable, being consecrated by the Holy Spirit. 17. Because of my union with Jesus Christ I have proud confidence in my work for God. 18. For I would not have the courage to speak of anything which Christ had not produced by me, to make the Gentiles obedient, by word and work, 19. through the power of the Spirit of God displayed in signs and marvels starting at Jerusalem and all around Illyricum, I have completely declared the good news of Christ. 20. I affirm that not only have I preached the gospel where Christ was known, but I strived to preach elsewhere and not to build upon another man's foundation: 21. but it is written, Those forgotten will see the glory of the gospel and those that have not heard shall understand the truth.

The Blessing of the Gospel
Romans 15:22-33

22. Previously I have been hindered from coming to you. 23. But now since the work here is completed, and having a great desire for many years to come to you; 24. when I travel to Spain, I will visit you: for I hope to include you in my journey and be aided forward after I have enjoyed your company for a while. 25. But first I must go to Jerusalem to deliver a collection to the saints. 26. For the provinces of Macedonia and Achaia have freely made a contribution for the poor saints in Jerusalem. 27. It was a pleasure for the Gentiles, being debtors and partakers of spiritual things, to feel responsible to minister in material things. 28. When I have finished this task and assured the delivery of the collection, I plan to visit you on my way to Spain. 29. And I am certain that when I visit you it will be in the fullness of the blessing of the gospel of Christ. 30. I appeal to you brothers, for the sake of the Lord Jesus Christ and the love the Spirit brings, that you earnestly pray; 31. that I may be delivered from the unbelievers in Judaea: and that my ministry in Jerusalem may be accepted by the saints; 32. that I may

come to you with joy by the will of God, and with you be refreshed. 33. Now the God of peace be with you all. Amen.

Who Labor in the Lord
Romans 16:1-16

1. I commend to you Phoebe our sister, who is a leader in the congregation at Cenchrea: 2. welcome her in the Lord as a believer, and provide any assistance she may need: for she has been most helpful in a difficult situation for many including myself. 3. Remember me to Priscilla and Aquila my fellow-workers in Christ Jesus: 4. who risked their own lives to save my life: unto whom not only I give thanks, but all the congregations of the Gentiles. 5. Also, give greetings to the congregation that meets in their house. Greet my well-beloved Epaenetus, who was the first convert to Christ in Achaia. 6. Greet Mary who has labored much for you. 7. Salute Andronicus and Junia, my countrymen and fellow prisoners, who are outstanding men among the messengers, who became Christians before me. 8. Remember me to Amplias, a dear friend in the Lord. 9. Greet Urbane, our fellow-worker in Christ and Stachys a dear friend. 10. Salute Apelles a tested and tried Christian. Salute those of Aristobulus' household. 11. Greet Herodion my countryman. Greet the believers in the household of Narcissus. 12. Salute Tryphena and Tryphosa who work hard for the Lord. 13. Remember me to Rufus chosen in the Lord, and his mother, who has been a mother to me, also. 14. Greet Asyncritus, Phlegon, Hermas, Patrobas, Hermes, and the brothers who are with them. 15. Salute Philologus, Julia, Nereus, and his sister, and Olympas, and all the believers who are with them. 16. Greet one another with a believer's greetings, even a sacred kiss. The assemblies of Christ send greetings to you.

Power to Establish You
Romans 16:17-27

17. I appeal to you brethren, make record of all who cause divisions and transgressions against the doctrine that you learned, and avoid them. 18. For such do not serve the Lord Jesus Christ, but are slaves to their base desires, and by pleasing words and smooth speeches deceive the hearts of the innocent. 19. The knowledge of your obedience has spread abroad. I am pleased, but want you to be wise unto all that is good and innocent concerning evil. 20. And the God of peace shall crush Satan under your feet shortly. The grace of our Lord Jesus Christ be with you. Amen. 21. Timothy, my fellow worker sends greetings and Lucius, Jason, and Sosipater, my countrymen. 22. I, Tertius, the scribe for this epistle, salute you in the Lord. 23. Gaius my host, and the whole congregation, send greetings. Erastus

the city treasurer sends greetings and Quartus, a brother. 24. May the grace of Jesus Christ be with you; 25. now to Him who has the power to strengthen you according to my gospel, and the preaching of Jesus Christ, according to the revelation of the sacred secret that was a mystery since the world began, 26. but now is made known by the writings of the prophets, and according to the commandment of the everlasting God made known to all nations for the obedience of faith: 27. to the only wise God be praises through Jesus Christ for ever. Amen.

THE LETTER TO THE COLOSSIANS

The letter to the Colossians was written by Paul about AD 61. The assembly at Colosse was established by Epaphras, a disciple of Paul. This letter was requested by Epaphras to bring the influence of Paul's ministry against certain problems in the assembly. Judaizers had gained access to this assembly and the confusing influence of both Greek Philosophy and Oriental Mysticism were added. As a result, angel worship and the importance of "spiritual" knowledge were added to the mix of legalism. Paul makes a distinction between the knowledge gained from teachers and books and the full knowledge one gains from personal experience.

Walk Worthy of the Lord
Colossians 1:1-14

1. Paul, an apostle commissioned by the will of God, and Timothy the brother, 2. to the consecrated and faithful believers at Colosse: spiritual blessings and peace from God our Father and the Lord Jesus Christ. 3. We continue to give thanks to God and the Father of our Lord Jesus Christ, constantly praying for you, 4. having heard of your faith in Christ Jesus, and the love which you show to all the saints, 5. for hope as a stored treasure for you in heaven, whereof you heard before in the true word of the gospel; 6. which reached unto you and to all the world; and yielding fruit also in you since the day you heard and knew the grace and truth of God: 7. and you were taught by Epaphras our beloved fellow servant, who is a faithful minister of Christ for you; 8. who also made known to us your love in the Spirit. 9. For this purpose, since the day we heard it, we have not ceased to pray for you and to desire that you might be filled with the knowledge of His will in all wisdom and spiritual understanding; 10. that you might behave worthy of the pleasing of the Lord, personally bearing good fruit and increasing in the full knowledge of God; 11. being empowered according to His glorious power, with a cheerful exercise of endurance and unlimited perseverance; 12. joyously giving thanks to the Father, who made us sufficient to partake of the inheritance of the saints who live in the light: 13. who has rescued us from the dominion of darkness, and has transformed us into the kingdom of His dear Son: 14. In whom we have redemption through His blood, even the forgiveness of sins:

Christ might have the Preeminence
Colossians 1:15-20

15. Who is the visible expression of the invisible God, the first creature of all creation: 16. because by Him all things were created, in heaven and on earth, things visible and invisible, whether thrones or authorities, or powers: all things were created by Him and for Him: 17. He existed before all things, and by Him all are sustained and held together.

18. He is head of the body, the church: He is the beginning and the first brought from the grave; that in all things Christ might have the pre-eminence. 19. For it pleased the Father that in Him divine perfection exists: 20. and, having made peace through the blood of His cross, by Him bringing the world and God together and all things unto Himself; by Him, all things in heaven and earth.

The Anticipation of Glory
Colossians 1:21-29

21. And you, were once estranged and mental enemies by evil deeds, yet now you are restored as friends, 22. through the death of His earthly body, to present you consecrated and blameless in His sight: 23. if you remain steadfast and fixed in your faith, and not removed from the hope of the gospel, which you heard that which was preached to the whole world; whereof I Paul was made a ministering servant; 24. and now my suffering for you is a joy as I complete in my body the full story of the sufferings of Christ for the sake of His body which is the church: 25. of which I became a servant, according to the stewardship God gave me for the Gentiles to fulfill the word of God; 26. even the sacred secret that was hid from past generations, but is now uncovered to His saints: 27. to whom God was pleased to manifest the wonder of this sacred truth among the Gentiles; which is Christ in you, the anticipation of glory: 28. whom we proclaim, admonishing and instructing every man in all knowledge; that we may present every man mature in Christ Jesus: 29. to this end I toil with all my physical strength, earnestly contending with spiritual energy.

Treasures of Wisdom and Knowledge
Colossians 2:1-5

1. For I wish you understood what an enormous struggle I have for you, and Laodicea, and for all who have not seen me face to face; 2. my exertion is so their hearts might be encouraged, and bound together in love, and obtain the full conviction of their understanding and acknowledge the sacred secrets of God, and of the Father, and of Christ; 3. in whom are the stored treasures of wisdom and knowledge, 4. and this I say lest any man entrap you with alluring words. 5. For though I am physically absent I am with you in spirit, witnessing with joy your steadfastness, and the solid firmness of your faith in Christ.

Entrenched and Growing in Christ
Colossians 2:6-12

6. Since you received Christ Jesus the Lord, so behave in union with Him. 7. Entrenched and growing in Christ, confirmed in faith, as you were taught, flourishing in faith with thanksgiving. 8. Be cautious lest any man stain your soul through a flawed viewpoint and worthless

deception, after human tradition, after the basics of the world, and not after Christ. 9. For in Him the fullness of the Godhead dwells incarnate. 10. And you are complete in Christ, who is the head of all authorities and powers: 11. in whom you wholly put away from yourself the sins of the flesh, without hands by a spiritual operation of Christ: 12. covered with Him in baptism, wherein you were raised with Him through faith in the operation of God, who stood Christ up from the grave.

Let no Man Defraud You
Colossians 2:13-23
13. And you, being dead through trespasses and your uncircumcised nature, were made alive together with Christ, because He pardoned all your sins; 14. cancelling the handwritten decrees that were against us and opposed us, and annulled them by nailing them to His cross; 15. and conquered authorities and powers, making a show of them openly, being fully triumphant. 16. Permit no man to judge what you eat or drink, or in respect to a holy day, or festivals, or Sabbaths: 17. all these things are a shadow of future events; but the real substance is in Christ. 18. Let no man defraud you of your reward with regard to fasting and the worship of angels, interfering with things because of false visions, puffed up by his worldly thoughts, 19. forgetting Christ the Head, on whom all the body depends for nourishment, and is knit together, and multiplied with the increase of God. 20. Wherefore if you died with Christ from the basic elements of the world, why are you lined up under worldly decrees as though you were living in the world, 21. (touch not; taste not; handle not; 22. are all decrees that perish;) after the commandments and doctrines of men. 23. These decrees appear to be wise with their self-imposed worship, their self-discipline, depriving the body; but are of no value against self-indulgence.

Set your Affections on Heavenly Things
Colossians 3:1-8
1. Since you are raised with Christ, keep on aspiring to heavenly things, where Christ is seated at the right hand of God. 2. Set your affection on heavenly things, not on earthly things. 3. You have already undergone death and your new life is hid with Christ in God. 4. When Christ, our life returns, then shall you be illuminated with Him in triumph. 5. Subdue your carnal nature: sexual immorality, filthy thoughts, wanton affection, evil desires, and greediness, which are forms of false worship: 6. For these things bring God's judgment on unbelievers: 7. which was once your behavior when you lived under their influence. 8. But now you must permanently put these away: rage, obsessive outburst, spite, profanity, and filthy words out of your mouth.

Let the Peace of God Rule
Colossians 3:9-17

9. Since you have stripped off the old nature and old practices, stop telling lies to one another; 10. having put on the new nature, which is being freshly renewed in full knowledge in the likeness of the Creator God: 11. all that matters is this new life in Christ and not nationality, the observance of the law, education or social position. 12. As the consecrated, loved and select ones of God, clothe yourselves with a tender heart, kindness, humility, gentleness, and long-suffering; 13. be generous with each other and overlook faults, forgiving all disagreements as Christ forgave you. 14. In addition to all these put on compassionate love, which binds believers together in harmony. 15. And let the peace of God rule in your hearts, this will produce harmony and thankfulness to the assembly. 16. Allow the word of Christ to remain in you as a treasure of wisdom; teaching and gently reminding one another in psalms and hymns and spiritual songs, singing with grace in your hearts to the Lord. 17. And whatever you do or say, do all in the name of the Lord Jesus, and through Him continue to give thanks to the Father.

Put your Heart into It
Colossians 3:18-25

18. Wives, line up under and adapt yourselves to your own husbands, as it is healthy in the Lord. 19. Husbands demonstrate warm affection to your wives, and do not permit bitterness to harm your relationship. 20. Children always abide by the rules of your parents: in doing so you show your love for the Lord. 21. Fathers, do not overcorrect your children and arouse resentment, lest they become discouraged. 22. Employees, abide by the rules of those in authority; not just when they are watching as if you only had to please men; but serve as a sincere expression of your devotion to God: 23. and whatever you do, put your heart into it as if you were serving Christ your Master. 25. All wrong doing will receive punishment: and there is no partiality with God.

Behave with Wisdom
Colossians 4:1-6

1.Employers, deal rightly and justly with those who work for you; knowing that you also have a Master in heaven. 2. Persevere in prayer and remain alert and thankful; 3. include us in your prayers, that God would give us an open door for the word, to speak of the sacred secrets of Christ, for which I am in prison: 4. that I may explain the secrets. 5. Behave with wisdom toward non-Christians, buying up every opportunity. 6. Always make your speech pleasing and tasteful, that you may know how to give a proper answer to every question.

Doing Faithful Prayer Work
Colossians 4:7-18

7. Tychicus, who is a beloved brother, faithful minister and fellow servant in the Lord, will tell you all that concerns me: 8. he was sent to you for this purpose, to gather news about you and to encourage your hearts; 9. with Onesimus, a faithful and beloved brother who is one of you. They will share with you everything that is happening here. 10. Aristarchus my fellow prisoner sends greetings, and Mark, the cousin of Barnabas, (instructions were given about him: if he comes to you make him welcome;) 11. and Joshua, who is called Justus, also sends greetings. These are the only converts from Judaism who have been fellow workers for the kingdom of God, who have been a comfort to me. 12. Epaphras, one of you and a servant of Christ salutes you, always doing faithful prayer work for you that you may stand mature and in full assurance and steadfast in the will of God. 13. Personally I can vouch that he has great passion for your welfare, and them that are in Laodicea, and in Hierapolis. 14. Luke, the well-loved physician, and Demas, greet you. 15. Greet the brethren that are in Laodicea, and Nymphas, and the congregation that is in her house. 16. And when this letter is read among you, send it to be read also in the assembly of the Laodiceans; and that you likewise read the letter from Laodicea. 17. A message for Archippus, attend to the ministry to which God called you, that you fulfill it. 18. The salutation by the hand of me Paul. Remember my bonds. May grace be with you. Amen.

THE LETTER TO THE EPHESIANS

While in prison in Rome about AD 61, Paul wrote the letter to the Ephesians. This is probably the general circulation letter the assembly at Colosse was instructed to receive from Laodicea and to send the letter already received on to Laodicea. In this letter Paul taught the importance of unity in the assembly, the redemptive work of Christ, the importance of a consistent Christian walk, a God-honoring home, and practical applications regarding true spiritual warfare.

Redemption Through His Blood
Ephesians 1:1-14

1. Paul, an apostle of Jesus Christ commissioned by the will of God, to the saints at Ephesus and the faithful in Christ Jesus: 2. grace and peace be granted to you from God our Father, and the Lord Jesus Christ. 3. Praise be to God and Father of our Lord Jesus Christ, who has graced us with all spiritual blessings that heaven enjoys in Christ: 4. before the foundation of the world He chose us in Christ, that we should be consecrated and blameless before Him in love: 5. having planned beforehand for our adoption to Himself by Jesus Christ, according to the good pleasure of His will, 6. to the manifest splendor of His grace, with which He has welcomed us in the beloved. 7. In whom we have redemption through His blood, the forgiveness of sins, according to His generous grace; 8. which He overflowed toward us in full wisdom and discernment; 9. having made known to us the sacred secret of His will, according to His purposed good pleasure in Himself: 10. that in the divine order that was to mark the fullness of times He might gather together in Christ all things, both in heaven and on earth; even in Him: 11. in whom we were made heirs, being chosen beforehand according to His purpose who works all things after the counsel of His own will: 12. that we who first trusted in Christ should manifest His glory. 13. In whom you also trusted, after you heard the word of truth, the gospel of your salvation: in whom after you believed, you were sealed with the Holy Spirit of promise, 14. which is the first installment until the full redemption of the purchased possession, to His praise and glory.

Cease Not to Give Thanks
Ephesians 1:15-23

15. Wherefore I also, after I heard of your faith in the Lord Jesus and your love for the saints, 16. cease not to offer unceasing thanks for you, remembering you in my prayers; 17. that the God of our Lord Jesus Christ, the most glorious Father, may give to you spiritual wisdom and insight into His knowledge: 18. the eyes of your heart being

enlightened: that you may know what is the anticipation of His calling, and what is the glorious treasure of His inheritance in the saints, 19. and how exceedingly great is the power given to us who believe, according to the working of His mighty power, 20. which He exercised in standing up Jesus from the grave, and placed Him at His own right hand in heaven, 21. far above all rule, authority, might and dominion, and any title of sovereignty that can be named, both in this world and the world to come: 22. and placed all things under His power, and made Him head over all things to the church, 23. the church is His body, the completeness of Him that fills the universe.

Salvation is His Handiwork
Ephesians 2:1-10
1. And you He made alive, who were in disobedience and sins; 2. for in the past you followed the ways of the world and lived in sin, and obeyed the evil prince of the air, the spirit that now works among the disobedient: 3. among whom we all once lived following the cravings of the body, obeying the desires prompted by our lower nature, and in our natural state were the offspring of God's displeasure, even as others. 4. Yet, God in His abundant mercy, and unlimited love with which He loved us, 5. even when we were without life in sins, has made us alive with Christ, (by unmerited favor you are saved;) 6. and stood us up together from the grave, and made us to rest together with Christ Jesus in heavenly places: 7. that for all time He might show the generosity of His grace and compassion toward us through Christ Jesus. 8. For through faith and His loving kindness are you rescued; it was not your action, but God's gift that saved you: 9. not personal action, lest any man should boast. 10. For our salvation is His handiwork, fashioned in Christ Jesus for good deeds, which God beforehand designed that good works should mark our behavior.

Built on the Foundation
Ephesians 2:11-22
11. Remember your nature as Gentiles, that you did not physically conform to the Jewish tradition; 12. that you were without Christ, being outside the commonwealth of Israel, and outside the covenants of promise, without hope, and without God in the world: 13. but now in Christ Jesus you who were outside are brought inside the promises by the blood of Christ. 14. For He is the bond of peace that unites both parts into one having dissolved the partition between us; 15. abolishing by His death the hostility, even the law with its decrees and rules; in order to bring together Jew and Gentile into one quality man and produce peace; 16. and unite both in God through His body on the cross, and thereby nullify the effect of their mutual hostility: 17. and

came and proclaimed peace from hostility to both far and near. 18. For through him we both have the right of entry to the Father's promises by one Spirit. 19. Therefore you are no more outsiders, but fellow citizens with the saints, and belong to the household of God; 20. and are now built on the foundation of the prophets and the apostles, Jesus Christ Himself being the foundation stone; 21. in whom the whole building is closely joined together and growing into a sacred temple in the Lord: 22. in Christ you are now assembled together in a spiritual sanctuary through the Spirit.

Fathomless Wealth of Christ
Ephesians 3:1-13
1. For maintaining the cause of you Gentiles, I Paul, am a prisoner of Jesus Christ, 2. if you have heard of the special consideration of God's grace given to me for you: 3. how by direct disclosure He made known to me the sacred secret; (as I wrote briefly*, 4. that when you read my explanation you may understand my knowledge of the secrets of Christ), 5. which in past generations was not made known to mankind, as it is now disclosed by the Spirit to His apostles and prophets; 6. that the Gentiles should become fellow heirs, and members of the same body, and partakers of His promise in Christ by the gospel: 7. for which I was called to serve according to the gift of grace given to me by the exercise of God's power. 8. Unto me, less than the least of all saints, was this grace given, that I should proclaim the fathomless wealth of Christ among the Gentiles; 9. and enlighten all men about the stewardship of the sacred secret, which from the beginning was hid in God, who created the world and collectively all things by Jesus Christ: 10. in order that now unto all the angelic powers might be known by the church the comprehensive wisdom of God, 11. in accordance with the eternal purpose which He intended in Christ Jesus our Lord: 12. in Him we have fluency of speech and confident access by faith. 13. Do not lose courage or be the coward at my troubles for you, which are for your benefit.

---
*See Colossians 1:26,27

Power at Work in Us
Ephesians 3:14-21
14. For this cause on my knees I beseech the Father, 15. of whom all fatherhood in heaven and earth derives its name, 16. that He would grant you, according to the wealth of His power, to be strengthened by His Spirit with power in your inner being; 17. that Christ may abide in your hearts by faith; firmly rooted and grounded in love, 18. may be able to understand with all saints what is the entire dimension

(breadth, length, depth, and height) of faith; 19. and to understand the love of Christ, which transcends all knowledge, that you are filled with the complete fullness of God. 20. Now unto Him who is able to do, over and above all we ask or think, according to the power at work in us, 21. may He be glorified in the assembly of believers through Christ Jesus for all generations world without end. Amen.

One Lord, One Faith, One Baptism
Ephesians 4:1-16

1. Therefore, the prisoner in the Lord, implore you to behave worthy of the mission to which you are called, 2. with humility and gentleness, patiently and lovingly bear with one another; 3. giving diligence to maintain the unity of the Spirit in the alliance of peace. 4. You are a single body with one Spirit, just as there is one hope in your calling; 5. One Lord, one faith, one baptism, 6. there is but one God and Father of all, who is over all and works through all, and lives in you all. 7. But each one is given his own special grace proportioned to the bounty of Christ. 8. The scripture said, He ascended on high and captured the enemies of His kingdom, and presented gifts to men. 9. (Now truly He ascended, but did He not first descend to the lowest level of the earth? 10. He who went down is the same who went up far above all heavens that the whole universe might know His presence.) 11. And He gave some to be messengers, and some preachers, and some missionaries, and some teaching pastors; 12. for the ultimate purpose of equipping the saints to do the work of serving and strengthening the body of believers in Christ: (See vs. 14-16) 13. until we all attain the same faith, and the experiential knowledge of the Son of God, unto mature manhood, unto the full measure of development in Christ: 14. that we no longer behave as young children, driven before the wind of each new teaching, by the trickery and sneakiness of men, whereby they ambush with deceitful schemes; 15. but arriving at truth in love, you may grow up into Him in all things, Who is the head, even Christ: 16. from whom the whole body is in harmony and compressed together by that which every joint supplies, according to the increase of every part (quality growth), so that the body is increased within itself in love.

Lesson you Learned from Christ
Ephesians 4:17-32

17. This I command solemnly in the Lord, that you henceforth behave not as Gentiles, in the arrogance of their mind, 18. having clouded powers of discernment, being estranged from the life of God, although ignorance prevails among them, because of the blindness of their heart: 19. having lost all sense of shame have given themselves over to sensuality, to practice all forms of immorality without restraint. 20.

This is not the lesson you learned from Christ: 21. if you have been instructed by Him and listened to the truth in Jesus. 22. For you learned concerning your former behavior, that the old man was corrupt according to deceitful passions; 23. and the spirit of your mind must be remade; 24. and that you fully clothe yourself as a new man, which after God is created in righteousness and the holiness of truth. 25. Wherefore speak every man truth with his neighbor without falsehood: for we are members bound one to another. 26. Have righteous anger without sin: let not the sun go down on your anger: 27. neither give an opportunity to the devil. 28. The thief must steal no more, but let him do honest work with his hands, that he may have something to share with the needy. 29. Let no unwholesome words come from your mouth, but only good words for enriching, that it may serve as a blessing to the hearers. 30. Never distress the Holy Spirit of God, whereby you have been marked for the day of redemption. 31. Let your bitter frame of mind, anger and violent outbreak or brawling, and abusive language, be put away from you with all hatred: 32. become gracious to one another, tenderly affectionate, ready to forgive one another, even as God for Christ's sake forgave you.

Habitually Behave in Love
Ephesians 5:1-14

1. Become imitators of God, as His beloved children; 2. and habitually behave in love, as Christ loved you, and was delivered for you as an offering and voluntary sacrifice to God to become a pleasing fragrance. 3. But as saints let not immorality, impurity or callous greediness, be named even once among you; 4. neither obscenity, nor corrupt talking, nor practiced suggestive speech, these are all unbecoming behavior: but rather give thanks. 5. For this you surely know, that no solicitor for prostitutes, or reckless spendthrift, or worshiper of idols, will have a place in the kingdom of Christ and of God. 6. Let no man mislead you with words devoid of truth: because these things bring the anger of God upon the disobedient. 7. Do not associate with such things. 8. For once your heart was in darkness, but now it is filled with light from the Lord: behave as the product of light: 9. (for the product of light is seen in all goodness, righteousness, and sincerity;) 10. be living proof of what is well-pleasing to the Lord. 11. And have no friendship with the activities of darkness, but rather admonish them. 12. For their secret actions are too disgraceful to even talk about. 13. But all things that are censured are made obvious by the light. 14. Wherefore it was said, *Awake sleeper and get up from among the dead, and Christ shall shine on you.**

---

*v14 These words do not appear in Scripture, Paul was quoting from another source.

Be Influenced by the Spirit
Ephesians 5:15-33

15. Look carefully how you walk, not foolishly, but in the light, 16. buying up every opportunity, because these are evil days. 17. Wherefore be not reckless, but prudently care for the future understanding the will of the Lord. 18. Stop excessively drinking wine, which influences riotous living; more willingly be influenced by the Spirit; 19. but speak to one another in exalted verse, songs of praise, and sacred music, singing and making melody with the music of your hearts, to the Lord; 20. continue giving thanks to God the Father for all things in the name of our Lord Jesus Christ; 21. line up under one another in reverence to Christ. 22. Wives, line up under and adapt to your own husbands, as unto the Lord. 23. For the husband is in charge of the wife, even as Christ is in charge of the church: and He is the champion of the church. 24. Therefore as the church is to line up under the authority of Christ, so let the wives line up under their husbands in all things. 25. Husbands, be devoted to your wives, even as Christ is devoted to the church, and gave Himself for it; 26. that He might consecrate and purify it with the cleansing water of the word, 27. that He might present the church to Himself as a glorious bride, without spot, wrinkle or blemish. 28. So must men love their wives as if they were their own body. He who loves his wife loves himself. 29. For no man ever loathed his own body; but nourishes and values it, even as the Lord values the church: 30. for we are members of his body. 31. For this reason shall a man leave his father and mother and cleave intimately to his wife, and they shall become one new body.* 32. This is a great sacred secret: but I speak concerning Christ and the church. 33. Nevertheless let each one in particular love his wife even as himself; and the wife should look to and pay attention to her husband.

*v31 A new body or "one flesh" is *sarx* which suggests a human body apart from the soul. Probably this is the bonding that comes with the first child and not only the emotional bonding of a couple when vows are physically consummated.

Discipline and Instruction of the Lord
Ephesians 6:1-9

1. Children, follow your parents in the Lord: for this is right. 2. Respect your father and mother; (this is the first commandment with promise;) 3. that you may prosper and have long life on earth. 4. And fathers provoke not your children to anger: but nurture them in the discipline and instruction of the Lord. 5. Servants *(employees)*, be respectful of

those who are over you, with concern and trepidation, with simplicity of motive, as serving Christ: 6. not just to please them when they are watching; but as the servants of Christ, doing the will of God from the heart; 7. give your service willingly, as to the Lord and not to men: 8. knowing that all men are rewarded for the good they do, whether bond or free. 9. Masters, (*employers*) deal with your servants in the same manner, there is no need for threats: remember that your Master is in heaven; neither does God show partiality.

The Complete Armor of God
Ephesians 6:10-23

10. Finally, my brothers, be strengthened in the Lord, and in the power of His unlimited resource. 11. Wear the complete armor of God, so you can stand against the strategy and assault of the adversary. 12. For our wrestling is not against a physical enemy, but against evil princes of darkness who rule this world, against hosts of spiritual wickedness in heavenly warfare. 13. Wherefore wear the complete armor of God that you may be able to withstand evil attacks when they come, and be found still standing. 14. Stand your ground, being protected by Truth, and having honest and strong moral principles for a breastplate; 15. and the gospel of peace preparing your feet for battle, 16. above all, take the shield of faith to extinguish all the fiery darts of the wicked. 17. And take the helmet, which is salvation, and the sword of the Spirit, which is the word of God: 18. praying on every occasion through petition in the Spirit, and be vigilant with unwearied perseverance and supplication for all saints; 19. and pray for me, that fluency of speech may be given me, that I may make known courageously the sacred secret of the gospel, 20. for which I am an envoy in a coupling-chain bound to a guard: that despite that detail I may speak bravely, as I ought to speak. 21. But that you may know what is happening to me, a beloved and faithful brother in the Lord, Tychicus, will make known to you all things: 22. whom I sent for the same purpose, that you might know about me, and that he might encourage your hearts. 23. Peace be to the believers, and love with faith, from God the Father and the Lord Jesus Christ. 24. Grace be with all who love our Lord Jesus Christ in sincerity. Amen.

THE LETTER TO THE PHILIPPIANS

The last letter Paul wrote during his first imprisonment was the letter to the Philippians about AD 63. Paul thanked the assembly for sending funds for living expenses while he awaited trial in Rome. He described the essence of humility in a psalm of praise to Jesus (2:5-11) in his presentation on the importance faithfulness to Christ and following His example of humility. Paul also warned against false teachers and against having confidence in the flesh, and encouraged them to follow his personal example of steadfast faith.

I Have You in My Heart
Philippians 1:1-11

1. Paul and Timothy, bondservants of Jesus Christ, to all the saints in Christ Jesus who are at Philippi, with the elders and ministers: 2. grace and peace to you from the Lord Jesus Christ. 3. Each occasion of my remembrance of you is a cause for thanksgiving, 4. always in my every prayer for you my request is with joy, 5. on account of your partnership in the gospel until this moment; 6. being persuaded that He who began a good work in you will carry it out until the day of Jesus Christ: 7. I have you in my heart and it is right for me to think this of you; inasmuch as both in my bonds, and in the defense and confirmation of the gospel, you are partakers of my grace. 8. For God is my witness, how greatly I yearn for you in the tender mercies of Jesus Christ. 9. And this I pray, that your love may abound yet more and more in knowledge and in all judgment; 10. teaching you to discern the good from the bad, that you may be kept pure and blameless till the day of Christ; 11. bearing the rich harvest of righteousness, which are by Jesus Christ, unto the glory and praise of God.

Advance the Gospel
Philippians 1:12-20

12. Now I would have you to understand, that which I have gone through will most likely advance the gospel; 13. so that my chains in Christ are known in all the praetorian guard and all the palace; 14. and many of the brethren have gained confidence by my chains, and are more fluent to speak the word with courage. 15. Some indeed do proclaim Christ out of jealousy and contention; but others preach Christ from good will: 16. the ones who preach Christ from motives of intrigue, without pure intent, think to add to my suffering in chains: 17. but another of love, knowing that I am set for the defense of the gospel. 18. What does it matter? Whether in pretence or in truth, Christ is preached; and I rejoice in this, yes, I will rejoice. 19. For I know that this will turn to my deliverance through your prayer, and the ample provision of the Spirit of Jesus Christ, 20. according to my earnest faith

and expectation, that in nothing I shall feel guilty, but with all fluency and courage, as always, now Christ shall be magnified in my physical body, whether by life or by death.

For Me to Live is Christ
Philippians 1:21-30
21. Living means Christ to me and death means gain. 22. But if living in this body means more fruitful labor: yet what I shall choose I know not. 23. This is my dilemma, having a desire to depart, and to be with Christ; which is far better: 24. nevertheless to abide in this body is more necessary for you. 25. Having this confidence, I know that I shall remain and continue working for you and furthering your joy of faith; 26. that your rejoicing for me may be more abundant in Jesus Christ by my presence with you again. 27. Only let your behavior be worthy of the gospel of Christ: that whether I am present or absent, I may hear that you stand fast in one spirit, with one mind striving together for the faith of the gospel; 28. and in no way alarmed by your adversaries: for their hostility is an evident token of punishment in hell, but to you salvation that is of God. 29. For you were granted on behalf of Christ, the privilege not only to believe on Him, but also to suffer for His sake; 30. having the same hard struggle which you once saw in me, and now hear the struggle continues in me.

Jesus Christ is Lord
Philippians 2:1-11
1. If there be any encouragement in Christ, if any reassurance in love, if any participation of the Spirit, if any tenderness and compassion, 2. fill up my joy by living in harmony, having the same love, being in one accord of one mind. 3. Let nothing be done through argument or excessive pride; but in true humility let each value others more than themselves. 4. Look not after your own interests, but practice looking after the interest of others. 5. Let your disposition and thoughts be the same as Christ Jesus: 6. although having a divine nature, did not cling to His equality with God: 7. but stripped Himself of His rightful divinity, and took upon Himself the nature of a servant, and was made in the likeness of men: 8. and appearing in human form, He humbled Himself, and became obedient even to death on the cross. 9. Wherefore God highly exalted Him, and gave Him a name that is above every name: 10. that at the name of Jesus every knee should bow, in heaven, and in earth, and things under the earth; 11. and that every tongue should openly confess that Jesus Christ is Lord, to the glory of God the Father.

Holding Forth the Word of Life
Philippians 2:12-18

12. Therefore, my dearly beloved, as you were always obedient, not as in my presence only, but much more in my absence, keep on working out the deliverance of the congregation with a humble frame of mind. 13. For it is God working in you to make you both willing and able to do His good pleasure. 14. Do all things without grumbling and disagreements: 15. that you may be above suspicion and unblemished, the children of God, with an untarnished reputation, in the midst of a warped and twisted nation, where you shine as lights in the world; 16. holding forth the Word of life; that you give me grounds for rejoicing on the day of Christ, that my course was run successfully, and my labor was fruitful. 17. Yes, and even if my blood must be poured out as a sacrifice to nurture your faith, I shall rejoice and share your joy. 18. And in the same manner you joy and share my rejoicing.

Hold in Honor Such Men
Philippians 2:19-30

19. But I hope in the Lord Jesus to send Timothy to you shortly, that I may be encouraged, when I know your situation. 20. For I have no other person as near my own attitude who will naturally care for your situation. 21. All others seem to be seeking their own aims, not the things that are of Jesus Christ. 22. You know that Timothy has proved himself, and that he has served me in the gospel, as a son would his father. 23. I hope to send him presently, just as soon as I can determine how my case is going here. 24. But I trust in the Lord that I also may visit shortly. 25. Yet I determined it necessary to send Epaphroditus to you now, he is my brother, companion in labor, and fellow soldier, but your messenger, and he ministered to my needs. 26. For he has been somewhat homesick for you since he heard that you knew of his sickness. 27. For indeed he was sick near to death: but God had mercy on him; and not him only, but on me also, lest I should have sorrow added to my suffering. 28. I sent him eagerly, that when you see him again, you may rejoice, and my own sorrow will be lessened. 29. Receive him with a joyful greeting in the Lord, and hold in honor such men: 30. because for the work of Christ he was near death, not regarding his life, to supply that which you could not because of distance.

Rejoice in the Lord
Philippians 3:1-11

1. Finally, my brothers, rejoice in the Lord. To repeat the same warning is not grievous to me, but for you it is reassuring. 2. Beware of backbiting (*Judaizers*), look out for workers of wickedness, beware of those who demand circumcision. 3. For we are the true circumcision, who worship

God in the Spirit, and rejoice in Christ Jesus, and have no confidence in outward ceremonies, 4. though I have basis for confidence. If others think they have whereof to trust in the flesh, I more: 5. circumcised the eighth day, of the stock of Israel, of the tribe of Benjamin, a Hebrew of Hebrew parents; as touching the law, a Pharisee; 6. in bitter hate I persecuted the church; and was blameless touching the standard of the law. 7. But what was once gain, I counted loss for Christ. 8. Affirmative, I count all things but loss for the exceeding value of the knowledge of Christ Jesus my Lord: for Christ I suffered the loss of all things, and count them as manure, that I may win Christ, 9. and in death actually be with Him, not depending on the righteousness of the law, but the righteousness which is of God by faith: 10. that I may have true knowledge of Him, and know the power of His resurrection, and the partnership of His sufferings, and sharing the likeness of His death; 11. if by any measure I might reach unto the standing up from the grave.

This One Thing I Do
Philippians 3:12-21

12. Not as though I had already won the battle or were already faultless: but I pursue, if I may catch that for which also I was captured by Christ Jesus. 13. Brothers, I have not yet reached my goal: but this one thing I do, forgetting those things that are behind, and stretching forth to those things that are before, 14. I press on to secure the goal and the prize of the high calling of God in Christ Jesus. 15. Let us therefore, as many as are mature, be thus minded: and if in any thing you be otherwise minded, God will reveal this to you. 16. Nevertheless, we must continue to live up to what we have attained, and behave the same rule, and mind the same thing. 17. Brethren, unite in imitating me and mark those who behave according to my example. 18. (For I have told you before and now tell you again weeping, that many behave as the enemies of the cross of Christ: 19. whose end is punishment in hell, whose stomach is their god, and are proud of their shameful behavior, and are absorbed in earthly matters.) 20. For our commonwealth is in heaven; from which place we look for the Savior, the Lord Jesus Christ: 21. who will change our contemptible body into one fashioned as His glorious body, according to the working of His power whereby He is able to subjugate all things unto Himself.

Keep on Being Focused
Philippians 4:1-9

1. Therefore, my dear brothers whom I long to see, you are my joy and crown, keep on standing fast in the Lord, my dearly beloved. 2. I requested that Euodias and Syntyche be of the same mind in the

Lord. 3. And I ask you also, true yokefellow, assist those women who labored with me in the gospel, with Clement also, and with others my fellow laborers, whose names are in the book of life. 4. Always rejoice in the Lord: and again I say, rejoice. 5. Let your gentleness be known to every one. The Lord is at hand. 6. Be anxious for nothing; but under all circumstances by general prayer and specific petition joined with thanksgiving let your personal needs be known to God. 7. And the authentic peace of God which transcends all comprehension shall guard your hearts and minds through Christ Jesus. 8. Finally, brethren, whatever things are genuine, whatever things are uncomplicated, whatever things are impartial, whatever things are unadulterated, whatever things are agreeable, whatever things are honorable; if there be any desirable quality, and if there be any acclaim, think on these things. 9. Model your behavior on those things which you both learned and received, and seen and heard of me, practice continually: and the God of peace will be with you.

I Have Learned
Philippians 4:10-23

10. But I rejoiced greatly in the Lord that at last your care of me has flourished again; wherein you were also concerned, but lacked opportunity. 11. Not that I speak in regard to need: for I have learned, in whatever circumstance I am, therewith to be self-sufficient. 12. I understand how to deal with humble circumstances, and I know how to have more than enough: every where and in all things I have learned to be well-fed and to be hungry, both to have plenty and to suffer need. 13. I can do all things through Christ who provides me strength. 14. Notwithstanding my circumstance, you have done well in contributing your share toward my hardship. 15. You Philippians know that in the beginning of the gospel, when I departed for Macedonia, no assembly but you, shared with me concerning financial matters. 16. For even in Thessalonica you sent funds twice to provide for my needs. 17. It was not a desire for financial gifts: but I desired that a harvest may abound to your account. 18. But I have more than enough: my needs are fully satisfied, having received of Epaphroditus the gifts you sent, they were like a sweet smelling sacrifice acceptable and well pleasing to God. 19. But my God shall supply all your needs according to the wealth of His glory by Christ Jesus. 20. Now to God our Father be praises for ever and ever. Amen. 21. Greet every saint in Christ Jesus. The brethren who are with me greet you. 22. All the saints salute you, especially Caesar's household servants. 23. The grace of our Lord Jesus Christ be with your spirit. Amen.

Section Four

Relational Letters

The Letter to Philemon
The First Letter to Timothy
The Letter to Titus
The Second Letter to Timothy
The Second Letter of John
The Third Letter of John

THE LETTER TO PHILEMON

Paul wrote the letter to Philemon in AD 61 from Rome. This letter is a plea to Philemon for forgiveness on behalf of a runaway slave named Onesimus. Philemon was evidently a convert of Paul's in Colosse, and Onesimus was somehow brought to Paul in Rome and became converted to Christ. This letter is a masterpiece of Christian courtesy and intercession. "If he has done you damage or owes you anything, put it on my account; I Paul in my own hand pledge to make it good:" (1:18, 19 EDNT)

Generosity in the Faith
Philemon 1:1-7
1. Paul, a prisoner of Christ Jesus, and Brother Timothy, to the well beloved Philemon, and fellow worker, 2. And to Apphia, a beloved sister, and Archippus, our fellow warrior, and to the assembly in your house: 3. grace and peace be yours from Father God and from the Lord Jesus Christ. 4. I always give thanks to my God, remembering you in my prayers, 5. for I hear accounts of your love and your faith, you show towards the Lord Jesus and towards all the saints; 6. I pray that your generosity in the faith may become operative in a full knowledge of every good thing in you for Christ. 7. It has been a joyful comfort to me, brother, to hear of the refreshment you have brought to the hearts of the saints.

Intercession for a Friend
Philemon 1:8-17
8. Wherefore, having fluency of speech in Christ to prescribe a sense of duty to you, 9. yet I prefer for love's sake to appeal to you as the old man, Paul, now a prisoner of Jesus Christ. 10. My appeal to you is for my son, Onesimus, a convert of my imprisonment: 11. the one formerly useless to you, but now useful both to you and to me: 12. whom I have sent back to you: receive him as a piece of my own heart. 13. I would rather keep him with me, to serve the gospel and my bonds in your place: 14. but I do not wish to do anything without your approval; that the good that you should do was willingly done and not of necessity. 15. Perhaps you lost him for a season, that he could be saved and with you eternally; 16. now receive him not as a slave, but as my well loved brother, even more to you, both as a man and as a believer in the Lord. 17. If you value our partnership, welcome him as you would receive me.

Pledge to a Brother
Philemon 1:18-21
18. If he has done you damage or owes you anything, put it on my account; 19. I Paul in my own hand pledge to make it good: not to

mention that you owe me a debt and even your own life. 20. Yes, brother, let me have treasure in you in the Lord: comfort my heart in the Lord. 21. Having trusted in your obedience I wrote to you, knowing that you will do even more than I request.

Confidence in Obedience
Philemon 1:22-25

22. And at the same time prepare for me lodging; for I hope that through your prayers I shall come to you. 23. Greetings to you from Epaphras, my fellow prisoner in Christ Jesus; 24. also, Mark, Aristarchus, Demas, Luke, my fellow workers. 25. The grace of our Lord Jesus Christ be with your attitude and frame of mind. Amen.

THE FIRST LETTER TO TIMOTHY

First Timothy is the first letter Paul wrote after he was freed from house arrest in Rome in AD 64. Timothy is in the assembly at Ephesus and this letter offered practical advice on dealing with false teachers. It gave guidelines for believers with regards to worship, prayer and outlined qualifications for leaders. Finally Paul gave practical, personal instruction to Timothy regarding his personal duties towards the congregation.

Charge Not to Teach Differently
1 Timothy 1:1-11

1. Paul, an ambassador of the gospel by the appointment of God our Savior, and of Christ Jesus our hope; 2. to Timothy, my own son in the faith: grace be yours, and mercy, and peace from God the Father and from Christ Jesus our Lord. 3. As I exhorted you to remain in Ephesus when I went to Macedonia that you might charge certain persons not to teach differently, 4. nor pay attention to legends or endless genealogies which brings questions, rather than provide a stewardship of God in faith. 5. Now the end of the charge is love out of a clean heart and a good conscience and faith without hypocrisy: 6. from which certain people have sharply changed direction to empty talking; 7. desiring to explain the law, without understanding the meaning of their words, or the subject on which they emphatically assert. 8. But the law is good if a man apply it lawfully; 9. remember the law was not made for those who live innocent lives, but for the lawless and disobedient, for the ungodly and the sinful, directed against people who attack their own parents, for murderers, 10. for the immoral, for sexual perverts, for slave traders, for those who lie or swear to lies, and for all other things that oppose sound moral teaching; 11. as set forth in the glorious gospel of the blessed God, this was entrusted to my care.

An Extreme Example of His Long-suffering
1 Timothy 1:12-17

12. Thanks I give to the one empowering me, Christ Jesus our Lord, because He deemed me faithful putting me in his service, 13. who was a blasphemer, a persecutor, a man of violence, author of outrage, and yet He had mercy on me, because I was acting in the ignorance of unbelief. 14. But the grace of our Lord was more than abundant with faith and love which is in Christ Jesus. 15. What a true saying and worthy of a favorable reception, that Christ Jesus came to the world to save sinners; of whom I rank first. 16. And yet I was pardoned, so that in me first Christ Jesus might give an extreme example of His long-suffering; I was to be a precedent for all those who will ever believe in Him and win eternal life. 17. Now to the King of the ages, incorruptible

and invisible only God, be honor and glory unto the ages of the ages. Amen.

Instructions to a Young Man
1 Timothy 1:18-20

18. This is the instructions I entrust to you, son Timothy, according to the prophecies that pointed to you, that you being equipped might fight a good fight; 19. with faith and a good conscience to assist you; which certain persons have rejected this duty and made shipwreck of their lives: 20. among them is Hymenaeus and Alexander; whom I have turned over to Satan, that they might learn not to speak profanely.

Prayers for All
1 Timothy 2:1-8

1. I exhort first of all, that petitions, prayers, intercessions, and thanksgivings, be made for all mankind; 2. for kings and all who hold high responsibilities; that we may lead a quiet and tranquil life with reverence and dignity. 3. It is good and to do this is pleasing in the sight of God our Savior; 4. who desires all men to be saved and come to the knowledge of the truth. 5. For there is one God, and only one go-between God and men, the man Christ Jesus; 6. who sacrificed Himself to ransom freedom for all mankind, a witness to God's timing. 7. For this I was appointed a herald and an apostle, this is true, I make no false claims; a teacher to the nations with a message of faith and truth. 8. I desire therefore the men to pray in every place lifting up holy hands with no anger in their hearts and no doubts in their minds.

Female Adornment and Behavior
1 Timothy 2:9-15

9. Also, I desire that women pray and clothe themselves in suitable apparel, in all modesty and self-restraint; not with elaborate hair styles, with gold or pearls, or expensive clothes; 10. but appropriately for women who profess devotion to God through good works. 11. Let the married women learn in quietness listening and respecting the authority of the teacher. 12. But I do not permit a married woman to instruct, or to obstinately disregard the rights of her husband, but to maintain quietness. 13. It was Adam that was first created, then Eve. 14. It was not Adam who was deceived by the serpent, but the woman being deceived was in the transgression. 15. But Eve was saved through the childbirth*, and this blessing is extended to all women who wisely walk the path that leads to love and sanctification.

---

*v15 The use of the Greek definite article refers to the birth of the Savior, which provided salvation not only for Eve but for all women who follow the path of santification; this blessing honors womanhood.

Criterion for Spiritual Leadership
1 Timothy 3:1-7
1. This is a faithful saying, if a man desire leadership oversight, he is aspiring to a noble task. 2. One holding an office of watchful care must be scrupulous, faithful to a certain woman, watchful, sensible, orderly, hospitable, experienced in teaching; 3. neither intemperate, nor quarrelsome, free from the love of money; but gentle, not contentious, not a craving for possessions; 4. he must be one who is a good head of his own family and keeps his children in order by winning their full respect; 5. if a man has not learned how to manage his own household, will he know how to govern God's church? 6. Not a recent convert, lest being puffed up he fall into judgment of the devil. 7. Moreover he must have a good report from those outside the church; that he not fall into reproach and into the snare of the devil.

Criterion for Spiritual Helpers
1 Timothy 3:8-16
8. Those who serve must be serious, sincere in their talk, not addicted to wine, not craving wealth; 9. keeping true, in all honesty of conscience, to the faith that has been revealed. 10. And let the ministers first be tested and undergo probation; then being found without accusation, let them function as a minister. 11. Even so must their wives be grave, not slanderous gossipers, temperate, faithful in all things. 12. Permit the ministers be a man married to a certain woman, and manage their own children and household well. 13. For those who have ministered well acquire for themselves a good position and fluency of speech of the faith founded on Christ Jesus. 14. I am writing these things hoping to come to you shortly; 15. but if I am delayed that you may know how you should conduct yourself in the family of God, which is the assembly of the living God, and the pillar and bulwark of the truth. 16. And confessedly great is the mystery of godliness: who was manifested in the flesh, was justified in spirit, was seen by angels, was proclaimed among nations, was believed in the world, was taken up in glory.

Blessed by Prayer and Word
1 Timothy 4:1-10
1. Now the Spirit speaks in words, that in later times some will depart from the faith, attending to misleading spirits and teachings of demons; 2. they will be deceived by the pretensions of imposters, whose conscience is hardened as if seared with a branding iron; 3. they discourage marriage and insist on abstinence from foods which God created to be received with thanksgiving by all who believe and know the truth. 4. For everything that God has created, there is

nothing that needs to be rejected if it is received with thanksgiving: 5. for it is blessed by prayer and the word of God. 6. If you put the brothers in remembrance of these things, you shall be a good minister of Jesus Christ, encouraged and fed by the words of faith and the good teaching that you have practiced. 7. But do not listen to childish fairy tales told by silly women, rather exercise yourself unto physical fitness. 8. Physical exercise has short-term value: while consecration is beneficial for your present life and for the future. 9. This is a saying that deserves to be accepted by all. 10. For to this we labor and struggle, because we have set our hope on a living God who is the Savior of all men, especially of believers.

Things Commanded and Taught
1 Timothy 4:11-16

11. These things learn and teach with authority. 12. Permit no man to look down on your youthfulness; show yourself a pattern of believers in speech, in behavior, in love, in faith, in sexual purity. 13. Until I come, grace the public reading of scripture with your presence and speak and teach encouraging words. 14. Do not neglect the spiritual endowment you possess, which was given you by means of prophecy, with the laying on of the hands of preaching elders. 15. Give attention to these things; give yourself wholly to them; that your progress may appear to all. 16. Take heed to yourself and continue in the teaching; for in doing this you will both save yourself and the ones hearing you.

Prescribed Relationships
1 Timothy 5:1-16

1. Do not reprimand an elder, but beseech him as a father; and the younger men as brothers; 2. treat the elder women as mothers; the younger women as sisters, with all transparency. 3. Respect widows that are truly alone. 4. But if any widow have children or grandchildren, let them learn first to show faithfulness at home, and to make suitable returns to their parents: for that is good and acceptable before God. 5. But the widow having really been left alone and has set her hope on God and continues in the petitions and the prayers night and day; 6. but the pleasure loving although alive is really dead. 7. Insist on these things that the women alone may not be condemned. 8. If anyone provides not for his own people, and especially his family, he has denied the faith, and is worse than an unbeliever. 9. Do not enroll a widow under 60 years of age, having been faithful to one man. 10. Being witnessed by good works; if she brought up children, if she entertained strangers, if she washed the feet of the saints, if she relieved the ones being afflicted, if she followed after every good work. 11. Refuse to enroll younger widows: for when they grow impatient with

Christian widowhood, they will marry; 12. for their decision to marry would go against the promise of Christian widowhood. 13. Because they learned to be idle, wandering from house to house; and not only idle, but gossip and interfere in things they ought not. 14. So I would have the younger women marry, bear children, guide the house, and give no occasion to the enemy for scandal. 15. For some have already turned out of the way to follow the path of Satan. 16. If any believing woman have widows, let her assist them, leaving the congregation to support the widows who are destitute.

Honor Senior Leadership
1 Timothy 5:17-25

17. Let the seniors who practice oversight well be counted worthy of two-fold money, especially those who labor preaching and teaching. 18. For scripture says, You shall not muzzle the ox treading out the corn. And, the laborer is worthy of his compensation. 19. Do not recognize an accusation against an elder unless there are two or three witnesses. 20. Give a public rebuke to all who sin that others may respect the consequences of sinning. 21. I urgently advise you before God, and the Lord Jesus Christ, and the chosen angels, that you observe these things without hasty judgment or partiality. 22. Do not be quick to lay hands on any man neither share the sins of others: Keep yourself pure. 23. No longer drink water, but use a little wine for your digestion and your frequent condition. 24. Some men's sins are plain for all to see, and are judged immediately; and some men their sins follow close behind. 25. Even so there are good deeds that are plain to see; and there are deeds that cannot be hidden for long.

Teach Respect for Authority
1 Timothy 6:1-2

1. As many as are under a yoke being slaves, let them deem their own masters worthy of all respect lest the name of God and the teaching be the cause of foul language. 2. And those whose masters belong to the faith, let them not look down on them because they are brethren; but rather render better service, because they who benefit are believers, worthy of their love. These things teach and encourage strongly.

Be Aware of Mercenary Teachers
1 Timothy 6:3-6

3. If anyone advocate different teaching and consent not to wholesome words, even the words of our Lord Jesus Christ, and to the teaching which is according to true righteousness; 4. then he is puffed up, without knowledge, but with an urge for speculation and controversy. 5. Perpetual quarrelings from corrupt minds, and men destitute

of the truth, who think of godliness as a way to enrich themselves: 6. but godliness with self-sufficiency is great gain.

Love of Money the Root of All Evil
1 Timothy 6:7-10
7. For we brought nothing into this world, neither can we carry out anything. 8. Let us be content with food and clothing. 9. But those who are determined to be rich are tempted and caught in a trap, and into many senseless and dangerous appetites, such desires cause men to sink into present destruction and later punishment in hell. 10. For the root of all evil is the love of money: while some craving money have wandered away from the faith and suffered many self-inflicted and discouraging sorrows.

Fight the Good Fight of Faith
1 Timothy 6:11-16
11. It is for you, servant of God, to run from these self-inflicted and discouraging sorrows; and pursue righteousness, godliness, faith, love, endurance, and be teachable. 12. Struggle to win the good fight of faith and grasp eternal life, to which you were called, now that you have witnesses to your noble profession. 13. I charge before God, the one making all things live and Christ Jesus the one having witnessed the good confession in the time of Pontius Pilate. 14. That you execute your charge without spot or blame, until our Lord Jesus Christ appears: 15. He will appear at His own time, who is the only Holy Potentate, the King of kings, and the Lord of lords; 16. He alone possess immortality, living in the glory that no man can approach; whom no man has seen, nor can see: to whom is ascribed eternal worship and power. Amen.

Guard the Truths Entrusted to You.
1 Timothy 6:17-21
17. Warn them who are rich in this present world not to think highly of themselves, not to trust in uncertain riches, but in the living God, who bestows on us all that we richly enjoy; 18. let them enrich their lives with charitable deeds, always ready to contribute and share with the fellowship; 19. some have laid up the foundation of a good treasure against the world to come that they may grasp true life eternal. 20. Timothy, keep safe what has been entrusted to you, avoiding profane and frivolous talk, and the contradictions of false knowledge: 21. some have missed the mark professing false knowledge concerning the faith. Grace be with you. Amen.

THE LETTER TO TITUS

Titus was a disciple of Paul who was trying to assist a troubled assembly on the island of Crete. Paul writes a personal letter to Titus about AD 64. The Letter included qualifications for leaders; guidelines for living a Godly life; an emphasis on faith that overcomes division among believers, and instruction on how to deal with heresy. The letter offered a great deal of practical advice on the personal ethics of a Christian leader. Paul explained that sound teachings would produce godly living.

A True Son of Faith
Titus 1:1-4

1. Paul, a servant of God and an apostle of Jesus Christ, according to the faith of God's chosen ones and full knowledge of the truth according to godliness; 2. in hope of eternal life which the truthful God promised before times eternal; 3. and now, in His time, He has made the meaning clear to us, through the preaching with which God, our Savior, has seen fit to entrust me. 4. To Titus, a true child according to a common faith: grace and peace from God the Father, and of Christ Jesus our Savior.

Deal with Unfinished Business
Titus 1:5-9

5. For this reason I left you in Crete, in order that the things wanting you should set in order, and should appoint in each city senior oversight as I had charged you: 6. always looking for one who is beyond reproach, faithful to one woman; one whose children hold the faith, not accused of reckless living. 7. For one who has oversight as the steward of God must be beyond reproach, not stubbornly self-willed, not easily angered, not given to wine, or one who comes to blows, nor greedy after material gain. 8. But hospitable, a lover of good things, sensible, just, holy, self-controlled, 9. holding to the faithful word according to the teaching, that he may be able by healthy teaching both to exhort and to convince the contradicting ones.

Silence the Disobedient Babblers
Titus 1:10-16

10. There are many rebellious spirits abroad, who talk of their own imaginations and deceive some; especially those who hold by circumcision: 11. they must be silenced, who subvert whole houses, teaching things that are false for material gain. 12. Even a prophet of their own said, The Cretans are always liars, wild and evil beasts, lazy gluttons. 13. This witness is true. Wherefore rebuke them severely, in order that they may gain a healthy faith; 14. not giving heed to Jewish tales and commandments of men, perverting the truth. 15. All things are clean

to the clean: but to the ones having been defiled and unfaithful nothing is clean, but both the mind and the conscience have been defiled. 16. They profess to know God; but by their works they deny Him, being repulsive and disobedient and useless for any good work.

Become a Wholesome Teacher
Titus 2:1-10

1. But you must speak those things that are appropriate for healthy teaching: 2. Charge the senior men to be sober, serious, prudent, healthy in Christian faith and love and endurance. 3. The senior women likewise must behave appropriately for a holy calling, not given to slanderous talk or given to wine, teaching others by good example: 4. in order that they may train the young women to be lovers of their husbands and child lovers, 5. to be sensible, pure, homemakers, good, lining up under the authority of their husbands lest the word of God be abused with foul language. 6. The younger men similarly exhort to be sensible, 7. about all things, showing yourself a pattern of good works in your teaching display purity of motive and seriousness. 8. Present a wholesome message that cannot be criticized; in this way your opponents may be ashamed, having nothing disparaging to say to you. 9. Encourage servants to line up under the authority of their masters and comply with their instructions; not being contentious; 10. not embezzling, but showing loyalty and faithfulness; that they may beautify the teaching of God our Savior in all things.

Teach with Authority
Titus 2:11-15

11. For the saving mercy of God has appeared to all mankind, 12. instructing us to deny all wickedness and worldly desires and to now live discreet, honest, and God-fearing lives in the world. 13. Looking for the blood purchased hope, and the magnificent appearing of the great God and our Savior Jesus Christ; 14. Who gave Himself for us, that He might ransom us from all wickedness, and purify a people as His personal treasure*, eager for good deeds. 15. Speak encouraging words about these things, and admonish with authority. Let no man look down on you.

---

* v14 The Greek word used for possession was "periousious" from the present participle feminine of a compound [peri] and [eimi] meaning "being beyond usual, i.e. special (one's own). Yet the KJB translators chose to use the word "peculiar" from the Latin [peculium] meaning one's own property or in Roman law meaning "private property". Although it did not essentially change the meaning for English readers because "peculiar" was common in 1611, but this translation became a problem later as some individuals used the concept of "being peculiar" as a standard for holiness..

Line Up Under Authority
Titus 3:1-7

1. Remind them they must line up under the authority of governments and comply with those in authority, and be willing to do honorable work, 2. they are not to speak injuriously of anyone and avoid quarreling, be gentle and demonstrate a willingness to learn. 3. For we all were once foolish, disobedient, being deceived and serving as slaves to various desires for pleasures, living in hatred and resentment, detestable ourselves, and hating each other. 4. Then the kindness and saving love of God was made manifest to all men, 5. it was not by personal works of righteousness that we did that saved us, but His mercy, with the cleansing power of rebirth, and restoring of the Holy Spirit; 6. which He poured out in abundance on us through Jesus Christ our Savior; 7. that being declared righteous by His grace, we should be made heirs of eternal life through faith and hopeful expectation.

Careful to Maintain Good Deeds
Titus 3:8-11

8. These things are faithful sayings that I want you to affirm confidently, that the believers in God might be careful to maintain good deeds. These things are good and profitable to all men. 9. But avoid foolishly searching for family pedigrees, and arguments and ruthlessness about the law; for they serve no useful purpose for anyone. 10. A man that holds to belief that contradicts these things after the second warning avoid his company; 11. You must know that such a man is perverted and under self-condemnation.

Support Workers and Meet Pressing Needs
Titus 3:12-15

12. After I send Artemas to you or Tychicus, make haste to come to Nicopolis; I have decided to winter there. 13. Zenas the lawyer and Apollo urgently send forward in order that nothing to them will be lacking. 14. Our brothers would be more fruitful if they learned to find honorable employment to meet their necessary demands, so they could contribute to others. 15. Everyone with me sends you greetings. Greet all who love us in the faith. Grace be with you all. Amen.

THE SECOND LETTER TO TIMOTHY

In AD67 Paul wrote a second letter to Timothy. Paul had been imprisoned again in Rome and understood the political climate suggested that his life was to be shortened. Most of his supporters had abandoned him. He was sick, suffering yet Paul struggled to write this last challenge to Timothy. Paul charged Timothy to be faithful and to be an effective minister. He writes about the coming apostasy and the need to guard and keep the spiritual truth that had been taught. Paul did not seek a divine intervention for his personal state but did identify the coming end of the apostolic era and the deception that would come to the church from false teachers

Remembering Genuine Faith
2 Timothy 1:1-7

1. Paul, a messenger of Christ Jesus by the will of God, according to the promise of life which is in Christ Jesus, 2. to Timothy, my own beloved child: grace, mercy, and peace, from God the Father and Christ Jesus our Lord. 3. I thank God, whom I serve with a pure conscience, as my forefathers did before me, that without ceasing I remember you in my prayers night and day; 4. remembering your tears, I greatly desire to see you again, that my joy might be full; 5. when I remember the genuine faith that is in you, which dwelt first in your grandmother Lois, and your mother Eunice; and I am convinced dwells also in you. 6. For which cause I remind you to fan the flame of the gift of God which is in you through the laying on of my hands. 7. For God has not given us the spirit of cowardice, but of power and of love and self-control.

Able to Guard My Deposit
2 Timothy 1:8-12

8. Never be embarrassed for the witness you give of our Lord, nor of me His prisoner: but be a participant in the sufferings of the gospel according to the power of God; 9. Who saved us and called us with a call to consecration, not according to our achievements, but according to His own purpose and grace, before the world began, 10. but is now made clear by the appearing of our Savior Jesus Christ, who hath abolished death, and hath brought life and immortality to light through the gospel: 11. whereunto I am appointed a preacher, and an apostle, and a teacher of the Gentiles. 12. For which cause, I also suffer these things: nevertheless I am not ashamed: for I know whom I have believed, and am persuaded that He is able to guard my deposit against that day.

The Standard of Healthy Words
2 Timothy 1:13-18
13. Retain the standard of healthy words in faith and love in Christ Jesus, which you heard from me. 14. Guard the trust that was committed to you by the Holy Spirit which dwells in us. 15. You know this, that all the ones in Asia have turned away from me; of whom are Phygellus and Hermogenes. 16. May the Lord give mercy to the Onesiphorus family; for he refreshed me often and was not ashamed of my chain: 17. when he was in Rome, he sought for me diligently, and found me. 18. And you know well how many times he ministered to me at Ephesus: the Lord grant that he may find mercy when that day comes.

Teach Others to Teach
2 Timothy 2:1-2
1. My son, keep empowering yourself in the grace that is in Christ Jesus. 2. And entrust the things you learned from me which were confirmed by many witnesses, to faithful men who will be competent to teach others also.

Share Hardships as a Soldier
2 Timothy 2:3-13
3. Join the ranks of those who share hardships as a soldier of Jesus Christ. 4. No active warrior entangles himself with ordinary affairs; so he may please the one who enlisted him as a soldier. 5. And also if anyone wrestles, he is not crowned unless he wrestles lawfully. 6. The hardworking farmer must be the first to partake of the fruits. 7. Consider what I say; for the Lord will give you understanding in all things. 8. Keep remembering that Jesus Christ, a descendent of David was raised from the dead and was the theme of my gospel: 9. this gospel for which I suffer, even in chains as an evil doer, but the word of God is not bound. 10. I endure everything therefore for the sake of God's chosen ones, in order that they too may obtain salvation and eternal glory which is in Christ Jesus. 11. This is a faithful saying: if we die with Him, we shall also live with Him. 12. If we endure suffering, we shall also reign with Him: if we deny Him, He will also deny us: 13. if we are without faith, He remains faithful: He cannot deny Himself.

The Foundation of God Stands Firm
2 Timothy 2:14-19
14. Remind them of these things, solemnly witnessing before God not to fight with words, for they are not useful but bring destruction to the ones hearing. 15. Be eager to present yourself approved to God, a workman unashamed, cutting straight the word of truth. 16. But avoid blasphemous and worthless chatter: for they will cause more disobeying of the word. 17. And their teaching will eat as does

gangrene: among them are Hymenaeus and Philetus; 18. who concerning the truth of the resurrection have behaved badly saying the standing up has already come: and cause the downfall of some in the faith. 19. However, the foundation of God stands firm, having this seal, the Lord knows those who are His. And Let everyone who names the name of the Lord stand clear from unrighteousness.

Prepared for Every Good Work
2 Timothy 2:20-21
20. In a great house there are not only vessels of gold and silver, but also of wood and earthenware; and some for honorable use, and some to dishonor. 21. Therefore if a man cleanses himself from the dishonor, he shall become a vessel of honor, set apart, and suitable for use by the master, having been prepared for every good work.

Flee Youthful Passions
2 Timothy 2:22-26
22. Flee youthful passions: but pursue righteousness, faith, love, peace with the ones calling on the Lord out of a clean heart. 23. But foolish and ignorant questions avoid, knowing they breed nothing but arguments. 24. And the servant of the Lord must not struggle with arguments; but behave kindly toward all men, teaching appropriately with unwearied tolerance, 25. understanding those who oppose in order to instruct properly; if perhaps God will change their mind to acknowledge the truth; 26. having been captured by the will of God they may remove themselves from the trap of the devil.

Know the Troublemakers
2 Timothy 3:1-9
1. Know this, that dangerous times will come in the last days. 2. For men will be self-lovers, lovers of money, arrogant boasters, treating God and sacred things disrespectfully, disobedient to parents, unthankful, wicked, 3. without family affection, trucebreakers, false accusers, without sexual restraint, violent, despisers of all that is good, 4. traitors, stubborn, lovers of pleasure more than lovers of God; 5. having an outward form of religion, but rejecting the collection of beliefs and contradicting the moral instructions: from such turn away. 6. These are the kind of men who sneak into homes and take captive foolish women weighed down with sins and driven by passions, 7. women always seeking new experiences, but never able to come to a full knowledge of the truth. 8. Just as Jannes and Jambres stood against Moses, so do they stand against the truth: men whose minds are corrupt, troublemakers concerning the faith. 9. But they will not

advance further: for their foolishness will be very clear to all men, as the madness of those became.

All Sacred Writings are God-breathed
2 Timothy 3:10-17

10. But you have closely followed my teaching, the conduct, the purpose, the faith, the long-suffering, the love, the endurance, 11. the persecutions, the sufferings, which happened to me in Antioch, Iconium, and Lystra; which persecutions I endured: but the Lord delivered me out of them all. 12. Yes, all who will live godly lives in Christ Jesus will be persecuted. 13. But wicked men and imposters will keep on going from bad to worse, misleading others and deceiving themselves. 14. But continue to hold fast the things you have learned and been convinced of, knowing the teachers from whom you learned them; 15. and from early childhood you have known the sacred letters, the ones able to make you wise unto salvation through faith in Christ Jesus. 16. All sacred writings are God-breathed, and serviceable for teaching, for warning, for correction, for instruction in righteousness, 17. in order that the man of God may be adequately equipped for every good work.

You must be Clear-headed
2 Timothy 4:1-8

1. I charge you before God, and the Lord Jesus Christ, being about to judge the living and the dead at the appearing of His kingdom; 2. Proclaim the word, immediately and at inconvenient times; warn, reprimand, urgently encourage and support with all long-suffering and teaching. 3. There will come a time when men will not tolerate healthy teaching; but following their own desires shall listen to many teachers because they are impatient to hear something to please and gratify their ears; 4. and they will stop listening to the truth and be turned aside to fictional tales. 5. You must be clear-headed in all things, endure hardships, declare the good news, fulfill your ministry. 6. For I am now ready for my blood to be poured out as a sacrifice, and it is my time to stand up for departure. 7. I have struggled for the prize, I have finished the course, I have kept the faith: 8. hereafter, there is reserved for me a crown of righteousness, which the Lord, the righteous judge, shall give me at that day: and not only to me, but to all those who have learned to love His advent.

Mark is Useful to My Ministry
2 Timothy 4:9-15

9. Hasten to come to me shortly: 10. for Demas forsook me, having loved this present age and went to Thessalonica; Crescens to Galatia, Titus to Dalmatia. 11. Only Luke is with me. Pick up Mark and bring him with you: Mark is useful to my ministry. 12. And Tychicus have

I sent to Ephesus. 13. When you come bring the topcoat I left at Troas with Carpus, and bring the scrolls, and especially the rolls of parchment. 14. Alexander, the coppersmith, did me much harm. The Lord will reward him according to his deeds. 15. You be on guard also; for he greatly opposed our words.

The Lord Stood With Me
2 Timothy 4:16-18
16. At my first defense no one was beside me, but all men forsook me: may it not be counted against them; 17. but the Lord stood with me and empowered me, in order that through me the proclamation might be accomplished and all the nations might hear: and I was delivered out of the mouth of the lion. 18. The Lord will deliver me from every wicked work, and will save me to His heavenly kingdom: to whom be the glory unto the ages of the ages, Amen.

Hasten to Come Before Winter
2 Timothy 4:19-22
19. Greet Prisca and Aquila, and the Onesiphorus family. 20. Erastus remained in Corinth: but Trophimus I left at Mileturn ailing. 21. Hasten to come before winter. Eubulus greets you, and Pudens, and Linus, and Claudia, and all the brothers. 22. The Lord Jesus Christ be with your spirit. Grace be with you. Amen.

THE SECOND LETTER OF JOHN

John, one of the original Twelve disciples, wrote three Letters (around AD 86), probably in Ephesus. They were general letters of counsel to Christians scattered throughout the Roman Empire. In the second letter John briefly addressed a special woman and her children. He encouraged her in the raising of her children and advised her in several doctrinal matters that troubled the early Christians.

The Way of Truth
2 John 1:1-4

1. The senior minister to an eminent Christian lady and her children, whom I love in the truth; and not I only, but also all they that have known the truth; 2. because of the truth remaining among us, and will be with us for ever. 3. Grace be with you, mercy, and peace, from God the Father, and from the Lord Jesus Christ, the Son of the Father, in truth and love. 4. It has given me great happiness, in meeting some of your children, to find that they followed the way of truth, obeying the command that came to us from the Father.

Early Lessons Taught Us to Follow
2 John 1:5-6

5. And now lady, I request not as though I wrote a new commandment to you, but that which we had from the beginning, that we love one another. 6. Love means keeping His commandments; love is itself the commandment which our early lessons taught us to follow.

Be on Guard
2 John 1:7-13

7. Because many deceivers went forth into the world, the ones not confessing Jesus Christ coming in the flesh; this is the deceiver and the antichrist. 8. See to yourselves lest you lose the things which we fashioned, and you may receive a full reward. 9. Whosoever goes back, who is not true to Christ's teaching, loses hold of God; the one who is true to the teaching, keeps hold both of the Father and of the Son. 10. If anyone comes to you and does not bring this teaching, do not receive him into your house and do not greet him on the street: 11. for he who greets him becomes a partner in his evil deeds. 12. Having many things to write to you, I purpose not to scribble with black ink: but I hope to visit you and convey it by word of mouth, to give you a full measure of happiness. 13. The children of your chosen sister greet you. Amen.

THE THIRD LETTER OF JOHN

John, one of the original Twelve disciples, wrote three Letters (around AD 86), probably in Ephesus. They were general letters of counsel to Christians scattered throughout the Roman Empire. This third brief Letter was addressed to a man named Gaius, who was well-known for hospitality. The letter simply commends Gaius for his Christian virtues, cautions him against Diotrephes, a scheming false teacher, and recommends a man named Demetrius. The letter gives Gaius personal praise and advice.

Walking in Truth
3 John 1:1-4

1. The senior minister to the beloved Gaius, whom I love in the truth. 2. Beloved, concerning all things I pray that you may prosper in business and be safe and sound in body, as your soul prospers. 3. For I rejoiced greatly when some brothers came bearing witness of you in truth, as you in truth walk. 4. I have no greater joy than to hear that my children are walking in truth.

Be Fellow Helpers to the Truth
3 John 1:5-8

5. Beloved you are faithfully serving when you show kindness to the brethren, even when they are strangers to you. 6. And they testify of your love before the assembly: if you send them on their journey as godly men, you do well: 7. because they went out for His name's sake, taking nothing from the Gentiles. 8. It is a duty to support such men, that we may show ourselves fellow workers with the truth.

Imitate the Good
3 John 1:9-11

9. I wrote something to the assembly: but Diotrephes, who loves to be in first place, received not the message: 10. wherefore, when I visit you, I will remember his deeds which he did ridiculing us with a malicious tongue: neither does he receive the brethren, and forbids others that would, and throws them out of the assembly. 11. Beloved, imitate the good and not the evil. He that does good is of God: but he that does evil has not seen God. 12. Demetrius has a good report of all men, and by the truth itself: yes, we also bear record; and you know that our record is true. 13. Having many things to write to you, I purpose not to scribble with black ink: 14. but I hope to visit you and speak to you face to face. Peace be to you. Our friends salute you. Greet the friends by name.

Section Five:

Letters to Scattered Believers

The General Letter of James

The First Letter of Peter

The Letter to the Hebrews

The Second Letter of Peter

The General Letter of Jude

The First Letter of John

The Revelation of John

THE GENERAL LETTER OF JAMES

James is considered the earliest of all the New Testament documents and was written to the scattered Jews who had embraced Christianity. Although they had accepted Christ, there were no designated Christian buildings and being of Jewish background they naturally gravitated to the synagogues as the traditional place of worship. It may have been as long as one hundred years before fixed places for Christian worship were built. Such believers still gathered in synagogues, similar to that at Berea that had embraced Christianity. James writes as head of the assembly in Jerusalem in a style of an old prophet. He presents a treatise on the ethical aspects of the Christian life that expresses the differences between intellectual apprehension of truth and the practical application of truth in life. The Letter is addressed to the twelve tribes of the Dispersion and tells them to endure, even enjoy, tribulations because these trials will strengthen their faith. The concept "the end is worth the journey: was strongly advocated by James.

That You May Be Complete
James 1:1-11

1. James subject to and serving God and the Lord Jesus Christ, to the twelve tribes which are scattered abroad, a cheerful personal greeting. 2. My cherished band of believers*, count it a jewel (precious stone) when you fall into adversity and testing that provides you a *choice of direction. 3. Knowing that your painful trial brings you assurance, trust and works patience. 4. But let suffering have her complete labor and make something of you, that you may be complete in all respects, without defect or omission and whole undivided, and unbroken. 5. If any of you lack wise judgment, let him express the craving by words to God, that gives to all men liberally, and does not defame, chide or snatch away your joy, and it shall be given him. 6. But let him ask in faith, nothing wavering, for he that shows doubt or indecision is like a wave of the sea driven with the wind and tossed. 7. Let not that man think that he shall receive anything of the Lord. 8. A two-spirited man is unsettled and wavering in all his direction, position or manner. 9. Let the brother* of low degree experience joy and gladness that he is exalted. 10. But the rich is depressed in pride and dignity because as the flower of grass shall pass away. 11. For the sun is no sooner near a vertical position with a burning heat, but it withers the grass, and the flower thereof falls, and the grace of the shape or figure of it perishes so also shall the rich man be extinguished and wither in his ways.

---

*v2 The way brethren and brother are used by James clearly includes all believers since it refers to a common womb or birth. *V2 Serving Satan required complete obedience to evil, but salvation brought believers a choice of behavior. The intent here is "rejoice because you have a choice."

The Enticement of Testing
James 1:12-18

12. Blood-related* and fortunate is the man who flinches not under the enticement of testing: for when he is proved trustworthy, he shall be given the wreath of honor that verifies vitality, which God promised to all who worship out of a benevolent heart. 13. Let no man say when he is enticed, God allured me to evil: for God does not use wickedness to validate the trustworthiness of any man. 14. But every man is attracted to wicked deeds, when he chooses action based on personal desire, and hope of pleasure. 15. Then when personal desire has joined together with enticement, it produces a voluntary transgression: and this offense produces separation from observant morality, and at the end separation from God. 16 . Do not wander from the right or deviate from the true course, my cherished band of brothers. 17. Every unspoiled and true benefaction is from above, and comes down from the Father of all light, with whom there is no changeableness, neither a dark side where there is no light. 18. Of His own determination procreated as a Father all of us with the expression of genuineness, that we should be the first matured and collected fruit of God's created beings.

---

* v12 To bless, in Middle English used at the time of KJV, had a meaning related to "blood" used to consecrate an altar; thus, the use of "blood-related."

A Teachable Spirit
James 1:19-27

19. Wherefore, my cherished band of believers, let every one be swift to hear, slow to speak, slow to wrath: 19. because of the righteousness of God, my cherished band of believers, let every one be ready listeners, slow to express our mind, slow to take offence: 20. for the anger does not bear fruit acceptable to God. 21. Wherefore put aside all moral corruption and the abundance of worthless behavior and receive with a teachable spirit the firmly established word, which is able to make safe that spiritual part of you that determines all behavior. 22. You must be honest with yourselves and live by the word not merely hear it. 23. But those who listen to the word, and do not behave it, are similar to a man seeing his own face in a mirror; 24. He observes his flaws, and immediately forgets the man he saw. 25. But whosoever bows down to observe the complete prescriptive usage and the unrestrained opportunity to continue in the word and not become a forgetful hearer, but one who behaves the prescribed deeds, this man shall by the blood be set apart for consecrated action. 26. If any man among you seems to be devout, and restrains not his unnatural language, he deceives his own heart and his service to God is ineffective.

27. Free from all that would dim the transparency in belief and conduct before God and the Father is this, to go see and relieve the orphans without a father's protection and the women lacking a husband in their distress, and to keep himself untainted with guilt.

Impartial Benevolence
James 2:1-13

1. My band of believers, you cannot really believe that the faith of our Lord Jesus Christ, the Lord of glory, can be mixed with partiality. 2. Suppose a man with a gold ring, having fine appearance, comes to your assembly and there come in also a poor man in cheap clothing; 3. will you pay attention to the well-dressed man and provide a place of honor and say unto the poor man, Stand over there, or sit here on the floor: 4. are you not introducing division and showing partiality in your judgment? 5. I command you to listen, my cherished band of believers, were not the poor of this world chosen to be rich in faith, and heirs of the kingdom promised to all who love God? 6. But you have dishonored the poor man. Do not rich men dominate you, and drag you before the law-courts? 7. Do they not blaspheme that worthy name by which you are called? 8. If you keep the noble law according to the scripture, you should unselfishly love your neighbor as yourself. 9. But if you flatter the great, you bring upon yourself guilt, and the law reckons you a transgressor. 10. For the man who fails at one point, but keeps the balance of the law, is liable for all the penalties. 11. For He who has forbidden adultery, also forbids murder. If you do not commit adultery but kill, you become a transgressor of the law. 12. You must speak and act as men already on trial before the law of freedom. 13. For he who acts without mercy will have judgment without mercy. Mercy triumphs over judgment.

Faith and Works
James 2:14-26

14. What is the benefit, my cherished band of believers, if a man says he has faith, and have not deeds? Can faith save him? 15. If a brother or sister is destitute of daily necessities and has no clothing, 16. of what use is it to say to the needy, Come in and be warmed, eat all you can and depart in peace; although you give them none of the essentials which are needful to the body? 17. Even so faith without praiseworthy deeds, is like an unburied corpse left alone. 18. Yes, a man may affirm that he has faith, and not have deeds; show me faith apart from deeds, and I will show you faith by means of my deeds. 19. You say you believe in one God; that is good. But the evil spirits also believe, and shake in fright. 20. Oh, worthless one, can you not perceive with certainty, that faith without deeds is a corpse? 21. Was not

Abraham our father accepted by action, when he presented Isaac his son on the altar? 22. See how his faith worked together with his deeds and how his belief was balanced by his deeds, 23. and so was fulfilled the Scripture, Abraham believed in God, and it was reckoned to him for righteousness, so that he was called the friend of God. 24. You see then that it is by deeds that a man is proved righteous, and not by faith alone. 25. How then did Rahab the harlot win Gods approval? Was it not by her action when she received the messengers and sent them away by a safe passage? For just as the body separated from the spirit is lifeless, so faith without works is a corpse.

The Danger of Being a Teacher
James 3:1-12

1. Do not be too eager, my cherished band of believers, to impart instruction to others; be certain that, if you do, you will be called to account more strictly. 2. There are many faults in us; but if a man never loses his language footing, he is a man completely able to keep the whole body under control. 3. We place bits in a horses' mouth to make them obedient, and we can turn their whole body. 4. Consider even the big ships, driven by ferocious winds, yet they are turned about, with a small helm, at the steersman's desire. 5. Yet the tongue a small part of the body but it boasts great power and can kindle a great fire. 6. And the tongue is a fire, and stands for a whole world of wickedness: so the tongue can defile the whole body, and start a fire in the world that is set on fire by the valley of everlasting fire. 7. Mankind can tame and has long since learned to tame the beasts of the field, birds, serpents and things in the sea. 8. But no human being has learned to tame the tongue; it is restless and depraved, full of deadly poison and evil influence. 9. The tongue is used to praise God and curse men, who are made after the likeness of God. 10. Commendation and cursing emerge from the same mouth, my band of believers these things should not be so. 11. Does a fountain gush out both fresh and salt water? 12. Can a fig tree bear olives or a grape vine figs? No more will salty water yield fresh?

Selfish Ambition Disqualifies a Teacher
James 3:13-18

13. Who among you is a wise man of knowledge and understanding? Let him give proof of this quality by providing a teachable spirit and good example of good judgment. 14. If in your hearts you have a zeal that is bitter and filled with selfish ambition, do not be arrogantly boastful about your attainments, for this boasting perverts the truth. 15. Such wisdom as yours does not come from above; it belongs to earth and to nature, and is inspired by the devil. 16. For where there is

jealousy and selfish ambition, there is disorder and various evil activities. 17. Whereas the wisdom that comes from above is marked by purity, then peacefulness; it is courteous and ready to be convinced, always taking the better part, it carries mercy with it and is a harvest of all that is good, undivided in mind, without hypocrisy. 18. Peace is the seed-ground of righteousness, and those who make peace will reap the harvest.

Reasons for Feuds and Fights
James 4:1-10

1. What causes feuds and quarreling among you? The source: they arise out of the appetites for pleasures which carry on a constant struggle within your bodies. 2. You desire but do not possess; you murder; you set your heart on something, and cannot have your will, so there is strife and quarreling. You have not, because you ask not. 3. You ask wrongly and do not receive, what you ask for is denied because you would squander it on your own pleasures. 4. You all adulterate your vows to God by adding another. Do you not know that companionship of the world breeds hostility toward God? Whoever seeks friends of the world becomes an enemy of God. 5. Do you think that scripture says to no purpose that the Spirit which dwells in you desires you with a jealous love? 6. Even so God gives more gratifying pleasure, and scripture says God refuses to accept the arrogant, but furnishes divine influence upon the heart to the self-effacing. 7. Be God's true subjects; stand firm against the devil, and he will vanish from you. 8. Bow down before God, and He will be near your hand. You who have erred and missed the mark must cleanse your hands, and you who have wavered or are two-spirited must free your thoughts and feelings from guilt. 9. Bow yourself down with sorrow and let weeping turn your delight to sadness. 10. Bring yourself low before God and He will exalt you.

Judging Others Based on Mistaken Confidence
James 4:11-17

11. Stop speaking judgmentally to one another. He who speaks harshly of his brother, or calls into question his brother, speaks evil of the law, and questions the law: but if you are a critic of the law, you are not a doer, but a censor of the law. 12. There is one Lawgiver and Judge who is able to save and destroy. Who are you to pass judgment on others near to you? 13. See how you say, today or tomorrow we will go to such a city, work there for a year, trade and make a profit. 14. When you have no means of knowing what tomorrow will bring. What is your life? It is a mist that appears and soon vanishes. 15. What you should say, If the Lord will, we shall live, and do this or that.

16. But your arrogant ways make boasters of you: all such bragging is wickedness. 17. Therefore if a man has the power to do good; and fails to do good it is sinful.

Social Passion and Selfishness
James 5:1-12

1. Come you rich men, bemoan yourselves and cry over the miseries that are coming upon you. 2. Corruption has fallen on your wealth and your fine clothes are food for moths. 3. Your gold and silver are corroded and poisoned by rust; and the decay is proof to you of how worthless your coins are. It is a canker which will eat into your very flesh like fire. These are your final days and you spent them storing up a personal destiny of retribution. 4. You have kept back the pay of the reapers who worked your land, and the great number of men in the Lord's army has heard their cries against you. God listened to their complaint. 5. You feasted on earth, your heart was comforted with luxuries but this day dooms you to slaughter. 6. You have condemned and murdered the innocent man who offered no resistance. 7. Have patience until the Lord comes. The gardener waits for the valuable fruit of the earth, and waits patiently for the early and latter rain. 8. Be patient, establish your hearts, wait for the early and latter rain. 9. Complain not one against another, brethren, lest you be condemned: behold, the Judge is already standing at the door. 10. Brethren, if you would learn by example how to work and wait patiently in evil times, think of the prophets who spoke in the Lord's name. 11. See how we congratulate those who have showed endurance. You have heard of Job's steadfast endurance; and you have read, in the story, the conclusion of his troubles, how kind and merciful the Lord was in rewarding his patience. 12. Above all, my brethren, bind not yourself by an oath, by heaven, by earth, or by any other pledge; but let your yes be a simple yes, and your no a simple no; otherwise you will be condemned for it.

Value of Prayer and Restoration
James 5:13-20

13. Is any among you troubled? Let him pray. Is any in good spirits? Let him sing hymns. 14. Is any sick among you? Let him personally identify and summons the senior leaders of the congregation; and let them earnestly perform their vows and pray with desire, anointing with oil in the name of the Lord: 15. Prayer offered in faithfulness will restore the sick, and the Lord will furnish relief; provided there were transgressions; the believer will be exempted from further penalty. 16. Acknowledge your failures and side steps one to another, and pray for yourselves and for one another, that you may be made spiritually

whole again. When a righteous man prays fervently there is great power in prayer. 17. Elijah was a man similar to us and he prayed earnestly that it should not rain, and for three years and six months no rain fell upon the earth. 18. And he prayed again and the heaven gave rain; and the earth put forth her fruit. 19. My band of believers, if any of you do stray from the true path, and one turn you about, 20. let the brother know, that he who turns one back from the error of his way into the right path, covers many faults and makes him safe, restoring his usefulness to the congregation.

THE FIRST LETTER OF PETER

The Apostle Peter wrote his first Letter (I Peter) in Rome AD 64 as a general letter to believers scattered throughout Asia Minor. Roman persecution was intensifying and many believers were wondering if they were abandoned. Peter understood suffering and his letter encouraged believers and offered hope in their suffering. He also wrote about a true Christ-like character and urged believers towards humility, sobriety and watchfulness.

Greetings to Outsiders
1 Peter 1:1-2

1. Peter, an apostle of Jesus Christ, to the outsiders spread throughout Pontus, Galatia, Cappadocia, Asia, and Bithynia, 2. chosen and destined by the previous knowledge of God the Father, through consecration of the Spirit, for obedience to give allegiance to Jesus Christ and be sprinkled with His blood; grace and peace be yours abundantly.

An Inheritance Kept Safe in Heaven
1 Peter 1:3-9

3. Set apart by the blood, that God, the Father of our Lord Jesus Christ, who in His great mercy has begotten us anew, making hope live in us through the resurrection of Jesus Christ from a lifeless corpse, 4. An inheritance imperishable, untainted, and unfading, kept safe in heaven for us, 5. Who by the power of God are afforded safe conduct until you reach heaven, this deliverance which is stored up to be revealed at the last time. 6. Herein you are triumphant, even if it is presently necessary to be saddened by trials of many sorts, 7. this must be so you can give proof of your faith, a more precious thing than gold tested by fire, this proof will bring you praise, and glory, and honor when Jesus Christ is revealed. 8. You never saw Him, but you learned to love Him, although you do not see Him, you believed in Him. And rejoice with triumphant joy. 9. You are receiving that which faith ultimately brings, the salvation of the soul.

Salvation was the Expedition
1 Peter 1:10-12

10. Salvation was the expedition of the prophets and the grace of which they prophesied has been reserved for you. 11. Seeking to find out when and how the Spirit of Christ in them witnessed in advance to the sufferings of Christ, and the worship that should follow. 12. It was revealed to them that their verbal message was not for them, but for those at a distance, the things that have been proclaimed to you through those who proclaim the gospel by the Holy Spirit sent from heaven, these things the angels desire to understand.

Have Childlike Obedience
1 Peter 1:13-16

13. Rid your minds of every encumbrance, keep full control of your senses, and set your hopes on the gift that is offered you when Jesus Christ appears; 14. have childlike obedience. Do not continue to live a life that matches the time you did not know you were controlled by the evil yearnings: 15. but show yourselves holy in all conduct; 16. because the One who called you is holy, you must be holy in all manner of living; you must be holy because the scripture declares: God is holy!

God the Impartial Judge
1 Peter 1:17-21

17. You appeal to God as your Father; but He also judges each man impartially by what he has done; look carefully then to the ordering of your lives while you live out your time on earth. 18. Knowing that the ransom that freed you from the vain observances of ancestral tradition was not by filthy lucre as silver and gold, 19. but with the precious blood of Christ, as of a lamb without blemish and without spot: 20. it was before the foundation of the world that He was ordained to His work that was made clear in the last days. 21. Through Him you have learned to be faithful to God, who raised Him up from the tomb, and gave Him glory; that your faith and hope might be centered in God.

The Discipline of Truth
1:22-25

22. Purify your souls with the discipline of truth through the Spirit, a cleansing that issues in sincere brotherly love. See that you love one another with a warm and sincere heart. 23. Your new life came from immortal parentage, through the word of God that lives and abides eternally. 24. All mortal things are as plant life and their splendor as the blossoms of the meadow, but the grassland withers and the blooms fall; 25. however, the word of the Lord continues perpetually. And this word is the good news announced to you.

Yearn for the Unadulterated Word
1 Peter 2:1-8

1. You must put aside all insincerity, jealous feelings, and all backbiting, 2. since you are newly born, yearn for the unadulterated milk of the word, so you may grow up until your soul thrives in good health. 3. Since you have tasked* (tasted) the Lord's kindness. 4. Draw near to him; He is the living fulfillment of the stone discarded by men but chosen of God. 5. You yourselves are lively stones built into a spiritual house; you must be a holy priesthood to offer up spiritual sacrifices acceptable to God by Jesus Christ. 6. The scripture contains these words, Behold, I lay in Zion a stone, a cornerstone, valued and those

who believe in Him shall not be put to shame. 7. You who believe He is of great value, but to the disobedient, the stone rejected by the builders, the same became the cornerstone over which they will stumble. 8. They trip because they disobey the word and the stone becomes a rock of offence a fate which is theirs.

---

*v3 When one tastes the goodness, the Lord is tasked to supply.

God's Private Property
1 Peter 2:9-16
9. But you are a chosen race, a royal priesthood, a dedicated nation, and a people God means to have for Himself, that you might show forth His praises who called you out of darkness into His amazing light. 10. There was a time when you were not a people, now you are God's people because you obtained mercy. 11. Beloved, I urge you, as strangers and sojourners, to abstain from the physical desires, which battle against the soul. 12. Your life among the Nations must be beyond reproach; even when they slander you. They must see only honorable conduct that you are behaving godly, and praise God when He comes to be their judge. 13. Line up under the authority of every human institution for the Lord's sake, whether the supreme authority is a man or a king. 14. Or to governors who send men to bring evildoers to justice and to commend those who obey the ordinances. 15. God expects you to silence the evil chatter of the foolish. 16. As free men, you are to serve God and never permit your freedom to become a pretext for wrong-doing.

Appropriate Godly Behavior
1 Peter 2:17-20
17. Give all men their due; to the band of believers your habitual love; to God, your worship; to the leader owed respect. 18. Respect the authority of those you serve, line up under the authority not only to those who are kind and considerate, but also to those who are hard to please. 19. It is a sign of grace when one bears up under unjust suffering because of moral goodness in his heart. 20. When you do wrong, do you suffer quietly a blow from the hand? But if you do things right and still suffer calmly, this is appropriate godly behavior.

The Shepherd Who Keeps Watch
1 Peter 2:21-25
21. You are engaged in this by a call from Christ who suffered for us; leaving an example for us to follow His path: 22. He did no sin neither was deceit heard from His mouth. 23. Who, when abusive language was hurled at Him, used not verbal abuse; when He endured pain and distress, and uttered no threats; but committed Himself to the

righteous judge: 24. on the cross His own body took our sins, that we might depart from sins and live righteously; it was His wounds that healed you. 25. Until then you were like straying sheep, but are now brought back to the Shepherd who keeps watch over your souls.

The Loving Behavior of Wives
1 Peter 3:1-7

1. Also, you who are wives line up under the authority of your own husbands; and if there are those who refuse to believe the word, they may be won to Christ because they have seen your pure and respectful behavior. 2. While they see your good manners without anticipation of ambush. 3. Whose appearance is not outward embellishment of elaborate hairstyles; and the wearing of golden ornaments, or expensive clothing, 4. but let it be the beautification of the heart that will not fade away, even a calm and teachable spirit, which in God's eyes is priceless. 5. It was this way that the holy women who trusted God in ancient times, made themselves attractive, and arranged their lives in an orderly manner with their own husbands: 6. think how Sara listened attentively to Abraham, and respected his authority: you have become her children, live honestly, and let no anxious thoughts disturb you. 7. You who are husbands must be disciplined and reside together as a family, providing respectful quarters for the wife who has less strength than your own. The grace of eternal life belongs to you both, and your prayers must not suffer interruption.

Called to Give Kind Words
1 Peter 3:8-12

8. Finally, you must think the same thoughts, share difficulties with one another, having automatic interdependence with brotherly kindness; be tender-hearted and humble-minded: 9. you must not repay injury with injury, or hard words with hard words, but bless those who curse you. For you were called to give kind words to others and come to a well-spoken eulogy at the end. 10. For the one wishing to love life and see prosperous days, let him avoid an evil tongue and cunning words. 11. Habitually avoid evil, and do good things; let him seek and follow peace. 12. Because the eyes of the Lord watch over the righteous, and his ears listen to their prayers: but the Lord looks directly into the eyes of wrongdoers.

Be Zealous for the Good
1 Peter 3:13-22

13. Who will do you harm, if your ambition is to do good things? 14. If you should suffer in the cause of right, you are blessed. Do not be disturbed at their threats; 15. put Christ on the throne in your hearts: if anyone asks you to give an account of the hope which you cherish, be

ready at all times to answer with a teachable spirit and a wonder that is inspired by a sacred trust. 16. Maintain a clear conscience, so that, whenever you are slandered as wrongdoers, they may be ashamed for defaming your holy life in Christ. 17. If it is the will of God, it is better to suffer for doing well, than for doing wrong. 18. Christ died once for all as a ransom, the innocent for the guilty, that He might present us to God. His flesh died, but He was made alive in the Spirit: 19. Alive in the spirit He preached to the spirits in prison. 20. These were disobedient at the time God patiently waited during the building of the ark by Noah, when only eight souls found refuge as they passed over the water. 21. A foreshadow of baptism through which you are now brought to safety, not the removal of physical stains, but a satisfying of a good conscience toward God by the resurrection of Jesus Christ. 22. He now is on the right hand of God; where the Powers in heaven are lined up under His authority.

The Rest of Your Mortal Life
1 Peter 4:1-6

1. Remembering that Christ suffered for us in the flesh, arm yourselves with the same attitude; he whose mortal nature has been crucified hath ceased from sin; 2. The rest of your mortal life should not be lived in the fleshly desires of mankind, your life must be ordered by the desire of God. 3. Sufficient is the past days of our life doing the will of the pagan world, when we lived in sensuality and debauchery, drunkenness, revelry and the profane worship of idols. 4. They are surprised when you do not rush headlong into wild extravagant spending, speaking evil of you: 5. they will give account to Him who is ready to judge the living and the dead. 6. For this cause the gospel was preached to the dead that they might be judged according to men in the flesh but live according to God in the Spirit.

Be Good Stewards of Grace
1 Peter 4:7-11

7. The end of all things is near: live wisely, and keep your senses awake to greet the times of prayer. 8. Above all embrace each other in love that is constant and intense: because love covers a multitude of sins. 9. Never begrudge the hospitality you show one another. 10. As each has received a gift from God, so let all use such gifts in the service of one another, as good stewards of God's multi-sided grace. 11. Should any man speak, let him speak words sent from God; if a man serves, let him do it with God-given ability: that God may be glorified in all things through Jesus Christ, to whom be praise and dominion for ever and ever. Amen.

Spirit of Glory Rests Upon You
1 Peter 4:12-19
12. My dearly loved brothers, do not think the test by fire kindling about you is some strange thing happening only to you. 13. Rather rejoice when you share in some measure the sufferings of Christ; so leap and rejoice, triumph will be yours, when His glory is revealed. 14. If you are denounced for the sake of Christ, rejoice you are blood-washed for the strength of glory and the Spirit of God rests on you: 15. let it not be said that any of you underwent suffering as a murderer, or thief, or slander, or busybody; 16. but if a man is punished for being a Christian, he has no need to be ashamed; but let him bear that Christian name and bring glory to God. 17. The time is ripe for judgment to begin with God's house: and if our turn comes first, what will be the end of those that disobey the gospel of God? 18. And if the righteous are saved narrowly, what chance will the godless have? 19. Wherefore let those who suffer in accordance with the will of God, entrust their souls in well-doing to the Creator who is trustworthy and true.

Be Shepherds to the Flock
1 Peter 5:1-5
1. And now as a fellow elder and witness of the sufferings of Christ, as a sharer in the glory that will be revealed, I have a charge to give to my fellow seniors among you: 2. be shepherds to the flock God has given you, do your watchful care, not out of an obligation, but willingly; not for gain, but freely; 3. Not as a noble with an inherited estate, but setting an example to the congregation. 4. But when the chief Shepherd appears, you will receive an unfading crown of honor. 5. In the same manner, the younger should respectfully line up under the authority of the older. High esteem must be given one another and you must wear the humble clothing of deference, because God opposes the proud and gives favor to the humble in spirit.

Bow Down; God Will Lift You Up
1 Peter 5:6-11
6. Bow down before the strong hand of God, that in His good time He may lift you up. 7. Throw back on Him the burden of your anxiety; because He cares for you. 8. Have a thoughtful demeanor, be on guard, because your enemy the devil, prowls about as an angry lion, seeking someone to greedily consume. 9. Be strong in faith and stand up to the devil, knowing that you share the same suffering with your brothers all over the world. 10. And the God of all grace who has called us to enjoy His eternal glory in Christ Jesus, after you suffer a little He will restore, strengthen, and establish you as a resident of heaven. 11. To Him be glory and power through endless ages, Amen.

Stand in the True Grace of God
1 Peter 5:12-14
12. I count Silvanus as a faithful brother; and through him I have written you these brief lines of encouragement; to assure you that the grace in which you are so firmly established is the true grace of God. 13. The believers in Babylon, chosen with you by God, send greetings; so does my son, Mark. 14. Greet each other with the kiss of love. Peace be with all who are in Christ Jesus. Amen.

THE LETTER TO THE HEBREWS

Although some debate the issue, it is reasonable to accept Paul as the writer of the Hebrews Letter. Composed soon after his release from a Roman prison about AD 65, the letter contained a strong argument for the superiority of Jesus Christ. It was sent to the Jewish population living in Rome and included a strong appeal to go forward and never go back to the old system. This was accomplished by showing contrasts between ritual law and faith with an emphasis on Christ as the "better" way.

God spoke in Many Ways
Hebrews 1:1-7

1. In times past God spoke in many and different ways to our fathers by the prophets, 2. now at last in these times He has spoken to us by His Son, chosen heir of all things, a Son by whose agency He made the universe, 3. being the radiant splendor of God's glory, and the full expression of His being, all creation depends on the support of His powerful word, when He had personally made purification for our sins, He took His royal seat at the right hand of God's splendor. 4. With a more excellent rank He was made much better than the angels. 5. Did God say at any time to any angel, Thou art my Son, this day have I begotten you? Did God ever say to an angel, I will be a Father and you shall be to Me a Son? 6. And again, when God brought His first born into the world, He said, And let all the angels of God worship Him. 7. And of the angels He said, Who makes His angels messengers as swift as the wind, and His servants that wait on Him a flame of fire.

The Oil of Gladness
Hebrews 1:8-14

8. And what of the Son? Thy throne, O God, stands firm forever and ever; the scepter of your kingship is a rod that rules true. 9. You have loved justice, and hated lawlessness, therefore God, has consecrated you with the oil of rejoicing more than those with you. 10. And Lord, you have laid the foundations of the earth at its beginning, and the heavens are the work of your hands: 11. they shall all perish, but you will remain unalterable; all of them will grow old as a threadbare garment: 12. and as a covering garment you will put them aside, and exchange them for new: but you shall never change, and your years will never end. 13. To which of the angels did He ever say, Sit on my right hand, until I make your enemies a footstool under your feet? 14. What are they but spirits waiting for service, dispatched on service for those destined to be the beneficiaries of salvation?

Pay Attention With Intensity
Hebrews 2:1-4

1. We must, therefore, with special intensity pay attention to things we have heard (understood) and run no risk of drifting away from them. 2. If the word spoken through spiritual messengers was valid, and every violation and infraction of it received an appropriate penalty; 3. how can we expect to escape, if we ignore so great a deliverance (rescue/safety), that had its origin in the words of the Lord, and then was guaranteed by those who had heard (understood) the Lord's spoken word, 4. and God added His own witness by a variety of miraculous powers, and giving them according to His own will, the Holy Spirit.

Nothing Outside His Authority
Hebrews 2:5-9

5. We are speaking of the world to come and that God did not entrust the ordering of that world to angels. 6. Somewhere in scripture a writer bears witness to this fact: What is man that you remember him or the son of man that you visit him? 7. For a little time you made him lower than the angels and crowned him with glory and honor; and set him over the work of your hands, 8. and placed all things under his authority. Observe, God has subjected all things to Him, and left nothing outside His authority. But all things are not in a state of subjection to Him. 9. But we see Jesus, who for a brief moment was made lower than the angels for the suffering of death, that He by the grace of God should taste death for every man and be crowned with glory and honor.

Children Share a Common Inheritance
Hebrews 2:10-18

10. For it was fitting, for whom and through whom all things exist, to guide many sons to His glorious salvation, to make the pioneer of salvation fully adequate for His destined work through suffering. 11. Since both the Son who sanctifies and the sons who are sanctified have a common origin, He does not hesitate to own them as brothers, 12. As he sang, I will tell your name to my brothers: I will sing hymns of praise to you unto the assembly 13. And again, I will put my trust in Him. Behold I, and the children which God has given me. 14. Since these children share a common inheritance of flesh and blood, He also took on flesh and blood, that through death He could destroy the Prince of death, that is, the devil; 15. and set free all those who through the fear of death were all their lifetime under the authority of death as a bond slave. 16. For He did not take on the nature of angels, but the nature of Abraham. 17. Wherefore in all things it was imperative that He be made like His brothers, in order to become God's compassionate and faithful high priest to atone for the sins of the people. 18. For whereas

He Himself has been tried by suffering, He is able to provide immediate assistance and comfort to those being tested.

We are the House of Christ
Hebrews 3:1-6

1. Wherefore sanctified believers who share a heavenly calling, regard Christ Jesus as the Apostle and High Priest of the faith which we profess; 2. He was faithful to Him who appointed Him, just as Moses was faithful in the household of God. 3. For He was attributed more honor than Moses, because He who builds and equips the house has more honor than the house itself. 4. Every house is prepared by someone, but God prepared and equipped all things. 5. And Moses in the management of God's house was a loyal servant; his purpose was to bear witness to those things that would someday be spoken; 6. but Christ was faithful as a Son in a household which was His own, we are His house provided we keep strong the confidence and pride of our hope to the end.

Beware the Evil Heart
Hebrews 3:7-19

7. For this reason the Holy Spirit warned, If you hear His voice speaking to you today, 8. do not harden your hearts, as they were hardened once when you put Me to the test in the wilderness. 9. Your fathers tested and tempted Me, and saw what I could do, all those forty years. 10. So I became the enemy of that generation, and said, Always they wander in their hearts; they have never learned My lessons. 11. So I swore in My anger that they shall never attain My rest. 12. Take care, brothers, lest that evil heart of disobedience be in any of you as to desert the living God. 13. But keep on urging each other day by day, while the word "today" still has a meaning, that none of you be hardened by the delusion of sin. 14. We have been given a share in Christ, but only on condition that we keep unshaken to the end. 15. While it is still possible to hear If today you will hear My voice, do not harden your hearts as when you provoked Me; 16. some, when they heard, provoked God: but not all who came out of Egypt under the leadership of Moses. 17. Against who was God's anger kindled for forty years? Was it not against those who had sinned and whose bones lay in the desert? 18. And to whom did God sware an oath that they should never attain His rest, it was those who refused to believe in Him. 19. So we see the consequences of unbelief: they were denied entrance to rest because of unbelief.

Don't Miss Your Rest
Hebrews 4:1-8
1. Let us be on guard, while the promise of entering His rest still holds; that none of you may be found to be delinquent and come up short. 2. The good news was proclaimed to us, as well as to them: but the word was not heard and therefore did not profit them, because it was not woven into the fabric of their faith when it was spoken. 3. This rest is only to be attained by those who have learned to believe; as He said, I took an oath in My anger, they shall never attain My rest, although his works were completed before the foundation of the world. 4. In another place scripture recorded of the Sabbath, God rested on the seventh day from all His labors; 5. and yet in this passage He is still saying, They shall not attain My rest. 6. And it is still left for some to attain the rest, since those to whom the message first came were excluded by unbelief: 7. Again He marked out a certain day, speaking so long after through the mouth of David, Today if you will hear My voice do not harden your hearts, 8. if Joshua had actually given them rest (in Palestine), God would not after that be speaking of another day.

Don't Fall Away in Unbelief
Hebrews 4:9-16
9. So a Sabbath rest remains for the people of God. 10. For those who enter God's rest has also rested from their own labor, as God did from His. 11. We must be diligent to enter this rest, lest we fall into the example (of the Israelites) and fall into the same kind of disobedience. 12. For the living word of God is effectual, and more cutting than a two-edged sword, and penetrating to divide the combined core of soul and the spirit, and scrutinizes the desires and intentions of the heart. 13. No creature can be hidden from Him; everything lies bare, everyone is brought face to face with whom we must give account. 14. We can claim a great high priest, Jesus, the Son of God, who has ascended into heaven, therefore, let us hold fast the faith we profess. 15. For we have a high priest who can lay a hand on our personal feebleness, because He has gone through every temptation, just the same way we have, and remains without sin. 16. Let us approach God with fluency of speech to the throne of grace, that we may find special favor, compassion and understanding to meet our needs just in time.

The Priesthood of Christ
Hebrews 5:1-10
1. Every high priest chosen from among men is appointed to offer gifts and sacrifices on behalf of sins for his fellowmen: 2. who can be patient with the ignorant and wayward; for he himself wears the garment of human weakness, 3. and for that reason he must needs

make sin-offerings for the people and himself. 4. No one on his own assumes this honor, but only when he is called of God, as was Aaron. 5. So also is it with Christ, He did not raise Himself to the dignity of the high priesthood; it was God that raised Him to it, when He said, You are my beloved Son; today I have begotten you. 6. Just so He says in another place You are a priest forever after the order of Melchizedek. 7. Jesus, in His earthly life offered up prayers and petitions with earnest cries and bitter tears unto God who was able to save Him out of death, and was heard because He feared God; 8. although He was a Son, He learned obedience in the school of suffering: 9. when His consecration was finished, He became the source of eternal salvation for all who obey Him; 10. And being made perfect, He became the Author of eternal salvation unto all those who obey Him; 10. being designated by God a high priest after the order of Melchizedek.

Grown Dull of Hearing
Hebrews 5:11-14

11. The story laid upon me is long and hard to explain, seeing you are so dull of hearing. 12. After all this time you should be teachers, yet you still need to be taught again the first principles of the divine revelation: you have gone back to needing milk instead of solid food. 13. Those who still have milk for their diet do not have the experience to speak of what is right: remains an infant. 14. But grown men can eat solid food, those who, through the development of the right kind of habit, have reached a stage when their perceptions are trained to distinguish between good and evil.

Don't Return to Lifeless Observances
Hebrews 6:1-12

1. So, then, let us leave elementary teaching about Christ behind us and pass on to full growth; no need to lay the foundations all over again, the change of heart which turns away from lifeless observations, the faith which turns towards God, 2. of the instructions about different kinds of baptisms, about the laying on of hands, and of resurrection from the dead, and upon that sentence that lasts all of eternity. 3. God willing, this is our plan. 4. It is impossible to renew to repentance those who were enlightened, those who tasted the free gift from heaven, and those who were partakers of the Holy Spirit. 5. And have tasted the goodness of the word of God, and felt the powers of the world to come, 6. if they fall away, they cannot attain repentance, seeing they crucify the Son of God a second time, and are exposing Him to public contempt. 7. For when the earth drinks in the rain that comes often upon it and when it brings forth herbage useful to those who work the ground. It receives a share of the blessing from God; 8. but if the earth

produces thorns and thistles it has lost its value; a curse hangs over it, and it will feed the bonfire. 9. But we are confident of better things of you, beloved, things that go together with salvation. 10. God is not an unjust God that He should forget all you have done as a labor of love that you displayed in that you have been and still are active in the service of God's dedicated people. 11. But our great longing is to see you all showing the same eagerness right up to the end: 12. so that you do not become lethargic, but imitate those who through faith and patience inherit the promises.

The Promise of God
Hebrews 6:13-20

13. When God made His promise to Abraham, since He was not able to swear by anyone greater, He swore by Himself, 14. Surely, I will bless you and multiply you. 15. Whereupon Abraham waited patiently, and saw the promise fulfilled. 16. Men swear by someone who is greater than themselves: and an oath serves for a guarantee beyond all possibility of contradiction, the end of all conflict. 17. And God, in the same way, eager to convince the heirs of the promise that His design was irrevocable, pledged Himself by an oath. 18. Two irrevocable assurances, over which there could be no question of God deceiving us, we who have fled to Him for refuge, might be strongly encouraged to lay hold upon the hope that is set before us. 19. This hope to us is an anchor of the soul, safe and sure, and it enters with us to the inner court beyond the veil. 20. Which Jesus Christ, our escort, has entered already, a high priest, now, eternally with the priesthood of Melchizedek?

King of Justice and Peace
Hebrews 7:1-10

1. It was this Melchizedek, King of Salem, and priest of the highest God, who met Abraham and blessed him on his way home, after the defeat of the kings; 2. to whom Abraham gave a tithe of all the spoils, and in the first place, his name means King of Justice and, in the second place, King of Salem means King of Peace; 3. that is all; no name of father or mother, no pedigree, no birth date or of death; there he stands, eternally, a priest, the true figure of the Son of God. 4. Consider how great this man was to whom the patriarch Abraham gave a tithe of the plunder. 5. Look at the difference, the sons of Levi, who received their priesthood, they received instructions from the law to receive a tithe from the people, their brethren, although they are descendants of Abraham. 6. Here is one with no common descent with them, taking tithes from Abraham himself. And blessed is the man to whom the promises had been made. 7. Beyond all argument, the

lesser is blessed by the greater. 8. In the one case the priests who received tithes are only mortal men; in the other, it is a priest who continues to live. 9. One might even say that Levi also received tithes and paid tithes through Abraham. 10. As the heir of Abraham, he was present in the person of his ancestor, when he met Melchizedek.

When a Fresh Priest Arises
Hebrews 7:11-22

11. If the desired effect could have been achieved by the Levitical priesthood (for under that priesthood the people became a people of the law), what further need was there to set up another priest and to call him a priest after the order of Melchizedek, and not be called after the order of Aaron? 12. When the priesthood is altered, the law, necessarily, is changed with it. 13. For the person of whom the statements are made belongs to another tribe altogether, from which no one ever served at the altar. 14. It is certain that our Lord took His origin from Judah, and Moses in speaking of this tribe, said nothing about priests. 15. And something further becomes evident, when a new priest arises to fulfill the type of Melchizedek, 16. not appointed to obey the law, with its outward observances, but with the power of an unending life; 17. for the witness of scripture: You are a priest forever after the order of Melchizedek, 18. if all that is true, on the one hand there emerges the cancellation of the previous injunction because of its own weakness and uselessness. 19. For the law never achieved perfection, but the introduction of a better hope did, through which we can come near to God. 20. Ratification by oath was evident this time: 21. none was taken when those other priests were appointed, but the new priest is appointed with an oath, when God says to him, The Lord has sworn an irrevocable oath, Thou art a priest forever after the order of Melchizedek: 22 in so far Jesus has become the surety of a better covenant.

Priesthood of Jesus is Forever
Hebrews 7:23-28

23. Of the other priests there was a succession, since death denied them permanence; 24. whereas Jesus continues forever, and His priestly office is unchanging; 25. that is why He can give eternal salvation to those who through Him make their way to God, He lives on still to make intercession on behalf of believers. 26. Such was the high priest that suited our need, holy and guiltless and undefiled, not counted among the sinners, lifted high above the heavens; 27. He does not need, as the high priests do, daily first to offer sacrifices for His own sins and thereafter for the sins of the people. This was done once for all when He offered Himself. 29. For the law appointed as

high priests men subject to weakness; but the word of the oath, which came after the law, appointed one who is a Son who is fully equipped to carry out His office forever.

Build According to the Pattern
Hebrews 8:1-6

1. Now to the central thread of things: this high priest is one who has taken His seat in heaven, on the right hand of that throne where God is in majesty, 2. a minister of the sanctuary and of the true tabernacle, set up by the Lord, and not man. 3. For every high priest is constituted to offer both gifts and sacrifices: this man must have an offering to make. 4. Whereas, if He were still on earth, He would be no priest at all; there are priests already to offer the gifts which the law demands, 5. who devote their service to the heavenly order which is but a shadowy outline. That is why Moses, when he was building the tabernacle, received the warning, Be sure to make everything in accordance with the pattern that was shown to you on the mountain. 6. But, as things are, He has been entrusted with a more honorable service, by how much also He is the dispenser of a nobler covenant, which was enacted based on nobler promises.

A New Covenant
Hebrews 8:7-9

7. If there had been no fault to find with the first covenant, there would have been no room for this second one. 8. But God does find fault, and said, Behold, says the Lord, a time is coming when I will ratify a new covenant with the people of Israel, and with the People of Judah: 9. it will not be the same covenant which I made with their fathers, on the day when I took them by the hand, to rescue them from Egypt; that they should break My covenant, and I, says the Lord, should abandon them."

Covenant Engraved on the Heart
Hebrews 8:10-13

10. It will be different because this is the covenant which I will grant the House of Israel when that time comes, says the Lord. I will implant my laws into their mind and I will engrave them upon their hearts, I will be their God, and they shall be my people: 11. There will be no need for neighbor to teach neighbor or no one will teach his brother, the knowledge of the Lord; all will know Me, from the lowest to the greatest. 12. I will graciously forgive their wrong-doings and I will not remember their sins any more. 13. Since He said, a new covenant, He has disqualified for age the first one. Now soon the antiquated must needs disappear.

Sacrifices Have No Power
Hebrews 9:1-10

1. Now even the first covenant had its own ceremonial ordinances, and a sanctuary belonging to the material world. 2. For the first tabernacle was constructed and in it there was the lamp stand and the table with and the loaves set out before God, and it was called the Holy Place. 3. And behind the second curtain there was the part of the tabernacle which was called the Holy of Holies; 4. With the golden altar of incense, and the Ark of the Covenant, gilded all round. In the ark rested the golden urn with the manna, Aaron's staff that budded, and the tablets on which the covenant (Ten Commandments) were inscribed; 5. above it was the cherubim of glory overshadowing the mercy seat; but this is not the place to speak about all these things in detail. 6. Into the outer tabernacle the priests made their way at all times, in the performance of their duties; 7. But into the second only the High Priest enters, and that once a year and not without blood, which he offers for himself and for the faults committed unknowingly by the people. 8. The Holy Spirit indicated that no way of access to the true sanctuary lay open to us, as long as the former covenant was still in force. 9. And that figure of speech still holds good at the present; here are gifts and sacrifices being offered, which have no power, where conscience is concerned: 10. to bring the worshipper to his full growth; they are but outward observances, connected with food and drink and ceremonial washings on this occasion or that, instituted to hold their own until better times should come.

A Greater and More Perfect Tabernacle
Hebrews 9:11-14

11. But Christ having appeared a high priest of blessings that is still in the future, He made use of a greater, a more complete tabernacle, which human hands never fashioned; 12. and not by the blood of goats and calves, but by His own blood, He entered once and for all into the Holy Place because He had secured everlasting redemption for us. 13. For if the blood of oxen and goats, and the ashes of a heifer, sprinkled over those who were ceremonially unclean, is sufficient for physical cleansing: 14. how much more will the blood of Christ who, through the eternal Spirit, offered Himself spotless to God, wash away impurities from your conscience so that you will be able to leave the conduct that brings death in order to become the personal followers of the living God?

The Testator of the New Covenant
Hebrews 9:15-18

15. Through His intervention, a new covenant has been bequeathed to us; His death must follow, to atone for all our transgressions under the old covenant, the purpose was to rescue them from the consequences of the transgressions which had been committed under the old covenant. And then the destined heirs were to obtain, forever, their promised inheritance. 16. For where there is a will, it is necessary that there be evidence of the death of the testator to make the will valid. 17. A will has no force while the testator is alive, and only comes into force with death. 18. Whereupon neither the first testament could be ratified without the use of blood.

Without Blood There is No Forgiveness
Hebrews 9:19-28

19. When Moses finished reading the guidelines of the law to the assembled people, he took blood of calves and goats, water, scarlet-dyed wool, and the potherb hyssop, and sprinkled the scroll itself and all the people in a solemn purification ceremony, 20. saying, this is the blood of the covenant which conditions God commended you to observe. 21. The tabernacle, too, and all the vessels of worship he sprinkled in the same way with blood; 22. And the law instructs that blood shall be used in almost every act of purification, unless blood is shed, there can be no forgiveness. 23. And if such purification was necessary for examples of the heavenly world, the heavenly things will need better sacrifices than these. 24. For Christ entered into a sanctuary not made by human hands, which is a vague and incomplete outline of the true, but entered heaven itself, where He now appears in God's presence for us. 25. Nor does He make a repeated offering of Himself when He enters the sanctuary, as the high priest, makes a yearly offering of the blood that is not His own. 26. If that were true He would have had to suffer again and again since the world was founded: but now once and for all, at the end of the ages, He has appeared with the sacrifice of Himself so that our sins could be cancelled. 27. And just as men are destined to die once with judgment following: 28. so Christ having been offered once for the sins of many; the second time sin will play its part no longer, He will be bringing salvation to those who eagerly expect His coming.

Where the Scroll is Unrolled
Hebrews 10:1-10

1. Since the law is only a shadow of the blessings which are to come and not a real image of these things, it can never really fit the fellowship of God for those who seek to draw near to His presence with the sacrifices which have to be brought year by year and which go on forever. 2. Should not the offerings have ceased before now? If they

could, there would be no guilt left to reproach the consciences of those who come to worship; they would have been totally cleansed. 3. But these annual sacrifices are a reminder again of sins. 4. It is impossible for the blood of bulls and goats to take away sins. 5. That is why He said when He entered the world: You did not desire sacrifice and offering; it is a body you have prepared for Me: 6. you have not found pleasure in burnt sacrifices, in sacrifices for sin. 7. Then I said, I am coming to fulfill what is written concerning Me, where the scroll is unrolled; to do your will, God. 8. In the scroll you did not demand sacrifice and burnt offerings and the sacrifice for sin, nor did you find pleasure in them; which are required by the law. 9. Then He said, I come to do your will. He abolished the kind of offering mentioned first in order to establish the kind of offering referred in the second. 10. In accordance with the divine will we have been sanctified by an offering made once for all, the body of Jesus Christ.

A Single Offering Completed His Work
Hebrews 10:11-18
11. One high priest after another must stand there, day after day, offering again and again the same sacrifices, which can never take away sins; 12. but this man offered one single sacrifice for sin and then took His seat forever at the right hand of God, 13. and for the future He waits until His enemies are made a footstool for His feet. 14. By a single offering He has completed His work in those who He sanctifies. 15. And to this the Holy Spirit is a witness: for after that He said, 16. The Lord says this is the covenant I will grant them, when that time comes, I will implant My laws in their hearts, engrave them in their innermost thoughts; 17. I will not remember their sins and transgressions any more. 18. Now, where there is forgiveness of sins, a sacrifice for sin is no longer necessary.

A New and Living Way
Hebrews 10:19-25
19. Having therefore, fluency of speech to enter the Holy Place by the blood of Jesus, 20. He has opened for us a new and living approach, by way of the veil, meaning His mortality. 21. Since we have a high priest over the house of God; 22. let us come forward with a sincere heart crammed full of faith, having our guilty consciences purified by sprinkling, and our bodies washed with pure water: 23. let us not waver in acknowledging the faith we profess; we have a promise from one who is true to His word. 24. Let us keep one another in mind, always ready with love and acts of piety, 25. let us not abandon our meeting together, as some habitually do, but let us encourage one another, and all the more as we see the great day drawing near.

Willful Sin Will Be Punished
Hebrews 10:26-31

26. If we continue sinning willfully, after the full knowledge of the truth had been granted to us, we cannot look forward to further sacrifice for sins; 27. There is nothing but a terrible expectation of judgment and looking for that flaming wrath which will consume the rebellious. 28. Let a man be convicted by two or three witnesses of defying the Law of Moses, and he dies, without hope of mercy: 29. how much worse do you think the punishment will be for that man who has trampled underfoot the Son of God, and failed to regard the blood of the new covenant, by which He was made sacred for God's presence, and who insulted the Spirit through whom God's grace comes to us? 30. For we know Him who said, Vengeance is for me, I will repay; and again, The Lord will judge His people. 31. It is a terrifying thing to fall into the hands of the living God.

Faith Brings Life
Hebrews 10:32-39

32. Remember those hard days, after you had been enlightened and you had to struggle with suffering; 33. there were times when you yourself were exposed to slander and harassment and partly because you came forward to share the suffering of your companions. 34. For you gave sympathy to my bonds, and the seizure of your goods with calm acceptance knowing that in heaven you have better and more material possessions that will endure in heaven. 35. Do not discard compensating self-confidence, for it is a self-reliance that has great reward. 36. For you need steadfastness, after you do the will of God, you must have staying power to receive the promise. 37. Only a brief moment before He who is coming will arrive; He will not linger on the way. 38. The justified man lives by faith; but if he withdraws, my soul is not well-pleased. 39. But we are not ones who draw back to destruction; but we are those who accept as true the personal consecration of the mind, will and human emotions which enable us to possess eternal life.

Substance of Hope is Faith
Hebrews 11:1-10

1. Now faith is the reality of things being hoped for, the proof of things not being seen. 2. By faith the saints of old took hold of a good witness. 3. It is faith that lets us understand how the worlds were fashioned by the word; so that what is seen came into being out of what is unseen. 4. It was by faith that Abel offered a better sacrifice than Cain, and thereby obtained justification, since God recognized his offering; through that offering although dead Abel still speaks. 5. By faith

Enoch was taken away not to see death, and was not found because God removed him: this is the account we have before he was taken, that he pleased God. 6. It is impossible to please God without faith. No one reaches God's presence until he has learned to believe that God exists, and that God is one who rewards those who are seeking him out. 7. By faith Noah, having been warned by God concerning things not yet seen, being devout prepared an ark for the salvation of his household, by which he condemned the world, and according to faith became heir to righteousness. 8. And Abraham showed faith when he left his home for a country which was to be his inheritance; obediently he left without knowing where his journey would take him. 9. It was by faith that he sojourned in a land promised as his own, encamping there with Isaac and Jacob, heirs with him of a common hope; 10. He was looking for a city which had foundations, whose architect and builder was God.

Power Through Faith
Hebrews 11:11-19

11. It was faith that enabled Sarah to receive power to conceive and bear a son, although she was past child-bearing age, she believed that God would be faithful to His promise. 12. So from one man who had lost his vitality, from him springs a race whose descendants rival the stars of the sky in multitude, as countless as the sand upon the seashore. 13. All these died without possessing the promises. They only saw them from far away and greeted them from afar, and they admitted that they were strangers and sojourners upon the earth. 14. Those who speak so make it clear that they have not yet found their home. 15. If they had been thinking of the land from which they had come, they would have had time and opportunity to return. 16. They were reaching out for something better, a heavenly country. It was because of their faithfulness that God was not ashamed to be called their God, for He had prepared for them a city. 17. Abraham showed faith when he was tested and offered up Isaac: he was willing to offer up his only son, 18. because it had been said, It is in Isaac that your descendants will be named: 19. he reckoned that God was able to raise him from the dead. Hence he did receive him back which is a figure of the resurrection.

Faith Brings Blessings
Hebrews 11:20-31

20. It was by faith that Isaac gave Jacob and Esau a blood-related blessing concerning future things. 21. It was by faith that Jacob, when he was dying, blessed both the sons of Joseph; and prayed leaning on his staff. 22. By faith Joseph when he came to the end of his life,

spoke of the departing of Israel from Egypt, and gave orders for the removal of his bones. 23. It was by faith that Moses was hid by his parents for three months, because they saw he was in good health and did not fear the edict of the king. 24. And Moses showed faith as he grew up and refused to be called the son of Pharaoh's daughter; 25. he chose to suffer with the people of God, rather than enjoy the transient pleasures of Pharaoh's house. 26. All the wealth of Egypt could not enrich him as the despised lot of Messiah's people; he had eyes for nothing but the promised reward. 27. It was by faith that he left Egypt, not fearing the anger of the king: for he endured as if seeing the coming Messiah. 28. In faith he performed the Passover rite and the pouring of the blood, to leave Israel untouched by the angel that destroyed the first born. 29. By faith they crossed the Red sea as if by dry land: whereas the Egyptians, when they ventured into the sea were drowned. 30. It was by faith that the walls of Jericho fell down, after they were encircled for seven days. 31. Faith saved Rahab, the prostitute, from sharing the doom of the disobedient, because she had welcomed the spies in peace.

Other Faithful Servants
Hebrews 11:32-40

32. And what more shall I say? Time will fail me to recount the story of Gideon, Barak, Samson, Jephthah, David, Samuel and of the prophets, 33. men who, through faith, mastered kingdoms, did righteousness, obtained promises, shut the mouths of lions. 34. Quenched the power of fire, escaped the edge of the sword, in their weakness they were made strong, showed courage in battle, made foreign armies yield. 35. There were women who received their dead children back to life: and others were tortured, not accepting deliverance; looking forward to a better resurrection: 36. and others experienced mockery and scourging, chains and imprisonment; 37. they were stoned, they were cut in pieces, they were tortured, they were slain with the sword; they wandered about, dressed in animal skins; being destitute, afflicted, tormented; 38. men of whom the world was not worthy: they wandered in desert places, and in mountains, and lived in caves and holes in the earth. 39. And these all, having obtained a good report through faith, received not the promise: 40. For us, God had something better in store. We were needed, to make the history of their lives complete.

Fix Your Eyes on Jesus

Hebrews 12:1-6
1. Therefore, since we are watched from above by such a cloud of witnesses, let us rid ourselves of all that weighs us down, and the concealed habits and misbehaviors that thwart our race, and let us run with steadfast endurance, the course that is marked out before us, 2. let this fix our eyes on Jesus the origin and the crown of all faith, who, to win His prize of blessedness, endured the cross and made light of its shame, Jesus, who now sits on the right of God's throne. 3. Consider Him who steadfastly endured such opposition at the hands of sinners, and compare your lives with His, so that you may not faint and grow weary in your souls. 4. you have not yet had to resist to the point of blood in your struggle against sin. 5. Have you forgotten the appeal, an appeal which reasons with you as sons? My son, do not treat lightly the discipline which the Lord sends; never lose heart when you are corrected by Him; 6. it is on whom He loves that He bestows correction; there is no recognition for any child of His, without chastisement.

The Discipline of the Father
Hebrews 12:7-13
7. Be patient, then, for while correction lasts; God is treating you as His children. Was there ever a son whom the father did not correct? 8. If you are left without discipline, that discipline which everyone must share, then you are illegitimate children and not sons. 9. We have known what it was to accept correction from earthly fathers, and with reverence; shall we not willingly line up under the authority of our spiritual Father, and live? 10. It was for a short time that our earthly fathers disciplined us as they thought best; but God disciplines us for our highest good, to give us a share in His holiness. 11. At the time all discipline is painful rather than pleasant; but afterwards, when it has done the work of discipline, it yields a harvest of good fruit in a righteous life for those trained by the experience. 12. So, then, lift up the drooping hands, and the weak knees; 13. and plant your feet in a straight path, lest someone who is weak stumble out of the path; but be restored to strength instead.

Avoid Any Cause for Animosity
Hebrews 12:14-17
14. Pursue harmony with all men, and strive for that consecration without which no man shall see the Lord: 15. watch that no one misses the grace of God; lest any cause for animosity grow up to trouble you, and thereby many be corrupted; 16. watch that no one falls into sexual impurity or follows a blasphemous person, as Esau, who for a scrap of food gave up the rights of the first born. 17. Afterward, he was eager

enough to have the blood related honor, but was rejected: he had no opportunity to change his mind, although he sought that blessing with tears.

Terrible Mountain or the City of God
Hebrews 12:18-24

18. For you have approached to a mountain that cannot be touched, and having been ignited with fire and to darkness and to deep gloom and to whirlwind, 19. and to a sound of trumpet to a voice of words, which the ones hearing entreated that not another word be spoken to them: 20. they could not bear the order that was given, and even if a wild beast touches the mountain, it shall be stoned, or thrust through with a dart: 21. and so fearful was the sight, that Moses said, I am terrified and trembling: 22. but you have approached mount Zion, and the city of the living God, the heavenly Jerusalem, and to a countless host of angels, 23. to the solemn gathering and congregation of the firstborn; to the assembly of the honored ones whose names are in the register of heaven, to that God who is Judge of all, to the spirit of just men who have come to that goal for which they were created, 24. and to Jesus, the mediator of the new covenant, to the sprinkled blood which has a message greater than the blood of Abel.

Beware of Excusing Yourself
Hebrews 12:25-29

25. Beware of excusing yourself from listening to Him who is speaking to you. If they who refused to listen to the one who brought the oracles of God upon earth did not escape, how much more shall we not escape if we turn away from Him who speaks from heaven? 26. His voice made the earth shake: but now He has promised, saying, Once more He has announced that He will shake not only the earth, but also heaven. 27. And that phrase, once more signifies the removal of the things that are shaken, because they are merely created things, in order that the things which cannot be shaken may remain. 28. The kingdom we have inherited is one which cannot be moved; in gratitude for this, let us worship God as He would have us worship Him, in reverence and godly fear: 29. for our God is a consuming fire.

Good Leaders Remember
Hebrews 13:1-8

1. Let brotherly love be with you always. 2. Do not forget to show hospitality; in doing this, men have unsuspectingly entertained angels. 3. Remember those who are in prison for you yourselves know what it is like to be a prisoner; remember those who are suffering ill-treatment for the same thing can happen to you so long as you are in the body. 4. Let marriage be held in honor among you and never let the marriage

bed be defiled: but God will judge the fornicators and those who adulterate the marriage vows. 5. Let your way of life be free from the love of money; and be content with the things you have: for He said, I will never leave you, nor forsake you. 6. So we may with fluency of speech say, The Lord is my helper, and I will not fear what man can do to me. 7. Remember them that have the rule over you, who spoke the word of God to you; follow their faith, observe how they made their exit from this life. 8. Jesus Christ the same yesterday, and today, and forever.

An Established Heart is Good
Hebrews 13:9-16

9. Do not be carried aside from your course by a maze of new teachings. For the heart is established with grace and not observances in the matter of food, which have never proved useful to those who follow those rules. 10. We have an altar of our own where those who serve the tabernacle have no right to eat. 11. For the bodies of the animals, whose blood is taken by the High Priest into the Holy Place as an offering for sin, are burned outside the camp. 12. That is why Jesus suffered outside the gate, so that He might make men fit for the presence of God by His own blood. 13. So then let us go to Him outside the gate, bearing the same reproach as He did, 14. for here we have no abiding city but are searching for the city which is to come. 15. It is through Him, then, that we must offer to God a continual sacrifice of praise, the tribute of lips that give thanks to His name. 16. You must remember to do good to others and give alms; God takes pleasure in the sacrifice of gifts.

Obey and Keep on Praying
Hebrews 13:17-21

17. Obey those who have rule over you, and line yourselves up under their authority: for they watch over your souls, because they know they will have an account to give. Make it a grateful task for them: it is your loss if they find it a difficult task. 18. Keep on praying for us, for we believe that we have a clear conscience, for we wish in all things to live in such a way that our conduct will be fair. 19. I urge you to do this all the more that I may the more quickly be enabled to return to you. 20. Now the God of peace, that brought again our Lord Jesus from among the dead, that great Shepherd of the sheep, through the blood of the everlasting covenant, 21. make you complete in every good work to do His will, working in you that which is well-pleasing in His sight, through Jesus Christ; to whom be glory forever and ever. Amen.

Bear Patiently With All These Words

Hebrews 13:22-25

22. I entreat you, fellow believers, bear patiently with all these words of warning; it is but a brief letter I am sending you. 23. You must know that our brother Timothy has been set at liberty; if he comes soon, I will bring him with me when I visit you. 24. Greet all those who are in authority, and all the saints. The brethren from Italy send you their greetings. 25. Grace be with you all, Amen.

THE SECOND LETTER OF PETER

Peter wrote his second Letter (II Peter) to the same believers in Turkey in AD 67. The main themes of this letter were: an exhortation to spiritual growth; the necessity of holding on to truth; warnings against false teachers; and advice on how to live in view of the Lord's return.

A Common Privilege of Faith
2 Peter 1:1-2
1. Simon Peter, a servant and an apostle of Jesus Christ, to them who share with us a common privilege of faith, justified as we are by our God and Savior Jesus Christ: 2. grace to you and peace, may it be multiplied to you through full knowledge of God and of Jesus our Lord.

Precious and Treasured Promises
2 Peter 1:3-7
3. Since His divine power has bestowed upon us all things that are necessary for true life and true worship, through the full knowledge of Him who called us to His own glory and moral uprightness: 4. since through these gifts He has bestowed upon us precious and treasured promises: you are to share the divine nature, leaving behind the corruption and passions of the world. 5. And you too have to contribute every effort on your own part, crowning your faith with moral excellence, and to moral excellence knowledge from books and teachers: 6. and to your knowledge self-control; and to self-control enduring steadfastness, and to enduring steadfastness godly worship; 7. and to godly worship brotherly kindness; and to brotherly kindness benevolent love.

An Abundant Entrance to the Kingdom
2 Peter 1:8-11
8. Such gifts, when they are yours in full measure, will cause you to be neither unproductive nor unprofitable in the full knowledge of our Lord Jesus Christ. 9. He who lacks them is no better than a short-sighted man feeling his way about; and has forgotten that his old sins have been purged. 10. So, believers, be the more eager to confirm your calling and your choice: for if you do practice these virtues, you will make no false steps: 11. and you shall be richly supplied the entrance into the kingdom of our Lord and Savior Jesus Christ.

Refresh Your Memory
2 Peter 1:12-21
12. It is for these reasons that I intend to constantly remind you of these things, although you know them well, and are grounded firmly in the present truth. 13. I think it right, as long as I am living, to refresh

your memory; 14. the Lord Jesus Christ has showed me that shortly I must fold my tent. 15. Moreover, I will make it my endeavor that after my departure you will always remember these things. 16. For we have not pursued deceitfully developed allegories, but were eyewitnesses to His majesty when we made known to you the power and presence of our Lord Jesus Christ. 17. For He received from God the Father honor and glory, when a voice came from the magnificent glory This is My Son, My beloved in whom I am delighted. 18. And we His companions on the holy mountain heard this voice coming from heaven. 19. So this makes the word of the prophets more certain for us: and you do well taking heed, as to a lamp shining in a gloomy place, until the day dawns and the morning star shines in your hearts; 20. knowing this firstly, that no prophecy of scripture becomes its own solution. 21. For no prophecy was brought forth by the will of man at any time: but men spoke from God being brought forth by the Holy Spirit.

Beware of Destructive Opinions
2 Peter 2:1-11

1. There were false prophets also among the people, and there will be false teachers among you, who secretly will bring destructive opinions among you, even denying the Master who bought them, and they will bring swift self- destruction. 2. Many will embrace their unashamed immorality and through them the True Way will be brought into disrepute. 3. And by greed with fabricated words they will make merchandise of you: their sentence was settled long ago, and now their damnation is not delayed. 4. Since God did not spare the sinning angels, consigning them to pits of gloom in a section of Hades reserved for punishment of the wicked until judgment. 5. And spared not the ancient world but guarded the eighth man Noah, a herald of righteousness, bringing a flood on a world of wicked men; 6. since He reduced the cities of Sodom and Gomorrah to ashes, when He sentenced them to destruction and gave an example of what happens to those who live ungodly; 7. and delivered righteous Lot, who was distressed by the immorality of lawless men, 8. for a righteous man to see and hear such lawless deeds was daily torment to his righteous soul. 9. The Lord knows how to deliver the righteous out of trials, and to keep the unrighteous for a day of judgment to be punished. 10. And especially those lives dominated by the polluting desires of the flesh and who despise authority. They are audacious, self-willed individuals who are not afraid to speak evil of those who hold a position or rank of honor. 11. Whereas angels being greater in strength and power do not bring on themselves any charges so abominable, before the Lord.

The Reward of Unrighteousness
2 Peter 2:12-16

12. But these false teachers were as natural animals, knowing only their instincts, born to be trapped and destroyed, speak evil of things they do not understand, and they shall perish through self-destruction; 13. they will have the reward they deserved. They regard daylight debauchery as pleasure. They are spots and moral flaws, reveling in their indulgences, carousing in their little circles among you. 14. With eyes full of adultery that cannot cease from sin; enticing unstable women: they have a heart trained in unrestrained ambition for things they have no right to have; producing cursed children: 15. these false teachers have deserted the correct path and gone off course following the path of Balaam*, the son of Bosor, the man who was willing to take pay in the cause of wrong. 16. A dumb donkey spoke with a human voice and ordered the prophet not to speak falsely.

---

*v15 Balaam is an example of the destructive influence of hypocritical teachers who attempt to lead God's people astray.

Beware of Dry Cisterns
2 Peter 2:17-22

17. These teachers are waterless cisterns, clouds driven before the storm; the eternal darkness is reserved for them. 18. They speak with big words with no meaning, they ensnare by appeals to sensual passions, those who have barely escaped from their heathen environment. 19. They promise freedom while they themselves are slaves of moral corruption: whatever influences get the better of man, becomes his master. 20. If they have escaped the contamination of the world by the full knowledge of the Lord and Savior Jesus Christ, and allow themselves again to become entangled and defeated, their last state is worse than the first. 21. Better for them never to have found their way to justification, than, after they have known righteousness, to turn from the holy commandment delivered to them. 22. In this case the truth of the proverb is clear: A dog turns back to his own vomit and Wash the sow, and she wallows again in the mud.

Remember the Words
2 Peter 3:1-9

1. This is my second letter to you, beloved; I write such letters as a reminder, to awaken your clear sense of truth. 2. That you may remember the words spoken before by the holy prophets, and our commandment as apostles of the Lord and Savior. 3. First, you are well aware that in the last days mockers will come, staggering after their own cravings, 4. saying, What has become of the promise that

He would appear? Since the fathers went to their rest, all things are the same as from the foundation of the world. 5. They willingly forget that the heavens were created long ago by the Word of God and the earth was standing out of water and in the water; 6. whereby the world that was, perished being overflowed with water. 7. But the present heaven and earth, by the same Word are stored up ready for the fire on judgment day and the punishment in hell of the disobedient and the wicked. 8. But, beloved, you must know this one thing, with the Lord one day is as a thousand years, and a thousand years as one day. 9. The Lord is not slow concerning His promise as some count slowness; but is long-suffering to all, not wishing any to perish, but desiring all to take the way of repentance.

What Kind of People Ought You to Be?
2 Peter 3:10-14
10. The day of the Lord is coming as a burglar in the night; the heavens will pass away with a great rushing sound, and the elements will be dissolved with burning heat and the earth and the works in it will be exposed and burned. 11. Since all these things are going to be dissolved, what kind of people ought you to be in your life of devotedness and true holiness. 12. How reverent toward God as you wait eagerly for the day of the Lord to come, for the heavens to be consumed with fire and the elements to melt in the heat? 13. Meanwhile, we have new heavens and a new earth to look forward to according to His promise, where dwells righteousness. 14. So, beloved, since these are the things for which you eagerly wait, be diligent to be found by Him at peace, blameless and without imperfection.

Steadfastness Prevents Destruction
2 Peter 3:15-18
15. Look upon our Lord's long-suffering as salvation; even as our beloved brother Paul has written according to the wisdom given to him; 16. also in all his letters, when he touches on these subjects, some things are hard to be understood, things which those who lack learning and a stable foundation in the faith twist, as they do other scriptures, to their own destruction. 17. For yourselves, beloved, be warned in time; do not be carried away by their impulsive errors, and lose the firm foothold you have won; 18. but grow up in grace, and in the knowledge of our Lord and Savior Jesus Christ. To Him be glory; now and for all eternity. Amen.

THE GENERAL LETTER OF JUDE

About AD 67, Jude, a brother of James and half brother of Jesus, wrote an open letter circulated among the scattered believers. His primary effort was to defend the apostolic faith against false teachers who were immoral, covetous, proud and divisive. These teachers suggested that being saved by grace permitted one to engage in all kinds of lawlessness and remain a believer.

Peace and Love
Jude 1:1-2
1. Jude, the servant of Jesus Christ, and brother of James, to the ones consecrated by God the Father, and having been kept and called in Jesus Christ: 2. mercy to you, peace and love, may it be multiplied.

Contend for the Faith
Jude 1:3-7
3. Beloved, making all haste to write to you of our common salvation, it was necessary for me to write to you, exhorting you to contend for the faith which was once delivered to the saints. 4. For certain men have found their way secretly, Godless men designated before for condemnation, who twist the grace of God into a justification of obvious immorality and who deny the only Master and our Lord Jesus Christ. 5. It is my intent to remind you, although you already possess full knowledge of how the Lord saved the people out of the land of Egypt, and afterward destroyed those that believed not. 6. And angels not having kept the rule of themselves, but having deserted their own territory, He has kept in everlasting bonds under obscurity for the judgment of the great day. 7. Even as Sodom and Gomorrah, and the cities around them that fell into the same debauchery, giving themselves over to sexual sins and strayed after perverted sexual immorality, are exhibited as a warning because they suffered the penalty of everlasting fire.

Filthy Dreamers Defile the Flesh
Jude 1:8-16
8. Likewise indeed these dreaming ones on the one hand pollute nature and on the other despise authority and use abusive language toward positions of dignity and honor. 9. Yet Michael, the Archangel, when debating the devil disputed about the body of Moses, did not bring abusive language against him in accusation, but said, The Lord rebuke you. 10. Such men sneer at the things they cannot understand; as animals without reason they are corrupted by their natural behavior

. 11. Woe to them, for they have followed in the path of Cain*, and ran greedily after the error of Balaam* for reward, and perished in the gainsaying of Korah*. 12. These men are hidden difficulties at your banquets, they eat sumptuously at your side, feeding themselves until they are fat: they are clouds that drop no water, but are blown by the wind. They are fruitless trees in harvest time, twice dead and torn up by the roots. 13. They are fierce waves of the sea, with shame for their crowns, wandering stars, with eternal darkness and storms awaiting them. 14. Enoch, the seventh from Adam, prophesied of these, saying, Behold, the Lord comes with ten thousands of His saints, 15. to execute judgment upon all, and to rebuke all that are profane among them of all their offensive deeds which they have blasphemously committed, and of all their abusive language which immoral sinners have spoken against Him. 16. These are whispering grumblers, complainers, walking after their own appetites; their mouths are ready with fine phrases, to flatter the great when it serves their ends.

---

*v11 Cain, offered a bloodless sacrifice, killed his brother, and did not repent. Korah, with two companions, resisted the civil authority of Moses. Balaam is an example of the destructive influence of hypocritical teachers who attempt to lead God's people astray.

You Must Remember the Words
Jude 1:17-21

17. But, beloved, you must remember the words once spoken before of the apostles of our Lord Jesus Christ; 18. how they told you there should be ridiculing spirits in the last time, who would make their ungodly appetites into a rule of life. 19. Such are the men who now keep themselves apart; fleshly creatures without the Spirit. 20. It is for you, beloved, to make your most holy faith the foundation of your lives, and to go on praying in the power of the Holy Spirit; 21. maintain yourselves in the love of God, and wait for the mercy of our Lord Jesus Christ, with eternal life as your goal.

Keep You From Slipping
Jude 1:22-25

22. And some, you must give a hearing and show them to be false; 23. and others you must pull out of the fire, and rescue them; while you shun them; even the outward fringe of what the flesh has defiled must be hateful to you. 24. Now unto Him who is able to keep you from slipping, and to present you blameless before the presence of His glory with exceeding joy, 25. to the only wise God our Savior, be glory and majesty, dominion and power, before time was, and now, and for all ages. Amen.

THE FIRST LETTER OF JOHN

John, one of the original Twelve disciples, wrote three Letters (around AD 86), probably in Ephesus. They were general letters of counsel to Christians scattered throughout the Roman Empire. John dealt with problems that were continuing to develop in the church because of false teachers. His letters were sent to encourage believers to maintain truth by maintaining their relationship with Christ. This first letter dwells on the nature of Christ, His mission, and His principle doctrines, in particular the Christian life. It also draws distinction between true and false believers.

The Word of Life
1 John 1:1-4
1. What was from the beginning, what we have heard, what we have seen with our eyes, what we beheld and our hands touched, concerning the Word of life; 2. and the life was manifested, and we have seen and we bear witness and we announce to you Life Eternal, who was with the Father and was manifested to us, 3. what we have seen and heard, we announce to you also in order that you may have fellowship with us, and indeed our fellowship is with the Father and with His Son Jesus Christ. 4. And these things we write in order that our joy may be fulfilled.

God is Light
1 John 1:5-10
5. This then is the message which we have heard of Him, and announce to you, that God is light, and no darkness can find a place in Him. 6. If we say that we have fellowship with Him, and at the same time walk in darkness, we lie, and are not living the truth: 7. but if we walk in the light, as He is in the light, we have fellowship one with another, and the blood of Jesus Christ His Son cleanses us from all sin. 8. If we say that we have no sin, we deceive ourselves, and the truth is not in us. 9. If we admit our sins, faithful is He and righteous in order that He may cleanse us from all wickedness. 10. If we deny that we have sinned, it means that we are treating Him as a liar; and that His word does not dwell in our hearts.

We Have an Advocate
1 John 2:1-11
1. My babes in Christ, the purpose of this letter is to keep you clear of sin. Meanwhile, if anyone does fall into sin, we have an Advocate to plead our cause before the Father, Jesus Christ the righteous: 2. and He made personal atonement for our sins: but not only concerning our sins, but also all the world. 3. And by this we know that we have known Him, if we keep His commandments. 4. The man who claims

knowledge of Him without keeping His commandments is a liar; truth does not dwell in such a man. 5. If a man keeps true to God's word, then it is certain that the love of God has reached its full level of respect in him; that is what tells us that we are dwelling in God. 6. He who claims that he abides in Him ought himself to live the same kind of life as He lived. 7. Beloved, it is not a new commandment which I am writing to you, but an old commandment which you had from the beginning; the old commandment is the word which you heard. 8. Again, yet it is a new commandment I am sending you, now that it is verified in Him and you; the darkness has passed away now, and true light shines instead. 9. He who claims enlightenment, and all the while hates his brother, is still in darkness. 10. He who loves his brother lives in the light; no fear of stumbling haunts him. 11. The man who hates his brother is in the dark, and takes his steps in the dark without being able to see where he is going; darkness has fallen, and blinded his eyes.

Love Not the World
1 John 2:12-17

12. I write to you, little children, because your sins have been forgiven on account of His name. 13. I write to you, fathers, because you have known the One from the beginning. I write to you, young men, because you have overcome the evil one. I write unto you, little children, because you have known the Father. 14. I wrote to you, fathers, because you have known Him that is from the beginning. I wrote to you, young men, because you are strong, and the word of God remains in you, and you have overcome the evil one. 15. Love not the world, nor the things in the world. If anyone loves the world, the love of the Father is not in him. 16. For all that is in the world, the forbidden desires of the flesh, and the forbidden desires of the eyes, and the vainglory of life, is not of the Father, but is of the world. 17. And the world is passing away, and the forbidden desires of it: but the one doing the will of God remains unto the age of eternity.

It is the Last Days
1 John 2:18-29

18. Young children, it is the last days, and now many antichrists have risen, even as you heard that an Antichrist was to come. That is how we know that it is the time of the last days. 19. They have gone out from among us but they are not of our number. Had they belonged to us they would have remained with us. 20. But you have an anointing from the Holy One, and you possess knowledge. 21. I wrote to you because you know the truth, and that no lie comes from the truth. 22. He who denies that Jesus is the Christ is a liar. He is an opponent of

the Messiah, denying the Father and the Son. 23. To disown the Son is to have no claim to the Father; it is by acknowledging the Son that we lay claim to the Father also. 24. Let what you heard from the beginning abide in you. If that first message stands firmly in you, you will also stand firm in the Son, and in the Father. 25. And He has promised us eternal life. 26. I wrote these things about those attempting to persuade you to stray from the truth. 27. Since the anointing you received from Him remains in you, there is no need for any man to instruct you; but since His anointing continues to teach you the truth without lies, follow those lessons, and dwell in Him. 28. And now, little children, be settled in Him; that when He appears, you will stand before Him confident and not be ashamed. 29. Since you know that He is righteous, you also know that everyone that lives morally upright is born of Him.

We Shall Resemble Him
1 John 3:1-3

1. See what kind of love the Father has given us, that we should be counted as His children: since the world did not recognize Him, they will not acknowledge us as God's children. 2. Beloved we are now the children of God, and it is not apparent now what we shall be: but we know when He appears and we observe Him at a distance, we shall resemble Him. 3. And everyone that holds this anticipation purges himself of all uncleanness, because God is virtuous.

Let No Man Deceive You
1 John 3:4-10

4. Everyone burdened with sin accumulates transgressions against the law: for wrongdoing is an offense against the commandments. 5. And you know that when God revealed Himself it was to take away our sins; and He was sinless. 6. Everyone who maintains a relationship with God does not miss the mark: everyone who misses the mark does not share in the prize nor do they speak positively of Him. 7. Little children, do not let anyone mislead you; the one who does right is the one connected with God. 8. He who lives sinfully takes his character from the devil; the devil was a reprobate from the first. The Son of God was revealed, that He might wipe out the deeds of the devil. 9. Whoever is a child of God cannot abide in or agree with sinning, because a divine life principle is planted in him, and he cannot live long offending God, because he is delivered by God. 10. This is how the children of God and the children of the devil are known apart: everyone who lives an unrighteous life and does not love his brother is not of God.

This is the Message
1 John 3:11-24

11. Because this is the message you heard from the first, that we should love one another. 12. Not of the wicked one, as Cain, who slew his brother. Why did he kill him? Because his own life was evil, and his brother's life was righteous. 13. Do not be surprised, my fellow believers, if the world hate you. 14. We know that we have moved out of death into life, because we love the congregation. The ones not loving remain in death. 15. Anyone who hates his brother is an assassin: and you know that no murder is abiding in eternal life. 16. God manifested His love to us by laying down His life for our sakes; we too must be ready to lay down our lives for the sake of the other believers. 17. But whoso has more worldly goods than he needs, and sees his brother in need, and closes up his heart to compassion, how does the love of God reside in him? 18. My little children do not let love be in word or unnatural language: but in a true test of action. 19. By this we shall know that we are of the truth, and shall reassure our consciences before Him. 20. But if our conscience condemn us it is because God is greater than our heart, and knows all things. 21. Beloved, if our heart does not condemn us, we can approach God with confidence. 22. Since we keep His commandments and live a life pleasing in His sight, He will grant our requests. 23. And this is His commandment that we should believe the authority of His Son Jesus Christ and love one another as He commanded us. 24. And the ones keeping His commandments remain in God. This is proof that He is dwelling in us, through the gift of His Spirit.

Test the Spirits
1 John 4:1-6

1. Beloved, not every prophetic spirit has credibility, test the spirits to see if they come from God: because many false prophets have gone forth into the world. 2. This is the test: every spirit that confesses that Jesus Christ came in the flesh is of God: 3. And every spirit which confesses not that Jesus is of God; is the spirit of the Antichrist, which you heard was coming, and now is already in the world. 4. You are of God, little children, and have overcome the false spirits: because greater is the One in you, than the one in the world. 5. They are of the world: therefore speak they of the world, and the world hears them. 6. We are of God: the ones knowing God hear us; the ones not of God do not hear us. From this we know the Spirit of Truth, and the spirit of error.

Atonement for Sins
1 John 4:7-10
7. Beloved let us love one another: for love springs from God; and everyone loving God, has been begotten and knows God. 8. The ones not loving knew not God, because God is love. 9. By this was the love of God manifested, because God sent His only begotten Son into the world in order that we might live through Him. 10. In this is love, not that we have loved God, but that He loved us and sent His Son as atonement for our sins.

Love One Another
1 John 4:11-21
11. Beloved, if God has showed such love to us, we too must love one another. 12. No man has ever seen God. If we love one another, then we have God dwelling in us, and the love of God has reached its full growth in our lives. 13. By this we know that we remain in Him and He in us, because He has given us of the Spirit. 14. And we have beheld and bear witness that the Father has sent the Son as Savior of the world. 15. Whoever confesses that Jesus is the Son of God, God remains in him and he remains in God. 16. And we have known and have believed the love which God has given to us. God is love; and the ones remaining in love remain in God and God in him remains. 17. Herein is our love made complete, that we may have confidence in the Day of Judgment, because as that one is, so are we in the world. 18. Love has no room for fear; and indeed, love drives out fear and when it is flawless love, it drives out the punishment of fear: since the one fearing has not been made complete in love. 19. We love Him, because He gave His love first. 20. If anyone says, I love God and hate his brother, he is a liar: for the one not loving the brother whom he has seen, how can he love God whom he has not seen? 21. And this is the divine commandment: anyone who loves God must also love his brother.

Faith Born of God Conquers
1 John 5:1-8
1. Everyone who believes that Jesus is the Christ has experienced the birth which comes from God; and everyone that loves the Father also loves the child. 2. This is how we know for sure we love the children of God, when we love God, and keep His commandments. 3. For loving God is to keep His commandments: which commandments do not cause severe suffering. 4. For faith born of God conquers the world. 5. And who is the one overcoming the world, except the one believing that Jesus is the Son of God? 6. This is the One coming through water and blood, Jesus Christ; not by the water only, but by the water and

by the blood. And the Spirit is the One bearing witness, because the Spirit is the Truth. 7. Because the Ones bearing witness are three, 8. the Spirit and the water and the blood, and the three are in the One.

That You May Know
1 John 5:9-15

9. If we receive the witness of men, the witness of God is greater: because this is the witness of God who has testified of His Son. 10. The one believing in the Son of God has the witness in himself. The one not believing has made God a liar, because he has not believed in the record that God gave of His Son. 11. And this is the true witness that God has given us eternal life and this life is in His Son. 12. He who has the Son has life; he who has not the Son has not life. 13. I wrote these things to you that believe on the name of the Son of God; that you may know that you have eternal life, and that you may go on believing in the authority of the Son of God. 14. And this is the freedom that we have to approach God that He listens when we ask anything according to His will. 15. And if we know He listens to us, whatsoever we ask, we know we have the requests made to Him.

All Wickedness is Sinful
1 John 5:16-21

16. If anyone sees his brother sin that is not a deadly sin, he should pray for him, and at his request, grant life to the brother who has not committed a deadly sin. There is a sin unto death: I do not ask that you pray for it. 17. All wickedness is sinful: and there is a sin not fatal. 18. The one born of God keeps clear of sin; because his divine origin protects him, and the evil one cannot lay a hand on him. 19. And even though the whole world lies in the power of evil, we can be sure that we are of God. 20. And we know that the Son of God is come, and has given us an understanding that we might know the True One; and we are in the True One, in His Son Jesus Christ. This is the true God and life eternal. 21. Little children keep on guard against giving value and worth to a heathen god. Amen.

THE REVELATION OF JOHN

John wrote his revelation to assist congregations undergoing persecution and difficult situations and to remind them that good would triumph over evil when Christ sets up His earthly kingdom. There are many perspectives on this unveiling of Jesus Christ. Of the many views, one is the symbolic view that Revelation portrays the continuing conflict between the forces of good and evil throughout the span of human history. With this view, the book was designed to give encouragement that good will triumph in the end. However, most likely the futuristic view is best and maintains that from chapter four to the end, Revelation deals with end-time events. Those who hold this perspective outline the work based on (1:19). Chapter one deals with the past; chapters two and three discuss things that were present at the time and throughout the church age; chapters four through twenty-two deal with things that are yet to come, including the Day of the Lord and the Second Coming of Christ (4:1). The key to understanding the book is based on three ways to be blessed from the words of this prophecy: read, hear, and keep (1:3). A close reading of the Revelation could greatly improve the "blessing of reading," bring vitality to prophetic preaching and understanding of the Last Days, and stimulate a desire for the return of the Lord Jesus Christ. When a desire for Christ's return is enhanced, the quality of Christian living is improved. (See Titus 2:13; 1 John 3:1-3)

Read, Hear, and Keeping
Revelation 1:1-6

1. This is the Revelation of Jesus Christ, which God unveiled and signified by His messenger to His Slave John: to uncover to His bondservants things that must shortly come to pass; 2. who exposed the record of the word of God, and of the testimony of Jesus Christ, and of all things that he saw. 3. Blessed is he who reads, and they who listen to the words of this message for the future, and is keeping those things written: for the time is at hand. 4. John to the seven assemblies which are in Asia: Grace be to you, and peace, from Him who is, and who was, and who is to come; and from the seven Spirits that are before His throne; 5. and from Jesus Christ, who is the Faithful Witness, and the First-Born of the dead, and the Prince of the Kings of the earth. To Him who loved us, and loosed us from our sins in His own blood, 6. and has made us a kingdom and priests unto God and His Father; to Him be glory and power unto the ages of the ages. Amen.

The Alpha and Omega
Revelation 1:7-20

7. Behold, He comes with clouds about Him; and every eye will see Him, and they also who wounded Him: and all tribes of the earth shall morn and weep because of Him. So it is to be, Amen. 8. I am Alpha

and Omega (the A and the Z), the beginning and the ending, says the Lord, the God who is, and who was, and who is to come, the Almighty. 9. I John, your brother and partner in persecution, and in the royal dignity and the steadfast endurance of Jesus Christ, was placed on the Isle called Patmos, because of the word of God, and for the testimony of Jesus Christ. 10. I was in the Spirit on the Lord's Day, and heard behind me a great voice, as of a war trumpet, 11. saying, What you see, write in a book, and send it to the assemblies in Asia; Ephesus, Smyrna, Pergamos, Thyatira, Sardis, Philadelphia, and Laodicea. 12. And I turned to see the voice that spoke to me. And as I turned, I saw seven golden lampstands; 13. and in the midst of the seven lampstands one similar to the Son of Man, clothed in a long garment, and a golden girdle about His breasts. 14. His head and hairs were as wool, as white as snow; and His eyes were as a flame of fire; 15. and His feet similar to burnished brass, as if refined in a furnace; and His voice as the sound of many waters. 16. And in His right hand were seven stars: and out of His mouth went a sharp two-edged sword: and His countenance was as the sun shining in its strength. 17. And when I saw Him, I fell at His feet as dead. And He laid His right hand upon me, saying, Fear not; I am the first and the last: 18. I am He who lives, and was dead; and, behold, I am alive for evermore, Amen; and have the keys of hell and death. 19. Write the things you have seen, and the things which are, and what must happen hereafter; 20. the mystery of the seven stars that you saw in my right hand, and the seven golden lampstands. The seven stars are the messengers of the seven assemblies: and the seven lampstands that you saw are the seven assemblies.

I Have Something Against You
Revelation 2:1-7

1. Unto the messenger of the assembly of Ephesus write; these things said He who holds the seven stars in His right hand, who walks in the midst of the seven golden lampstands; 2. I know your works, and your weariness, and your steadfast endurance, and how you cannot tolerate evil-doers: and you have tested those who say they are apostles, and are not, and found them false: 3. and have steadfastness, and have carried a heavy load for My name's sake have labored and not despaired 4. Nevertheless, I have "something" against you, because you have left your first love. 5. Remember therefore from where you have fallen and repent, and live as you did at first; or else I will come quickly, and remove your lampstand from its place, except you repent. 6. But this is in your favor, that you hate the deeds of the Nicolaitans,* which I also hate. 7. He who has an ear let him listen to what the Spirit

says to the assemblies; to him who overcomes will I give to eat out of the tree of life, which is in the Paradise of God.

---

*v6 The Nicolaitans taught that to master sensuality, one had to experience the whole range of immorality. These heretics were hated and expelled by the assembly in Ephesus, but tolerated by Pergamum.

I Will Give You a Crown of Life
Revelation 2:8-11

8. And to the messenger of the assembly in Smyrna write; these things said the first and the last, which was dead, and is alive; 9. I know the affliction and poverty you endure, (but you are rich) and I know the slandering and abuse from those who say they are Jews, and are not, but are the assembly of Satan. 10. Fear nothing that you may suffer: soon, the devil will throw some of you into prison, that your faith may be tested; and you will have ten days of tribulation: be faithful unto death, and I will give you the crown of life. 11. He who has an ear let him listen to what the Spirit says to the assemblies; he that overcomes shall not experience wrong from the second death.

I Know Where You Live
Revelation 2:12-17

12. And to the messenger of the assembly in Pergamos write; these things said He who has a sharp two-edged sword; 13. I know where you live, a place where Satan sits enthroned: and you hold fast My name, and have not denied My faith, even in the days when Antipas was My faithful martyr, who was slain among you, where Satan lives. 14. But I have a few things against you, because you have among you those who hold the teaching of Balaam, who taught Balac to cast a stumbling block before the children of Israel, to eat things sacrificed to idols, and to commit fornication. 15. So hast thou also them that hold the teaching of the Nicolaitans, which thing I hate. 16. Repent or else I will quickly come to you, and make war against such men with the sword of My mouth. 17. He who has an ear, let him listen to what the Spirit says to the assemblies; to him that overcomes I will give to eat of the hidden manna, and will give him a white stone, and on the stone a new name written, that no man knows saving he who receives it.

You Tolerate the Woman, Jezebel
Revelation 2:18-29

18. And to the messenger of the assembly in Thyatira write; these things said the Son of God, who has eyes like flaming fire, and feet like burnished brass; 19. I know your works, your love, ministry, faith, and enduring steadfastness; and how in these last days you

are more active than at first. 20. Notwithstanding, I have a few things against you, because you tolerate the woman, Jezebel, who calls herself a prophetess, to teach and to seduce My bondservants to sexual immorality, and eating things sacrificed to idols. 21. And I gave her time to repent of her fornication; and she would not repent her immorality. 22. Watch, I have a bed of punishment ready for her, and great suffering for those who committed adultery with her, unless they repent of their wickedness. 23. Also I will permit her children* to be put to death; and all the assemblies will know that I am one who probes the innermost of their hearts: and I will also give each one of you according to your works. 24. But to you I say, and to the rest in Thyatira, as many as do not accept this teaching, and who have not known, the so called, depths of Satan; I will place no fresh burden on you. 25. But hold on to what you already have until I come. 26. And he who overcomes, and keeps until completion my works, to him will I give authority over the nations: 27. and he shall rule them with a rod of iron; as the vessels of a potter they will be broken together: even as I received of My Father. 28. And I will give him the bright star of the morning. 29. He who has an ear let him listen to what the Spirit says to the assemblies.

---

*v23 The children were not participators, but were associated with the evil. This speaks to those who cause their children to stumble or enticed them to sin by their example.

Wake Up and Watch
Revelation 3:1-6

1. And to the messenger of the assembly in Sardis write; these things said He who has the seven Spirits of God, and the seven stars; I know your reputation that you are alive, but are dead. 2. Wake up and watch and strengthen the things that remain, that are ready to die: for I have not found your works fulfilled before God. 3. Remember what you heard and what you received as a permanent deposit, and hold fast, and repent. If therefore you will not wake up, I will come as a thief, and you will not know what hour I will come. 4. But you have a few people in Sardis who have not sullied the purity of their lives: and they will walk with Me in white: for they are worthy. 5. He who overcomes, the same will be clothed in white raiment; and I will never blot his name out of the book of the life, but I will openly confess his name before My Father, and before His angels. 6. He who has an ear let him listen to what the Spirit says to the assemblies.

My Lesson of Endurance
Revelation 3:7-13

7. And to the messenger of the assembly in Philadelphia write; these things said He who is holy and genuine, He has the key of David, no man can shut when He opens; or open when He shuts; 8. I know your works: watch, I have set an open door before you, and no man can shut it: for you have a little strength, and have kept My word, and have not renounced My name. 9. Watch, I will make them of the assembly of Satan, who say they are the People of God, and are not, but do lie; watch, I will make them to come and bow down at your feet, and to learn that I loved you. 10. Because you did keep true to My lesson of endurance, I also will keep you safe in the hour of testing that will come upon all the world, to test those who dwell upon the earth. 11. I come quickly: hold fast to what you have, that no man may take your crown. 12. I will make him who overcomes a pillar in the temple of My God, and he shall never leave it again: and I will write upon him the name of My God, and the name of the city of My God, that is new Jerusalem, that comes down out of heaven from My God: and I will write upon him My new name. 13. He who has an ear let him listen to what the Spirit says to the assemblies.

I Am About to Spit You Out
Revelation 3:14-19

14. And to the messenger of the assembly of the Laodiceans write; these things said the Amen, the faithful and unerring witness, the source of the creation of God; 15. I know your works, that you are neither cold nor hot: I would you were cold or hot. 16. So then because you are lukewarm, and neither cold nor hot, I am about to spit you out of My mouth. 17. Because you say, I am rich, and increased with goods, and have need of nothing; yet you are unaware that you are desolate, deprived, broke, sightless, and exposed: 18. My counsel for you is to obtain from Me gold tried in the fire, that you may become rich; and white garments, that you may be clothed, and cover the shame of your nakedness; and salve to anoint your eyes so you may see. 19. As many as I love, I correct and chasten: be zealous therefore, and repent.

I Am standing at the Door
Revelation 3:20-22

20. Behold, I am standing at the door, and continue knocking: if any man listens to My voice, and opens the door, I will come in to him, and will feast with him, and he with Me. 21. To him who overcomes will I grant to sit beside Me in My throne, even as I also overcame, and am

set down beside My Father on His throne. 22. He who has an ear let him listen to what the Spirit says to the assemblies.

A Door Opened in Heaven
Revelation 4:1-5

1. Then I saw a vision, behold, a door opened in heaven: and the same voice I heard as a war trumpet talking with me; saying, Come up here, and I will show you things that will come after this. 2. Immediately, I found myself under the power of the Spirit: and saw a throne positioned in heaven, and One sitting on the throne. 3. And He who sat appeared as a multi-colored stone: and there was a rainbow around the throne shining as an emerald. 4. And around the throne were four and twenty seats: and upon the seats I saw four and twenty elders, clothed in white raiment; and they had on their heads crowns of gold. 5. And out of the throne came lightning and thundering and voices: and there were seven lamps of fire burning before the throne, these are the seven Spirits of God.

You are Worthy, Lord
Revelation 4:6-11

6. And before the throne there appeared a crystal-like glassy sea: and in the center of a circle around the throne, were four living creatures with eyes before and behind. 7. And the first creature was of a lion, and the second creature was of a calf, and the third creature had the face of a man, and the fourth creature was like a flying eagle. 8. And the four creatures each had six wings; and were full of eyes: and they had no rest day and night, saying, Holy, Holy, Holy, Lord, God Almighty, who was, and is, and is to come. 9. And when those creatures gave glory and honor and thanks to Him who sat on the throne, who lives forever and ever, 10. the four and twenty elders fall down before Him who sat on the throne, and worship Him who lives forever and ever, and cast their crowns before the throne, saying, 11. You are worthy, Lord, to receive glory and honor and power: for you have created all things, and nothing was ever created, but in obedience to your will.

The Lion of the Tribe of Judah
Revelation 5:1-7

1. And I saw in the right hand of Him who sat on the throne, a scroll written on the front and the back, sealed with seven seals. 2. And I saw a strong messenger proclaiming with a great voice, Who is worthy to open the book, and to break its seals? 3. And no man in heaven, nor anyone living or dead in the earth, was able to open the scroll, neither to take a single look. 4. And I was weeping, because no man was found worthy to open and to read the scroll, neither take a single look. 5. And one of the elders said, Stop weeping: watch, the Lion of

the tribe of Judah, the Root of David, has prevailed to open the book, and to break its seven seals. 6. And I saw in the midst of the throne and the four beasts, and the elders, a Lamb standing with marks of being slain, having seven horns and seven eyes, which are the seven Spirits of God dispatched to all the earth. 7. And He came and took the scroll out of the right hand of Him who sat upon the throne.

They Sang a New Song
Revelation 5:8-10
8. And when He took the scroll, the four beasts and four and twenty elders fell down before the Lamb, each one having a harp, and golden bowls full of incense, which are the prayers of saints. 9. And they sang a new song, saying, You are worthy to take the scroll, and to open the seals: for you were slain, and have redeemed us to God by your blood out of every tribe, tongue, people, and race; 10. and made them a kingdom of priests to our God: and they will reign on the earth.

Worthy is the Lamb
Revelation 5:11-14
11. Then in my vision, I heard the voice of many angels around the throne and the living creatures and the elders: and the number was ten thousand times ten thousand and thousands of thousands; 12. saying with a great voice, Worthy is the Lamb who was slain to receive the power, and the riches of God, wisdom and strength, honor and glory, and praise. 13. And every created creature that is in heaven, and on the earth, living and dead, I heard crying, Praise and honor, and glory and dominion, be to Him who sits on the throne and to the Lamb for the ages of ages. 14. And the four living creatures said, Amen. And the four and twenty elders fell down and worshipped Him who lives for ages of ages.

The Voice of Thunder
Revelation 6:1-17
1. And I saw when the Lamb opened one of the seven seals, and I heard, as the voice of thunder, one of the four living creatures saying, Come. 2. And I saw, and behold a white horse: and the rider had a bow; and a crown was given to him: and he went forth conquering, and to conquer. 3. And when he opened the second seal, I heard the second living creature say, Come. 4. And there went out another horse that was flame-colored: and power was given to the rider to take peace from the earth that men would kill one another: and he was given a great sword. 5. And when he had opened the third seal, I heard the third living creature say, Come. And I saw a black horse; and the rider had a balance in his hand. 6. And I heard a voice coming from the fourth living creature say, A silver piece for a measure of

wheat, and three measures of barley for a silver piece; and do not damage the oil and the wine. 7. And when he had opened the fourth seal, I heard the voice of the fourth living creature say, Come. 8. And I looked, and behold a pale horse: and the rider was named Death, and Hell followed with him. And power was given to them over the fourth part of the earth, to kill with sword, and famine, and with pestilence and by the wild beasts of the earth. 9. And when he had opened the fifth seal, I saw under the altar of sacrifice and blood of them that were slain for the word of God, and for the testimony which they held fast: 10. And they cried with a loud voice, saying, How long, Lord, Holy and True, will you refrain from judging and avenging our blood on those who dwell on the earth? 11. And white robes were given to each one of them; and they were asked to wait patiently a little time, until their fellow bondservants and their brethren, that should be killed as they were, should be completed. 12. And I beheld when he had opened the sixth seal, there was a great earthquake; and the sun became dark as coarse black cloth, and the full moon was red as blood; 13. and the stars of heaven fell to the earth, even as unripe figs fell untimely from fig tree, when shaken by a mighty wind. 14. And the heaven departed as a scroll when it is rolled together; and every mountain and island were removed from its place. 15. And the kings of the ungodly earth, with their noblemen and their captains, and the rich ones, and the chief captains, and the mighty men, and every slave, and every free man, hid themselves in the caves and in the rocks of the hills; 16. and said to the mountains and rocks, Fall on us, and hide us from the face of Him who sits on the throne, and from the wrath of the Lamb: 17. For the great day of His wrath is come; and who will be able to survive.

God Will Wipe Away All Tears
Revelation 7:1-17

1. And after these things I saw four angels standing at the four quarters of the earth, holding firmly the four winds of the earth, so the wind should not blow on the earth, nor on the sea, nor against any tree. 2. And I saw another angel ascending from the sunrise, with a seal belonging to the living God: and he cried with a loud voice to the four angels, who were empowered to hurt the earth and the sea, 3. saying, Hurt not the earth, neither the sea, nor the trees, until we have sealed the bondservants of God in their foreheads. 4. And I heard the number of those who were sealed: and there were sealed an hundred and forty and four thousand of all the tribes of the children of Israel. 5. Of the tribe of Judah were sealed twelve thousand. Of the tribe of Reuben, twelve thousand. Of the tribe of Gad, twelve thousand. 6. Of the tribe of Aser, twelve thousand. Of the tribe of Nepthalim, twelve thousand. Of the tribe of Manasses, twelve thousand. 7. Of the tribe

of Simeon, twelve thousand. Of the tribe of Levi, twelve thousand. Of the tribe of Issachar, twelve thousand. 8. Of the tribe of Zebulun, twelve thousand. Of the tribe of Joseph, twelve thousand. Of the tribe of Benjamin, twelve thousand. 9. After this I saw, a great crowd, which no man could number, of all race, and all tribes, and people, and tongues, standing before the throne, and before the Lamb, clothed in white robes, and palms in their hands; 10. And shouted with a great voice, saying, Salvation to our God which sits on the throne, and to the Lamb. 11. And all the angels stood round about the throne, and about the elders and the four living creatures, and fell before the throne on their faces, and worshipped God, 12. saying, Amen: Blessing, and glory, and wisdom, and thanksgiving, and honor, and dominion, and strength, be to our God for ages of ages. Amen. 13. And one of the elders answered, saying to me, What are these arrayed in white robes? From where did they come? 14. And I said to him, Sir, you know. And he said to me, These are they who came out of great tribulation, and have washed their robes, and made them white in the blood of the Lamb. 15. Therefore are they before the throne of God, and serve Him day and night in His temple: and He who sits on the throne will dwell among them. 16. They will hunger no more, neither thirst anymore; neither will the sun heat them. 17. For the Lamb who is in the midst of the throne shall shepherd and lead them to living fountains of waters: and God will wipe away all tears from their eyes.

Silence in Heaven
Revelation 8:1-5
1. And when he opened the seventh seal, there followed silence in heaven about half an hour. 2. And I saw the seven angels who stand before God; and seven trumpets were given to them. 3. Another angel came and stood at the altar, having a golden censer; and there was given to him much incense, that he should add it to the prayers of all saints on the golden altar that was before the throne. 4. And the smoke of the incense that came with the prayers of the saints, ascended up before God out of the angel's hand. 5. And the angel took the censer, and filled it with fire of the altar, and threw it upon the earth: and there were sounds of thundering, and flashes of lightning, and an earthquake.

Trumpets Prepared to Sound
Revelation 8:6-13
6. And the seven angels that had the seven trumpets prepared to sound them. 7. The first sounded, and there followed hail and fire mingled in blood, and they were cast upon the earth: and the third part of the earth was burned, and all pale grass was burned. 8. And

the second angel sounded his trumpet, and what appeared to be a large burning mountain was thrown into the sea: and the third part of the sea became blood; 9. and the third part of the living creatures in the sea, died; and the third of the ships were destroyed. 10. And the third angel sounded his trumpet, and there fell a great meteor, blazing as a torch from heaven, and it fell on the third part of the rivers, and on the springs of waters; 11. and the name of the meteor is called Wormwood: and the third part of the waters became bitter-tasting; and many died because of the bitter waters. 12. And the fourth angel sounded his trumpet, and the third part of the sun was affected, and the third part of the moon, and the third part of the stars; that the third part of them were darkened, and the third part of the day and night were darkened. 13. And I saw and heard one eagle flying through the circle of heaven, saying with a great voice, Woe, woe, woe, to the population of the earth because of the remaining three trumpets of the three angels, that are about to sound!

Key to the Bottomless Abyss
Revelation 9:1-12

1. And the fifth angel sounded, and I saw a star falling from heaven to the earth: and to the angel was given the key of the bottomless abyss. 2. And he opened the bottomless abyss; and there arose a smoke out of the abyss, as the smoke of a great furnace; and the sun and the air were darkened because of the smoke of the abyss. 3. And there came out of the smoke grasshoppers swarming on the earth: and they were given the power of scorpions on the earth. 4. And they were ordered not harm the grass of the earth, neither any green thing, neither any tree; but only those men who did not have the seal of God on their forehead. 5. They were not permitted to kill, but to torment them for five months: with the sting of a scorpion. 6. And in those days the men will seek death, and not find it; and will earnestly seek to die, and death will flee from them. 7. And in likeness the swarming grasshoppers appeared as horses prepared for battle; and on their heads were crowns like golden horns, with the human faces of men. 8. And they had hair of women, and their teeth were as the teeth of lions. 9. And their breastplates, resembled the plates of horse armor; and the sound of their wings was as the sound of many-horsed chariots running to battle. 10. And they had tails with sharp-pointed scorpion tails: and the power to torment men five months. 11. And they had a sovereign over them, who is the angel of the bottomless abyss, whose name in the Hebrew tongue is Destruction, but in the Greek tongue hath his name Destroyer. 12. One woe has past; and, watch, there are two woes to come.

Neither Did They Repent
Revelation 9:13-21

13. And the sixth angel sounded his trumpet, and I heard a voice from the four horns of the golden altar that is before God, 14. saying to the sixth angel who had the trumpet, Loose the four angels who are bound at the great river Euphrates. 15. And the four angels were loosed, who were prepared for the hour appointed by God, to kill the third part of men. 16. And I heard the number of troops of their cavalry to be twenty- thousands times ten-thousands. 17. And I saw the horses and the riders in the vision, as having breastplates of fiery red, dull blue and sulfurous yellow: and the heads of the horses were like the heads of lions; and out of their mouths issued fire, smoke and brimstone. 18. With the plagues of fire, smoke, and brimstone that issued from their mouths, a third part of men were killed. 19. For their power is in their mouth, and in their tails: for their tails and heads were similar to serpents, and with them they do torment. 20. And the rest of the men who were not killed by these plagues yet repented not of the works of their hands, that they should not worship devils, and idols of gold, silver, brass, stone, and wood: which neither can see, nor hear, nor walk: 21. neither did they repent of their murders, nor of their sorceries, nor of their immorality, nor of their thefts.

The Secret Purpose of God
Revelation 10:1-7

1. And I saw another mighty angel come down from heaven, clothed in a cloud: with a rainbow on his head, and his face was as it were the sun, and his feet as pillars of fire: 2. and he had in his hand a little scroll open: and he set his right foot on the sea, and his left foot on the earth, 3. and cried with a loud voice, as the roar of a lion: and when he had cried, seven thunders sounded. 4. And when the seven thunders had sounded, I was about to write: and I heard a voice from heaven saying, Seal up those things that the seven thunders sounded, and do not write them. 5. And the angel that I saw standing on the sea and on the earth lifted up his hand to heaven, 6. and swore by Him that lives for ages and ages, who created heaven, and the things that are therein, and the earth, and the things that are therein, and the sea, and the things that are therein, that there shall be no more waiting: 7. but in the days of the voice of the seventh angel, when he is about to sound, and the secret purpose of God would be completed, as He announced to His bondservants the prophets.

Make a Fresh Prophecy
Revelation 10:8-11

8. And the voice which I heard from heaven spoke again, and said, Go and take the little scroll that is open in the hand of the angel that was standing on the sea and on the earth. 9. And I went to the angel, and said, Give me the little scroll. And he said to me, Take it, and eat it; it will be sweet as honey to your mouth, but bitter to your stomach. 10. And I took the little scroll out of the angel's hand, and ate it; and it was sweet as honey in my mouth: and as soon as I had eaten, it was bitter to my stomach. 11. And he said, You are to make a fresh prophesy, that concerns many peoples, and races, and languages, and many kings.

Prophecy of the Two Witnesses
Revelation 11:1-14

1. And there was given me a measuring staff: and the angel stood, saying, Rise, and measure the Temple of God, and the altar, and those who worship there. 2. But the court outside the temple do not measure; for it was given to the Gentiles: and they will trample on the Holy City for forty and two months (1260 days). 3. And I will give power to My two witnesses, and clothed in sackcloth, they will prophesy a thousand two hundred and sixty (1260) days. 4. These are the two olive trees, and the two lampstands standing before the Lord of all the earth. 5. And if anyone desires to hurt them, fire proceeds out of their mouth and devours their enemies: and whoever tries to hurt them, they must be killed in this manner. 6. These have power to shut up the heaven so the rain will not wet the earth in the days of their prophecy: and have power over waters to turn them to blood, and to smite the earth with all plagues, as often as they will.

The Beast of the Bottomless Abyss
Revelation 11:7-14

7. And when the two witnesses have finished their testimony, the beast that ascended out of the abyss will make war against them, and overcome them, and kill them. 8. And their carcass will lie upon the street of the great city, allegorically called Sodom and Egypt, where also their Lord was crucified. 9. And they of the people and tribes and languages and races will see their dead bodies three and a half days, and will not permit their bodies to be buried. 10. And they that dwell on the earth will rejoice over them, and make merry, and send gifts one to another; because these two prophets tormented them. 11. And after three and a half days the Spirit of life from God entered into them, and they stood upon their feet; and great fear fell on those who saw them. 12. And they heard a great voice from heaven saying, Come up hither.

And they ascended up to heaven in a cloud; and their enemies beheld them. 13. And at that hour there was a great earthquake, and the tenth part of the city fell, and in the earthquake were slain seven thousand men: and the rest were terrified, and acknowledged the glory to the God of heaven. 14. The second woe is past; and, behold, the third woe comes quickly.

Temple of God Opened in Heaven
Revelation 11:15-19

15. And the seventh angel sounded his trumpet; and there were great voices in heaven, saying, The kingdoms of this world have become the kingdoms of our Lord, and of His Christ; and He will reign for ages and ages. 16. And the four and twenty elders, who sat before God on their seats, fell upon their faces, and worshipped God, 17. saying, We give you thanks, Lord God, the Almighty, who was and are; because you have taken your great power, and have become King. 18. And the nations were angered, and your anger came, and the time of the dead was vindicated, that you should give reward to your bondservants the prophets, and to the saints, and those, small and great, who fear your name; and should destroy those who corrupt the earth. 19. And the Temple of God was opened in heaven, and there was seen in His temple the Ark of His Covenant: and there was lightning, and voices, and thundering, and an earthquake, and great storm of hail.

A Man Child
Revelation 12:1-6

1. And there appeared a great sign in heaven; a woman arrayed with the sun, and the moon under her feet,* and on her head a crown of twelve stars: 2. And she was in sorrows being with child, travailing in birth, and tormented in delivered. 3. And there appeared another sign in heaven; and behold a great flame-colored dragon, having seven heads and ten horns, and seven crowns on his heads. 4. And his tail swept the third part of the stars of heaven, and did cast them to the earth: and the dragon stood in front of the woman that was ready to give birth to devour her child as soon as it was born. 5. And she brought forth a man child, who was to rule all nations with a rod of iron: and her child was snatched away to God, and to His throne. 6. And the woman fled to the desert, where she had a place prepared by God, so they could care for her for a thousand two hundred and sixty (1260) days.

---

*v1 Some suggest that this woman is a symbol representing the church.

War Against the Dragon
Revelation 12:7-17

7. And there arose war in heaven: Michael and his angels going to war against the dragon; and the dragon and his angels fought them, 8. and prevailed not; neither was their place found any more in heaven. 9. And the dragon, the great old serpent, called the Devil and Satan, who deceived the whole world, was cast out into the earth, and his angels were cast out with him. 10. And I heard a great voice saying in heaven, Now comes to pass the salvation, and the power, and the kingdom of our God, and the authority of His Christ: because the accuser of our brethren is cast down, who accused them before God day and night. 11. They have overcome him by the blood of the Lamb, and by the word of their witness; and they loved not their lives to the death. 12. Rejoice, therefore, you heavens, and you that dwell in them. Woe to the inhabitants of the earth and of the sea! Because the devil came down to you, having great anger, because he knows that he has but a short time. 13. When the devil saw that he was cast to the earth, he persecuted the woman who brought forth the man-child. 14. The two wings of a great eagle were given to the woman so she could fly to the desert, to her place, where she is nourished for three and a half years (1260 days), from the face of the serpent. 15. And the serpent cast out of his mouth water as a river after the woman that he might cause her to be carried away by the flood. 16. And the earth helped the woman and opened and swallowed up the flood that the dragon cast out of his mouth. 17. And the dragon was enraged with the woman, and went to make war with the rest of her family, who keeps the commandments of God, and have the witness of Jesus.

Faith of the Saints
Revelation 13:1-10

1. And I stood upon the sand of the sea*, and I saw a living creature coming up out of the sea, having seven heads and ten horns, and upon his horns ten royal crowns, and on his heads I saw blasphemous names. 2. And the living creature that I saw was similar to a leopard, with the feet of a bear, and the mouth of a lion: and the dragon delegated him his power, and his throne, and great authority. 3. And I saw one of his heads as it were wounded to death; and his deadly wound was healed: and all the world wondered after the creature. 4. And they worshipped the dragon because he gave power to the creature: and they worshipped the beast, saying, Who is like unto this creature? Who is able to make war with him? 5. And there was given to him a mouth speaking great things and blasphemies; and power was given to him to continue forty-two months. 6. And he opened his mouth for blasphemy against God, to blaspheme His name, and His tabernacle,

and those who dwell in heaven. 7. And it was given to him to make war against the saints, and to overcome them: and power was given him over all tribes, and languages, and races. 8. And all that dwell on the earth shall worship him, whose names are not written in the Book of Life of the Lamb slain from the foundation of the world. 9. If any man has an ear, let him listen. 10. He who brings together captives will go into captivity: he who kills with the sword must be killed with the sword. Here is the steadfast endurance and the faith of the saints.

---

*v1 The best manuscripts place this phrase at the end of the previous chapter.

The Beast on the Earth
Revelation 13:11-18

11. And I saw another living creature coming up out of the earth; and it had two horns like a lamb, and roared as a dragon. 12. And acts for the first beast before him with the same authority, and causes the earth and the inhabitants to worship the first beast, whose deadly wound was healed. 13. And it performed great signs, so that he makes fire come down from heaven on the earth in the sight of men, 14. it deceives the inhabitants on the earth with power to do miracles in the sight of the beast; saying that they should make an image to the beast that had the wound by a sword, and did live. 15. And it had power to give life to the image of the beast, that the image should both speak, and cause as many as would not worship the image of the beast should be killed. 16. And it caused all, both small and great, rich and poor, free and bond, to receive a mark in their right hand, or in their foreheads: 17. and that no man might buy or sell, without the mark, or the name of the beast, or the number of his name. 18. Here is wisdom. Let him who has understanding count the number of the beast: for it is the number of a man; and his number is six hundred and sixty-six.

Steadfast Endurance of the Saints
Revelation 14:1-12

1. And I looked, and -the Lamb stood on the mount Zion and with Him a hundred forty-four thousand, having His Father's name written in their foreheads. 2. And I heard a voice from heaven, as many waters, and as a great thunder: and I heard harpers playing on their harps: 3. and they sang a new song before the throne, and before the four living creatures, and the elders: and no one could learn that song but the hundred and forty-four thousand, who were purchased from the earth. 4. These are they who were not corrupted by women; for they are virgins. These are they who follow the Lamb wherever He goes. These were purchased from among men, being the first-fruits to God and to the Lamb. 5. And in their mouth was found no falsehood: for they are without blemish before the throne of God. 6. And I saw another angel

fly in the center of heaven, having the eternal gospel to preach to them who dwell on the earth, and to every race, and tribe, and language, and people, 7. saying with a great voice, Fear God, and give glory to Him; because the hour of His judgment is come: and worship Him that made heaven, and earth, and the sea, and the springs of waters. 8. And there followed a second angel, saying, Babylon fell, that great city, because she made all nations drink of the wine of the wrath of her fornication. 9. And the third angel followed them, saying with a great voice, If any one worships the beast and his image, and receive his mark in his forehead, or in his hand, 10. the same shall drink of the wine of the wrath of God that is poured out without mixture into the cup of His indignation; and he shall be tormented with fire and brimstone in the presence of the holy angels, and in the presence of the Lamb: 11. and the smoke of their displeasure ascends up for ages and ages: and they have no rest day or night, who worship the beast and his image, and whoever receives the mark of his name. 12. The steadfast endurance of the saints: here are they who keep the commandments of God, and the faith of Jesus.

Winepress of the Wrath of God
Revelation 14:13-20
13. And I heard a voice from heaven saying, Write, blood-related are the dead who die in the Lord from henceforth: Yea, says the Spirit that they may rest from their labors; and their works do follow them. 14. And I looked, and behold a white cloud, and upon the cloud one sat like unto the Son of Man, having on His head a golden crown, and in His hand a sharp sickle. 15. And another angel came out of the temple, crying with a great voice to Him who sat on the cloud, Thrust in your sickle and reap for the time is come for you to reap; for the harvest of the earth is ripe. 16. And he that sat on the cloud thrust in His sickle on the earth; and the earth was reaped. 17. And another angel came out of the temple that is in heaven, he also having a sharp sickle. 18. And another angel came out from the altar, which had power over fire; and cried with a loud cry to him who had the sharp sickle, saying, Thrust in your sharp sickle, and gather the clusters of the vine of the earth; for her grapes are fully ripe. 19. And the angel thrust in his sickle into the earth, and gathered the vine of the earth, and cast it into the great winepress of the wrath of God. 20. And the winepress was trodden without the city, and blood came out of the winepress, even unto the horse bridles, by the space of two hundred miles.

Seven Last Punishments
Revelation 15:1-8

1. And I saw another sign in heaven, great and marvelous, seven angels having the seven last punishments; for in them is finished the wrath of God. 2. And I saw as it were a sea of glass mingled with fire: and those who were victorious over the beast, and over his image, and over his mark, and over the number of his name, standing beside the sea of glass, having harps of God. 3. And they sang the song of Moses, the bondservant of God, and the song of the Lamb, saying, Great and marvelous are your works, Lord God Almighty, King of the ages; just and true are your ways. 4. Who shall not fear you, Lord, and glorify your name? For you only are holy: for all nations will come and worship before you; for your judgments are made manifest. 5. And after that I looked, and, behold, the temple of the tabernacle of the testimony in heaven was opened: 6. and the seven angels came out of the temple, having the seven punishments, clothed in pure and white linen, and having their breasts girded with golden girdles. 7. And one of the four creatures gave to the seven angels, seven golden vials full of the vengeance of God, who lives for ages and ages. 8. And the temple was filled with smoke from the glory of God, and from His power; and no man was able to enter the temple, until the seven punishments of the seven angels were completed.

Vessels of God's Vengeance
Revelation 16:1-12

1. And I heard a great voice out of the temple saying to the seven angels, Go your ways, and pour out the vessels of the vengeance of God upon the earth. 2. And the first went, and emptied his vessel upon the earth; and there fell a malignant ulcerous sores on the men who had the mark of the beast, and on those who worshipped his image. 3. And the second angel emptied his vessel upon the sea; and it became as the blood of a dead man: and every living thing died in the sea. 4. And the third angel emptied his vessel upon the rivers and springs of waters; and they became blood. 5. And I heard the angel of the waters say, You are righteous, Lord, who was and are and will be, because you are just in your judgments. 6. For they have shed the blood of saints and prophets, and you have given them blood to drink; this is what they deserve. 7. And I heard another out of the altar say, Even so, Lord God Almighty, true and righteous are your judgments. 8. And the fourth angel emptied his vessel upon the sun; and power was given to him to blister men with fire. 9. And men were blistered with great heat, and blasphemed the name of God, who had power over these punishments: and they repented not to give Him glory. 10. And the fifth angel emptied his vessel upon the seat of the beast; and

his kingdom was full of darkness; and they chewed their tongues in anguish, 11. and blasphemed the God of heaven because of their pains and their sores, and repented not of their deeds. 12. And the sixth angel emptied his vessel upon the great river Euphrates; and the water dried up, that the way of the kings of the east might be prepared.

Punishment was Exceedingly Great
Revelation 16:13-21

13. And I saw three unclean spirits as frogs come out of the mouth of the dragon, and out of the mouth of the beast, and out of the mouth of the false prophet. 14. For they are the demonic spirits, working signs, that go forth to the kings of the earth and of the whole world, to gather them to the battle of that great day of God Almighty. 15. Behold, I come as a thief. Blood-related is he who watches and keeps his garments ready so he does not walk naked, and expose his shame to men. 16. And they gathered them together into a place called in the Hebrew language, Armageddon. 17. And the seventh angel emptied his vessel into the air; and there came a great voice out of the temple of heaven, from the throne, saying, It is done. 18. And there were voices, and thunders, and lightning; and there was a great earthquake, such as was not from the beginning of time, so mighty an earthquake, and so great. 19. And the great city was divided into three parts, and the cities of the nations collapsed: and great Babylon was remembered before God, to give unto her the cup of the wine of the fierceness of his vengeance. 20. Every island vanished and the mountains disappeared. 21. And there fell from heaven upon men great hailstones, every stone weighing about one hundred pounds: men blasphemed God because of the pestilence of the hail; for the punishment was exceedingly great.

The Woman and the Scarlet Beast
Revelation 17:1-13

1. And there came one of the seven angels that had the seven vessels, and talked with me, saying, Come here; I will show you the judgment of the great whore who sits on many waters: 2. with whom the kings of the earth have committed fornication, and the inhabitants of the earth have been made drunk with the wine of her immorality. 3. So he carried me away in spiritual rapture to a desert: and I saw a woman riding on a scarlet-colored wild beast, covered with blasphemous names, having seven heads and ten horns. 4. And the woman was arrayed in purple and scarlet color, and decked with gold and precious stones and pearls, having a golden cup in her hand full of abominations and lewdness of her sexual immorality: 5. and on her forehead was a secret meaning name written, Babylon, the Great, the Mother of Harlots and abominations of the earth. 6. And I saw the woman drunken with

the blood of the saints, and with the blood of the martyrs of Jesus: and when I saw her, I was greatly astonished. 7. And the angel said to me, Why did you wonder? I will tell you the symbolic meaning of the woman, and of the beast that carried her, that had the seven heads and ten horns. 8. The animal you saw was, and is not; and will ascend out of the bottomless abyss, and go into perdition: and the inhabitants of the earth will wonder, whose names were not written in the Book of Life from the foundation of the world, when they behold the beast that was, and is not, and yet is. 9. And there is the need for a mind with wisdom. The seven heads are seven hills, on which the woman sits. 10. And there are seven kings: five are fallen, and one is, and the other is not yet come; and when he comes, he must continue a short space. 11. And the beast that was, and is not, even he is the eighth, and is of the seven, and goes into perdition. 12. And the ten horns which you saw are ten kings, who have received no royal authority yet; but will receive authority as kings for one hour in the presence of the beast. 13. These have one mind, and give their power and strength to the beast. 14. These shall make war with the Lamb, and the Lamb will conquer them: for He is Lord of Lords, and King of Kings: and those with Him are called, and chosen, and loyal. 15. And he said to me, The waters that you saw, where the whore is seated, are peoples, and crowds, and races, and languages. 16. And the ten horns that you saw upon the beast, will hate the whore, and will make her desolate and naked, and will devour her flesh, and burn her in the fire. 17. For God has put in their hearts to perform His purpose, and to agree, and give their royal power to the beast, until the words of God are fulfilled. 18. And the woman you saw is that great city that has dominion over the kings of the earth.

Fallen is Babylon
Revelation 18:1-8

1. And after these things I saw another angel come down from heaven, having great authority; and the earth was illuminated by his splendor. 2. And he cried mightily with a mighty voice, saying, Fallen, fallen is the great Babylon, and is become the dwelling-place of demons, and the stronghold of every unclean spirit, and a refuge for every unclean and hateful fowl. 3. Because the nations have drunk of the wine of the wrath of her fornication, and the kings of the earth have committed fornication with her, and the merchants of the earth are grown rich with the wealth of her depravity. 4. And I heard another voice from heaven, saying, Come out of her, my people, lest you be partakers of her sins, and share in her punishments. 5. For her sins have reached to heaven, and God has remembered her immorality. 6. Repay her even as she dealt with you, and double and repay her twice over

according to her works: brew double for her in the cup she brewed for others. 7. How much she has overvalued herself, and lived in luxury, so give her an equal measure of suffering and mourning: for she said in her heart, I sit a queen, and am no widow, and shall see no grief. 8. Therefore will her punishments come in one day, pestilence and grief and famine; and she will be utterly burned with fire: for the Lord God who judges is strong.

Lament over Babylon
Revelation 18:9-20

9. The kings of the earth, who have committed fornication and lived luxurious with her, will grieve and lament for her, when they see the smoke of her burning, 10. standing afar off horrified at her torment, saying, Sadly, the great city Babylon, the mighty city! In a single hour your judgment came. 11. And the merchants of the earth shall weep and mourn over her; for no man buys their merchandise anymore: 12. the merchandise of gold, silver, precious stones, pearls, fine linen, purple, silk, scarlet, and all citrus woods, all manner vessels of ivory, all manner vessels of precious wood, brass, iron, and marble, 13. and cinnamon, incense, ointments, frankincense, wine, oil, fine flour, wheat, large animals, sheep, horses, chariots, slaves, and human souls. 14. The fruit your soul desires are no longer within reach, and all things which were seasoned with fat and extravagant are departed, and you will find them no more. 15. The merchants of these things, who were made rich by her, shall stand at a distance for the fear of her torment, weeping and wailing, 16. and saying, Sadly, that great city, that was clothed in fine linen, purple, scarlet, and decked with gold, precious stones, and pearls! 17. In one hour so great riches came to naught. And every ship's captain and all the passengers in ships, and sailors, who make a living from the sea, stood at a distance, 18. and cried, when they saw the smoke of her burning. They said, What city is like unto this great city? 19. And they cast dust on their heads, and cried, weeping and wailing, saying, Sadly, for the great city, wherein all that had ships in the sea by reason of her extravagance! For in one hour she is made desolate. 20. Rejoice over her, heaven, and you holy apostles and prophets; for God has exacted vengeance for you on her.

Babylon Cast Down with Vengeance
Revelation 18:21-24

21. And a mighty angel took up a stone similar to a great millstone, and cast it into the sea, saying, With a rush will that great city Babylon be thrown down, and will never again be found. 22. And the sound of harps, minstrels, flute-players, and trumpeters, will never again be

heard; and no craftsman, whatever craft, will never again be found; and the sound of a millstone shall never again be heard; 23. and the light of a lamp will never again shine; and the voice of the bridegroom and of the bride will not again be heard: for your merchants were the great men of the earth; for by your witchcraft were all nations deceived. 24. And in her was found the blood of prophets, and saints, and of all who were slain upon the earth.

Judgment of the Great Whore
Revelation 19:1-10

1. And after these things I heard a great voice of many people in heaven, saying, Praise the Lord; Salvation, and glory, and honor, and power, belong to our God: 2. for true and righteous are His judgments: for He has given sentence against the great whore, that did corrupt the earth with her sexual immorality, and has avenged the blood of His bondservants at her hand. 3. And again they said, Praise the Lord. And her smoke rose up forever and ever. 4. And the four and twenty elders and the four creatures fell down and worshipped God that sat on the throne, saying, Amen; Praise the Lord. 5. And a voice came out of the throne, saying, Praise our God, all of His bondservants, and you who fear Him, both small and great. 6. And I heard as it were the voice of a great crowd, and as the voice of many waters, and as the voice of mighty thundering, saying, Praise the Lord: for the Lord God omnipotent reigns. 7. Let us be glad and rejoice, and give honor to Him: for the marriage day of the Lamb has come, and His bride has made herself ready. 8. And to her was granted that she should be arrayed in fine linen, clean and white: for the fine linen is the righteousness of saints. 9. And he said to me, Write, blood-related are they who are called to the marriage supper of the Lamb. And he said to me, These are the very words of God. 10. And I fell at His feet to worship God. And He said to me, You must not do that: I am your fellow bondservant, and of your brothers who have the testimony of Jesus: worship God: for the witness of Jesus is the spirit of prophecy.

The Righteous Judge
Revelation 19:11-21

11. And I saw heaven opened, and behold a white horse; and the rider was called Faithful and True, and His judgment and warfare are just. 12. His eyes were as a flame of fire, and on His head were many crowns; and He had a name written, that only He knew. 13. And He was clothed with a vestment sprinkled in blood: and His name is called, The Word of God. 14. And the armies that were in heaven followed Him on white horses, clothed in fine linen, white and clean. 15. And out of His mouth came a sharp sword, and with it He could

smite the nations: and He will rule them with a scepter of iron: and He treads the winepress of the fierceness and wrath of Almighty God. 16. And He has on His vestment and on His thigh a name written, King of Kings, and Lord of Lords. 17. And I saw an angel standing in the sun; and he cried with a great voice, saying to all the fowls that fly in the midst of heaven, Come and gather yourselves together to the supper of the great God; 18. that you may eat the flesh of kings, and the flesh of captains, and the flesh of mighty men, and the flesh of horses, and of the riders, and the flesh of all men, both free and bond, both small and great. 19. And I saw the beast, and the kings of the earth, and their armies, gathered together to make war against Him who sat on the horse, and against His army. 20. And the beast was taken, and with him the false prophet that wrought signs before him, with which he deceived them that had received the mark of the beast, and them that worshipped his image. These both were cast alive into a lake of fire burning with brimstone. 21. And the remnant was slain with the sword of him who sat upon the horse, which sword proceeded out of His mouth: and all the fowls were filled with their flesh.

Satan Bound for a Thousand Years
Revelation 20:1-6

1. And I saw an angel coming down from heaven, with the key of the bottomless abyss and a great chain upon his hand. 2. And he laid hold of the dragon, that ancient serpent, who is the Devil and Satan, and bound him for a thousand years, 3. and cast him into the bottomless abyss, and locked him up, and set a seal over him, that he might no longer deceive the nations, until the thousand years were completed: and after that he must be set free for a little time. 4. And I saw thrones, and those who judged sat upon them: and I saw the souls of those who were beheaded for the witness of Jesus, and for the word of God, and who had not worshipped the beast, nor his image, neither had received his mark upon their foreheads, or in their hands; and they lived and reigned with Christ a thousand years. 5. The rest of the dead lived not again until the thousand years were completed. This is the first resurrection. 6. Blood-related and holy is he who has part in the first resurrection: on such the second death has no power, but they will be priests of God and of Christ, and will reign with Him a thousand years.

Lake of Fire and Brimstone
Revelation 20:7-10

7. And when the thousand years are completed, Satan will be set free of his prison, 8. and will go out and deceive the nations which are in the four quarters of the earth, Gog, and Magog, to assemble them for w ar: their number is as the sand of the sea. 9. And they went up

on the broad plain of the earth, and encircled the camp of the saints, and the beloved city: and fire came down from heaven and devoured them. 10. And the devil who deceived them was cast into the lake of fire and brimstone, where both the beast and the false prophet were, and they will be tormented day and night for ages and ages.

The Book of Life
Revelation 20:11-15
11. And I saw a great white throne, and one setting on it, from whose quick look the earth and the heaven disappeared; and there was found no place for them. 12. And I saw the dead, small and great, standing before the throne; and the books were opened: and another book was opened, which is the Book of Life: and the dead were judged out of the things written in the books, according to their works. 13. And the sea rendered up the dead in it; and death and hell rendered up the dead in them: and they were judged every man according to their works. 14. And death and hell were cast into the lake of fire. This is the second death. 15. And everyone who was not found written in the Book of Life was cast into the lake of fire.

A New Heaven and New Earth
Revelation 21:1-5
1. And I saw a new heaven and a new earth: for the first heaven and the first earth were passed away; and the sea was no more. 2. And I saw the holy city, Jerusalem, coming down new out of heaven from God, adorned as a bride for her husband. 3. And I heard a great voice out of heaven saying, Behold, the dwelling-place of God is with men, and He will dwell with them, and they shall be His people, and God Himself will be with them, and be their God. 4. And He will wipe away every tear from their eyes; and there will be no more death, neither grief, nor crying, neither will there be any more pain: for the first things are gone. 5. And He who sat upon the throne said, Behold, I make all things new. And He said to me, Write: for these words are true and trustworthy.

Water of Life
Revelation 21:6-14
6. And He said to me, It is done. I am Alpha and Omega, the beginning and the end. I will give to him who is athirst of the fountain of the water of life without price. 7. He that overcomes shall inherit these things; and I will be his God, and he shall be My son. 8. But the cowards, the unbelieving, the defiled, and murderers, and fornicators, and those who claim magical powers, and the worshiper of idols, and all teller of lies, will have their part in the lake that burns with fire and brimstone: which is the second death. 9. And there came to me one of the seven

angels which had the seven vessels full of the seven last punishments, and talked with me, saying, Come here, I will show you the Bride, the Lamb's wife. 10. And he carried me away in the Spirit to a great and high mountain, and showed me the holy city, Jerusalem, descending out of heaven from God, 11. having the glory of God: its light was like unto a stone most precious, even like a jasper stone, clear as crystal; 12. and had a wall great and high with twelve gates, and at the gates twelve angels, and names written on the gates, which are the names of the twelve tribes of the sons of Israel: 13. on the east three gates; on the north three gates; on the south three gates; and on the west three gates. 14. And the wall of the city had twelve foundations, and on them were the names of the twelve apostles of the Lamb.

The Golden Rod
Revelation 21:15-27
15. He who talked with me had a golden measuring rod to measure the city, the gates, and the wall. 16. And the city was four-square, and the length was the same as the breadth: and he measured the city with the rod, about 1500 miles. The length and the breadth and the height were equal. 17. And he measured the wall about 216 feet, according to the measure of the angel. 18. And the building of the wall was of jasper: and the city was pure gold, like unto clear glass. 19. And the foundations of the wall of the city were adorned with all manner of precious stones. The first foundation was jasper; the second, sapphire; the third, a chalcedony; the fourth, an emerald; 20. the fifth, sardonyx; the sixth, carnelian; the seventh, chrysolith; the eighth, beryl; the ninth, a topaz; the tenth, a chrysoprase; the eleventh, a jacinth; the twelfth, an amethyst. 21. And the twelve gates were twelve pearls: every gate was a single pearl: and the street of the city was pure gold, as it were transparent glass. 22. And I saw no temple: for the Lord God Almighty is the temple and the Lamb. 23. And the city had no need of the sun, neither of the moon, to shine in it: for the glory of God did illuminate it, and the Lamb is the lamp thereof. 24. And the nations of those who are saved will walk in the light of it: and the kings of the earth do bring their glory and honor into it. 25. And the gates will not be shut by day: for there shall be no night there. 26. They will bring the glory and honor of the nations into it. 27. And there will in no wise enter into it anything that defiles, neither whatever makes abomination, or makes a lie: but those who are written in the Lamb's Book of Life.

River of Life
Revelation 22:1-6

1. And he showed me a river of water of life, clear as crystal, proceeding from the throne of God and of the Lamb. 2. In the center of the street, and on either side of the river, was the tree of life, that produced twelve kind of fruits, and yielded fruit every month: and the leaves of the tree were for the healing of the nations. 3. And there will be no more curse: but the throne of God and of the Lamb will be there; and His bondservants will serve Him: 4. and they will see His face; and His name will be on their foreheads. 5. And there will be no night there; and they need no light of a lamp, neither light of the sun; for the Lord God gives them light: and they will reign for ages and ages. 6. And he said to me, These sayings are faithful and true: and the Lord God of the holy prophets sent His angel to show to His bondservants the things that must shortly happen.

Jesus Will Come Quickly
Revelation 22:7-11

7. Watch, I come quickly: blood-related is he who keeps the words of the prophecy of this book. 8. And I John am he who heard and saw these things.. And when I had heard and seen, I fell down to worship before the feet of the angel who showed me these things. 9. Then said he to me, See that you do not do this: for I am your fellow bondservant, and of your brothers, the prophets, and of those who keep the words of this book: worship God. 10. And he said to me, Seal not the sayings of the prophecy of this book: for the time is at hand. 11. He who is unjust, let him be unjust still: and he who is filthy, let him be filthy still: and he who is righteous, let him be righteous still: and he that is holy, let him be holy still.

Bright and Morning Star
Revelation 22:12-17

12. Watch, I come quickly; and My reward is with Me, to render to every man according to his works. 13. I am Alpha and Omega, the beginning and the end, the first and the last. 14. Blood-related are they who wash their robes that they may have right to the tree of life, and may enter in through the gates into the city. 15. For without are dogs, and workers of magic spells, and fornicators, and murderers, and those who worship idols, and whoever loves and does a lie. 16. I, Jesus, have sent My angel to witness to you these things in the assemblies. I am the root and the offspring of David, and the Bright and Morning Star. 17. And the Spirit and the Bride say, Come. And let him who hears say, Come. And let him that is athirst come. And whosoever will, let him take the water of life free of charge.

Come, Lord Jesus
Revelation 22:18-21

18. For I testify to everyone who hears the words of the prophecy of this book, If any man add to these things, God will add to him the punishments that are written in this book: 19. And if anyone will take away from the words of the book of this prophecy, God will take away his part out of the Book of Life, and out of the Holy City, and from the things that are written in this book. 20. He who verifies these things said, Surely, I come quickly. Amen. Even so, come, Lord Jesus. 21. The grace of our Lord Jesus Christ be with you all. Amen.

Appendix One

THE KING JAMES VERSION

The King James Version was based on six previous English translations: (1) Tyndale's Bible (1526); (2) Coverdale's Bible (1535); (3) Matthew's Bible (1537); (4) Great Bible (1539); (5) Geneva Bible (1560); (6) Bishop's Bible (1568). This would make the King James Version, the seventh in this line of modern English translations of the Bible. When Queen Elizabeth died in 1603 a draft act was in Parliament for a new version of the Bible: "An act for the reducing of diversities of bibles now extant in the English tongue to one settled vulgar [common] translated from the original." When James I succeeded Elizabeth one of the first things done by the new king was the calling of the Hampton Court Conference in January of 1604 "for the hearing, and for the determining, things pretended to be amiss in the church." Here were assembled bishops, clergymen, and professors, along with four Puritan theologians, to consider the complaints of the Puritans.

Although Bible revision was not on the agenda, the Puritan president of Corpus Christi College, John Reynolds, "moved his Majesty, that there might be a new translation of the Bible, because those which were allowed in the reigns of Henry the eighth, and Edward the sixth, were corrupt and not answerable to the truth of the Original." The king responded "...I wish some special pains were taken for an uniform translation, which should be done by the best learned men in both Universities, then reviewed by the Bishops, presented to the Privy Council, lastly ratified by the Royal authority, to be read in the whole Church, ..." Accordingly, a resolution came forth to translate the whole Bible.

The actual selection of the men who were to do the translation began in July of 1604, James wrote to Bishop Bancroft that he had "appointed certain learned men,..., for the translating of the Bible." These men were the best biblical scholars and linguists of the day. Although fifty-four men were nominated, only forty-seven were known to have taken part in the translation work. *The Translators to the Readers* stated, "In this confidence and with this devotion, did they assemble together; not too many, lest one should trouble another; and yet many, lest many things haply might escape them." The work began to take shape in 1604 and progressed steadily until completion in 1611.

The translators were organized into six groups, and met respectively at Westminster, Cambridge, and Oxford. Ten at Westminster were assigned Genesis through 2 Kings; seven had Romans through Jude. At Cambridge, eight worked on 1 Chronicles through Ecclesiastes, while seven others handled the Apocrypha. Oxford employed seven to translate Isaiah through Malachi; eight occupied themselves with the Gospels, Acts, and Revelation. Fifteen general rules were advanced for the guidance of the translators:

1. The ordinary Bible read in the Church, commonly called the Bishops Bible, to be followed, and as little altered as the Truth of the original will permit.

2. The names of the Prophets, and the Holy Writers, with the other Names of the Text, to be retained, as nigh as may be, accordingly as they were vulgarly used.

3. The Old Ecclesiastical words to be kept, viz. the word Church not to be translated Congregation.

4. When a word hath divers Significations, that to be kept which hath been most commonly used by the most of the Ancient Fathers, being agreeable to the Propriety of the Place, and the Analogy of the Faith.

5. The Division of the Chapters to be altered, either not at all, or as little as may be, if Necessity so require.

6. No Marginal Notes at all to be affixed, but only for the explanation of the Hebrew or Greek Words, which cannot without some circumlocution, so briefly and fitly be expressed in the Text.

7. Such Quotations of Places to be marginally set down as shall serve for the fit Reference of one Scripture to another.

8. Every particular Man of each Company, to take the same Chapter or Chapters, and having translated or amended them severally by himself, where he thinks good, all to meet together, confer what they have done, and agree for their Parts what shall stand.

9. As any one Company hath dispatched any one Book in this Manner they shall send it to the rest, to be considered of seriously and judiciously, for His Majesty is very careful in this Point.

10. If any Company, upon the Review of the Book so sent, doubt or differ upon any Place, to send them Word thereof; note the Place, and withal send the Reasons, to which if they consent not, the Difference to be compounded at the general Meeting, which is to be of the chief Persons of each Company, at the end of the Work.

11. When any Place of special Obscurity is doubted of, Letters to be directed by Authority, to send to any Learned Man in the Land, for his Judgment of such a Place.

12. Letters to be sent from every Bishop to the rest of his Clergy, admonishing them of this Translation in hand; and to move and charge as many skilful in the Tongues; and having taken pains in that kind, to send his particular Observations to the Company, either at Westminster, Cambridge, or Oxford

13. The Directors in each Company, to be the Deans of Westminster, and Chester for that Place; and the King's Professors in the Hebrew or Greek in either University.

14. These translations to be used when they agree better with the Text than the Bishops Bible: Tyndale's, Matthew's, Coverdale's, Whitchurch's Bible, Geneva.

15. Besides the said Directors before mentioned, three or four of the most Senior and Serious Theologians, in either of the Universities, not employed in Translating, to be assigned by the vice-Chancellor, upon Conference with the rest of the Heads, to be Overseers of the Translations as well Hebrew as Greek, for the better observation of the 4th Rule above specified.

The KJV Translation Process

Each group was given a portion of the Bible to translate. Initially, each member of the group would make an individual translation. There were evidently at least seven members in each group, so each passage would be translated a minimum of seven times at this stage. Each group would then go over the work together and come up with a joint translation. The translations were then passed along to the five other companies for their review and correction. For the final review of the entire translation, a general committee was made up of two men from each of the original groups. In addition, other scholars not on the formal committees were encouraged to give comments and suggestions throughout the translation process. By using this method, each passage was closely gone over at least 14 times. After all, it was a group effort, and this at times leads to compromise.

NOTE: One of the most historically significant translations of the Bible into the English language was the Geneva Bible, preceding the King James translation by 51 years. It was the Bible of the Reformation and the one used by the early colonists fleeing oppression by the Church of England. Printing of the Geneva Bible stopped in 1644 due to exclusive rights given to the Royal Printers for the KJB. Most American

Protestants embrace the KJB without knowing that ninety (90) percent of the 1611 text is the same as the Geneva Bible.

Any difficulties found in the Authorized (1611) King James Bible (KJB) were not the fault of classical scholarship, but the restrictive Royal Instructions given the translators and the many provisions for individuals to change their work. Indeed the KJB was a Church of England document limited by the culture and nature of the English language. Most are not aware of the many changes made to the 1611 text; mainly in these years: 1613, 1616, 1617, 1618, 1629, 1630, 1633, 1634, 1637, 1638, 1640, 1642, 1653, 1659, 1675, 1679, 1833, 1896, 1904. The original changes were to correct typographical errors, add notes, and omit the Apocrypha between the Testaments, but there has always been scholarly opposition to the process. This produced more translations and more versions. Few realize that the Church of England now recommends six (6) versions in addition to the 1611 text.

Translators Choice of Words

Words in 1611 did not mean the same as the average English language reader understands them to mean. Modern English was not formalized until about 1650. For example, when Queen Elizabeth died in 1603 a draft act was in Parliament for a new version of the Bible: "An act for the reducing of diversities of bibles now extant in the English tongue to one settled vulgar translated from the original." Note the word "vulgar" in English at the time of the KJV meant "common or popular" but presently has different connotation. Vulgar could mean rude, offensive, bad, earthy, naughty, etc. in the vernacular of today.

Another example sheds light on the reasons for using an Unabridged English Dictionary to discover what a particular word meant in English during the King James period. Note the following examples:

Literal Greek translation of Titus 2:14 -- who gave Himself on behalf of us in order that he might ransom us from all lawlessness and might cleanse for Himself a people (his) own possession, zealous of good works.

King James Version of Titus 2:14 --Who gave Himself for us, that he might redeem us from all iniquity, and purify unto Himself a peculiar people, zealous of good works.

Devotional New Testament of Titus 2:14 -- Who gave Himself for us, that He might ransom us from all wickedness, and purify a people as His personal treasure, eager for good deeds.

The Greek word used for possession was "periousios" from the present participle feminine of a compound [peri] and [eimi] meaning "being beyond usual, i.e. special (one's own). Yet the King James translators chose to use the word "peculiar" from the Latin [*peculium*] meaning one's own property or in Roman law meaning "private property."

Although it did not essentially change the meaning of the verse at the time of translation; it did use a word that was not in the original Greek text and demonstrated the strategy of the translators. This presumptive change causes one to wonder what other liberties the translators took in the 1611 version of scripture. The word "peculiar" was in common use in Old England. There was in the Church of England the Court of Peculiars. Also, a particular parish or church located outside a diocese was classified as a Peculiar Church. And England had a bottled beer called "old peculiar." The first English readers of the KJV understood the word "peculiar" but current Western readers of English have a different perceptions of the word.

Each Book has a Message

Just reading the ancient translation or only listening to a teacher or preacher is not sufficient. There must be personal attachment to the truth of the Book. To do this one needs to know the exact meaning of words used in the sacred scripture. One should remember that the Bible means exactly what the first persons who heard it understood it to mean. Another fact, relative to the KJV, is that many of the words used by the translators had different meanings in 1611 than they do today. It is clear that the people in the churches of England understood the words because they were in common use. The general public presently sees some old words in a different light.

Each book of the New Testament has a special message: Matthew declared that Jesus was King of the Jews, Mark said Jesus was a Servant, Luke deals with Jesus as a man, and John reveals the Deity of Christ. Yet these books are presented out of sync. The chronological order would be Mark, Luke, Matthew, and John. How does this change the understanding of Jesus? Mark (servant); Luke (man); Matthew (King of Jews); John (Deity of Christ). First, one needs to see Jesus as an active Servant. Forty times Mark wrote that Jesus did this or that and "straightway" or "immediately" moved to additional action. Mark is a much better place to start reading the Gospel narrative. Luke presents Jesus as a man to a Roman audience to demonstrate human involvement in the divine plan and to show what Jesus "began to do and teach." Matthew reviewed the facts that Jesus came through the Jewish Nation to become the Redeemer King. John then puts a cap on the process by declaring Jesus to be Divine, King of Kings, and Lord of Lords.

The message of each book deals with a logical development of God's Plan for mankind. The Bible was given in books and should be read and studied by books. The New Testament was written in common Greek with all capital letters and no punctuation. There were no verses or chapters, just the Book or Letter. Scholars later divided the books into chapters and the chapters into verses and incorporated the punctuation. Unless one considers the New Testament book by book much of the value and meaning is lost. A roughly chronological order provides an opportunity to witness the design of God's message to mankind. The New Testament should be viewed as events occurring over many years. The record was given over time in books, yet they are not placed in the New Testament in chronological order. Each book has a theme and the material included in the book is there to support the purpose of the book. When read in an approximate chronological order, the message has greater meaning.

Remember, when Jesus told His disciples they were not ready to hear and understand a particular message? At times new converts to the Christian faith are given a Bible and told to read it from cover to cover. When they start at the Gospel of Matthew, it is easy to get bogged down in the "begets." This reminds me of a Bible Reading Marathon in the Chapel of Oxford Graduate School. The New Testament was being read in a 24-hour period in chronological order by books. The reading began at 6:00 PM and continued through the night. A small boy wanted to read and the place was Matthew. He began reading but soon stumbled over a few big words and some proper names. His mother instructed "Just say steamboat and go on!" The young lad read: "And steamboat begat steamboat; and steamboat begat steamboat; and steamboat begat Jacob." Everyone had a good laugh, but it pointed out the difficulty of reading such a difficult passage as a young believer.

The Old Testament was placed in roughly chronological order, but the New Testament remains in an early arrangement made before the dating process was attempted. The New Testament is in the same order found in major translation and it has been the same since it was printed in 1456. It was organized this way because an Augustinian Monk thought this order made it easier to study doctrine. The average reader is not attempting to scholarly study doctrine, but simply desires to understand the written message and apply it to their lives. If one took any book and put the sections or chapters out of order, the author's intended message would be lost. With this in mind, the New Testament is presented in roughly chronological order by books.

Another Difficulty is Chronology

The New Testament was given to mankind in books. There were no chapters, paragraphs or sentence punctuation. The Greek language

Appendix One: The King James Version

has a special process of determining which words are in an emphatic position, which words go together and where thoughts and ideas begin and end. It has to do with the endings of the words. In reality each book was one long sentence written in capital Greek letters with one basic theme or thought. The stories in each book related directly to the purpose of the book. Facts taken out of context cause the meaning to change. Therefore, the New Testament is best understood when it is studied book after book in as near a chronological order as possible. This assists the understanding of the progressive nature of scripture. When the New Testament is read randomly or here a little -- there a little, the purpose of the book is often missed. It is similar to viewing a movie with the segments out of order.

Academics who have devoted a lifetime of study do not entirely agree on the chronology of the New Testament. Absolute accuracy is not claimed for the order presented here; however, it is roughly chronological by books. Part of the problem of a divided Christianity is the 27 books of the New Testament being read out of sync. The chronological order of the New Testament that follows is to enable you to familiarize yourself with the order the original scriptures were written (a space of several decades). God did not intend for scripture to be difficult to understand. Neither did God propose a Book that required a highly educated scholar to read and understand. The historical record is clear that when churchmen restricted scripture in a language uncommon to the people, the world went into hard times. The Prophet Isaiah wrote: 35:8. "And an highway shall be there, and a way, and it shall be called the way of holiness; the unclean shall not pass over it; but it shall be for those: the wayfaring men, though fools, shall not err therein."

Order and Record of Chronological Readings

Read the books and letters of the New Testament chronologically to get a feel of the *progressive nature of God's revelation to mankind*. Always keep in mind both the human writer of the passage and the inspiration of the Holy Spirit that prompted and motivated the writing of the words. There were eight (8) human writers of the New Testament; however, the Holy Spirit was the true Author. Simon Peter wrote about this (2 Peter 1:21) *"For no prophecy was brought forth by the will of man at any time: but men spoke from God being brought forth by the Holy Spirit."*(EDNT)

You may keep a record of your reading using the following Order and Record of Chronological Reading by circling the Chapter numbers as they are completed:

The writer is marked after the name of the Book or Letter. The code for writers is: **[J]** James; **[JD]** John, the Disciple; **[JJB]** Jude, Jesus' Brother; **[JM]** John Mark; **[L]** Luke; **[M]** Matthew; **[P]** Paul; **[SP]** Simon Peter.

Order and Record	Of	Chonological Reading
BOOK	**WRITER**	**CHAPTERS**
James	(J)	1,2,3,4,5
Mark	(JM)	1,2,3,4,5,6,7,8,9,10,11,12,13,14,15,16
I Thessalonians	(P)	1,2,3,4,5
II Thessalonians	(P)	1,2,3
Galatians	(P)	1,2,3,4,5,6
I Corinthians	(P)	1,2,3,4,5,6,7,8,9,10,11,12,13,14,15,16
II Corinthians	(P)	1,2,3,4,5,6,7,8,9,10,11,12,13
Romans	(P)	1,2,3,4,5,6,7,8,9,10,11,12,13,14,15,16
Luke	(L)	1,2,3,4,5,6,7,8,9,10,11,12,13,14,15,16, 17,18,19,20,21,22,23,24
Matthew	(M)	1,2,3,4,5,6,7,8,9,10,11,12,13,14,15,16, 17,18,19,20,21,22,23,24,25,26,27,28
Philemon	(P)	1
Colossians	(P)	1,2,3,4
Ephesians	(P)	1,2,3,4,5,6
Philippians	(P)	1,2,3,4
Acts	(L)	1,2,3,4,5,6,7,8,9,10,11,12,13,14,15,16, 17,18,19,20,21,22,23,24,25,26,27,28
I Timothy	(P)	1,2,3,4,5,6
Titus	(P)	1,2,3
II Timothy	(P)	1,2,3,4
I Peter	(SP)	1,2,3,4,5
Jude	(JJB)	1
Hebrews	(P)	1,2,3,4,5,6,7,8,9,10,11,12,13
II Peter	(SP)	1,2,3
John	(JD)	1,2,3,4,5,6,7,8,9,10,11,12,13,14,15,16, 17,18,19,20,21
I John	(JD)	1,2,3,4,5
II John	(JD)	1
III John	(JD)	1
Revelation	(JD)	1,2,3,4,5,6,7,8,9,10,11,12,13,14,15,16, 17,18,19,20,21,22

New Testament Books with Authors and Themes

Taking into account all the efforts to place the New Testament in chronological order, the following is the best practical order. It is in approximate order in which the books were written. Personal preference is to study the books of authors together. The issue here is chronology. The books of the New Testament are classified in five (5) categories: Relational Letters; Letters to Scattered Believers; Letters to Assembled Believers; Letters to Theophilus; and, Narrative About the Life of Jesus.

Use the guide on the previous page to record the chapters you have read by placing a circle around the chapter number.

James – James wrote a treatise on the ethical aspects of the Christian life that expresses the differences between intellectual apprehension of truth and the practical application of truth in life.

Mark – John Mark presented Jesus as a person of action in the context of an evangelistic message to those living outside of Palestine who had not witnessed the events in the life of Jesus.

I Thessalonians – Paul wrote about the expected return of Christ and to relieve concerns that those who had already died would miss the return of Christ. Paul also dealt with the believer's attitude during persecution and that they should never return to paganism.

II Thessalonians – Paul explained that certain events must take place before the return of Christ and exhorted steadfastness in the midst of persecution. He encouraged believers to reject worldliness and to live a principled life.

Galatians – Paul's purpose was to combat the heresy that claimed Christ alone was not sufficient for salvation.

I Corinthians – Paul wrote to a prosperous cosmopolitan city of the Roman Empire to provide balance to new converts who were having difficulty breaking pagan habits of their former lifestyle. Paul dealt with sexual misconduct, abuse of spiritual gifts, problems with the Lord's Supper, and confusion concerning the resurrection.

II Corinthians – Paul reinforced his apostleship and told converts to always be faithful to Christ. Paul softened his approach from the first letter and expressed love for the people. He taught about financial support for the needs of others.

Romans – Paul wrote to a Gentile audience to educate them on the basic doctrines related to salvation and to introduce himself. Paul discussed major themes of grace, faith, righteousness, and justification. His point was that Christ was not just for Jews.

Luke – Luke the only Gentile writer of the New Testament wrote to a Gentile audience to explain "All that Jesus began to do and teach." Luke's gospel is the best written book in the New Testament. His strong academic background is demonstrated by his choice of words as he explains the work and teachings of Jesus.

Matthew – Matthew was one of the original disciples and wrote to a Jewish audience to verify that Jesus was the Messiah. As one of the original 12 Disciples, Matthew had a good foundation to share the story of Jesus, the awaited King of Israel.

Philemon – Paul wrote from prison that the all-sufficiency of Christ gives meaning to life and causes people to serve Him even to their death. Philemon speaks of forgiveness and receiving new converts as believers.

Colossians – Paul wrote at the request of the minister from Colosse demonstrates that all things are fulfilled in Christ and the people did not need to listen to the Judaizers about the worship of angels or some so-called spiritual knowledge. He wanted them to experience the full knowledge of the will of God for themselves.

Ephesians – Paul stressed unity in the church, the redemptive work of Christ, and a Godly family life. He wrote about doctrine and practical Christian living and illustrations to present God's plan to bring all believers together using a body, a building, a bride and the individual parts of a body that must operate as a unit.

Philippians –Paul thanked the people for sending funds and dealt with the value of being faithful to Christ. He wrote concerning the all-sufficiency of Christ that gives meaning and value to life.

Acts – Luke wrote this second book to tell how the Gospel was spread beyond the confines of the Jewish community to the larger world. The first half is about Peter (Apostle to the Jews); the second half is about Paul (Apostle to the Gentiles). Luke demonstrates good research skills by comparing Peter and Paul.

I Timothy -- Paul expressed his feelings as he prepared to pass his ministry on to others. He offered advice on dealing with false teachers and gave the qualification for leaders.

Titus – Paul encouraged Titus to preach sound doctrine in spite of false teachers and to use good judgment in selecting leaders in the church.

II Timothy – Paul wrote to encourage Timothy in the work of the ministry and to warn him that he would encounter persecution and turmoil from false teachers and that Timothy should strictly keep the teachings of scripture.

I Peter – Simon Peter wrote to encourage believers to endure persecution and to be prepared for difficult times.

Jude – Jude the brother of Jesus was alarmed at the number of false teachers who taught one could live anyway and still be forgiven.

Hebrews – Paul wrote to assure Jewish believers that their faith in Jesus as the Messiah was secure and legitimate. He encourages them to go forward and to never go back to the old ways.

II Peter – Simon Peter warned of false teachers, and living in view of Christ's return. He exhorts spiritual growth and the importance of holding on to the truth.

John – John one of the original disciples presented the signs and wonders of Jesus to convince the readers that Jesus was the Christ, the Son of God and that salvation came through faith.

I John – John one of the original disciples wrote to provide direction to believers who faced new challenges to their faith. He encouraged believers to maintain a spiritual life by keeping a relationship with Christ.

II John – John further warned against traveling false teachers who went from assembly to assembly.

III John – John encouraged leaders to assist those who were spreading the gospel and teaching the truth.

Revelation – John wrote his revelation to assist assemblies undergoing persecution and difficulty and to remind them that good would triumph over evil when Christ sets up His earthly kingdom.

Important Facts about Bible Reading and Study

Five important facts should be understood by those who wish to read, study, learn and follow scriptural teachings.

1. The deep truths of God are revealed by the Spirit (1 Corinthians 2:9-13).
2. The teaching ministry of the Holy Spirit is not available to the unconverted (1 Corinthians 2:14-16).
3. A carnal or unspiritual person will not come to the fullness of spiritual truth (1 Corinthians 3:1-4).

4. Truth requires believing; believing requires behaving. The spiritual admonition is to hear and do (James 1:22-25); Believe and behave (John 15:14).

5. Truth demands obedience. The Bible becomes a closed book to those who persist in disobedience (Mark 4:23-25).

New Testament Reading Plus Listening

Although study plans are important, they are no substitute for the teaching ministry of the Holy Spirit (John 16:13-15), nor are they a substitute for believers assembling together for worship (Hebrews 10:23-25) or for witnessing and sharing (Acts 1:8). In addition to personal devotional reading and study, each believer needs to listen carefully to the preaching/teaching ministry of a local congregation. Listening carefully may not mean taking notes; in fact, more can be learned by disciplined listening and doing follow-up study based on the passage used in the message. The believers in Berea were good listeners and good students: "They received the word with all readiness of mind, and searched the scriptures daily."(Acts 17:11). Private study alone is not sufficient for spiritual growth. Each believer needs the guidance of the Holy Spirit and the fellowship of other believers. At times this guidance comes through a local pastor; at other times it comes through prayer and meditation as one shares their personal study of the Word with family and friends.

Steps in Devotional Reading and Study

Meditate a moment in prayer to clear the mind. Read the selected passage silently; then read it again aloud. Read with an honest desire to receive what God is saying.

Seek to understand what the Bible means, free from personal prejudices. Read each verse again, meditating on important words. Single words often teach essential spiritual truths. Write down the words you do not understand.

Study the passage prayerfully, depending on the Holy Spirit to illuminate its meaning. Look for the obvious. Watch for key words and use your Unabridged English Dictionary (UED) if you do not know the meaning. Ask questions. The Bible has answers. Raise your hand! You are in God's school. Write down your thoughts. Does the passage bring to mind any prayer concerns? The Holy Spirit is the Teacher. (John 16:13-15)

Determine the message for you and make notes. You will be surprised what you learn.

Apply the truth to your personal life, family, work, or life situation. Permit the Holy Spirit to bring your life into joyful compliance with the teaching of the passage. Let the Word speak directly to you. Permit the Bible to have an affect on your life.

Pray for the Lord to use the truth in your life to ensure spiritual growth.

Share what you have learned with someone: a family member, a study group, or a friend. Use the telephone, E-mail, write a letter. Remember, much of the New Testament is letters.

A Systematic Study of the New Testament

This devotional reading and study plan is designed to activate lay involvement in a systematic study of the New Testament. For many years congregants have passively sat through both song and sermon without taking home a useable kernel of truth. Often the worship service has been geared to entertainment rather than instruction in righteousness. It seems that one can attend religious services for years without learning the basic tenants of the faith. One of the major problems relates to a lack of preparation on the part of the audience. The only one making advance preparation is the clergy. A professor in graduate school is remembered because when an individual had not done their homework, they were counted absent. The professor's statement "How can you participate in class when you don't know what I am talking about?"

Clergy spend years in studying scripture and perfecting the art of homiletics without learning communication skills. The pulpit is filled with oratory and gymnastics, but little or no food to nourish the soul of the congregants during the coming week. If this trend continues, The Empty Pulpit that Clyde Reid wrote about has become the empty heart and the empty pew (Reid 1967). The empty pulpit syndrome in the intervening decades since 1967 has produced a half-filled church behind stained glass windows with half-hearted commitment to the basic tenets of the faith. The pulpit today is empty in the sense that there is often no message heard, no results seen, and no power felt. The emptiness of which I speak is an absence of meaning, a lack of relevance, and a failure in communication. To be sure, this is a relative emptiness, not absolute. But it is emptiness, nevertheless.

Since most people can do little to improve the quality of the public ministry, the answer is in a serious and systematic reading and study of scripture by individuals. This Devotional New Testament is designed to provide a reading and study plan, to correct the lack of scriptural understanding of individuals. Personal growth will come through regular and interactive reading of the New Testament together with a systematic study plan.

Structured Scripture Reading

Structured scripture reading twice a day, evening and morning, takes the reader through the New Testament at a regular pace. Each session should range from ten (10) to thirty (30) minutes depending on the seriousness of the study suggested in the paragraph (expository unit) read. Those who have more time are encouraged to spend additional time in study and prayer.

Reading as an Art

Art is the disposition or modification of things by human skill. Reading is an art. As such one can learn how to read and learn how to read better; consequently, most students need assistance with reading and interpreting what is read. The concept of reading for a degree in Europe was rejected in early education in the New World because there were no libraries. The teacher was the only repository of knowledge and was the basis for transferring knowledge to students. As libraries were constructed and books placed on the shelves, the teachers gave assignments to do collateral reading but continued to lecture. The constant lecturing and the many reading assignments extended the required time to earn a degree. The reading was considered supplemental to the lecture, while in Europe it was instead of the lecture. Over time this process has continued and has slowed the process of educational development.

In English/European universities students complete a course of study in about two and one-half years. Yet English language students are required to take four or five years of their life to reach the bachelorette level of certification. Distance education attempts to give the student back some of the lecture time for reading and thus speed the process of learning. In this way the student becomes a self-directed learner and is no longer dependent on the pedagogical process of instruction. It is in this regard that the Devotional New Testament is presented. Individual believers need to read and study the New Testament for themselves in a self-directed manner and have less dependency on someone else to explain the meaning of the inspired text.

Learning, Listening and Learning More

The emphasis is on both listening and learning. As one listens carefully to a message delivered in a worship setting, they become aware of areas where more study is needed. The Devotional New

Testament advances a plan to prepare a listener to identify areas for more study and thereby do word studies to better understand what was taught. During the execution of self-study the individual will grow in grace and knowledge and become a more effective listener and learner.

Evening and Morning Readings

Why do we suggest that the reading be done first in the evening and then in the morning? Genesis declared "And the evening and the morning were the first day." This continued for each day of Creation and established that the evening before the daylight goes with the next light. The Jewish religion recognized this and began the Sabbath on Friday evening at sundown until sundown the next day. Although the Resurrection of Christ caused the followers of Christ to worship on Sunday rather than Saturday, the pattern was clear. The slave culture of the day forced over one-half of the people in servitude, yet they could worship of the evening (Saturday) at sundown which in reality was the beginning of the first day of the week. Although the modern church has lost the real impact of the "Sunday punch" the reality of an "evening and morning" reading and study plan could take one back to a fundamental understanding of the Creator's master plan. To wait until the morning to begin a devotional is to lose the "sundown to sunup portion of the day." A full discussion can be found in chapter one of Why Churches Die. ISBN 978-0-9796019-0-3. (Green, 1972, 2007)

Divided into Expository Units

This book includes a guide to read the New Testament book by book in evening and morning units in a general chronological order. Why this order? Genesis was clear "the evening and morning" were the parameter of the day. This organization of the text is designed to witness God's progressive dealing with mankind and see the process as a direct benefit for today. The evening and morning selection is designed to place the reader in a creative atmosphere for renewal. Since it is obvious that the scriptures were written over a period of time and that no writer received all of God's special revelation at once, it is logical to assume that each writer was progressive in the expression of the revelation; consequently, the work of each writer needs to be read chronologically in turn to see clearly this progression.

Chronology to Provide Order

The chronological listing is to provide order to the reading process. This provides a creative frame of reference and places you in a special place to listen and learn. For your convenience the various books and the chapters have been divided into expository/study units that function similar to a paragraph. There is a central idea and a logical development of thought. Each unit is connected to the previous one and the following one. It is important that you discover the transitional connections of ideas as they are presented in the scripture passage. God's Word is "line upon line, precept upon precept."

As you follow the reading plan feel free to depart on occasion to follow-up on a study based on what you heard while listening to someone else expounding scripture. This may be in church, on TV, radio, CD, or some other recorded means. In other words, study those areas that are relevant to your current thinking and digress to study those "thoughts" that come to you providentially. However, do not forget the systematic chronological study. This remains the best routine to understand the progressive revelation presented in scripture.

A Systematic Reading

A systematic reading of the Bible is important. The evening is the time to prepare for the day. The habit of thinking differently about the day is not easy to form or to maintain, but it is most rewarding. — even priceless! A daily quiet time which promotes regular reading of the Word in a general chronological pattern will be an encouragement to spirituality. Write down the key thoughts. What affect did the Word have on you? Develop the habit of asking questions:

- **Who** wrote the book?
- **Why** was it written?
- **What** was the message?
- **What** does it say to my heart?
- **What** is the command, promise, or warning?
- **Was** there an example to follow or an error to avoid?

APPENDIX TWO

INTERACTIVE STUDY USING INTERROGATIVES

The Learning Process

Basic questions for hermeneutics, the science of interpretation, relate directly to how one gathers facts, interprets these facts, uses these facts and stores them in the long-term memory. This is the learning process. One should engage scriptural material with at lease five questions: (1) What does the written material say? (2) What does the written material mean? (3) How may the written material be paraphrased to clearly express the original intent? (4) How can my understanding of the written material be supported? And (5) How may what is learned be utilized or applied? These questions interpret the written material at five levels:

1. **Memorization** – what it says.
2. **Understanding** – what it means.
3. **Expressing the thought** – your own words.
4. **Providing evidence** -- support
5. **Applying knowledge** -- use

A Methodical Path

A methodical path is required to understand what is written. Method is based on the Greek word *methodos,* which literally means "a way or path of transit." Method implies orderly, logical, and effective arrangement and may denote either an abstraction or a concrete procedure. Method is a way of doing things which carefully maintains and fosters conditions conducive to understanding and development.

Interrogatives

An interrogative is a question, normally, using who, what, when, where, why, and how. To develop the basic context of the writer and the subject at hand, asks formal questions. Both an understanding of written material and an adequate use of printed information may be developed through the interrogatory process.

WHO is the writer?
WHERE was the material written?
WHEN was the material written?
WHY did the writer write this composition?
WHAT does the writer say?
WHAT does the writer mean?
HOW may the meaning be paraphrased?
WHERE can collateral evidence be found?
HOW may the material be applied?

The method of interpretation is the process by which a reader understands the meaning of words. The sense may be clarified by considering seven key words:

SEE – Observe the link between subject and object.

INQUIRE – Inquisitiveness is required to find the meaning.

ANSWER – Re-creating the attitude of the writer is a source of answers.

SUMMARIZE– Integrate and summarize to discover the primary message.

EVALUATE – Determine the subject or universal value of the meaning.

APPLY - A true understanding should be applicable to real life.

ASSOCIATE - The meaning of a message must be associated with others in the same work and with data outside the source to develop the ultimate correlation.

Major components of a written passage

TERMS – primary use of a word

STRUCTURE – relationship between terms

GENERAL LITERARY FORMS – format used to communicate the message

ATMOSPHERE – underlying tone or spirit of written material

Useful Assumptions in Interpretation

What is read should be an objective body of information. A methodical approach is required to gain this information. The information communicated by the author is distinct from the interpreter. The interpreter must use an objective approach to extract the intended message. There is no absolute objectivity or pure induction, because of bias. A method that stresses induction should be more impartial and accurate than any other method one could use. The method of Devotional Bible Study should discover a better understanding of a scriptural passage by obtaining the sense of individual words. These particular facts make for sound interpretation of scripture.

Inductive Study

Induction is the process of reasoning or drawing conclusions from particular facts and individual words. In induction one observes a sufficient number of facts, and on the grounds of reason, extends what is true of them to others of the same class, thus arriving at assumptions or a general sense of the meaning of words. The opposite is true of deduction. One begins with a general truth, and seeks to connect it with some individual case by means of a middle term or class of objects known to be equally connected with both. Thus, one deduces the specific from the general, attributing to the former the distinctive qualities of the latter. The idea of induction is to read out of the text by being an objective observer and a logical interpreter. The systematic process begins with observation.

Observation

Taking into account the above, a basic step in constructing the meaning of words is observation. This step determines the components of a written document. This step involves perception and is essentially awareness of the process which causes the interpreter to become saturated with the particulars and concerns for the existence of terms and requires definition of terms used in a given context. Observation assists in discovering the structure of a passage through the relations and interrelations between terms (various structural units: phrases, clauses, sentence, paragraph, segment, subsection, section, or division.) Observation identifies the general literary form or forms which cause terms to communicate ideas. Observation opens the interpreter's eye to the atmosphere or underlying tone or spirit of the passage. (Some moods by which a written portion may be characterized: despair, thanksgiving, awe, urgency, joy, humility, or tenderness.)

Interpretation

The next phase is interpretation. One must objectively read out of the text, not subjectively read into the passage. This logical step is to determine the meaning of words in relationship to the purpose or objective of the passage. Since a paragraph is one idea fully developed and an expository unity of scripture functions as a paragraph, what is the basic idea? Does the author mean exactly what is written? Why was it written? To whom was it written? Was it written to inform, persuade, interpret or answer a question or solve a problem? This requires empathy or projection into the consciousness of the author. Keep in mind that the writer's of scripture were inspired by the Holy Spirit; consequently, one may need the assistance of the spirit to fully understand the message. The interpreter must be identified with the author to understand what is written. This requires the recapturing of the author's attitudes, motives, thoughts, and emotions at the time of the writing.

Always Incomplete

Interpretation is always incomplete, because the interpreter cannot fully reproduce the circumstance of the writer or fully understand the motives of the author. The basic meaning of the components must be determined through logical steps based on the "original idea expressed by the unit." This is a definitive phase which corresponds to the function of dictionaries and lexicons. The meaning is not sufficient, the underlying reasons why the statements are made must be determined. There may be a general reason related to the whole of the written work or a particular reason for a particular part. The author had a reason for choosing specific words. What about the historical situation or the literary context of the writing? The inter-relatedness of facts is the outgrowth of presuppositions and becomes the assumptions behind the choice of words. The implication of statements is more than the explicit expression. This requires that interpretive questions be applied to the written word. The interpreter must be aware of potential erroneous or inaccurate expositions.

Possible Areas of Concern

Some of the concerns are: (1) Treating a chapter or paragraph as a collection of isolated sentences that may be understood apart from the immediate context. (2) Searching scripture with preconceived ideas to substantiate certain personal beliefs. (3) Attempting to rationalize and make written material fit one's bias and thereby eliminate the true meaning. (4) Viewing a scriptural passage purely from the historical without realizing that all writing contains more than history. (5) Explaining parables for example, as allegories or extended metaphors and, consequently, pressing every detail for some meaning instead of understanding the purpose of the narrative. (6) The reader should see all scripture as accurately explaining the writer's intent to communicate the factual meaning.

Avoidable Dangers

There are other avoidable dangers in interpretation. Some relate to misinterpretation and others a failure to determine the full meaning or seeing more than is actually present in the written passage under consideration. Some avoidable dangers are: (1) Viewing what an author writes without considering the time (date) of the writing. (2) Assuming that an isolated fact is useful without seeing it in the context of the whole work. (3) View an author's work as a maze of cross-references and not interpret each book in its own right before associating it with the other works of the same author or other authors. (4) Seeing a written work as exhaustive rather than seeing it as part of a whole story. (5) See the work as great literature rather than its use of literary form to communicate a message.

Evaluation and Application

The process of evaluation and application is a phase of induction. Written statements need to be evaluated and applied for both edification and learning. The worth of each statement must be assessed and its relevance or usefulness determined.

Evaluation should follow interpretation and must not interfere with the process. Evaluation must precede application. Following interpretation, the relevance and worth of the passage is determined with the view of application. Adequate assessment suggests valid application. Application is the final objective of all developmental readings or serious study and must be preceded by a process of evaluation.

Evaluation is both general and specific. The facts may be relevant to a larger study and useful for an intermediate effort. The worth and value of a writer's work is the general step in evaluation. Specifically, the exact worth of a particular portion of writing is necessary because different parts of a work may address specific questions, situations, and consequently, have degrees of relevance and value to support another position or work. The task of evaluation is to distinguish between those facts which are of limited value and those that are timeless and of general use.

When a timeless or general value is determined, a specific use must be analyzed to ascertain whether or not it falls within the scope of a present task or written work. The interpreter must search for a contemporary problem to which the facts are relevant. Application naturally follows. Facts from another source must be applied in an appropriate manner regardless of the consequences.

Correlation

The concluding step of inductive study is correlation. Some correlation occurs during the process of interpretation and application because it is the natural outgrowth of the examination of written material. In order to develop data useful to build or support a written work, the findings from inductive study must evolve into a synthesized concept that supports the new works thesis or purpose. Facts in a written work must be related to other facts within the same work and facts in other works. The weakest part of inductive study is at this point of generalizations. Most of the interpreter's energy is concentrated on the search for facts and little effort is giving to synthesizing and correlating those facts before they are included in another work. This correlation should be both formal and informal.

An attempt must be made to see another author's work as a whole and determine if it supports the direction of a new work. Even individual chapters of a book should not be interpreted without considering the purpose of the whole book. An effort must be made to see the inter-relatedness of facts rather than superficial compartmentalization to fit a new work. This is often called, "the use of proof texts." The ultimate goal of developmental readings is to add to one's knowledge and understanding of scripture.

APPENDIX THREE

ORDER OF NEW TESTAMENT BOOKS

Chronological Order

AD45 -- AD60

The General Letter of James	page 337
The Gospel According to Mark	page 24
The First Letter to the Thessalonians	page 229
The Second Letter to the Thessalonians	page 234
The Letter to the Galatians	page 237
The First Letter to the Corinthians	page 244
The Second Letter to the Corinthians	page 265
The Letter to the Romans	page 279
The Gospel According to Luke	page 123
The Gospel According to Matthew	page 58

AD61 – AD68

The Letter to Philemon	page 318
The Letter to the Colossians	page 300
The Letter to the Ephesians	page 305
The Letter to the Philippians	page 312
The Acts of the Apostles	page 175
The First Letter to Timothy	page 320
The Letter to Titus	page 326
The First Letter of Peter	page 344
The General Letter of Jude	page 373
The Letter to the Hebrews	page 351
The Second Letter of Peter	page 369
The Second Letter to Timothy	page 329

AD85 -- AD95

The Gospel According to John	page 82
The First Letter of John	page 375
The Second Letter of John	page 334
The Third Letter of John	page 335
The Revelation of John	page 381

Alphabetical Order

Acts	p 175
Colossians	p 300
Corinthians, I	p 244
Corinthians, II	p 265
Ephesians	p 305
Galatians	p 237
Hebrews	p 351
James	p 337
John	p 82
John, I	p 375
John, II	p 334
John, III	p 335
Jude	p 373
Luke	p 123
Mark	p 24
Matthew	p 58
Peter, I	p 344
Peter, II	p 369
Philemon	p 318
Philippians	p 312
Revelation	p 381
Romans	p 279
Thessalonians, I	p 229
Thessalonians, II	p 234
Timothy, I	p 320
Timothy, II	p 329
Titus	p 326

Traditional Order

Matthew	p 58
Mark	p 24
Luke	p 123
John	p 82
The Acts	p 175
Romans	p 279
I Corinthians	p 244
II Corinthians	p 265
Galatians	p 237
Ephesians	p 305
Philippians	p 312
Colossians	p 300
I Thessalonians	p 229
II Thessalonians	p 234
I Timothy	p 320
II Timothy	p 329
Titus	p 326
Philemon	p 318
Hebrews	p 351
James	p 337
I Peter	p 344
II Peter	p 369
I John	p 375
II John	p 334
III John	p 335
Jude	p 373
Revelation	p 381

APPENDIX FOUR
C.A.F.E. Logo Data

The C.A.F.E. logo represents integration of the church and community. All faith-based congregations can work together to reach the community and families with basic Christianity to show *pure religion in the community. The psychology of color shows that black and white have many meanings; however, the colors can also symbolize the starkness of decison-making when one is confronted with hard *choices.

The Squares are black and white and have four equal sides and four right angles. The four sides represent equality: personal, social, spiritual and racial. The center square represents structured or established congregations working together in fellowship to advance commonalities of religious faith. It is common ground, not differences, that advance knowledge and understanding.

An X is interwoven with the center square representing the church and with itself representing the integration of basic Christianity. The X-shaped cross, commonly called the St. Andrew's Cross, was named for Simon Peter's brother, Andrew, who was martyred by crucifixion on an X-shaped cross at his own request, because he deemed himself unworthy to be crucified in the same manner as Christ. The X-shaped cross signifies his resolution or resolve.

The fish symbol occurred early in Christian history and was placed in the center of the cross. After the crucifixion believers were persecuted and the fish became a symbol Christians would recognize, but others would not. Therefore, believers could connect through this symbol without being exposed to their oppressors. The Greek word for fish, ΙΧΘΥΣ, was used as an acrostic to advance the Christian faith by giving the meaning "Jesus Christ God's Son Saviour" to the early believers. They also saw the X-shaped cross in the tail of the fish. The FISH symbol was placed in the center of the cross to represent a central concept in religion.

*Free from all that would dim the transparency in belief and conduct before God and the Father is this, to go see and relieve the orphans without a father's protection and the women lacking a husband in their distress, and to keep himself untainted with guilt. James 1:27 EDNT

*My cherished band of believers, count it a jewel (precious stone) when you fall into adversity and testing that provides you a choice of direction. James 1:2 EDNT

Quick Reference

Alphabetical Order		Traditional Order	
Acts	p 175	Matthew	p 58
Colossians	p 300	Mark	p 24
Corinthians, I	p 244	Luke	p 123
Corinthians, II	p 265	John	p 82
Ephesians	p 305	The Acts	p 175
Galatians	p 237	Romans	p 279
Hebrews	p 351	I Corinthians	p 244
James	p 337	II Corinthians	p 265
John	p 82	Galatians	p 237
John, I	p 375	Ephesians	p 305
John, II	p 334	Philippians	p 312
John, III	p 335	Colossians	p 300
Jude	p 373	I Thessalonians	p 229
Luke	p 123	II Thessalonians	p 234
Mark	p 24	I Timothy	p 320
Matthew	p 58	II Timothy	p 329
Peter, I	p 344	Titus	p 326
Peter, II	p 369	Philemon	p 318
Philemon	p 318	Hebrews	p 351
Philippians	p 312	James	p 337
Revelation	p 381	I Peter	p 344
Romans	p 279	II Peter	p 369
Thessalonians, I	p 229	I John	p 375
Thessalonians, II	p 234	II John	p 334
Timothy, I	p 320	III John	p 335
Timothy, II	p 329	Jude	p 373
Titus	p 326	Revelation	p 381

www.ingramcontent.com/pod-product-compliance
Lightning Source LLC
Chambersburg PA
CBHW020345170426

43200CB00005B/55